Reprints of Economic Classics

A VIEW OF THE
ART OF COLONIZATION

Also by EDWARD GIBBON WAKEFIELD

In REPRINTS OF ECONOMIC CLASSICS

England and America [1834]

A

VIEW

OF THE

ART OF COLONIZATION

IN PRESENT REFERENCE TO THE
BRITISH EMPIRE

IN LETTERS BETWEEN
A STATESMAN AND A COLONIST

EDITED BY

(ONE OF THE WRITERS)

EDWARD GIBBON WAKEFIELD

[1849]

REPRINTS OF ECONOMIC CLASSICS

AUGUSTUS M. KELLEY · PUBLISHERS
NEW YORK 1969

First Edition 1849

(London: John W. Parker *West Strand* 1849)

Reprinted 1969 by
AUGUSTUS M. KELLEY · PUBLISHERS
New York   New York   10001

Reprinted from a copy in the Collections of the
Oberlin College Libraries

. . . .

S B N   678 00561 3

L C N   68 30548

. . . .

PRINTED IN THE UNITED STATES OF AMERICA
by SENTRY PRESS, NEW YORK, N. Y. 10019

A VIEW OF THE

ART OF COLONIZATION.

" There need be no hesitation in affirming, that Colonization, in the present state of the world, is the very best affair of business, in which the capital of an old and wealthy country can possibly engage." — JOHN STUART MILL.

A

VIEW

OF THE

ART OF COLONIZATION,

WITH PRESENT REFERENCE TO THE
BRITISH EMPIRE;

IN LETTERS BETWEEN A STATESMAN AND A COLONIST.

EDITED BY

(ONE OF THE WRITERS)

EDWARD GIBBON WAKEFIELD.

LONDON:
JOHN W. PARKER, WEST STRAND.
M DCCC XLIX.

THIS BOOK

IS AFFECTIONATELY DEDICATED

TO

JOHN HUTT, ESQ.,

LATELY GOVERNOR OF WEST AUSTRALIA,

WHO, MORE THAN ANY OTHER INDIVIDUAL KNOWN TO ME,

HAS COMBINED STUDY AND EXPERIENCE

IN LEARNING THE

ART OF COLONIZATION.

PREFACE.

SOME time ago, one of the most accomplished of our public men invited me to write to him on a question relating to the colonies. This question really involved the whole subject of colonization and colonial government. The correspondence that ensued, was neither intended nor suitable for publication; but it was shown confidentially to various persons. Some of them, being most competent judges on such a point, have repeatedly expressed their wish that the letters should be published; of course, with such alterations as would render them not unfit for the public eye. This suggestion is now adopted. The actual correspondence has been altered by omission, modification, and large additions. The following letters, there-

fore, are very different from those which passed
through the post-office. But the difference
consists mainly in workmanship and form, not
in materials or substance. In aim, scope, and
tenour—as respects the subjects examined, and
the ideas propounded—the two sets of letters
are nearly alike. I indulge a hope, that the
fictitious correspondence may make an impression on many, not unlike that which the real
one has left on a few: for if so, systematic
colonization, which is at present only a vague
aspiration of some of the more intelligent minds,
would ere long become a fruitful reality.

The name of the statesman who was a party
to the actual correspondence, it would be at least
idle to exhibit in this publication. It is therefore kept out of view by the omission of dates,
addresses, and the formal expressions with
which real letters usually begin and end. The
letters purporting to have been written by him,
are described merely as Letters from a Statesman: my own are called Letters from a

Colonist. I fancy myself justified in assuming that title, as being indicative of my acquaintance with colonial topics: for I really was a colonist in Canada (having been a member of its House of Assembly) under the administration of two of its governors, Sir Charles Bagot and Lord Metcalfe, who in practice had more concern with the question of responsible government for colonies than Lord Durham, under whose administration the theory was first officially propounded, and I was a busy actor in colonial politics; whilst under that of Lord Sydenham, I was a diligent observer of them on the spot. But if these are not sufficient grounds on which to call myself a colonist, then I would claim the title on the ground of sympathy with the class of our fellow-subjects who have the misfortune to be nothing but colonists; a sympathy, the force of which will be understood when I add, that it was acquired partly by residence and frequent sojourn in British North America, as well as in some States of the

American Union, which in one sense of the
word are still colonies of England; and yet
more, by a very active participation, for nearly
twenty years, in the labours by which the two
youngest of England's colonies, South Australia
and New Zealand, have been founded in spite
of the most formidable opposition from the
colonial branch of the government of the empire.

REIGATE,
   30th January, 1849.

CONTENTS.

LETTER XI.

From the Colonist.

LETTER XII.

From the Colonist.

LETTER XIII.

From the Colonist.

LETTER XIV.

From the Colonist.

LETTER XV.

From the Statesman.

LETTER XXXI.

From the Colonist.

LETTER XXXII.

From the Colonist.

LETTER XXXIII.

From the Statesman.

LETTER XXXIV.

From the Colonist.

LETTER XXXV.

From the Colonist.

APPENDIX.

No. I.

A VIEW

THE ART OF COLONIZATION.

LETTER I.

From the Statesman.

THE STATESMAN INVITES THE COLONIST TO *VIVÂ-VOCE*
DISCUSSIONS OF THE SUBJECT.

YOU will be glad to learn that on coming to town,
I find certain friends of mine resolved to bring the
question of colonization before the House of Commons
next session. Two of them probably will take an
active part in the discussion; and they all wish that I
should co-operate with them. This I have engaged
to do, provided always that I shall be able in the time
to acquire the indispensable knowledge. Thus I am
pledged at all events to study the subject; and your
wish on that point will at last be realized.

Now, therefore, I am in need of all the assistance
you can render me. In one word, I want to be
crammed. Indulge on me as much as you please,
your turn for preaching and teaching about colonization. You shall find me at any rate an assiduous

pupil. I will endeavour to read whatever you may think likely to be useful, and will give up as much time to *vivâ-voce* discussion, as may turn out to be necessary, and I can possibly spare. The latter mode of learning, however, would most effectually give me the benefit of your studies and experience; besides that, as nothing like a complete treatise on colonization exists, I should be glad to avoid the cost of time and trouble attendant on picking up information bit by bit from a variety of books, parliamentary papers, and other sources.

I have, therefore, to request that you will do me the favour to call here when you shall be next in town, giving me a day or two's notice. We should then, I hope, as it is my intention to be near London throughout the recess, be able to make arrangements for frequent meetings.

Not doubting that you will be equally pleased with my news and my proposal to give you all this trouble, and trusting that your health is improved, &c. &c.

LETTER II.

From the Colonist.

I AM indeed pleased by your letter, but also not a little annoyed. The determination of your friends is most agreeable to me; and I rejoice at hearing that you intend to continue your inquiries into a subject which interests me beyond all others. But in proportion to my satisfaction on these points, I am really distressed at having to inform you that, it is not in my power to comply with your wish for *vivâ-voce* communication with me. My health, instead of improving, has got worse lately, and will probably never mend. It is a disorder of the nerves which has long hindered, and now absolutely precludes me from engaging in the oral discussion of subjects that deeply interest me, more especially if they are subjects involving argument and continuous thought. You must have observed how I suffered towards the end of our last conversation. At length, I cannot disobey the doctors' injunction to stay at home and be quiet, without effects that remind me of a bird trying to fly with a broken wing, and knocking itself to pieces in the vain exertion. As respects earnest conversation, I am a helpless cripple. I would try at all risks, if there were the least chance of my being able to do what is more desired by me than it can be by you: as it is, I am under the necessity of declining your flattering and most gratifying invitation.

But there occurs to me an alternative, which I am in hopes you may be disposed to adopt. With the seeming caprice of most nervous disorders, mine, which forbids talking, makes far less difficulty about letting me write. The brain suffers greatly, only when it is hurried—as with old hunters "'tis the pace that kills" —but can work somehow when allowed to take its own time. Leisurely, in writing, I could answer questions at any length, and could save you some trouble by pointing out the most available sources of instruction in print. I venture to suggest, therefore, the substitution of a correspondence by letter for the proposed but impossible conversations.

The alternative might not be a *pis-aller*. The interchange of thought would be indeed less brisk and agreeable; but the greater trouble would fall principally on me, and would consist for both writers of that more careful thinking, which even the sagest of talkers bestow on the written communication of their ideas: so that, probably, the discussion would be more complete and effective. As you have a reputation for success in your undertakings, which means of course that you only undertake what you have resolved to do as well as possible, I imagine that you may prefer my suggestion to your own proposal.

If it should prove so, have the goodness to let me know what the topics are on which you wish for information. Conversations would naturally have been led by you. I can only place myself at your disposal, promising to take the direction in which, from time to time, it shall please you to point.

LETTER III.

From the Statesman.

THE STATESMAN DESCRIBES THE CONDITION OF HIS OWN
KNOWLEDGE, CALLS FOR SOME DEFINITIONS, AND ASKS
QUESTIONS RELATING BOTH TO THE SUBJECT, AND TO
THE STATE OF IT AS MATTER OF PUBLIC OPINION.

I DEEPLY regret the cause of your inability to comply with my request.

At first I did not relish the proposed alternative; but on reflection and trial I am inclined to prefer it. After considering in order to reconcile myself to the more troublesome course for both of us, I see that, for my purpose, written communications, which remain, will be better than oral, which soon pass from the memory when the subject of them is not one of lasting personal concern: and a first trial of writing has confirmed your view of its advantages; for on sitting down to give you a statement of the points on which I wish for information, I discover the full difficulty of the task I have undertaken. I undertook it on the supposition, that I had definite ideas about what our colonization is and ought to be; and that I had only to learn the best method of improving it: but on examining the matter further, as the necessity of writing has compelled me to do, I find that in reality my knowledge is very scanty and superficial. As in fact I do not know enough for telling you satisfactorily what it is I want to learn, my best course probably will be to describe the state of my impressions on the subject.

In common with not a few men in public life, I have lately thought that this subject is unwisely neglected by us. I see with them, that colonization is a natural means of seeking relief from the worst of our social ills, and of thus averting formidable political dangers. I see with every body who reads the newspapers, that our colonies cost us money, much trouble, and not a little shame, without rendering any important services to us in return. All of them at one time or another seem to get into a state of disorder and disaffection; just now the number of disturbed colonies is more than commonly large; and there is not one of the whole forty (that, I believe, is the sum of them) of which an Englishman can feel proud. All of them together provide for fewer emigrants than the United States; Canada, which receives the greatest number of emigrants, we are by all accounts only peopling and enriching for the Americans to possess ere long: and of the only other part of the world to which British emigrants proceed, the population, after seventy years of what is termed colonization, amounts to no more than 300,000, or about that of the town of Glasgow. The West-India colonies are in a lamentable state, both economically and politically: so is South Africa, politically at least, with its colonist rebellions and Caffre wars: so is Ceylon with its uproarious governor and native insurrection: so is our youngest colony, New Zealand, as the seat of a deadly feud between colonist and native, of a costly military occupation in order to maintain British authority at all, and of the wildest experiments in colonial government: so is, on one account or another, every one of the colonies of England, more or less. I go merely by our own newspapers for the last year or two, which hardly at any time mention a colony but when it is disturbed. To my mind, therefore, nothing could be more unsatisfactory than our colonization as it is. On that one point at least, my notions, however general, are sufficiently clear. On the question of what our colonization ought to be, my ideas are even more general, and utterly indistinct. I find indeed on attempting to write them down, that they consist of a most vague hope, that something very useful and important might be done by us, if we pursued colonization systematically. But as I confess a profound ignorance of what is, so I have no conception of the means by which my hazy aspirations could be realized. My fancy pictures a sort and amount of colonization that would amply repay its cost, by providing happily for our redundant people; by improving the state of those who remained at home; by supplying us largely with food and the raw materials of manufacture; and by gratifying our best feelings of national pride, through the extension over unoccupied parts of the earth of a nationality truly British in language, religion, laws, institutions, and attachment to the empire. But when I descend from the regions of imagination to inquire into the wherefore of the difference between this picture and the dismal reality, I have no ideas at all; I have only a feeling almost of shame at my own want of ideas. With such blindness as to causes, suitable remedies, of course, are far out of my sight: if indeed suitable remedies are to be found; for now, as writing leads to thinking in earnest, I almost despair of the parliamentary project of my friends, and wish that I had declined to share in its execution.

I say this with no present thought of drawing back from my engagement, but to show you that in order to qualify myself for performing it, I must begin with the alphabet of our subject; and that there is hard work for both of us. In order, then, to learn my letters, I proceed at once to ask for some definitions. Is British India a colony? Is Jersey one? Are the United States of America colonies of England? and, if they are not, why do we give the name of colonies to the states which the ancient Greeks formed in Sicily and Asia Minor, but which were always completely independent of their parent states? Then what is colonization? If French Canada, when we took it, became a colony of England, the mere conquest and government of a foreign people is colonization; which cannot be. Is it the sending forth of people and their settlement in a distant country already inhabited? or must we deem it a condition of colonization, that the land of the new country should be wholly or in a great measure unoccupied? Does colonization include government, or relate solely to emigration from an old country, and the settling of the emigrants, independently of government, in their new home? Even as I write these questions, some answers occur to me; but I own that I have hitherto talked, and rather fast too, about colonies and colonization, without at the time exactly knowing what I meant by the words. But not many among our statesmen could honestly point at me for this. The confession is singular, not the utter ignorance and indifference. The last word leads to another question. What is the cause of the general indifference to the subject of colonization? Quite recently indeed, a lively interest has been professed in the subject by many; and it may perhaps be said even that public attention is turned that way: but the sort of interest is not, I fear, very real. I apprehend that it somewhat resembles the interest which a parrot feels about your health, when it says in a tone of tender anxiety, "How do you do?" There is a good deal of pretty and seemingly earnest talking and writing about colonization; but what else I know not. Colonization, I take it, is something to be done, not something to be merely known, like geography or astronomy. Who is there that can tell us what he would have Parliament do? Who proposes any plan? Who is seriously looking to important practical results? Besides, with all the talking and writing about colonization, and "systematic" colonization too, people in general seem to possess no greater knowledge of the subject than the ignorance that I have avowed. At least, I know not where to seek real knowledge, save by applying to one of a few who have made the study of the subject a business for years, and who are therefore a marked exception from the general rule. Generally, there is still as much ignorance as ever. Ignorance implies real indifference, however copious the wordmongering. Does the public care so little about colonization because it knows so little, or know so little because it cares so little? If the indifference does not arise from ignorance, what, I repeat, is its cause? This last question is of great importance to me, practically and personally, who am not disposed to waste precious time on mere speculation. Is it worth while to study the subject? Shall we ever overcome the general indifference? Is there any prospect of action? Returning to my primer, I want to know what, if any, is the substantial distinction, which, in words at least, many people now draw between emigration and colonization. The most popular newspapers say now, let us have colonization, not emigration. What does this mean? Again one hears a good deal about " systematic," as distinguished, I suppose, from systemless colonization. But what is meant by " systematic"? With reference to what system is this epithet employed? Is there any known system? Are there several to choose amongst? Or do the advocates of systematic colonization mean that a system ought to be devised? I ask these questions without forgetting that there is a project of colonization which goes by your name, and which is sometimes called a system. Lord Grey calls it so. I remember seeing a letter of his written two years ago, which was shown about for the information of persons then very desirous of promoting a great emigration from Ireland, in which he said that if he continued in office your system would be largely carried into effect. Has anything been done with it? It has been tried, I know, in some of the Australian colonies; but if I am to believe an official acquaintance, who ought to know all about it, with only failure and disappointment hitherto. At all events, be so good as to tell me what I ought to read in order to understand the project, of which I have but a vague, perhaps an erroneous conception.

If I am not mistaken, your project of colonization relates exclusively to matters of an economical nature, such as emigration and the sale of waste land, leaving untouched the question of political government for colonies? But I have heard lately in society of a plan of government for colonies, which is praised by some of your friends, and which they call a plan of municipal government. What is this? Is there any publication which would enable me to comprehend it without troubling you on that point? I think I heard somebody say, that Lord Grey's constitution for New Zealand was founded upon this plan of colonial government. If that were true, I should fear that the plan cannot be a very sound one; for the New-Zealand constitution was, to speak plainly, so impracticable and absurd, that Lord Grey himself seized the first opportunity of destroying it; and the offer of its extension to New South Wales was scornfully declined by that colony. If, therefore, Lord Grey really adopted or copied from the plan lauded by your friends, I must ask you to put me in the way of examining some other plan or plans of colonial government. Indeed I should like to read anything on this branch of our subject, that you may be disposed to recommend. I take it for granted that the topic has been handled by philosophical writers, but cannot recollect by whom.

In particular I wish to understand the theory of what Lord Durham in his Report, I think, called " responsible government for colonies." Or are those words the title of a little book, the joint authorship of which I have some faint recollection of having heard attributed to yourself and Charles Buller?* Is not that theory now carried into full effect in Canada? And if it is, how does it work? Charles Buller's name reminds me of his capital speech on colonization in 1843. I say capital, because it excited universal admiration at the time, and had the effect of placing the speaker in the first rank amongst philosophical statesmen. I heard the speech myself, and thought that I should never forget it; so strong and pleasing was the impression which it made on me. But I have entirely forgotten it; and I find that it has escaped from the memory of others who praised it to the skies at the time of its delivery. Even now they say that it was a capital speech; but they cannot tell why: they say that they have forgotten all about it except that it was a first-rate speech; and this is just my own predicament.

Is it desirable that I should wade through the evidence taken by the recent committee of the Lords on emigration? A cursory glance at it has left me with the impression that it consists of an immense mass of facts, or statements of fact, heaped up without form or order, without regard to any guiding principles, and without producing in any degree the only desirable result; that, namely, of a comprehensible

---

* The manuscript of this book was nearly ready for the press before Mr. Buller's death. Not a word of it has been altered in consequence of that event. How greatly for the better it might have been altered if he had lived a few weeks longer, every reader will understand when I add, that it would have passed through his hands for critical revision on its way to the publisher. I have wished and tried to say something about him here, but cannot.

theory or a feasible plan. Are there any other inquiries by committees of Parliament which you think that it would be well for me to study?

In the session before last, the House of Commons, on a motion made by Lord Lincoln, presented an address to the Queen, praying that an inquiry might be instituted into the subject of colonization for Ireland in particular. The motion for an address was at first strenuously opposed by the Government, who only gave way when they found that they would be beaten on a division. The address having passed, an answer from the Queen promised that the wish of the House of Commons should be realized. If common usage had been followed, a Royal Commission of Inquiry would have been appointed. Nothing of the sort was done. No commission was appointed; and there has been no inquiry by other means. The address and answer have been utterly disregarded by the Government. I have endeavoured, but in vain, to get at the why and wherefore of this curious official neglect. Other members of the Government merely refer me to the Colonial Office, where, however, I can learn nothing. My official acquaintance, who is a member of that department, answers me with a vacant look, and a reference to Lord Grey, to whom he well knows that I should not apply for information. What does all this mean?

I see by the newspapers that several societies have recently been formed with a view of promoting colonization. There is one called the Colonization Society, another the Canterbury Association; I forget the names of others. Have any of these societies a plan to go upon, or theory to guide them? If not, I

should only lose time in examining their schemes:
for I must needs obtain a general and abstract view of
the subject before attempting to form any opinion on
particular or practical questions.

At the same time, let me warn you that mere theory
or abstract science has no charms for me now. I
have now no leisure to bestow on it. I could not
become interested about a theory of colonization
which was applicable to other countries, but not to
our own. It is with a view to practical results for
this United Kingdom of Great Britain and Ireland,
that I wish to master the subject of our inquiry. I
am in hopes, therefore, that as far as possible, without
discarding abstract considerations as aids in the pursuit of truth, you may be disposed and able to keep
practice always in view, and practice for our own
country especially.

LETTER IV.

From the Colonist.

YOUR letter, which I have read with much interest,
leaves me without a doubt concerning the topic
to which you would first direct my attention. After
calling for some definitions, which are indeed required
with a view to accuracy and clearness throughout our
correspondence, your questions in fact ask for an
account of what may be termed the state of the subject. Here I will confine myself to the definitions,
offering besides a few remarks, not-on the condition of
the public knowledge and opinion with regard to colonization, to which a separate letter must be devoted,
but on a preliminary point which is suggested by one
or two of your inquiries.

I am not surprised at your asking what is meant by
the words colony and colonization; for both words are
commonly used without a definite meaning, and even
with different meanings. This vagueness or confusion
of language arises from vagueness or confusion of
ideas, which arises again from indifference. Only a

very few people have thought it worth while to form a clear conception of the very marked difference of feature or circumstance belonging to the numerous outlying portions of a wide-spread empire. A full account of those differences is given in Mr. Cornewall Lewis's *Essay on the Government of Dependencies;* but this statement I need not repeat, because it will suffice for the present purpose if I mention briefly what it is that, in writing to you, I shall never mean, and what it is that I shall always mean, by the words colony and colonization.

By the word colony, I shall not mean such a country as either British India, which is a great dependency, or the Mauritius, which was a colony of France, but is only a dependency of England: still less would I term Malta or the Ionian Islands a colony. Nor does the process by which these places became dependencies of England, partake in any degree of the character of colonization. Of colonization, the principal elements are emigration and the permanent settlement of the emigrants on unoccupied land. A colony therefore is a country wholly or partially unoccupied, which receives emigrants from a distance; and it is a colony of the country from which the emigrants proceed, which is therefore called the mother-country. To the process by which the colony is peopled and settled, and to nothing else, I would give the name of colonization. Unquestionably, the process of colonization comprises government; for in the first place the settlers must be governed somehow; and secondly, the amount and character of the emigration to a colony are deeply affected by the manner in which the emigrants are governed. Besides, the national character of the states formed by colonization must greatly depend on the character of the institutions of government which the first settlers obtain. Regarding colonial government, therefore, as an essential part of colonization, the question remains whether the government of the colony by the mother-country is equally so. Is the subordination of the colony to the mother-country, as respects government, an essential condition of colonization? I should say not. The independent sovereign states which we term colonies of ancient Greece, I shall suppose to be properly so called. To my view, the United States of America, formed by emigration from this country, and still receiving a large annual increase of people by emigration from this country, are still colonies of England. I divide colonies into two classes; the dependent and the independent, like Canada and Massachussetts. Which kind of government is the best for colonists, which most conduces to rapid and prosperous colonization, and whether or not a combination of the two is preferable to either, are questions foreign to my present purpose of mere definition, but which we shall have to examine with care; since it is clearly indispensable in colonizing to establish some kind of government for the colonists. It may be good or bad government, and may make the colonization itself good or bad; but the forming of it, and the carrying of it on if it is dependent government, are essential parts of the whole process of colonization. And so here end my definitions, which have been purposely framed to make them state and limit the subject of our inquiry.

With regard to your specific questions about that subject, and about the state of it in the public mind, I would suggèst the expediency of their being answered, not at once, nor in the order in which I have received them, but in the course of what I shall have to say on both topics. Sooner or later they must needs be answered; but to exclusively occupying ourselves with them now I see a twofold objection. It would be inconvenient and troublesome to notice these particulars before touching upon generals; it would be useless besides, because in disposing of generals, the particulars would be disposed of too. For example, several of your questions relate directly to what you call my " system" of colonization. Now, if that theory, as I must call it, comprises, as indeed it does, the subjects of emigration, settlement, and colonial government, then such an account of it as some of your questions require, would be all that I have to say about colonization. It is about that theory alone, that I can furnish you with informaticn; or rather, all the information I could furnish, would be nothing but an exposition of that theory. Again, your questions about the state of opinion with regard to colonization, would be best answered by a general account thereof, which would also supply some information on that point for which you have not specifically asked.

Subject to your approval, therefore, I intend to abstain for the present from giving a specific answer to. any of your questions: but I think it safe to promise that they will be answered somewhere in the course of what I shall write about colonization as an art, and colonization as a subject of public opinion.

The latter topic will occupy my next letter.

LETTER V.

From the Statesman.

THE STATESMAN OBJECTS TO THE PROPOSED COURSE OF INQUIRY AS BEING CONFINED TO A PARTICULAR PROJECT OF THE COLONIST'S, AND DESIRES THAT A MORE GENERAL VIEW OF THE SUBJECT MAY BE EXPOUNDED.

YOUR letter just received, shows me that my last was deficient in candour, which this shall not be. Coming to the point at once then, I state explicitly, what something in my last was intended to convey, that in asking you to afford me the benefit of your long studies and experience in colonization, I meant to beg for a great deal more than an account of your own particular project. I must of course examine it, along with others probably; but the mere examination of that or any other scheme exclusively, would be a most inadequate method of endeavouring to master the whole of so comprehensive a subject. Very probably your plan is the best. Many clever people think so; and I bow to such an authority as Mr. Mill, who in his great new book speaks of it in the highest terms. But with all proper deference to his singular acuteness and sagacity, I have a responsibility of my own to consult, which commands me to "prove all things," and "hold fast that which is good." It is, for one purpose, with a view of being able to judge of particular plans, that I wish to acquire a general knowledge. A general and comprehensive view of the subject is what I require, including, not instead of, those special schemes which may seem worth careful examination.

Amongst these, I think it probable that yours will take the highest place in my opinion; and I say this in spite of a sort of prejudice against it, which I ought to have avowed before. It has arisen as follows.

Believing that, however it may be with broth and cooks, a learner cannot have too many teachers if he has time to hear them all, I no sooner engaged to speak about colonization in Parliament, and asked for your assistance in preparing myself, than I also improved my acquaintance with one of the chief clerks in the Colonial Office, a gentleman of no common attainments and ability, whom the facilities of railway travelling have induced to reside with his family in this neighbourhood. It was to him that I alluded in my last. I told him that my object was to obtain information from him, and to use it in Parliament, but of course without quoting him as my authority. He at first tried hard to dissuade me from the enterprise, but finally acceded to my request that he would permit me at least to refer to him occasionally. I then told him of my intention to consult you; whereupon he appeared better disposed to lend me his assistance; and indeed he said, that if I listened much to you, I should be in want of well-informed counsel. Having heard of some of your differences with the Colonial Office, I did not mind his obvious aversion to you, but went on to mention your plan of colonization, and to ask his opinion of it. He expressed no opinion, but said that Lord Grey has done his utmost to make something of the project, but that somehow or other it breaks down wherever it is tried. He afterwards sent me several pamphlets and blue-books of official documents, with passages marked relating to your scheme, which show at least that it has not worked well in New South Wales, and that there, as well as in other colonies, it is very much disliked. Not satisfied with this evidence, however, though it seems very complete as far as it goes, I spoke to one who is in the way of knowing about such things. He approves of your plan as a theory, and is rather friendly than inimical to yourself. But he said, that in practice the plan disappoints expectation; that Lord Grey, as Colonial Minister, has done it full justice by discarding some parts of it which experience had shown to be faulty, and by carrying the rest into effect with all the power of his office; but that, just as my official informant said, the plan breaks down in the working. He said, further, that Lord Grey (whose knowledge of political economy and talent for mastering principles we must all admit, notwithstanding his conspicuous failure in the office for which he was deemed particularly fit), whilst he gives you credit for inventing the plan, wholly objects to parts of it which you maintain to be sound, and now doubts, after having believed that great things might be done with it, whether it can be turned to much account. I must own that this judgment of Lord Grey, considering his talents and experience, has great weight with me; and the more because his frequent mention of you as the author of a scheme which he once so warmly approved, shows that he has no personal ill-will to you like that of my acquaintance in his office.

You will now see why, though I wish to understand your scheme thoroughly, I am far from wishing to be taught nothing else; and why, therefore, I rather invited you to separate it from the general subject, so that we might dispose of it before entering upon that. I ought to have been more explicit at first. My plain-speaking now requires no apology, though I could offer one in the form of some compliments.

LETTER VI.

From the Colonist.

THE COLONIST EXPLAINS THAT HE ALWAYS INTENDED
TO EXPOUND A THEORY, NOT TO RECOMMEND A PRO-
JECT.—NARRATIVE CONCERNING LORD GREY.—LORD
GREY'S STATE OF MIND AND HIS PROCEEDINGS WITH
REGARD TO COLONIZATION, DESCRIBED.

I REJOICE at your plain-spoken letter, and thank
you for it.

To speak plainly in my turn, you have been led
astray by certain misnomers, which, I see, were suggested to you by your Downing-street acquaintance.
You are in the state of mind with regard to me and
my view of the Art of Colonization, which David
Hume would have been in towards Adam Smith, if
the latter, before publishing his view of the Causes of
the Wealth of Nations, had seriously told his friend
that it was a scheme for making the nation rich. In
that case, David would have fought as shy of Adam
and his theories, as most people do of projectors
and their schemes. The words " scheme" and " project" have led you to fear that I should dwell continually on some object of my own, instead of laying
before you such a general view or theory as would

become yours if we agreed about it after discussion. But this last is what alone I intended, and proposed to you. The theory may at present be so far mine as it has been formed in my head by the studies and experience which you value; but otherwise I have no more property in it, than Lindley Murray had in that view of the art of English composition which is set forth in his *Grammar*. Verily I have had schemes and projects many, relating to colonization. Some of these succeeded; some failed. It was by pursuing them into action, that I gained the experience on which my present view of the art is in a great measure founded. Therefore in conveying the view to you, I shall frequently refer to that experience for the purpose of illustration. But I hereby undertake that it shall be for no other purpose. Have I said enough on this point? Your prejudice against the theory you wish to understand, must surely be removed in so far as it was occasioned by misleading words.

In so far as it was caused by misrepresentation, something more must be said. As so occasioned, the prejudice is felt by most people who have heard of the theory but have not examined it. The misrepresentation is that the theory has been submitted to the test of practice, and especially by Lord Grey. By the Colonial Office, and by Lord Grey in particular, the theory has been tried in practice as Charles the Tenth carried into effect the British constitution when he upset his throne by taking ministry after ministry from the minority in parliament; or as the plan of steam navigation with screw propellers would be tried, by placing the screw forward, at the bottom of the ship, instead of aft. What Lord Grey has done with the theory, has been to pick out bits of it here and there, turn them into crotchets of his own, and then call them mine. Or rather, whilst he was thus mauling an important part of my theory in practice, he has professed to be carrying it into effect, and has thus brought it into great discredit. Most true is it, that what Lord Grey calls a trial of the theory, has worked ill in New South Wales, and is greatly disliked there, as well as in other colonies. But my statement is, that the theory has never had anything like a fair trial anywhere; that the professed trials of it have been something not only different from it, but utterly at variance with it in reality, though some likeness has been kept up by professions and forms of words. The opposition between the so-called trials and the theory itself, is as great as the contradiction between my statement and the one that has imposed on you. Before we have done, you will have ample means of determining for yourself which of those statements is correct.

But even now, without delay, considering both Lord Grey's deserved reputation for the talent of mastering questions of principle in political economy, and his almost unlimited power in matters relating to the colonies, I must give you some insight into his feelings and doings with regard to my views of colonization. It is really of moment to yourself, if you would examine them without prejudice, that you should be enlightened on this point.

You think that he does not share the personal aversion of the gentlemen in the Colonial Office to one who has caused them infinite trouble. This is a great mistake. His aversion to me is rather a fierce antipathy. I am telling no secret, betraying no confidence, but only report what many know and openly talk about, and what Lord Grey has had the satisfaction of making me feel very severely. And yet, it is equally true, as you say, that before the public he rather goes out of his way to couple my name with a " system " of colonization which he also professes to be most desirous of carrying into effect. Before the public, therefore, he seems to patronize and befriend me. The contradiction will be explained by reference to certain facts, and to Lord Grey's peculiar temper and intellect.

In 1831, Lord Howick, being then a very young statesman, and parliamentary Under-Secretary for the Colonies, was made acquainted with a part of the theory of colonization which has since been attributed to me. At that time, it was attributed to nobody : the part of it in question was a suggestion without an author, which anybody was at liberty to appropriate. He adopted the principle of it at least; and being the son of the Prime Minister, with other near connexions in the Cabinet and a strong will of his own, he forced the Colonial Office, though sorely against the grain, to do so likewise. For doing this, he was diligently praised in public as a vigorous colonial reformer, and the author of a valuable improvement in colonization. This praise, which I think he deserved, he received plentifully, and certainly did not dislike. But some believers in the theory, including myself, were dissatisfied with the manner in which a part of it was submitted to the test of practice by Lord Howick; and we determined to try the whole theory, if possible, by getting a colony established upon its principles. Hence the first attempts to found South Australia. In these attempts, we were at first warmly encouraged by Lord Howick, but in the end roughly defeated by the Colonial Office. Subsequently, for no reason that we could divine, except that our comprehensive theory cast his small doings as a colonizer into the shade, and also called in question his mode of giving effect to a bit of that theory, he became one of the most zealous of our opponents. A sort of rivalry as colonizers was established between him and us, during which the two parties disparaged and assailed each other. Among the partizans on our side, I was certainly the most active, as he afterwards came to know. About the same time, not I, but others, publickly attributed to me the theory of which he had adopted a part when it was anybody's who chose to father it; and thus he found himself in the unpleasant position of having caused a revolution in the economical policy of many colonies at the suggestion of one who was at open war with him.

Then came our first attempt to found New Zealand. On this occasion, though Lord Howick was no longer in the Colonial Office, we were again placed in official communication with him, because when, passing by the Colonial Office, for fear of its inevitable hostility to our scheme, we applied to Lord Melbourne (then prime minister) for the requisite powers, he desired us to communicate with Lord Howick as the organ of the Government *prô hac vice*. For a while, he encouraged us to proceed with our undertaking, which was therefore considered safe as respects the grant of powers by the government; when I went to Canada with Lord Durham, one of the chief promoters of the New-Zealand scheme.

Among the numerous plans for settling the then distracted condition of British North America, which were placed in Lord Durham's hands, there was one so excellent in theory that it must have been adopted if it had been practicable; but it happened, in consequence of actual circumstances which its able author had quite overlooked, to be utterly impracticable at the time.   The author of that plan was Lord Howick: it was rejected by Lord Durham on the ground of its impracticability; and I am mistaken if Lord Howick did not learn that Lord Durham's view of its impracticability was first suggested to him by me.   At all events, whilst Lord Durham was still in Canada, and I there with him, Lord Howick zealously opposed our New Zealand scheme which he had before patronized. The history of his patronage and opposition is to be found in the evidence taken by Lord Eliot's (now St. Germans) Committee of the House of Commons about New Zealand in 1840.

Lord Howick was one of the Cabinet by which, as Lord Durham died believing, his Canadian mission was upset; and upon that point the brothers-in-law differed as men so nearly connected are apt to differ when they disagree at all.   I of course sided with Lord Durham; Lord Howick well knew with what staunchness and activity.   At this time Lord Howick's ill-will to me was violent and undisguised, but nevertheless was destined to increase.

The New-Zealand project, on the success of which Lord Durham had set his heart, having been defeated for a time, and mainly by Lord Howick, a Committee of the House of Commons was, on Lord Eliot's motion, appointed to inquire into the matter; and Lord Howick was naturally appointed a member of it. Before this Committee I was examined for several days, Lord Howick not being present.   When my examination was closed, he attended the Committee for the first time, and complained of certain statements made by me as a witness, which he declared to be untrue. At his instance, a day was fixed when I was to attend the Committee for the single purpose of being cross-examined by him, and destroyed if he made his charges good. When we met in the Committee-room, it contained, besides a full attendance of members of the Committee, other members of the House, who came there to witness the anticipated conflict. But hardly any conflict took place. Lord Howick, after arranging on the table a formidable mass of notes and documents, put some questions to me with a view of establishing one of his accusations. The answers established that I had spoken the exact truth; and that my accuser himself was mistaken. Instead of proceeding to another charge, he hastily gathered up his papers, and left the room without a remark. The Committee's blue-book reports the words that passed: if it had also described the scene, you would probably, upon reading it, agree with the lookers-on, that in this murderous attack upon me, Lord Howick was provokingly worsted. How eager he was to make the attack, and how the repulse of it affected his passions, is shown by two facts. On the day of the attack, Lord Durham, whom, as the first governor of the New Zealand Company, I almost represented before the Committee, was dying: and he was dead, but unburied, when Lord Howick attended the Committee once more, to vote with a Government majority of the members in rejecting a Report favourable to his brother-in-law's much-cherished objects, which was drawn up by the chairman, Lord Eliot.

The next occasion on which I met Lord Howick, was of a totally different kind. After the early successes of the New-Zealand Company, in rescuing " the

Britain of the South" from Louis Philippe's purpose of making it a convict colony of France, I was going to Canada with some chance of remaining there for years. Just before my departure, my brother-directors of this company invited me to a sort of public or complimentary dinner at the Clarendon Hotel, to which they also invited a number of public men, such as Lord Eliot, and others who were interested about colonization generally and New Zealand in particular. To the great surprise and satisfaction of many besides myself, Lord Howick attended this dinner of compliment to me. We sat on either side of the chairman, conversed across him during dinner, and after dinner addressed the company in civil speeches about each other. I relate the facts without comment.

On returning from Canada, I met Lord Howick at a private dinner table, when his manner was rather friendly than as disagreeable as it usually is towards his inferiors. He was now out of office. The colonization of New Zealand was struggling for existence against the hostility of the Colonial Office under Lord Stanley. We (I mean the colonizers of New Zealand) confiding in Lord Howick's power of grasping a complicated question, and still more in his pugnaciousness and resolution, were pleased to learn that he was disposed to take up our cause: and this he did, not in form, of course, as an advocate, but in fact to our entire satisfaction. By very difficult and careful management we got him to be chosen chairman of a Committee of the House of Commons on New-Zealand affairs, which was now appointed on the motion of Mr. Aglionby: and we supplied him with information, both written and oral, which enabled him to induce the Committee, most of whom were friends of the

Government, to adopt a Report highly condemnatory of the proceedings of the Colonial Office and Lord Stanley. In the following session, we carried on within the House, during debates which occupied nine days, the war whose first battle had been fought in Committee: and here again Lord Howick was our victorious champion. Lord Stanley retired from office in consequence of disagreeing with Sir Robert Peel about free-trade: his most prominent antagonist became the leader of the colonial reformers, and the statesman to whom public opinion pointed as the future Colonial Minister. Nay, some people, influenced solely by his colonial reputation (for he had no other) thought him in a fair way of becoming prime-minister, either instead of or immediately after Lord John Russell. I may confidently add, that for the whole state of the public mind with regard to him, he was largely indebted to the assiduous celebration of his name by colonizing partizans, who had various means of exalting it and making it familiar to the public ear.

In an early stage of the New-Zealand proceedings in Parliament, I was warned that Lord Howick disliked my taking an open part in them, lest it should be supposed that he acted on prompting from me: and I was urged (for the sake of the cause) to keep entirely in the background. This advice I took, but without relaxing my exertions, or ceasing to communicate indirectly with Lord Howick upon the subject of his exertions.

Still, although the colonizers of New Zealand had gained their cause in Parliament, nothing was done to accomplish their objects with regard to the state of the colony. When Mr. Gladstone succeeded Lord Stanley, therefore, it became a question whether we

should press those objects on the attention of the new
minister, or wait for the time, which everybody thought
to be near at hand, when Lord Howick would be in
power.   The latter course was recommended by the
common belief that the weeks of Mr. Gladstone's
tenure of office were numbered before he accepted the
seals; by our conviction that Lord Howick entirely
agreed with us in opinion as to what ought to be done
in order to make colonization prosper; and by a fear
lest, having regard to his jealous disposition, we might
displease him by relying on Mr. Gladstone: but on
the other hand, the desperate state of the colony demanded immediate remedies; there was just a chance
that the Peel ministry might not retire after carrying
its free-trade measures; and some of us deemed Mr.
Gladstone perfectly able to seize, and not likely to
despise, the opportunity of establishing in one instance
a system of colonization and colonial government,
that might serve as a model for the reform of other
colonies and for after time.   Moved by the latter considerations, I submitted to Mr. Gladstone by letter a
plan for the settlement of New-Zealand affairs, but too
late for enabling him to come to any official decision
upon it.   A copy of that letter was confidentially
placed in Lord Howick's hands by one of his coadjutors
in the attacks on the Colonial Office under Lord
Stanley.

Lord Howick became Lord Grey, and Colonial
Minister.   Mr. Hawes, who had for years been a
convert to my theoretical views and an active coöpe-
rator with me in attempts to give them effect—who
had no claim to being deemed fit for the administration
of colonial affairs, save that he had made a sort of colonial reputation as a disciple and coadjutor of mine—

CABINET CHANGES. 33

became Lord Grey's Parliamentary Under-Secretary.
Besides a semi-official announcement that Mr. Charles
Buller, between whom and me the relation as colonizers was that of each other's *alter ego*, was to take
an active part with Lord Grey in colonial affairs
whilst holding the somewhat sinecure office of Judge
Advocate General, Lord Grey himself solemnly told Mr.
Buller that it should be so. I could not doubt that now
at last, after long years of toil and trouble, I should be
rewarded by the utmost happiness which God vouch-
safes to man on earth, the realization of his own idea.

The question which most urgently demanded Lord
Grey's decision, was that of the settlement of the
affairs of New Zealand; and this question embraced
the entire subject of colonization and colonial government. Upon this subject, with relation to New Zealand, Lord Grey's mind had been long made up, and his
opinions given to the public. Amongst those opinions,
the one which he had most emphatically uttered,
was, that comprehensive, vigorous, and prompt action
was absolutely necessary. Yet as Minister he would
not move a step. He seemed incapable of deciding
officially any one of the points which, out of office, he
had so lately and so completely determined in his own
mind. Those who had made the colony, and recently
co-operated with Lord Grey in exposing its grievances
to Parliament, were utterly confounded. In the blindness of their dismay, they fancied that if they could
bring about an interview between Lord Grey and me,
he might be persuaded to fulfil his late professions and
promises. I believe they hoped that the sight of me
(for I was very ill at the time) might revive in him
the generous impulse which took him to the Clarendon-
Hotel dinner. How they induced him to consent to

an interview I never knew; but I reluctantly consented to it; and the meeting took place at the house and in the presence of Mr. Buller.

Considering how his rank and official station placed me greatly at his mercy, and that I could hardly stand or speak from illness, his reception of me was perfectly brutal. Bearing this with outward meekness at least (for I had promised not to quarrel with him), I endeavoured to perform my allotted task, but without the least success. He listened to me with impatience, would scarcely let me complete a single sentence, and, addressing himself rather to Mr. Buller than to me, talked in angry and contemptuous terms of the principal suggestions contained in my letter to Mr. Gladstone. Though he did not mention either Mr. Gladstone's name or the letter, I now saw that the attempt to make an impression on him was utterly hopeless; and I therefore remained silent till, after one or two fruitless attempts by Mr. Buller to mollify him, he got up, and hurried out of the room and the house as if we had been insulting him.

Some days later, I had a dangerous attack of illness, of a kind that is commonly produced by overwork and anxiety. Continued ill-health has ever since compelled me to abstain from meddling with New-Zealand affairs and colonization in general. When I was no longer in the way, the New-Zealand Company and Lord Grey made a settlement of the affairs of that colony, which leaves every question unsettled, and under which, as I believe, nothing good can be done. Lord Grey and the Company naturally persuade themselves, and would persuade the public, that this arrangement gives effect to the views of colonization and colonial government which they jointly proclaimed whilst at war with Lord Stanley; but when you shall have compared that arrangement, including Lord Grey's short-lived New-Zealand constitution, with the views that I am about to lay before you (views nearly identical in substance with those submitted to Mr. Gladstone), you will see that the resemblance between my recommendations and Lord Grey's doings is altogether unreal, and only so far apparent as to preserve some show of consistency between his principles in opposition and his practice in office. Indeed, I think you will perceive in the end, that as regards many questions besides those relating to New Zealand, a greater ingenuity than Lord Grey's has been employed to make his practice look like his opinions and unlike mine.

I am assured that my letter to Mr. Gladstone is still Lord Grey's *bête noire;* that he is still sensitively fearful of being supposed to adopt opinions of mine, and even more afraid that his fear on that point should be perceived. The latter apprehension partly accounts for his going out of his way to couple my name in public with one of those opinions, with which his own name is inseparably coupled. I enclose some extracts from a letter of Lord Grey's, to which you have alluded.* He is not afraid, not he, of being

Downing Street, March 8th, 1847.
* "You will remember that in North America, the profuse grants made to private persons, and the surrender of the territorial revenue by the Crown to the Provincial legislature, leave to the Government no power of adopting with effect the Wakefield principle of colonization, as to the soundness of which I am quite of the same opinion as yourself. Such are the difficulties which stand in the way of doing more than has been hitherto done by the Government to promote Emigration to North America."

    *   *   *   *   *

"With regard to Australia, I would observe to you, that every thought to get ideas about colonization from me; for does he not himself proclaim the fact? Add that, if he did not sometimes avow the fact, as to this particular suggestion, he would be open to the suspicion of rather too parental an adoption of it. Think of his well-known pride; bear in mind that he can only preserve, or rather recover, his reputation as a colonial statesman, by trying to do a great deal in colonization; do not forget, what his surprising break-down in high office proves, that with a more than common talent for understanding principles, he has no originality of thought—which compels him to take all his ideas from somebody, and no power of working out theory in practice—which compels him to be always in some-body's hands as respects decision and action: apply these considerations to the above narrative, and you will be at no loss to comprehend his state of mind and his conduct on the subject of our correspondence.

You are now forewarned against misrepresentations on that subject which mislead others, and against any injustice towards Lord Grey that I may be betrayed into by a resentment which it is impossible not to feel.

possible facility is now given to the purchase of land in this country, and the application of the purchase-money in carrying out emigrants.

*   *   *   *   *

" Be assured that the colonization of Australia for its own proper objects, which I consider as valuable as you do, and which I am no less anxious to promote, affords no means of immediate relief from such a calamity as that which has now fallen upon Ireland, and cannot be hastily carried into effect. That it may be gradually very largely extended, I have no doubt, and, if I continue to hold my present office, I trust to be enabled to prove."

*   *   *   *   *

" Though I have marked this letter " private," you are quite at liberty to show it to any of the persons with whom you are in com-munication upon the subject to which it relates, that you may think proper."

LETTER VII.

From the Colonist.

MR. MOTHERCOUNTRY INTRODUCED.

IT seems right to inform you, that I know the name of your Downing-street acquaintance. He does indeed possess uncommon attainments and ability. He also knows a great deal more about the colonies than I possibly can. I hope, therefore, that you will continue to consult him as occasion for it may arise. We three may, perhaps, throw useful light on points that are still in obscurity. Besides, his remarks will probably afford me the best possible opportunity of leading you into certain dark recesses of the Colonial Office, which it much behoves you to explore. Rest assured that I will not betray his participation in our discussions. Indeed, as it is unwise to mention frequently a name that one wishes to conceal, and as "your Downing-street acquaintance" is an awkward designation, I would propose that we call him by the appropriate name of Mr. Mothercountry. You will learn by-and-by how well the appellation suits any of his class.

LETTER VIII.

From the Statesman.

FOREWARNED is forearmed; and I feel obliged by *your* plain-speaking. Pray go on.

LETTER IX.

From the Colonist.

TWENTY years ago, colonization was in no respect a subject of public opinion: the public neither knew nor cared anything at all about it. There existed indeed at that time, a controversy between Mr. Wilmot Horton and Mr. Michael Thomas Sadler concerning emigration, which the infinite zeal of the disputants forced into some public notice: but as the only question between them was, whether, as Mr. Sadler contended, paupers ought to " dwell in the land" in order to be fed, or, as Mr. Wilmot Horton proposed, be sent abroad out of the way, the public took no real interest in the dispute.   Still less did Mr. Horton, notwithstanding his singular perseverance, excite a general interest in his plans of mere pauper emigration. Then, as now, the "shovelling out of paupers," as Charles Buller afterwards happily termed it, was a displeasing topic; and though Mr. Horton rode his hobby so as to induce Parliament to try on a small scale a costly and deterring experiment of his well-meant suggestions, he soon rode it to death.   Excepting the stir which his strenuous efforts made for a while, I can recollect no mark, previous to 1830, of the slightest public interest even in emigration; and at that time, the word colonization was devoid of meaning to the public ear.   I will now describe briefly the change which has taken place in public opinion during the last eighteen years.

When Englishmen or Americans have a public object, they meet, appoint a chairman and secretary, pass resolutions, and subscribe money: in other words, they set to work for themselves, instead of waiting to see what their government may do for them.   This self-relying course was adopted by a few people in London in 1830, who formed an association which they called the Colonization Society.   The object they had in view was, in general terms, to substitute systematic colonization for mere emigration, and on a scale sufficient to produce important effects on the mother-country.

They were an unknown and feeble body, composed chiefly of very young men, some of whose names, however, have long ceased to be obscure, whilst others are amongst the most celebrated of our day. They used to say at the time, that they were an exceedingly small minority, as indeed they were; for whilst the outside number of the founders of the Society did not pass a dozen, the great public was either hostile or utterly indifferent to their views. The objectors formed two distinct classes. Belief in the doctrine of superabundant population was, at that time, confined to a few; and even these denied the possibility of a superabundance of capital. Thus some took offence at the notion of sending people out of the country; and others contended that the grand object in our political economy should be, instead of sending capital abroad, to accumulate the utmost quantity at home. But all the objectors united, though comprising nearly everybody who noticed the subject, were far from numerous. The public at large cared nothing about the matter, and could not be brought to take the slightest interest in it. If opponents had been many and much in earnest, converts would not have been wanting: the general inattention was too complete for an opposition that might have proved useful. We could not even get up a controversy, except with Mr. Wilmot Horton and Colonel Torrens;*

---

* Colonel Torrens afterwards became a zealous and valuable convert to our views of colonization as opposed to mere emigration, and

to which, though it put an end to our infant society, the public was utterly indifferent.

We supposed, however, that the Minister for the Colonies, as the guardian and organ of colonial interests, which were manifestly and deeply involved in the question, would bestow on our suggestions his serious attention at the least. He merely told us, that the Government rather wished to discourage emigration: there was more already than they knew how to deal with. When requested to observe that the scheme was not one of emigration, but of colonization, which itself would deal with the emigration, his reply showed that he had not conceived the distinction, nor ever paid any attention to any part of the subject.

That subject presented before 1830 one very remarkable feature; namely, an immense amount of practice without any theory. The practice of colonization has in a great measure peopled the earth: it has founded nations: it has re-acted with momentous consequences on old countries, by creating and supplying new objects of desire, by stimulating industry and skill, by promoting manufactures and commerce, by greatly augmenting the wealth and population of the world: it has occasioned directly a peculiar form of government—the really democratic—and has been, indirectly, a main cause of the political changes and tendencies which now agitate Europe. Yet so lately as twenty years ago, no theory of colonization had set forth what should be the objects of the process, still

also chairman of the commission for founding South Australia in accordance with some of our principles.

less what are the best means of accomplishing them. There were long experience without a system, immense results without a plan, vast doings but no principles.

The two chief nations of the world were, each of them, founding a new colony at the time in question; France in North Africa, England in West Australia. In both cases, the means of a great success were unusually large: such large means as respects capital and population, the main elements of colonization along with waste land, were never before at the disposal of a colonizing nation. In both cases, the failure has been complete. The French government has spent fifty millions sterling with a really anxious desire to colonize Algeria, but without colonizing it in the least: the miserable doings of England at Swan River or West Australia do not merit the name of colonization. The causes of failure in both cases will be examined hereafter. It will then be apparent that whatever France and England did as nations, was perfectly calculated to defeat the object in view: it will be seen, that in modern times the practice of colonization has deteriorated in proportion to the greater means of improvement, as much as its theory was always deficient. Indeed the colonizing measures of our own time have been so paltry in comparison with those of ancient nations, and of our own forefathers, that we now reckon colonization amongst the arts which have been lost. Formerly there was practice without theory, art without science: now, with wants and means exceeding those of all preceding time, we have neither theory nor practice, neither science nor art. Present colonization is only remarkable for its pretence to importance and its real nothingness.

The ideas of the founders of the Colonization Society of 1830 grew out of the first proceedings of the British government in settling the Swan River or West Australia. A perception of the utter inadequacy of the means employed on that occasion—the curious fact of a government elaborately, though unconsciously providing for inevitable failure, with copious elements of success at its easy disposal—led to a careful examination of the whole subject. True it is, that the blind blundering at Swan River directed attention rather to the means than to the objects of colonization; but when the means at the disposal of this country had been weighed, the importance of the attainable objects was perceived: and thus, at length, a system was framed, which embraced both objects and means. The means and the objects were not confounded, but first separated, and then brought together, compared, and fitted. The subject was further divided into two parts; into matters economical, such as the selection of poor emigrants, or the disposal of waste land, and into matters political, such as the effects of extensive colonization on home politics, or the nature of colonial government. In a word, the colonizers of 1830 framed a theory.

It was not in this respect only that they differed from the rest of the community and so formed a party or school: they had faith in the goodness of their purpose. But they were rather a party than a mere school: for it happened that those of them who had chiefly framed the new theory, were constitutionally disposed rather to action than to preaching and teaching. Accordingly, when they found that they could make no impression on the public by argument, they set about endeavouring to get their theory submitted to the test of experiment.

Their first effort, in 1831, was easily successful. It must be briefly described, because in the first place there is no more instructive fact relating to modern colonial government by England, and secondly because its results intimately belong to the present state of the subject.

It will be understood at once, by even the reader who has never thought at all about colonization, that in the business of settling a new country, the mode in which waste or public land is disposed of by the government, must necessarily exercise an all-important influence; an influence similar in importance, for example, to that which the supply of cotton and coal has upon the manufactures of Lancashire. Down to 1831, the general practice of the British government had been to grant land for nothing, and without stint as to quantity: the new theory proposed, among other changes, to substitute for this plan, that of uniformly selling the land for a price in ready money. A change therefore was proposed, which would be a perfect revolution in the most important function of colonial government. The colonies, if they had been consulted, would have earnestly objected to this revolution, as they afterwards protested against it; the colonial governments and the members of the Colonial Office as a body greatly disliked it, because it went to deprive them of patronage and power; the very few persons who at that time desired this change, were obscure and feeble: and yet all of a sudden, without inquiry by Parliament or the Executive government, without a word of notice to those most concerned, and without observation from anybody, out came an Imperial decree, by which, in the principal colonies of England, the 'plan of selling waste land was completely substituted for that of free grants. At the same time, another leading suggestion of the Colonization Society was adopted by the government: as respects New South Wales and Van Diemen's Land, it was further enacted, that the purchase-money of the waste land should be used as an emigration fund in defraying the cost of the passage of labouring persons to the colonies. Apparently, effect was about to be given to the whole economical theory of the Society, apart from the subject of government.

But the authors of that theory attached the highest importance to the subject of government, believing that the best economical arrangements would not work well without provisions for a good political government of the colonists. Now, in New South Wales and Van Diemen's Land, to which alone the new economical theory was, even in form, completely applied, the system of government was the very reverse of what we deemed the best, being in the first place completely arbitrary, and secondly as distant as, in this world of twenty-four thousand miles in circumference, a government can possibly be from its subjects. Those settlements, moreover, had been planted with convicts, a mode of colonization which the theorists of 1830 regarded with the same abhorrence as all the world would feel of a proposal from France to pour her convicts into England or Germany. And lastly, whilst we could not deny that the new regulations for the disposal of waste land and the promotion of emigration, were founded on the principles of our economical theory, we saw very distinctly that the official method of giving effect to those principles was really calculated to defeat them, and to prevent them from obtaining public favour. Instead of being pleased, therefore, we were much dissatisfied with the awkward workmanship of Lord Howick and the Colonial Office upon materials which we believed to deserve more careful and skilful handling.

We hoped indeed to encourage Lord Howick to improve himself as a systematic colonizer; and we therefore praised his awkward attempts; but we also resolved to try and establish a fresh colony, in which both our economical and political views should obtain a fair trial. This determination led to the foundation of South Australia. At that time the extensive country now known by that name, was a nameless desert, about which nothing was known by the public or the government. Some information concerning its natural features was with difficulty acquired by the would-be colonizers, who now formed a plan for the intended settlement, and at last, by dint of great exertion for a long while, got together a body of people disposed to embark their fortunes and persons in the adventure. These, along with the colonizing theorists, were at first encouraged by the Colonial Office, which afterwards refused their only request for a charter of organization. This refusal broke up and scattered the first body of South-Australian colonists; many of whom, though till then without any turn for politics, now joined the rebellious Political Unions of the time, whilst others sailed for the United States, where they have prospered, though they resemble Irish Americans in their feelings towards England. It was clear to us that the part of our South Australian-plan to which the Colonial Office most objected, was a provision for bestowing on the colonists a considerable amount of local self-government. As we could not move an inch without the sanction of that Office, we now resolved to abandon the political part of our scheme, in the hope of being enabled to realize the economical part. The latter part of the scheme was explained in a book,* the publication of which enabled us to get together another body of colonists. With these, however, and their theoretical prompters and guides, the Colonial Office played as it had done before, and as the angler plays with the fish on his hook. We were at the last gasp, when the Principal Secretary of State was succeeded by another, from whom we managed, before he had set foot in Downing-street, to obtain a sufficient promise, that the Colonial Office should not prevent our measure, which required an act of Parliament, from passing the two Houses. Somehow or other, therefore, though not without many a squeak for its life, we got the South-Australian Bill into the House of Lords. A Prince of the Blood asked, " Pray, where is this South Australia?" and the Lord Chancellor, renowned for the surpassing extent and variety of his knowledge, answered, " Somewhere near Botany Bay." It will be supposed, that in an assembly where the exhibition of such complete indifference to colonial matters was thought nothing

* To which the publisher, in the author's absence from England, took on himself to give the puffing title of *England and America.*

strange, our humble project would not be opposed at any rate. Nevertheless, an apparently dangerous opposition met us at the first step. For reasons that will be made plainer further on, the Colonial Office has always cordially disliked the interference with their domain, the poaching on their manor, of the new school of colonizers; and although on this occasion the promise of their chief, luckily obtained before they had any opportunity of setting him against us, disabled them from openly thwarting us, they found means of raising against us in the House of Lords an active opposition, which threatened to prove fatal, because, though it was confined to a few peers, not a single one, except the proposer of the bill, had any active good will towards our measure. The Ministers, however bound by their colleague's promise of neutrality, would give us no assistance in either House; and for a time, the loss of the bill in the House of Lords seemed inevitable. In this extremity, one of us thought of endeavouring to interest the Duke of Wellington in our favour. He assiduously examined our plan, came to the opinion that "the experiment ought to be tried," and then, with a straight-forward earnestness that belongs to his nature, and with a prompt facility for which his great personal influence accounts, lifted our poor measure over all obstacles. In order to mark our gratitude to him, we intended, and told him so, that the metropolis of the new colony should bear his name; but this intention was shabbily frustrated by some whom I abstain from mentioning.*

* The leaders of the first settlement afterwards planted in New Zealand were made aware of this circumstance, by the person who had applied to the Duke of Wellington in the South-Australian case,

The South-Australian Act, in the opinion of its authors, was defective in many points, and contained some vicious provisions.   In order to get the Bill first through Downing-street, and then through the House of Commons, we had curtailed it and added largely to it against our will.   We struck out this provision because it displeased somebody, altered another to conciliate another person, and inserted a third because it embodied somebody's crotchet.   Upon the whole, at last, our plan was so disfigured, that we should have disowned it, if enough of the original stuff had not remained to let us hope, that with very good execution, the new principle of colonization would come well out of the trial.   This, therefore, was peculiarly one of those cases in which everything depends, as in cases of political experiment everything must necessarily depend for a time, upon the suitableness of the executive hands.   The South-Australian Act confided the business of colonization apart from government to a commission, the members of which were to be appointed by the Crown; that is, by the Colonial Office. The commissioners were not to be paid.   It was a grand point, therefore, to find three or four persons, masters of the theory, willing to undertake the task, and likely from their personal character to perform it under a strong sense of honourable responsibility. Such persons were found, but were not appointed. Instead of four commissioners such as Mr. Woolryche

and who requested them, as a personal favour in return for much exertion on their behalf, to give the name of Wellington to the spot most likely to become the metropolis of the Britain of the South. Hence *Wellington* on one side of *Cook's* Strait, *Nelson* being on the other.

Whitmore, Mr. William Hutt, Mr. Grote, and Mr. Warde Norman, who consented to act, only one of these gentlemen was appointed; and to him were joined eight others, few of whom knew or cared anything about the subject. As a whole, it was a commission composed, begging their pardon, of ignorant and careless amateurs. I am bound to add, that for this grievous mistake, the Colonial Office, then under Lord Aberdeen, was not in the least to blame.

Notwithstanding this grievous mistake, and numerous mistakes into which the commissioners fell, the plan worked even better than its authors now expected. A fine colony of people was sent out; and for the first time the disposal of waste land, and the emigration of shipfulls of labourers to the other side of the world, was managed with something like system and care. As respects the emigration of poor people to Polynesia, the first large ship of the South-Australian Commission served as a model for all the subsequent proceedings of that kind: and from that day to this, though it was then found difficult to persuade a shipfull of poor labourers to embark for so distant a part of the world, there have always been more applicants of that class for a passage to the antipodes of England, than funds wherewith to grant their petitions.

It will be understood, however, that the theorists of 1830 were far from being satisfied. In order to promote attention to the subject, they obtained, in 1836, an inquiry by a Select Committee of the House of Commons into their theory of colonization apart from government. The Report of this Committee on

Colonial Lands and Emigration, (whose labours were most ably conducted by Mr. Henry George Ward), had a considerable effect in spreading a knowledge of the subject. It also led Lord John Russell, in pursuance of one of its recommendations, to appoint a Commission of Colonial Lands and Emigration; which, though a mockery of what a commission bearing that title ought to be, has been of service, through the recognition by the Crown of the principle, that the disposal of waste land in the colonies, and the superintendence of emigration, are functions of government which it requires a special authority to perform. I shall take an opportunity of explaining somewhere why this Commission has not realized the intentions with which we must presume that it was created.

One of the members of Mr. Ward's Committee was Mr. Francis Baring, then and now M.P. for Thetford. The inquiry induced him to lead the theorists of 1830 in forming the New-Zealand Association of 1837; and this association founded the company and the colony, whose battles with the Colonial Office have since, more than anything else, helped to form the present state of public opinion upon the subjects of colonization and the government of dependencies by the Colonial Office.

When the New-Zealand controversy began, the efforts of the colonizers of 1830 had been principally directed to matters relating to their views on colonization apart from government. In 1838, the rebellions in Canada gave them an opportunity of promoting the realization of some of their opinions on colonial government. One of them was the Chief Secretary in Lord Durham's mission; and another took a part in it, which was to some extent described in a despatch from Lord Durham to Lord Glenelg, since " mislaid " by the Colonial Office. Hence, the much agitated question of " responsible government for colonies," with which even the British public was for a time made almost familiar by Lord Durham's Report and other writings of a similar tenour. Amongst these, one of the most efficient was a newspaper entitled the *Colonial Gazette*, which was established, and was for some years carried on, by members of the Colonization Society of 1830. This journal exercised an influence very much greater than its circulation. In consequence of the smallness of the demand for such a publication in the mother-country, and the very small sale for it in the colonies, because the local newspapers, one and all, reprinted its contents, it could not be carried on without a loss of money, and was finally abandoned on that account: but whilst it lasted, it may be said to have had more influence than the Colonial Office on the government of Canada: it produced important changes of opinion in the West Indies upon both economical and political questions: it originated in many colonies an ardent longing for self-government: above all, it continually applied a stimulating goad to the sluggish Colonial Office, which it thus urged into the performance of some good, besides stripping and exposing it to the public gaze.

Leading members of the Colonial Office never miss an opportunity of saying, that every labour of the new school of colonizers has proved a failure. There is a great deal of truth in the assertion; but it is not quite true. A comparison of failure and success would exhibit a large balance of failure; but the success is not quite despicable. Two important colonies—South Australia and New Zealand—have been founded by the hands of the theorists of 1830. The prosperity of a third, Port Philip or Australia Felix, has been wholly derived from a realization, however defective, of their economical theory. The sale of waste land in the Southern colonies has produced about three millions of money, which used, though but in part, as an emigration fund, have carried out to that part of the world a large proportion of its present white population exclusive of convicts. The great evil of Clergy Reserves in Canada has been abated. In all the British-American colonies, but especially Canada, the inhabitants have acquired a great deal more of local government, and of the reality of free institutions, than they ever possessed before. In the West Indies, the causes of economical stagnation and ruin, as well as of want of government and of political disturbance, have been made familiar to the colonists. Exertions, commenced by Archbishop Whately, for the purpose of getting convict colonization abolished, were vigorously followed up for a time by members of the new school of colonizers, led by Sir William Molesworth, and have never been entirely relaxed: and those labours have at least had the effect of shaking the abomination, by forcing the Colonial Office to make change after change in it; changes which only more fully show the impossibility of reforming it; the absolute necessity of abolishing it with a view to prosperous colonization in the South. Lastly, our success has been considerable in a matter which, on account of its novelty and importance, deserves separate consideration. When the theorists of 1830 had been some time engaged in the business of colonization, they discovered, and some of them became deeply convinced, that it cannot be done satisfactorily, still less as well as possible, without ample provisions of a religious nature. I shall have to dwell at length on this point hereafter. Here it is only needful to state, that we managed to give some effect to our opinions by proceedings which I will briefly describe.

Episcopacy is surely an essential attribute of the Church of England. Until the Association was formed which made New Zealand a British colony, nobody had proposed to establish bishoprics in new settlements: it was only in old colonies, which had made considerable progress in population, and in which most of the settlers had become Dissenters either from the Church of England or from all religion, that bishops had hitherto been appointed. We asked for a bishop for the first settlement in New Zealand. Everybody laughed at us. We could obtain hardly any serious attention to our proposal. The Colonial Office, which hated our whole proceedings, sneered at the episcopal scheme, and at us for making it, all the more openly because the public, so far as the public thought at all about the matter, supported the gentlemen of Downing-street in treating us as visionary enthusiasts. On account of our scheme of a bishopric, the newspapers turned us into ridicule; public men of mark refused us their support generally; and even leading members of the Society for the Propagation of the Gospel, with the Bishop of London at their head, thought our proposal absurdly impracticable. We persevered, however. At length one of us, Dr. Hinds, the present Dean of Carlisle, converted the

late Archbishop of Canterbury to our view. By degrees
the suggestion made way in high quarters, and became
the parent of the bishoprics of Tasmania, South Australia, South Africa, Australia Felix, &c., &c. I hear
you say, Well and what has come of it as respects the
improvement of colonization? Little or nothing certainly as yet: but I think that a foundation of much
good has been laid. When I shall come to the arguments by which we recommended episcopacy for infant
settlements, you will perceive why colonization has not
yet been much improved by the institution of these
bishoprics. But these arguments had a considerable
effect on opinion in this country. We took care to
sow them about in all directions, with a view to that
result, as well as to our immediate object. They took
strong root in many quarters. I have watched the
growth of the plants: the harvest time is not yet come:
but even at present there is a promising crop in the
new and lively, though too vague interest in the subject of colonization, which is now taken by the clergy of
the Church of England, and by laymen who peculiarly
sympathize with them. It is amongst religious churchmen, both lay and clerical, that this novel interest is
most felt. This is a very important improvement in
the state of opinion on the subject of colonization:
how and why important, will be made plain when I
shall come to the arguments for religious provisions
in the very founding of colonies, in the spread of which
the change of opinion took its origin.

But it was not by addressing himself to English
churchmen only, that the author of the New-Zealand
bishopric persuaded men of various religious denominations to assist him in compelling the Colonial

Office to adopt the principle of episcopacy for the Church of England in new settlements: by general arguments in favour of religious provisions for colonists of whatever denomination, he induced not only Roman Catholics, Scotch Presbyterians, and Dissenters, but also men of the world who had formerly ignored the vast influence of religion in politics, and who at first *pooh-poohed* his suggestions, to co-operate with English churchmen in the endeavour to make religious provisions *for every body* a part of the business of colonization. Accordingly, as a colonizing body, composed, like the legislature, of people differing in creed, we determined to assist all denominations of settlers alike, with respect to religious provisions. We have assisted Roman Catholics according to their numbers, and the Church of Scotland on the same principle. In founding the settlement of Otago, we have intimately co-operated with the General Assembly of the Free Church of Scotland, for whose emigrating members this spot has been adapted by special provisions for religion and education according to their tenets; and we are co-operating with the Canterbury Association, the names of whose members I inclose.* Amongst

* The Archbishop of Canterbury, *President.*

The Archbishop of Dublin.	The Bishop of Oxford.
The Duke of Buccleugh.	Bishop Coleridge.
The Marquis of Cholmondeley.	Viscount Alford, M.P.
The Earl of Ellesmere.	Lord Ashburton.
The Earl of Harewood.	Lord Lyttelton.
The Earl of Lincoln, M.P.	Lord Ashley, M.P.
Viscount Mandeville, M.P.	Lord Courtenay, M.P.
The Bishop of London.	Lord A. Hervey, M.P.
The Bishop of Winchester.	Lord J. Manners.
The Bishop of Exeter.	Sir Walter Farquhar, Bart.
The Bishop of Ripon.	Sir Wm. Heathcote Bart., M.P.
The Bishop of St. David's.	Sir Wm. James. Bart.

us, thus aiding English bishops to found a Church-of-England settlement, there is an eminent and very religious Jew: which may not surprise you on learning, that he did not join us till our principle of strict equality as respects religious provisions for all sorts of colonists, had been manifested to his people by a circumstance, which, though trifling in itself, is a good illustration of the principle. Among the first emigrants to New Zealand were some Jews, who asked us "with bated breath and whispering humbleness," if a priest authorized to kill animals for meat according to Jewish custom, could have accommodation in their ship. We treated their inquiry as a request, and granted it with alacrity, taking care besides that every arrangement should be made to satisfy their religious scruples. The Jews of England have since done the New-Zealand Company's settlements more than one service; and if they were an emigrating class, many of them would have been attracted thither. But how powerfully religious provisions for emigrants tend to promote colonization, is a question into which I must not enter here. In

Sir Willoughby Jones, Bart.	Edmund Halswell, Esq.
Right Hon. H. Goulbourn, M.P.	Ven. Archdeacon Hare.
Right Hon. Sidney Herbert, M.P.	Rev. E. Hawkins.
Hon. Sir Edward Cust, K.C.H.	Rev. Dr. Hinds.
The Dean of Canterbury.	Rev. Dr. Hook.
C. B. Adderly, Esq., M.P.	John Hutt, Esq.
W. H. Pole Carew, Esq., M.P.	G. K. Richards, Esq.
Hon. R. Cavendish.	J. Simeon, Esq., M.P.
Hon. F. Charteris, M.P.	A. Stafford, Esq., M.P.
Thos. Somers Cocks, Esq., M.P.	Hon. J. Talbot.
Rev. E. Coleridge.	Rev. C. M. Torlesse.
W. Forsythe, Esq.	Rev. R. C. French.
Rev. G. R. Gleig.	E. Jerningham Wakefield, Esq.
J. R. Godley, Esq.	Ven. Archdeacon Wilberforce.

this place, I will only say further, that our small doings in this matter are an example which a really colonizing legislature would not despise.

On the other hand, it must be admitted, that not one of the objects of the theorists of 1830 has been fully accomplished. South Australia, as an experiment of their economical theory, has rather failed than succeeded: the experiment did not attain the success of being fairly tried. In New South Wales, the experiment, as such, has been little more than a make-believe, whilst it has proved very injurious to the colonists in another point of view. New Zealand altogether, as respects both colonization and government, is a miserable mess. There is no part of the colonial empire of Britain, no portion of the colonizing proceedings of the mother-country apart from government, still less any instance of colonial government, which the theorists of 1830 can regard without disappointment and regret. The only aspect of the subject that is agreeable to them, is the present state of opinion both at home and in the colonies. Everywhere in the British Empire, they find ideas about colonization prevailing, and a lively interest in it, which twenty years ago were exclusively their own; and when they trace the birth and progress of these opinions to their own exertions, they almost forget the painful disappointments which they have suffered, in the hope that the time is now not distant when their conceptions may at length be realized.

It would be affectation to pretend, that in the labours of the theorists of 1830, I have had any but the principal share. Whilst thus claiming my own for the first time, I long to dwell on the more brilliant efforts, and the public-spirited sacrifices of time, money, and comfort, which others have made in the endeavour to colonize in spite of the Colonial Office: above all, I would speak of the generous sympathy and aid, by which many have laid me under deep personal obligation: but these topics alone would fill a long letter, and I have no right to intrude them on you. I will therefore pass on, after saying, however, that by far the heaviest of my debts of gratitude is due to the proprietor and editor of *The Spectator* newspaper. You have not to learn what the influence of that journal has been during its disinterested labours of near twenty years in the cause of colonial reform and systematic colonization.

I however entirely agree with you, that the present ideas about colonization consist for the most part of mere aspiration; of opinions concerning aims or objects, with but little regard to the means of accomplishment. Opinion of the most enlightened and respectable order in the mother-country knows what it thinks ought to be, wishes for large and definite results, dislikes and despises what has been and what is, but is still in the dark with respect to the mode of setting about the realization of its wishes. In the colonies, ideas with respect to means are somewhat better defined; for there, opinion generally longs for a permanent supply of labour as the indispensable means of economical prosperity, and for local self-government as the *sine quâ non* of a tolerable colonial existence. Whether the colonists are right in these views, is a point upon which opinion at home is in a state not merely of doubt, but of what the late Mr. Thomas Peregrine Courtenay called, being like a sheet of white paper. It is to opinion at home, therefore, that you must address yourself in Parliament.

In the endeavour to assist you, it will not be in my power to do more than repeat what others as well as myself, theorists of 1830, or subsequent converts to our opinions, have already written or spoken. The exposition of our theory (let me call it so once more) is scattered about in a great variety of publications. These are books, blue-books, pamphlets, reports of speeches in Parliament and elsewhere, and many newspapers published in different places. But most of them are forgotten, as you have forgotten Charles Buller's speech; still more are out of print, and difficult of access. My object, therefore, will be to collect these dispersed thoughts, and lay them before you with such corrections and additions as the most recent experience has suggested. Your remarks from time to time, especially with the aid of Mr. Mothercountry's objections and great information, will probably suggest other improvements, besides correcting errors. The order of our inquiry remains to be pointed out by you.

LETTER X.

From the Statesman.

THE STATESMAN DIVIDES THE SUBJECT INTO FOUR MAIN PARTS, AND INDICATES THE ORDER OF INQUIRY.

I AM now sufficiently interested at least, to have a conception of the order in which I should like our investigation to proceed. In describing it, I must recur to thoughts and expressions which you have adopted from my previous letters.

It strikes me that the distinction which terms colonization an art rather than a science, is not pedantic, but highly useful. Colonization, as I have said before, is something to be done, not merely something to be known; and a knowledge of it consists of knowing how to do something. In colonization, as in watchmaking or navigation, the doing has certain results in view. In order to learn how these objects may be best secured, they must be clearly ascertained before the means of securing them are considered: for, of course, when there is something to be done, the character of the means depends altogether on the character of the objects. Our first topic, therefore, is the objects of a systematic colonization. I wish to learn what you think our colonization *ought to be*, as respects the objects of the mother-country.

This question being disposed of, I think that we should do well to compare our aspirations with the present state of things. Our second step, therefore, should be to examine colonization *as it is*.

Since we are sure to be dissatisfied with colonization as it is, and since, in order to improve it, a knowledge of the causes of its actual state is indispensable, but more especially of the causes of what is most objectionable in it, I would propose that our third step should be to examine colonization with a view of determining *why it is what it is*.

This done, we shall be in a condition to work with effect at the more practical, I would call it, the planning part of our task, by considering colonization for the purpose of learning *how to make it what it ought to be*.

To recapitulate: we should divide colonization, as a subject of inquiry, into four parts.

1. What it ought to be, as respects the objects of the mother-country.

2. What it is; or the points in which our colonization differs from what it ought to be.

3. Why it is what it is; or the causes of the above difference.

4. How to make it what it ought to be; or the means of attaining the desired objects.

LETTER XI.

From the Colonist.

THE COLONIST PROPOSES A FURTHER DIVISION OF THE SUBJECT, AND SETTLES THE ORDER OF INQUIRY.

I CORDIALLY adopt the suggested division of our subject, but would propose that we divide it further into two distinct parts, into which, indeed, the nature of things has divided it. This separation, however clear to the mind, cannot be described in a sentence, nor neatly at all by words, in consequence of the unfortunate title given to Political Economy.

The politics of a colony—that is, all things relating to colonial government as there is government in an old country—are totally distinct from the economy of a colony—that is, all things relating only to immigration and the disposal and settlement of waste land—which are matters pertaining to colonies. This marked separation in fact would I think be usefully observed in dealing with each of your four divisions, though less completely with regard to some of them than to others. I would suggest, therefore, that in treating of what British colonization ought to be, what it is, why it is what it is, and how to make it what it ought to be, we more or less separate considerations relating to politics from those relating to economy.

This separation might be the least complete in the first branch of the subject; because, though the objects of the mother-country in colonization are both economical and political, the two classes are so far blended in fact, and dependent on each other, that they may be examined at the same time without confusion, but with a due regard to the difference between them. In the other three divisions, which relate almost exclusively to the colonies, and in which we have to deal with the unaccustomed elements of waste land, immigration, and settlement, the separation between economy and politics should be more complete, though not equally so as to all of them. The most convenient course, as it strikes me, would be, after entirely disposing of the objects, to examine colonization as it is both economically and politically. Under this head would come *all* the impediments to a colonization sufficient for the objects of the mother-country. I would then proceed to the causes of the political impediments, and go on to the means of removing them by a reform of colonial government. Lastly, the causes of economical impediments should be considered, with a view to their removal by means of a plan of colonization apart from government, which would conclude our work.

If you do not write objecting to this arrangement, I shall suppose that you approve of it, and shall proceed at once to the objects of colonization.

LETTER XII.

From the Colonist.

DIFFERENT OBJECTS OF COLONIZATION FOR DIFFERENT
PARTS OF THE UNITED KINGDOM. — WANT OF ROOM
FOR ALL CLASSES A CIRCUMSTANCE BY WHICH GREAT
BRITAIN IS DISTINGUISHED FROM OTHER COUNTRIES.
—COMPETITION AMONGST THE LABOURING CLASS A
MOMENTOUS QUESTION. — INFLUENCE OF ECONOMICAL
CIRCUMSTANCES IN POLITICAL REVOLUTIONS.

IN order to determine the objects of this United
Kingdom in promoting colonization, it seems necessary to mark the different circumstances of different
parts of the country. The economical and political
circumstances of Ireland on the one hand, are so different from those of Great Britain on the other, that
like effects might not be produced in both countries
by the going forth of people and capital to plant or
extend colonies; and if so, colonization would be undertaken with different objects for Ireland from those
which would be had in view for England and Scotland.
For example, it is certain that Ireland cannot spare
any capital, although in Great Britain, on the contrary, capital sometimes accumulates so far beyond
the room for productive investment, that a great mass
of capital is wasted, both at home and abroad, in all

sorts of unproductive enterprises. For Great Britain accordingly, but not for Ireland, it may be an object of colonization to provide a productive field of employment for superabundant capital. This example will suffice to explain why I propose to consider how Great Britain might be affected by colonization, separately from the question of how Ireland might be affected by it.

There is a general circumstance, comprising many particulars, by which Great Britain is at present distinguished from all other countries. That circumstance may be termed a want of room for people of all classes. The peculiarity consists, not in mere want of room, for that is felt by some classes in old countries generally, but in the extension of the want to all classes. In Ireland there is a want of room for the poor, but plenty of room for capitalists if they could be got to go or to grow there: in France there is a remarkable want of room for the literary class, though not for capitalists, who would be far more numerous without hurtful crowding if there were more security against revolutions: in Russia, where trade is despised by the nobility, there is a great want of room for cadets of that class; whilst if capital were more abundant, there would be plenty of room for more people of the labouring class, or else waste land would not abound, and slavery would not continue: but in Great Britain all classes suffer from the want of room; the labourers, the small and great capitalists, the professional classes, and even the landed and monied aristocracy, who are yet more puzzled than other people to know what to do with their younger sons and their daughters.

By a want of room, I mean a want of the means of a comfortable subsistence according to the respective standards of living established amongst the classes, and obviously arising from the competition of the members of each class with one another. Whatever the fund for the maintenance of any of the classes, it is divided amongst too many people; there are too many competitors for a limited fund of enjoyment. It may be said that the fund is too small, not the competitors too many; but, take it either way, whether we say that the competitors are too many or the fund is too small, there is a want of room. At all events, there are too many competitors in proportion to the fund; there is actually a want of room; and the immediate cause of it is over-crowding.

The hurtful competition of labourers with each other is an old story amongst political thinkers; that of the other classes had not been noticed till it was pointed out by the colonizing theorists of 1830. Indeed it was then a new circumstance in our political economy, having grown up from 1815, with the cessation of war, which promoted a rapid increase of capital; with the improvement and spread of education, which augmented the numbers of the educated classes; and with the diminution of public expenditure, which cut down the fund for the maintenance of the children of the gentry. Since 1830, this competition of capital with capital, of education with education, and of place-hunting with place-hunting, has been continually on the increase. It has at length, along with the competition of labour with labour, produced a state of things which requires some notice in detail.

I am not going to harp upon the well-worn string

of the labourers' competition: the topic is too stale and familiar. But some features of this competition are peculiar to Great Britain, and others are new even there. These I will briefly notice.

In Great Britain, far more than in any other part of the world, the labourers' competition is a momentous question: and the reason for this is, that in consequence, partly of the growth of manufacturers, and partly of the decrease of small proprietorship in land and small land-holdings amongst tenants, there is now in Great Britain a larger proportion of labourers for hire —of people whose subsistence depends wholly on wages —than in any other part of the world: in Great Britain, though nowhere else, I rather think, labourers for hire do constitute the bulk of the people.

In the next place, the bulk of the people in this country has been taught to read. It is the fashion to praise this so-called education, and to insist that all sorts of good will grow out of it. I hope so: I think so: but I must be allowed to add that the good has hardly yet begun to grow. Thus far, the education of the common people has not improved their lot; it has only made them discontented with it. The present fruits of popular education in this country are chartism and socialism.

There is a tradesman in the Strand, who was a special constable on the 10th of last April, and who has no doubt that chartism and socialism were put down for ever on that day. I mention him as an instructive " foolometer:" his opinion is common enough amongst very dull people of the middle and highest classes. Others know that chartism and socialism were not rampant on that day, but only a pretence of chartist agitation by a few scatter-brained English busy-bodies, and some Milesian-Irish settlers in Liverpool, Manchester, and London. Chartism, and still more socialism, are not yet ripe: but they are growing apace: and they present, I think, some fearful dangers in the prospect.

I look upon chartism and socialism as representatives of discontent. The honest chartists and socialists (not meaning thereby any of the rogues who trade in the discontent of the working class) are people of the working class, who have got more education than the rest. All those of the working class who are the best educated—that is, who know most—who in stolid ignorance least resemble the bulk of the peasantry—are not indeed chartists and socialists; but chartists and socialists are mainly composed of that class; and I cannot help expecting that as education spreads—as the dullest of the common people become more knowing—chartism and socialism will spread likewise, and in the same proportion. If so, in the end, chartism and socialism will be able to disturb the peace of this country. I do not pretend that either is likely to triumph for a long while yet: ages hence perhaps, both will have triumphed; chartism first, then some kind of socialism: but it seems plain to my apprehension, that with the continuance of discontent and the spread of education amongst the common people, chartism and socialism will have many a struggle for the mastery over a restricted franchise and private property: and in these struggles I perceive immense danger for everybody.

Political disturbance is the form in which these struggles would appear. Now, I say that this country is less capable than any other in the world is, or ever was, of undergoing great political disturbance without mortal injury. The nature of the injury and the probability of its occurrence depend upon certain peculiarities in our condition.

There is not, and probably never was, a country in which credit played so important a part as it does now in Great Britain. In this country alone among the more populous nations, have barter and payment of wages in kind entirely ceased. All transactions are carried on by money of one sort or other. Of the money, the currency of which does not depend upon credit—that is, the precious metals, which owe none of their value to credit—there does not and cannot exist more than enough for carrying on a very small proportion of the transactions, by means of which the whole nation is fed and society held together. The rest of the money, composed of bank-notes, bills of exchange, book-debts, credits, and all kinds of securities or engagements to pay something, owes its currency entirely to credit. Overturn, or only shake the belief, that the promises will be kept, and you thoroughly destroy the value of this credit money. Now the belief, that the promises to pay, which constitute the great bulk of our money, will be kept, depends altogether on the preservation of political order; if there were political disturbance enough to cause a general and serious doubt of the steady execution of the laws, credit would cease: and if credit ceased in this country, what would happen?

Bank-notes would not pass; sovereigns would be hoarded; there would be no buying and selling. Such a state of things could not last long anywhere. If it lasted in a country like France, or Ireland, or one of the United States of America, where the bulk of the people live upon the land and have food under their hands, means might be found to feed the town population. In such a case, the town population might be fed by the government, because it bears so small a proportion to the rural population. But in Great Britain the rural population, which can always feed itself in case of extremity, bears a small proportion to the town population: in Great Britain so large a majority of the people live in towns, and are totally dependent on credit for their daily bread, that political disorders which should destroy credit, would inevitably occasion famine in our towns. If credit ceased, the town markets would be bare of food; and we should have great masses of people in a state of hunger and starvation. This would surely increase the political disturbance. Whatever course events might then take, there would be a high probability, to say the least, of the ruin of our country.

There is a great gap in the history of the French Revolution, which may perhaps be yet filled up. Throughout that history one meets with indications of an all-important influence on events arising from purely economical circumstances, and especially from those relating to the supply of food in towns. One sees, for example, that the bloody fury of the reign of terror may have been a lunacy of the populace occasioned by the maddening horrors of famine, and caught or simulated by the demagogues. But these incidental glimpses of the truth are very unsatisfactory. We want a distinct and full account of the political economy of the French Revolution. To France just now it would be a book

of inestimable value: I cannot help thinking that it
would bring the minds of our statesmen to reflect on
national dangers, which they now seldom heed because
the ugly prospect is too indistinct, the danger too far
off, to be remembered except under the pressure of
immediate uneasiness occasioned by some passing
aspect of chartism and socialism. Without the instruction of such a history, however, we may surely
see enough in this country for arriving at these two
conclusions; that the singular state of our political
economy renders us peculiarly liable to injury from
merely political disturbance; and that it is well worth
while to try colonization, or anything that affords a
chance of reducing that competition amongst the working classes which is the cause of their political discontent. If other motives are required for inducing us
to adopt some practical solution of the " condition-of-
England question," they are plentifully furnished by
the present state of Europe, and in particular by the
infectious character of the communist and socialist
agitation in France and Germany.

Whether colonization would have the desired effect,
can only be finally determined by an attempt to make
it do so: but the mere attempt, if set about in the
spirit that actuates such men as Lord Ashley, and
that formed the unceasing public motive of the late
Mr. Walter, would go a long way towards softening
the hearts of the common people, and inducing them
to bear their lot with patience. Do you doubt that
Mr. Walter's battling for the rights of paupers, and
Lord Ashley's agitation of the Ten Hours factory
question, had a conservative effect upon the popular
mind? I feel as sure of it, as that the Parliamentary-

Fare law and Rowland Hill's Penny Postage had far
more to do with keeping the peace of the country on
the 10th of April last, than all Sir George Grey's
special constables, and all the Duke of Wellington's
excellent precautions. If the classes who alone wield
political power according to law, cannot always serve
the people by legislation, they can at least show that
they would if they could: and the oftener they do this,
the more, we may rely upon it, the common people
will take the will for the deed.

LETTER XIII.

From the Colonist.

COMPETITION FOR ROOM IN THE RANKS ABOVE THE LA-
BOURING CLASS.——THE ANXIOUS CLASSES.——WOMEN IN
THE ANXIOUS CLASSES. —— HOARDING, SPECULATION,
WASTE, AND THE SPIRIT OF THE GAMBLER.

THE competition of the other classes, apart from
that of the labourers, is as obvious as theirs, and,
like the large proportion which labourers for hire bear
to the other classes, as peculiar to the condition of
Great Britain. If it is not so obviously dangerous,
we may yet believe that it is an element of political
danger: for it is a competition even more distressing
to behold than that of the labourers, because the other
classes feel more acutely than the common people, the
uneasiness and anxiety arising from excessive competition.   Thus we have considerable numbers capable

of exerting the power which knowledge gives, who are dissatisfied with their lot, and prone to attribute its evils to the actual order of things political. It was this sort of discontent that induced the middle classes to join heartily in the agitation for the Reform Bill: a like discontent amongst the section of them who live in large towns, formed the Anti-Corn-Law League, and would have led to most dangerous political agitation if Sir Robert Peel's practical conservatism had not been there to avert it: and, notwithstanding the present calm in our politics, occasioned in some measure by exhaustion, and the breaking up of parties after the Corn-Law struggle, though probably more by late events in Europe, which naturally indispose our middle classes to political agitation, there are symptoms of restlessness and a vague longing for change, which indicate that another storm may not be very distant. It is true that agitation raised by the middle class alone, however it carried along with it men of the highest class actuated by motives of party rivalry and personal ambition (as always happens when agitation is seen to be real), would only be dangerous if it did not accomplish its object: it is a kind of agitation that may be bought off by concessions: but on the other hand, concessions as such, only whet the appetite for more; the tendency of all our concessions is towards democracy; and there is always a risk that concession to middle-class agitation may not be made in time to prevent the middle and the working classes from combining in a greater agitation, which, in the present state of this country, might easily prove a revolution.

But there is a less selfish point of view than that of political conservatism, in which competition in the

classes above the common people has lately obtained
the notice of conservative statesmen. The misery and
vice of the bulk of the people, as produced by this
competition with each other, is a stale topic, by dwelling on which in the House of Commons you might
only weary your audience: but a fervent sympathy
would attend you there and " out of doors" if you
painted a true picture of the misery and corruption
of the other classes as arising from excessive competition. What class does this competition not affect
painfully and corruptingly?. One only; those alone
who are in the actual enjoyment of incomes derived
from property and equal to their reasonable wants.
If the income is not derived from property transmissible after death, there is extreme anxiety for the
future welfare of children: and, in most cases, however large the transmissible property may be, the
custom of primogeniture by means of settlement and
will, places the daughters and younger sons amongst
the uneasy class. Speaking generally, then, the class
which alone does not suffer from competition, is a
very small one. The others are always suffering from
it in a variety of forms, as great as the variety of their
positions in the community and modes of subsistence.
In every kind of trade, from the banker's to the cos-
termonger's, the complaint is that there are too many
dealers: but in truth there is too much capital, as is
manifested in the banker's trade by the low rate of
interest occasioned by the competition of capital with
capital in the money market. In the professions, one
and all, the same competition prevails, but manifested
here by the excess of qualified numbers snatching the
bread out of each others' mouths. All trades and

professions being full to overflowing, the risk of entering either career is very great; and thus the competition for employment in the public service, where
there is no risk after gaining the object, is even more
severe than in commerce, law, and physic. But all
this relates only to one sex. With regard to the other,
the mention of one fact will suffice for that mere in-
dication of the symptoms of excessive competition in
all ranks of the middle class, which alone I pretend to
submit to you. Assuredly there is not in the world
a community, in which the proportion of women past
the marriageable age, but condemned to forego the
joys of marriage and maternity, is as large as in this
country at this time. Was there ever a country in
which grown-up unmarried women were as numerous
in proportion to the married? In this respect, Great
Britain differs from all other countries at all times,
and, surpassing those countries in which the institution
of nunneries has most flourished, is the greatest and
the saddest convent that the world has seen. I say
nothing of the monastic life of the unmarried men,
who, if there were as much room here as in America,
would be the husbands of our countless miserable nuns.
The unhappiness! the vice! These topics, you will
excuse me for saying, would be best brought before
the House of Commons by Lord Ashley, who, besides,
is in spirit a zealous friend of colonization.

With regard to the competition of capital with
capital, I would only explain further, that it appears
to be the immediate cause of all the other competitions.
Our power of increasing capital seems to be unlimited.
If the continually-increasing capital of Great Britain
could be continually invested so as to yield high profits,

the labourers' competition would cease, because there would be ample employment at good wages for the whole class. Trade of every kind would present an unlimited field of employment for classes above the common people; the professional field of employment would be equally large in proportion to the cultivators; and in all ranks, neither daughters nor younger sons would be more in excess than the eldest sons of men of assured fortune are at present. The one thing needful for all society is more room for the profitable employment of capital: it is in the excess of capital above the means of profitable investment, that this country differs injuriously from the United States. Do you adopt this proposition? if not, you will not go along with me in deeming colonization a suitable remedy for our social ills. So anxious am I for our agreement on this point, that I will trouble you with one more illustration of the superabundance of capital in Great Britain.

I allude to the necessity in this country of an occasional destruction of capital on the grandest scale. Perhaps if a less energetic people had too much capital, they would waste a little of it continually, so as to keep down the amount without fully exhibiting the destruction; but this is not our mode of proceeding. The practice with us seems to be to hoard up capital till we know not what to do with it, and then to throw it away as rapidly as possible till the quantity for use is brought to a level with the field of investment. Thus one observes for a time a general care and prudence in the making of investments: mere speculation is almost unknown: everybody that saves, saves now. Presently, a decreasing rate of interest on good securities shows that a want of room for capital is growing; and the least prudent turn an eye to unsafe securities which yield a higher return: but the hoarding goes on. At length, interest on good securities is so low, or so nearly reduced to nothing, that the annoyance of risking to lose becomes less than that of the certainty of not gaining: and all the world, everybody being afraid lest his neighbour should get before him, rushes headlong into speculation. Capital without end is thrown into operations from which large returns are expected, but which turn out more or less ruinous: a great amount of capital has disappeared. The ruin and misery thus brought upon individuals frighten the whole body of capitalists: and now another set of people are ruined by the difficulty or impossibility of obtaining capital for safe undertakings. By degrees the panic subsides; steady hoarding goes on again; and after a while the same process is repeated.

The alternations of hoarding, wasting, and panic, are full of evils of various kinds. The misery which they occasion by the breaking down of fortunes, adds to the number of needy or desperate people, not ignorant populace, whose position could not be made worse, and might be improved by a revolutionary state of things. A ruined man is a dangerous citizen; and I suspect that there are at all times in this country more people who have been ruined than in any other country. During the time of speculation indeed, some gain; those who are fortunate or sharp enough to "get out" of bad speculations before their badness is generally known. These gain suddenly and largely: they are, for the most part, gamblers for life. Their success is an example which induces others to become gamblers when the speculation-time comes round again. Indeed, during the time of speculation most people are gamblers. I know of nothing for which these violent alternations of "prosperity" and "distress," of speculation and panic, are more to be regretted than for their effect in nurturing the spirit of the gambler. Ever since capital began to be superabundant in England, the spirit of the gambler has been growing amongst our commercial and manufacturing classes. The old-fashioned, steady, plodding, prudent, and honourable merchant or manufacturer has become a rare exception from the general rule: speaking generally, our men of business of all ranks and kinds are, in comparison with their predecessors of the last century, unsteady, in haste to be rich, fearless of risk, sharp or ready to take advantage of all opportunities, rather than signally honest and true. A similar change has doubtless taken place in America, but from totally different causes, to be noticed hereafter. There, the *general* standard of honour and honesty has been lowered during this century, and especially within the last thirty years: here, on the contrary, it seems higher than ever. Out of business, all sorts of people are more strict than their grandfathers: it is in the various ranks of business only, that the standard of right conduct has sunk. I can find no cause for the change but the spread of the spirit of gambling and unscrupulousness, produced by the excessive competition of capital with capital.

LETTER XIV.

From the Colonist.

THE PECULIAR CHARACTERISTIC OF COLONIES IS PLENTY
OF ROOM FOR ALL CLASSES; BUT WAGES AND PROFITS
ARE OCCASIONALLY REDUCED BY GLUTS OF LABOUR
AND CAPITAL; AND WHILST COLONIAL PROSPERITY IS
ALWAYS DEPENDENT ON GOOD GOVERNMENT, IT ONLY
ATTAINS THE MAXIMUM IN COLONIES PEOPLED BY THE
ENERGETIC ANGLO-SAXON RACE.

WHILST it is the peculiar characteristic of Great
Britain to exhibit a want of room for all classes,
it is that of colonies or new countries to exhibit plenty
of room. In colonies, the field of production is unlimited; and the use of it may be enlarged faster than
capital and population can possibly increase. In
colonies, therefore, the greatest increase of capital and
people occasions no mischievous competition. Both
profits and wages are always at the maximum. And
this happens not only in spite of the greatest increase
of capital and people in the colony, but also in spite
of a further increase by means of the importation of
capital and people. Do what we may in colonies, we
cannot overcrowd the field of employment for capital
and labour.

But this proposition must be qualified. There may be

a temporary excess of capital and people in a colony; and this sometimes happens in small colonies. It happens when a sudden importation of capital, exceeding the actual supply of labour, or of labour exceeding the supply of capital, disturbs the ordinary state of things. In some of the newest, and therefore smallest colonies, we have witnessed at times such a redundancy of capital in proportion to labour, that wages rose to an enormous pitch; the labourers got nearly all, or all, the capital of their employers, and spent a good deal of it in drinking stuff called port wine and champagne. It was not unusual at Adelaide in South Australia, and Port Philip in Australia Felix, for half a dozen common labourers to leave their work, go to a public house, and order a case of wine for their present drinking. I have known the same thing happen at Wellington in New Zealand. In these newest colonies, desert spots are pointed out where a public house once stood, and where now nothing remains but a hillock of broken glass, the debris of bottles of porter, ale, and wine imported from England, and sold to these common labourers at the rate of 2s. per bottle for the ale and porter, and 5s., 6s., and 7s. for the wine. On the other hand, in these newest colonies, a sudden importation of labour exceeding the demand for labour—that is, the supply of capital —has knocked down wages to a very low rate, and even occasioned a total want of employment for some labourers. In all these very new colonies, there has been what we call here " distress " amongst the labouring class. But whether as respects labour or capital, these disturbances of the ordinary state of things do not last. An excessive capital is soon wasted; an excess of labour is soon remedied by fresh importations of capital, or by the rapid increase of capital in the colony. These rare events might be averted by care; but even if they could not, they would only be rare exceptions from the general rule. The general rule is a continual state of high profits and high wages.

But there is another case of exception from this general rule which must not be overlooked. In many colonies, and in quite modern times, neither capital nor labour has always obtained a high remuneration. Algeria, I believe, is one of them. A list of them would contain most of the colonies, lately dependencies, of Spain in South America. In the newest English colony, New Zealand, profits have at times been low, most of the capitalists for the time being were ruined, and a large proportion of the labourers were thrown out of employment, by causes altogether independent of any excess of capital in proportion to labour, or of labour in proportion to capital. The cause of the mischief in such cases, is one that has at all times prevailed over the greatest portion of the world; it is insecurity of property. If there is not a fair prospect of enjoying the proper fruits of enterprise and industry, enterprise and industry are feeble: they are paralysed if there is a well-founded fear of never enjoying their fruits; of reaping instead nothing but loss and disappointment. Security of property is the indispensable foundation of wealth, let all other circumstances be what they may. Security of property depends wholly on government. In order, therefore, that profits and wages should be constantly high in a colony, it is essential that the colony should be tolerably well governed; well enough, that is, to hold out a fair prospect that enterprise and industry will enjoy their proper fruits. In all the cases that I can call to mind, of low profits and low wages in a colony, not occasioned by the disturbing causes above mentioned, the cause has been a stagnation of enterprise and industry, arising from insecurity of property; and the insecurity of property arose from defective or vicious government. I lay it down as an axiom therefore, that tolerably good colonial government is an essential condition of that state of continual high profits and high wages, which moderately well-governed colonies exhibit.

Provided, then, that care is taken to prevent temporary gluts of either capital or labour in very young colonies, and provided also that colonial government is tolerably good, it may be affirmed with confidence, that neither too much capital nor too many people can be sent to a colony; for the more of both the colony receives, the more readily will fresh importations of capital and people find profitable employment; certainly without any decrease, perhaps with an increase, in the rates of profit and wages.

The normal state of high profits and wages, notwithstanding the utmost importation of capital and people, in colonies where the proper fruits of enterprize and industry are secured by good government, arises partly from the manner in which the produce of colonial industry is distributed; partly from the great productiveness of industry in a country where only the most fertile spots need to be cultivated. In colonies, as compared with old countries, the landlord and the tax-gatherer get but a small share of the produce of industry : the producer, therefore, whether capitalist or labourer, gets a large share : indeed, they get nearly the whole : and this whole, as before observed, is very large in consequence of the great natural fertility of all the cultivated land, or the small cost of production. Both the labourer and the capitalist, therefore, get more than they consume. The labourer saves, and the capitalist saves : capital augments rapidly. But as nearly all the colonists are either capitalists or labourers, who have more than they can consume, the whole colony has more than it can consume. Colonies, therefore, are, may I say, naturally exporting communities : they have a large produce for exportation.

Not only have they a large produce for exportation, but that produce is peculiarly suited for exchange with old countries. In consequence of the cheapness of land in colonies, the great majority of the people are owners or occupiers of land ; and their industry is necessarily in a great measure confined to the producing of what comes immediately from the soil ; viz., food, and the raw materials of manufacture. In old countries, on the other hand, where the soil is fully occupied and labour abundant, it may be said that manufactured goods are their natural production for export. These are what the colonists do not produce. The colony produces what the old country wants ; the old country produces what the colony wants. The old country and the colony, therefore, are, naturally, each other's best customers.

But of such great surplus production in a colony as renders the colony a best-possible customer of its mother-country, there is an essential condition over

and above good government.   At least, I rather think
so.   I doubt whether the singular energy of British
industry — that characteristic of our race, whether
here or in America—is not necessary to the production of a very large surplus produce under any circumstances: and looking at the present state of what
may be termed the colonial world, I think that this
notion is borne out by facts.   I doubt whether a
purely Milesian-Irish or Celtic-French colony, however well it should be governed, would be anything
like as good a customer of its mother-country, as a
purely English or Lowland Scotch colony.   Numerous
illustrations of this will occur to you: I would only
mention two.   The United States of America, which
have been chiefly colonized by English blood, are
the best customers that ever mother-country had;
and secondly, of the whole produce exported from
Canada to England, which purchases the whole export from England to Canada, nineteen-twentieths,
I feel confident, are raised by the enterprise and
energy of British, that is, of Scotch and English
blood, although a good deal more than half the population of Canada consists of Celtic-French* and Milesian-Irish blood.   I speak of enterprise and energy
only, not of mere labour for hire; for in Canada,
labour, hired and guided by men of English and Low-
land-Scotch extraction, is principally that of Canadians of French origin and Milesian-Irish emigrants.
Mere labour, without the enterprise and energy required for rendering a wilderness productive, will not
raise a large surplus produce from even the most fertile

* Brittany more than France in general is the mother-country of
French Canada.

soils. In the business, therefore, of creating customers by colonization, Great Britain, like the older States of the American Union, would create better customers than most other countries could.

LETTER XV.

From the Statesman.

THE STATESMAN OBJECTS TO A GREAT DIMINUTION OF THE WEALTH AND POPULATION OF GREAT BRITAIN, AND COMPLAINS OF A PATRIOTIC HEAD-ACHE.

SO far as my judgment is under the influence of reason, I adopt your conclusions with respect to the point in which this country and our colonies in general most signally differ: but from these conclusions an inference is reasonably drawn, which offends some sentiment or prejudice not under the control of reason. The inference is, that in order to prevent overcrowding here, where there is too little room, we must send our whole superabundance of capital and people to the colonies, where the room for both is at all times unlimited. You propose, therefore, to diminish very considerably the wealth and population of Great Britain. The removal of so great a number of capitalists and labourers would, I dare say, be beneficial to those who were not removed; but the idea of it is disagreeable to me.

> " I do not like thee, Dr. Fell :
> The reason why, I cannot tell,
> But I do not like thee, Dr. Fell."

Is it a feeling of national pride, or the vulgar anti-Malthusian prejudice, that leads me, as I am persuaded it would lead the House of Commons and the public, to prefer the manifest evils of excessive competition to such a diminution of our wealth and numbers as must lower our country in the scale of nations? Since I have reflected seriously about colonization, my wish has been to learn by what means we could bring about a sufficient emigration of capital and people, to have the effect of raising profits and wages here: but now that I perceive what a vast amount of capital and population must be removed in order to produce this effect, I begin to sympathize with the school of political economists who think that no country can ever have too much capital, and even with the very different school who deny that population can be superabundant. To think of seeing England less wealthy and populous makes me uncomfortable. I am out of order this morning. Can you prescribe a remedy for this sort of head-ache?

LETTER XVI.

From the Colonist.

AS A CURE FOR THE STATESMAN'S PATRIOTIC HEAD-
ACHE, THE COLONIST PRESCRIBES THE DOCTRINE, THAT
EMIGRATION OF CAPITAL AND PEOPLE HAS A TEN-
DENCY TO INCREASE INSTEAD OF DIMINISHING THE
WEALTH AND POPULATION OF THE MOTHER-COUNTRY.

I HOPE that it will not prove impossible to reconcile your judgment with your patriotism; but in
order to do so we must look a little more closely into
the effects of colonization on the wealth and population
of the mother-country.

Let us begin by defining what we mean by want
of room. Room signifies the fund for the maintenance
of all classes according to their respective standards
of living. This fund is the whole annual produce of
the industry of the country. If the fund were larger,
population not increasing and the present distribution
into shares holding good, there would be more for all
classes; more rent, more profit, higher wages, a larger
income for everybody. So, likewise, if the produce
remained as it is, and the number of people in every
class were diminished, everybody would get more. It
appears, consequently, that there are two ways of

remedying excessive competition; either by increasing the whole annual produce of the country, or diminishing the number of competitors in all classes. A time may come when people in all classes will have the sense, which some few classes of people have now (such as the Quakers), to keep their numbers within their means of comfortable subsistence; but at present we must endeavour to increase the whole annual produce. Why does not the whole annual produce increase fast enough for the object in view? It does so in America. In this country there is want enough, capital enough, industry and skill enough: there are all things except one, which abounds in America, but which cannot be increased here; and that is land. It is the want of more land which stops us, and which is at the bottom of the excessive competition.

It is not a want of more acres, but of more capacity of production, whether by means of more acres, more fertility in the acres we have, or more skill for making those acres yield more. If we could suddenly make the land of Great Britain produce double what it does now, with the present outlay of capital and labour, all classes would be in a state of high prosperity until their numbers increased up to the limit of the augmented fund. There has been an unremitting increase of all classes for centuries, with hardly any importation of food until lately: it arose from and was wholly dependent upon agricultural improvements, by which the fund of maintenance was augmented without any acreable increase of the land. But unfortunately, it seems to be in the nature of agricultural improvements to advance very slowly: they never have advanced, and probably never will advance, faster than the increase of people in all classes.   This being, apparently, a law of nature in the present state of human impulse and self-restraint, competition is unaffected by an increase of produce arising from agricultural improvements.   Along with the improvements, there are more people of all classes to consume the greater produce; and the competition is unaltered. As a remedy for competition, therefore, it is more land that we want.

But it is not more land here.   It is not the land that we want, but the use of it.   The use of land may be got elsewhere.   It may be got by means of exchange.   If, without any increase of capital or people, we could purchase with manufactured goods twice as much food as we obtain now by various means, everybody here would enjoy the same prosperity as if our land were doubled, or as actually happens in America and other new countries.   Every fresh importation of food by means of exporting more manufactured goods, is an enlargement of the field of production; is like an acreable increase of our land; and has a tendency to abolish and prevent injurious competition.   This was the best argument for the repeal of our Corn-Laws. It was little urged in words, but, if I may use the expression, much felt instinctively by the sufferers from competition.

The question remains, however, whether the importation of food can outrun the increase of people. It never has done so yet; and apparently, it never can do so in the present state of the world.   For to every importation there are two parties; the buyer and the seller of the thing imported.   We could make goods for exportation much faster than population can possibly increase; but where would be the buyers? We could buy the food; but who would have it to sell? It is not manufactured goods only that we want to increase rapidly, but also customers who would buy them with food. Now, in countries where food can only be increased by agricultural improvements, the increase of food is very slow, like the advance of those improvements: in such countries, the increase of food will probably not advance much more quickly than the increase of their own population. A great many such countries, besides, almost exclude our manufactured goods by means of hostile tariffs; and not a few of them are just now in a state of political convulsion which threatens to diminish their food-exporting, goods-importing power. There remain countries where food is increased by taking fresh land into cultivation; new countries; North America and the British colonies. There, the power of increasing food is practically unlimited; and the pace at which food is increased in such countries might (as I shall take pains to show by-and-by) be very much accelerated. It does seem possible, therefore, that Great Britain, without Corn-Laws, might enlarge her whole field of production more quickly than her population could increase.

But this is an unsolved problem; and time is required for its solution. For the meanwhile, at all events, there must be a pressure of all classes upon their means of subsistence; the field of employment for capital, labour, knowledge, and ambition, must be too small for the number of cultivators; and mischievous competition must last. For we have now to observe a distinct and very important phenomenon.

Neither by improvements of agriculture, nor by the importation of food, if these fall short of the power of the people to increase, is the competition of excessive numbers in all classes diminished in the least. By whatever means the field of employment for all classes is enlarged, unless it can be enlarged faster than capital and people can increase, no alteration will take place in profits or wages, or in any sort of remuneration for exertion: there is a larger fund, but a corresponding or greater increase of capital and people, so that competition remains the same, or may even go on becoming more severe. Thus a country may exhibit a rapid growth of wealth and population—such an increase of both as the world has not seen before—with direful competition within every class of society, excepting alone the few in whose hands very large properties have accumulated. This is our own case now. In whatever light, then, this matter is viewed, we trace the competition to want of room; that is, to a deficiency of land in proportion to capital and people, or an excess of capital and people in proportion to land.

After reaching this conclusion as to the nature of the malady, the appropriate remedy almost suggests itself. If we could sufficiently check the increase of capital and people, that would be an appropriate remedy; but we cannot. Can we then sufficiently enlarge the whole field of employment for British capital and labour, by means of sending capital and people to cultivate new land in other parts of the world? If we sent away enough, the effect here would be the same as if the domestic increase of capital and people were sufficiently checked. But another effect of great importance would take place. The emigrants would be producers of food; of more food, if the colonization were well managed, than they could consume: they would be growers of food and raw materials of manufacture for this country: we should buy their surplus food and raw materials with manufactured goods. Every piece of our colonization, therefore, would add to the power of the whole mass of new countries to supply us with employment for capital and labour at home. Thus, employment for capital and labour would be increased in two places and two ways at the same time; abroad, in the colonies, by the removal of capital and people to fresh fields of production; at home, by the extension of markets, or the importation of food and raw materials. It is necessary and very interesting to observe, that colonization has a tendency to increase employment for capital and labour at home. When a Hampshire peasant emigrates to Australia, he very likely enables an operative to live in Lancashire or Yorkshire. Besides making food in the colony for himself, he makes some more to send home for the manufacturer, who in his turn makes clothes or implements for the colonist. Accordingly, if colonization proceeded faster than capital and people increased, hurtful competition would be at an end; and yet capital and people might increase here in Great Britain faster than they do now. At what rate capital increases here nobody can tell; but it is said that people increase here at the rate of 1,000 a day: if there were colonization enough, they might increase at the rate of 1,100 a day or more. The common idea is that emigration of capital and people diminishes the wealth and population of the mother-country. It has never done so; it has always increased both population and wealth at home. And the reason is obvious. In the case supposed of a great colonization, and of our actual free trade, viewing Great Britain and all new countries as one country for the purposes of production and exchange, there would be in the whole of this great empire an increase of production exceeding the utmost possible increase of capital and people. Capital and people, therefore, would increase as fast as possible. Some of the increase would take place in the new-country or colony part of the empire; some here: and it might well happen that our share of the increase would be greater than our present increase of wealth and population. " To appreciate," says Mr. Mill, " the benefits of colonization, it should be considered in its relation, not to a single country, but to the collective economical interests of the human race. The question is in general treated too exclusively as one of distribution; of relieving one labour-market and supplying another. It is this, but it is also a question of production, and of the most efficient employment of the productive resources of the world. Much has been said of the good economy of importing commodities from the place where they can be bought cheapest; while the good economy of producing them where they can be produced cheapest, is comparatively little thought of. If to carry consumable goods from the places where they are superabundant to those where they are scarce, is a good pecuniary speculation, is it not an equally good speculation to do the same thing with regard to labour and instruments? The exportation of labourers and capital from old to new countries, from a place where their productive power is less, to a place where it is greater, increases by so much the aggregate produce of the labour and capital of the world. It adds to the joint wealth of the old and new country, what amounts in a short period to many times the mere cost of effecting the transport. There needs be no hesitation in affirming that colonization, in the present state of the world, is the very best affair of business, in which the capital of an old and wealthy country can possible engage."*

Nor is it necessary that the increase of capital and people at home should be wholly dependent on, and therefore in proportion to the importation of food from new countries. Of course, before there can anywhere be any increase of people under any circumstances, save one, there must be the one circumstance of an increase of food. The food must come first; then the people. And further, capital must consist for the most part of food; for if capital employs people, of course it feeds them: the feeding of labourers whilst the produce of their labour is coming to perfection, is the main business of capital. More food is a condition precedent of more capital and people. But all the new food need not come from abroad. Colonization has the effect of increasing the production of food at home. Compare the agriculture of England now with what it was before we began to colonize. Can you doubt that the flourishing manufactures of Yorkshire and Lancashire, for example, and in so far only as they grew out of colonization, have stimulated and improved the agriculture of England, and been the means of in-

* *Principles of Political Economy, with some of their Applications to Social Philosophy.* By JOHN STUART MILL.

creasing the quantity of food and the number of people in the mother-country? An intimate connexion in the form of cause and effect, between the English colonization of the West Indies and America on the one hand, and the improvement of agriculture, with the consequent increase of food and people in England, on the other, would be exhibited by a review of the facts since the time of Elizabeth: and many other instances might be cited, in which colonists, by furnishing to their mother-country new objects of desire, new materials of manufacture, and new markets for the disposal of goods, in return not for food, but for such luxuries as sugar and tobacco, have been the not very indirect means of stimulating agricultural industry and enterprise in the country from which they emigrated. France, with her wretched agriculture, is a country that stands in the utmost need of this effect of colonization; and we are very far from having brought our agriculture to such perfection as to make this effect of colonization no longer an object of importance to us. An increase of food grown at home by means of improved agriculture is, I think, one of the objects of colonization. If you think so, and if you agree with Mr. Mill and me as to the natural effect of colonization in augmenting the wealth and population of the mother-country by means of the importation of food and other produce grown on fresh land, your judgment as an economist and your patriotism as an Englishman must have made up their quarrel.

My next letter, however, will be exclusively addressed to your patriotism.

LETTER XVII.

From the Colonist.

FURTHER OBJECTS OF THE MOTHER-COUNTRY IN PRO-
MOTING COLONIZATION.—PRESTIGE OF EMPIRE.—BRI-
TISH " SUPREMACY OF THE OCEAN" FOR THE SECURITY
OF SEA-GOING TRADE.

I THINK that an old country has objects in promoting colonization, over and above those which
we term economical objects. In explaining my view
of some of them, I must needs dispose, in part at least,
of a question, the whole of which at first sight may
seem to belong to the means rather than the objects
of colonization. The question is, whether it is desirable that a colony should be dependent or independent
as respects government. At first sight it would
appear, that this question requires solution only with
a view to ascertaining whether the objects of colonization would be best promoted by dependent or independent colonial government as a means; but if we
look a little further, we shall see that the possession of
colonies may be good or bad for the mother-country;
that is, may or may not be an object of colonization.
And it is in this point of view alone, that I propose
now to examine the question. The question thus

restricted, and moreover put into a practical form, is whether or not it is desirable that this country should retain possession of its colonies, not as possession or dependence would best promote colonization, but independently of colonizing purposes.

I once heard a discussion of this question at the Political-Economy Club. With its usual neglect of the most important colonial subjects, the Colonial Office had permitted the question of the boundary of New Brunswick towards Maine to grow into a question of peace or war between England and the United States. The Americans would have readily agreed with us upon this boundary question when it was of no practical moment: when in consequence of the progress of settlement in Maine and New Brunswick, large interests came to be involved in it, they seemed quite unmanageable, and would not, I believe (for I was a keen observer on the spot), have been managed except by war, or by that diplomacy of perfect candour and straight-forwardness, combined with resolution and a capital cook, by means of which they were managed by the late Lord Ashburton. The near prospect of war produced in this country an interest about New Brunswick; and the question of her boundary was discussed in all companies. At the Political-Economy Club, a mere man of science contended that the loss of a part, and still more the whole, of New Brunswick would be a gain to England. Of what use, he said, is this colony to the mother-country, that it would not be if it were independent? It is of no use except as a market; and it would be as good a market if independent as it is now. We need not possess a country in order to trade with it. Its dependence is of no use to us; but it is an injury, since the ordinary defence of the colony as British territory is costly; and the possession of the colony is apt to involve us in costly and otherwise mischievous disputes with foreign countries. This was the whole of his argument.

The other side of the question was argued by a London banker, whose sagacity and accomplishments are unsurpassed. He began by admitting that possession of a colony may not make it better as a market; that it costs something in ordinary times; and that it exposes us to the risk of disputes with foreign nations, from which we should be free if the colony were independent. He admitted the whole argument of the merely scientific economist. But, on the other hand, said he, I am of opinion that the extent and glory of an empire are solid advantages for all its inhabitants, and especially those who inhabit its centre. I think that whatever the possession of our colonies may cost us in money, the possession is worth more in money than its money cost, and infinitely more in other respects. For by overawing foreign nations and impressing mankind with a prestige of our might, it enables us to keep the peace of the world, which we have no interest in disturbing, as it would enable us to disturb the world if we pleased. The advantage is, that the possession of this immense empire by England causes the mere name of England to be a real and a mighty power; the greatest power that now exists in the world. If we use the power for our own harm, that is our fault; the being able to use it for our good is, to my mind, an inestimable advantage. You tell us of the cost of dependencies: I admit it, but reply that the cost is the most beneficial of investments, since it converts the mere sound of a name into a force greater than that of the most costly fleets and armies. If your argument is good for New Brunswick, it is good for all our dependencies. Suppose that we gave them all up, without losing any of their utility as markets: I say that the name of England would cease to be a power; and that in order to preserve our own independence, we should have to spend more than we do now in the business of defence. It would be supposed that we gave them up because we could not help it: we should be, with respect to other nations, like the bird which has been wounded, and which therefore the others peck to death. You talk as if men were angels, and as if nations were communities always under the influence of Christian love for each other: whereas men are to some extent devils; and nations take a pleasure in subjugating one another when they can. Vanity, emulation, jealousy, hatred, ambition, love of glory, love of conquest and mastery; these are all national attributes: and whether any nation is independent of a foreign yoke, is always a question merely of whether, either by forces of her own, or by the aid of a powerful ally whom jealousy of some other nation induces to befriend her, she is able to resist aggression. Let all our dependencies be taken away or given up, and the name of England would go for nothing: those of our dependencies which are weak, would be seized by other nations, which would soon want to seize England herself, and would be strongly tempted by our apparent weakness, by the loss of the prestige of our greatness, to try their hand at seizing us. Or would you have

England, after giving up her dependencies, continue to defend them from foreign aggression? Most of them could not maintain their own independence if we gave it to them; and the maintenance of it for them by us would cost incalculably more without the prestige of a mighty empire, than our dependencies now cost with that important adjunct of real, effective power. I am for retaining New Brunswick; and though I think that we shall be under vast obligation to Lord Ashburton if he should enable us to keep it without a war, I would devote all the means of the empire to a war for preserving it.

The banker's argument satisfied me. But he was not aware of a peculiarity of colonies, as distinguished from dependencies in general, which furnishes another reason for wishing that they should belong to the empire. I mean the attachment of colonies to their mother-country. Without having lived in a colony— or at any rate without having a really intimate acquaintance with colonies, which only a very few people in the mother-country have, or can have—it is difficult to conceive the intensity of colonial loyalty to the empire. In the colonies of England, at any rate, the feeling of love towards England and of pride in belonging to her empire, is more than a sentiment; it is a sort of passion which all the colonists feel, except Milesian-Irish emigrants. I have often been unable to help smiling at the exhibition of it. In what it originates, I cannot say: perhaps in a sympathy of blood or race, for the present Anglo-Americans (not counting those Milesian-Americans who pass for belonging to the Anglo-Saxon race) feel in their heart's core the same kind of love and respect for

England, that we Englishmen at home feel for the memory of Alfred or Elizabeth: but, whatever may be its cause, I have no doubt that love of England is the ruling sentiment of English colonies. Not colonists, let me beg of you to observe, but colonial communities; for unfortunately the ruling passion of individuals in our colonies is a love of getting money. How strong the collective love of England is, how incapable of being even much diminished by treatment at the hands of England which is calculated to turn love into hatred, you will be better able to judge when I shall come to our system of colonial government. Here I must beg of you to take my representation in a great measure upon trust. If it is correct, the fact shows, that the possession of dependencies which are also colonies, conduces to the might, security, and peace of the empire, not merely by the prestige of greatness, as other dependencies do, but also by the national partizanship for England of the communities which she plants. To her own strength there is added that of a large family of devoted children. The empire is preserved, not alone by its greatness, but by the strong cohesion to the centre of its colonized, as distinguished from its conquered portions.

The possession by England of colonies which she plants, conduces, I fancy, to another national advantage. It is an advantage reaped exclusively by these islands. For some time, these little islands, with their thirty millions of people, have been becoming, and they are sure to be still more, dependent on the continuance of sea-going trade as the only means of preventing famine and horrible convulsion. The steady continuance of sea-going trade depends for these islands, on the inability of foreign nations to stop or harass our commercial marine. The British " supremacy of the ocean," which has been a boast and a benefit, has become a necessity. If I were prime minister of England, now that the Corn Laws are repealed, I should not be able to sleep if I thought that the war marine of England was not stronger than that of all the nations combined, which there is the least chance of ever seeing engaged in a conspiracy for our destruction. The strength of our war marine is greatly dependent on that of our commercial: for a war marine is composed of practised sailors as well as ships and guns; and it is a commercial marine alone that makes plenty of first-rate sailors. We are about to repeal the Navigation Laws, which were designed to foster, and which, for anything that we can yet positively know to the contrary, had the effect of fostering, our commercial marine. There is some risk that a larger proportion than at present of our external trade may be carried on by the commercial marine of other nations; a smaller proportion by our own. It behoves us therefore to maintain and augment our commercial marine by all the reasonable means in our power. The means of restraint and bounty, on the principle of the Navigation Laws, are dying out. But, notwithstanding ample freedom of commercial navigation, the trade between a dependent colony and its mother-country would almost inevitably be carried on by the mother-country's ships and sailors. Moreover, an independent colony, like Massachussetts, cultivates a commercial marine of its own for its own defence, and is likely to convert the sailors of the mother-country into foreign sailors : if a dependent colony has a marine of its own (as New Zealand, for example, is sure to have in course of time, for coasting and intercolonial purposes), this colonial marine belongs to the empire; it adds to the number of our sailors in case of war.

How colonization itself, irrespective of colonial dependency, adds to the commercial marine of the country which founds the colonies, is a distinct question on which you would do well to consult an intelligent ship-owner. He would tell you that in our own time the little that has been done in the way of systematic colonization, has had a visible effect in adding to the demand for shipping, and especially for ships of the first class making a voyage round the world. He would show you two numbers of a London daily newspaper, in the front page of which passenger ships are advertised; the first published at a time when the founding of South Australia, Australia Felix, and New Zealand, was most active; the second published when these colonizing operations were much impeded by the success of some anti-colonizing policy of the Colonial Office; and then your own eyes would tell your understanding of the bustle of business in the docks at the one time, and the comparative stagnation at the other of the trades of the outfitter, the provision-merchant, and the first-class ship-owner. The temporary briskness of these trades was solely occasioned by the sale of waste land in the aforesaid colonies, and the outlay of some of the purchase-money as an emigration fund: the single cause of the dulness (as I shall have to prove hereafter) was the stoppage of this species of colonization by bureaucratic statesmanship, when a few different strokes of the official pen would have continued and augmented it beyond assignable limit. I cite this case because it occurred lately, and may be proved by living testimony. But this is an insignificant case, because the colonizing operation was stopped. Turning to greater cases, in which colonizing enterprise was not put down by a Colonial Office—which indeed took place before we had a Colonial Office—I would point to the effects on the ports of London, Bristol, Liverpool, and Glasgow, of the colonization of the West Indies and North America by our forefathers. It created a large proportion of the trade of the port of London: at Bristol, Liverpool, and Glasgow, it may be said to have called ports into existence, with their docks, ships, and sailors. But that was long ago, I hear a politician of the pure Manchester school object, when trade with foreign countries was fettered, and colonization produced shipping because with colonies alone was the mother-country free to trade; but now that we are free to trade with all the world as we please, it is not necessary to have colonization in order to have plenty of ships: our trade with foreign nations will support an ample commercial marine. I ask, in reply, with what foreign nations? With the United States, says he. But the United States, like the ports of Bristol, Liverpool, and Glasgow, were called into existence by colonization; and they are still, as regards trade, colonies of England, with the exception always of their hostile tariff. Take the United States, however, with their hostile tariff, and all the other colonies of England, which, being dependencies likewise, have no hostile tariffs; and see what proportion the shipping engaged in our trade with them, both independent and dependent colonies, bears to that employed in our trade with foreign countries. The countries colonized by England, carry it hollow; more especially if we add those, such as British India, in which, without colonizing them, we have substituted better for worse government, and some security for utter insecurity of property. And the reasons are as plain as the fact. They are the reasons before set forth, why British colonists are the best of their mother-country's customers: for British colonization called the town as well as the port of Glasgow into existence, Manchester as well as Liverpool; and every new piece of our colonization adds to our commercial marine, not merely by the demand which it occasions for emigrant ships, but further in proportion as it augments our sea-going trade of import and export.

LETTER XVIII.

From the Colonist.

THERE remains for consideration only one more
particular in which the mother-country has an
end to attain by colonization. It would be gratifying
to our national pride, if our colonies were made to
resemble their parent; to be extensions of the mother-
country, as you have said, over the unoccupied parts
of the earth of a nationality truly British in language,
religion, laws, institutions, and attachment to the
empire. How this aim might be accomplished is
indeed a question of means; but in order to the
adoption of effectual means, we must have a distinct
view of the object. The object is charmingly
described in the inclosed paper, which I have copied
from an appendix to *Thoughts on Secondary Punish-
ments*, by the Archbishop of Dublin. That work was
published in 1832, and has been long out of print.
The author of the little essay on colonization, which I
extract from it, is the present Dean of Carlisle. You

will learn on reading it, that there has been one colonizing theorist besides those of 1830, who only obtained in 1837 the advantage of Dr. Hinds' acquaintance, counsel, and co-operation. His dissertation on colonizing, however brief and slight in texture, is full of the spirit of kindness and wisdom which belongs to his character. I would earnestly press you to read it now; that is, before we dismiss the question of objects, to take up that of colonization as it is with a view of ascertaining the best means of making it what it ought to be.

There is only one point on which I differ from Dr. Hinds. I think that he underrates the social position at home of the emigrants who led the old English colonization of America. But on this point I shall have to dwell at some length in the proper place.

" COLONIZATION.

" SUPPOSING the system of stocking colonies with criminals to be, as may be hoped, abandoned, never to be restored, it becomes an important question, what steps shall be taken in respect of the now convict-colonies; of our other existing colonies; and of any that may hereafter be contemplated. Shall everything be left to go on as it is, with the single exception of no longer transporting criminals? Or shall any means be thought of for remedying the mischiefs done to our convict-colonies, and assimilating them to the character of our other colonies? Or shall we consider whether important improvements may not be introduced into those also, and into the whole of our plans of founding and conducting colonies?

" In order to discuss these questions profitably, it will be necessary to premise a brief statement of some general principles that have been usually overlooked, which has been attempted in the following suggestions for the improvement of our system of colonization.

" It is remarkable, that notwithstanding the greater facilities which modern times afford for the settlement and growth of colonies, the ancients were more successful with theirs than we are with ours. If we look back on the history of Greek emigrations especially, we find many ruinous enterprises indeed, owing sometimes to the situation for the new settlement being ill-chosen, sometimes to the difficulties and dangers of rude and unskilful navigation ; sometimes again, to the imprudence of settlers, or the jealousy of neighbours embroiling the infant state in quarrels before it was strong enough to protect itself. But supposing the colony to escape accidents of this kind, it was generally so efficient in itself, so well organized and equipped, as to thrive; and this at far less cost, it would seem, and with less looking after, on the part of the parent state, than is usually bestowed (and often bestowed in vain) on our colonial establishments. After a few years, a colony was seen, not unfrequently, to rise into a condition of maturity that afforded support or threatened rivalry to the state that had lately called it into existence.

" Our colonies are, in fact, far less liable to those accidents which have been alluded to as occasionally interfering with the success of those of ancient times, both from the greater stock of useful knowledge, and from the greater power and wealth possessed by those who now send out colonies. And yet how many instances are there of modern European states, carefully providing for a new plantation of its people—expending on it ten times as much money and labour as sufficed in earlier ages ; and still this tender plant of theirs will be stunted and sickly ; and, if it does not die, must be still tended and nursed like an exotic. At length, after years of anxious looking after, it is found to have cost the parent state more than it is worth ; or, perhaps, as in the case of the

United States, we have succeeded in rearing a child that disowns its parent—that has acquired habits and feelings, and a tone and character incompatible with that political στοργη which colonies formerly are represented as entertaining, through generations, for the mother-country.

" The main cause of this difference may be stated in few words. We send out colonies of the limbs, without the belly and the head ;—of needy persons, many of them mere paupers, or even criminals ; colonies made up of *a single class* of persons in the community, and that the most helpless, and the most unfit to perpetuate our national character, and to become the fathers of a race whose habits of thinking and feeling shall correspond to those which, in the meantime, we are cherishing at home. The ancients, on the contrary, sent out *a representation of the parent state—colonists from all ranks.* We stock the farm with creeping and climbing plants, without any trees of firmer growth for them to entwine round. A hop-ground left without poles, the plants matted confusedly together, and scrambling on the ground in tangled heaps, with here and there some clinging to rank thistles and hemlocks, would be an apt emblem of a modern colony. They began by nominating to the honourable office of captain or leader of the colony, one of the chief men, if not the chief man of the state,—like the queen-bee leading the workers. Monarchies provided a prince of the blood royal ; an aristocracy its choicest nobleman ; a democracy its most influential citizen. These naturally carried along with them some of their own station in life,—their companions and friends; some of their immediate dependents also—of those between themselves and the lowest class ; and were encouraged in various ways to do so. The lowest class again followed with alacrity, because they found themselves moving *with*, and not *away from* the state of society in which they had been living. It was the same social and political union under which they had been born and bred ; and to prevent any contrary impression being made, the utmost solemnity was observed in transferring the rites of pagan superstition. They carried with them their gods—their festivals—their games; all, in short, that held together, and kept entire the fabric of society as it existed in the parent state. Nothing was left behind that could be moved,—of all that the heart or eye of an exile misses. The new colony was made to appear as if time or chance had reduced the whole community to smaller dimensions, leaving it still essentially the same home and country to its surviving members. It consisted of a general contribution of members from all classes, and so became, on its first settlement, a mature state, with all the component parts of that which sent it forth. It was a transfer of population, therefore, which gave rise to no sense of degradation, as if the colonist were thrust out from a higher to a lower description of community.

"Let us look now at the contrast which a modern colony presents, in all these important features, and consider the natural results. Want presses a part of the population of an old-established community such as ours. *Those who are suffering under this pressure* are encouraged to go and settle themselves elsewhere, in a country whose soil, perhaps, has been ascertained to be fertile, its climate healthy, and its other circumstances favourable for the enterprise. The protection of our arms, and the benefit of free commercial intercourse with us and with other nations, are held out as inducements to emigrate. We are liberal, perhaps profuse, in our grants of aid from the public purse. We moreover furnish for our helpless community a government, and perhaps laws; and appoint over them some tried civil or military servant of the state, to be succeeded by others of the same high character. Our newspapers are full of glowing pictures of this land of milk and honey. All who are needy and discontented—all who seek in vain at home for independence and comfort and future wealth, are called on to seize the golden moment, and repair to it.

"'Eja!
Quid statis? Nolint. Atque licet esse beatis!'

Those who do go, have, for the most part, made a reluctant choice between starvation and exile. They go, often indeed with their imaginations full of vague notions of future riches, for which they are nothing the better : but they go, with a consciousness of being *exiled;* and when they arrive at their destination, it is an exile. I am not now alluding to the morbid sensibilities of a refined mind : I am speaking of the uneducated clown, the drudging mechanic. His eye and his heart miss in all directions objects of social interest, on the influence of which he never speculated ; but which he never theless felt, and must crave after. He has been accustomed, perhaps, to see the squire's house and park ; and he misses this object, not only when his wants, which found relief there, recur ; but simply because he, from a child, has been accustomed to see gentry in the land. He has been used to go to his church ; if the settlement be new, there is no place of worship. He has children old enough for school ; but there is no schoolmaster. He needs religious comfort or instruction, or advice in the conduct of his life ; there is no parson, and no parson's wife. His very pastimes and modes of relaxation have been so associated with the state of society, in which he learnt to enjoy them, that they are no longer the same to him. In short, no care has been taken, as was the custom formerly, to make especial provision for the cravings of his moral nature; no forethought to carry away some of the natural soil about the roots of the tree that has been transplanted. We have thought of our colonist, only as so much flesh and blood requiring to be renewed by food, and protected by clothing and shelter ; but as for that food of the heart, which the poor man requires as much as the more refined, although of a different quality, it has not been thought of.

" Nor is this defect in our system of colonization, one that merely affects the happiness of the emigrant-colonist, by adding to the strangeness of his condition, and keeping alive a mischievous regret for his old country. He was a member of a community made up of various orders ; he was a wheel in a machine of a totally different construction ; it is a chance if he answers under circumstances so different. He must adapt his habits of thinking and acting to the change ; and in doing this he ceases to be an Englishman. He has no longer, probably, his superior in wealth to ask for pecuniary assistance ; his superior in education to ask for instruction and advice. His wits are, doubtless, sharpened by the necessity of doing without these accustomed supports ; but whilst he learns to be independent by sacrificing some objects, or by otherwise supplying some, he finds himself and those around him gradually coalescing into a community of a totally different character from that which they left at home. Witness the United States of America. Let any thoughtful observer consider the traits of character that distinguish these children of our fathers from Englishmen of the present day ; and the probable causes of the difference. We are apt enough, indeed, to ridicule as foibles, or to censure as faults, their national peculiarities—their deviations from our habits. But it would be wiser and worthier of us to trace them to their causes, and to add the result of our inquiry to our stock of legislative experience. We sent them forth, poor and struggling only for the means of subsistence. Is it we that should taunt them with becoming a money-making, trafficking people ? We severed the humble from the nobles of our land, and formed the embryo of a plebeian nation. Is it we that should find fault with their extravagant abhorrence of rank, or their want of high breeding and gentle blood which we so sparingly bestowed on them ? We gave for the new community only some of the ingredients that enter into our own. Can we wonder at the want of resemblance, and of congenial feeling, which has been the result ?

" And yet our American colonies, including the islands which are still attached to us, were not altogether without an admixture of the higher ranks of the British community ; and no doubt their early advance to wealth and strength was greatly promoted by this circumstance. But the advantage, such as it was, was accidental. It made no part of our legislative project. Whoever of birth or fortune betook themselves to the settlements of the New World, did so from no design, of their own or of their government, to benefit the colonies. They went into 'exile through the influence of political or other evils at home, such as drive out some of the better portions of the community, as a portion of the life-blood is forced from a wound, and not as a healthy secretion. Our later colonies have not had even this scanty and ill-administered aid. They are regular communities of needy persons representing only one class in the parent country,—persons who carry away with them the habits of a complex fabric of society to encounter the situation of a solitary savage tribe, each member of which has been trained from infancy to live among equals; to shift for himself, however rudely, and to perform, though with barbarian clumsiness, almost all the offices of life. The military and civil appointments attached to them form really no exceptions; for these are no parts of the permanent community, but extraneous to it— temporary props, instead of stones to the edifice. They live to themselves, and are always in readiness to shift their quarters.

" Much has been said lately about enlarging our colonies, or establishing new ones, in order to relieve Great Britain of a portion of its needy population. Our success, experience shows, must be purchased, if at all, at an enormous rate, and the final result must be the rise of states, which, like those in America, may be destined to influence the character and manners of the whole world, and to form important portions of civilized society, without deriving from us any of that national character, on which we so much congratulate ourselves; owing their national character, in fact, to chance, and that chance a very unpromising one.

" But what is to be done ? Are we to force our nobles and gentry to join the herd of emigrants ? They have no need to go,—no inclination to go ; and why should they go ? Can we afford to bribe them ? They may, I conceive, be bribed to go ; but not by pounds, shillings, and pence. Honour, and rank, and power, are less ruinous bribes than money, and yet are more to the purpose, inasmuch as they influence more generous minds. Offer an English gentleman of influence, and competent fortune (though such, perhaps, as may fall short of his wishes) a sum of money, however large, to quit his home permanently and take a share in the foundation of a colony; and the more he possesses of those generous traits of character which qualify him for the part he would have to act, the less likely is he to accept the bribe. But offer him a patent of nobility for himself and his heirs,—offer him an hereditary station in the government of the future community; and there will be some chance of his acceding to the proposal. And he would not go alone. He would be followed by some few of those who are moving in the same society with him,— near relations, intimate friends. He would be followed by some, too, of an intermediate grade between him and the mass of needy persons that form the majority of the colony,— his intermediate dependents,—persons connected with them, or with the members of his household. And if not *one*, but some half-dozen gentlemen of influence were thus tempted out, the sacrifice would be less felt by each, and the numbers of respectable emigrants which their united influence would draw after them so much greater. A colony so formed would fairly represent English society, and every new comer would have his own class to fall into; and to whatever class he belonged he would find its relation to the others, and the support derived from the others, much the same as in the parent country. There would then be little more in Van Diemen's Land, or in Canada, revolting to the habits and feelings of an emigrant than if he had merely shifted his residence from Sussex to Cumberland or Devonshire,—little more than a change of natural scenery.

" And among the essential provisions which it would then be far easier to make than at present, is the appointment of one or more well-chosen clergymen. It is so great a sacrifice to quit, not simply the place of abode, but the habits of society, to which an educated man is brought up, that, as our new colonies are constituted, it would be no easy matter to obtain accomplished clergymen for them. In truth, however, it makes no part of our colonization-plans; and when a religious establishment is formed in any of these settlements, it has to contend with the unfavourable habits which have been formed among Christians, whose devotions have been long unaided by the presence of a clergyman or a common place of worship. By an accomplished clergyman, however, I do not mean a man of mere learning or eloquence, or even piety; but one whose acquirements would give him weight with the better sort, and whose character and talents would, at the same time, answer for the particular situation in which he would be placed.

"The same may be urged in respect of men of other professions and pursuits. The desirable consummation of the plan would be, that a specimen or sample, as it were, of all that goes to make up society in the parent country should *at once* be transferred to its colony. Instead of sending out bad seedlings, and watching their uncertain growth, let us try whether a perfect tree will not bear transplanting: if it succeeds, we shall have saved so much expense and trouble in the rearing; as soon as it strikes its roots into the new soil it will shift for itself. Such a colony, moreover, will be united to us by ties to which one of a different constitution must be a stranger. It will have received from us, and will always trace to us, all its social ingredients. Its highest class will be ours,—its gentry ours,—its clergy ours,—its lower and its lowest rank all ours; all corresponding and congenial to our manners, institutions, and even our prejudices. Instead of grudgingly casting our morsels to a miserable dependent, we shall have sent forth a child worthy of its parent, and capable of maintaining itself.

" These suggestions are obviously no more than prefatory to a detailed scheme for the formation of a colony on the general principle which I have been advocating; but, supposing that principle to be sound, the details of the measure would not be difficult. Certain it is that our colonies prove enormously expensive to us: such a system promises an earlier maturity to them, and consequently a speedier release from the cost of assisting them. Our colonies are associated in the minds of all classes, especially of our poorer classes, with the idea of banishment from all that is nearest to their hearts and most familiar to their habits. Such a system would remove much that creates this association. Our colonies are not only slow in growing to maturity, but grow up unlike the mother-country, and acquire a national character almost necessarily opposed to that of the parent state;—such a system would remove the cause of this, too. And lastly, among the disadvantages under which the colonist is now placed, none is more painfully felt by some, none so mischievous to all, as the want of the same religious and moral fostering which was enjoyed at home. This, too, is a defect whose remedy is proposed in the above scheme. It contemplates a colony in short, that shall be an entire British community, and not merely one formed of British materials,—a community that shall carry away from the soil of Great Britain the manners, the institutions, the religion, the private and the public character of those whom they leave behind on it; and so carry them away as to plant them in the new soil where they settle.

" Should it be replied, however, that all this is indeed theoretically true, but cannot be reduced to practice in modern times, it is at least some advantage, though it may be a mortifying one, to know where we actually stand, and to be aware of our own inferiority, in this point, to the Greeks and Romans, if not in political wisdom, at least in the power of applying it. If the art of founding such colonies as theirs be indeed one of the *artes perditæ*, it is well to be sensible of the difference and the cause of it, that we may at least not deceive ourselves by calculating on producing similar effects by dissimilar and inadequate means. But if we are ashamed to confess this inferiority, we should be ashamed to exhibit it: we should consider whether we may not, from candidly contemplating it, proceed to do something towards at least diminishing, if we cannot completely remove it.

" It may be necessary to notice an objection that is not unlikely to be raised against the practical utility of the foregoing remarks. These views, it may be said, might have been advantageously acted on when we first began to colonize. But we have not now to form a system of colonization; this has been long since done. Wisely or unwisely, we have adopted a different course, and are actually proceeding on it. The practical and pressing questions, therefore, about colonization, are those which relate to the state of things as they are in these settlements of ours,—the best remedies which may be applied to the evils existing in them,—the best method of improving them now that they have been founded.

" And it must be admitted that, with respect to our old colonies, this is true ; but our new colonies are not yet out of our forming hands. There is one, especially, in the constitution of which we are bound to retrace, if possible, all our steps,—bound on every principle of expediency and national honour ; nay, on a principle (if such a principle there be) of national *conscience*. It will be readily understood that this one is the convict colony in New South Wales,—a colony founded and maintained on principles which, if acted upon by an individual in private life, would expose him to the charge of insanity or of shameless profligacy. Imagine the case of a household most carefully made up of picked specimens from all the idle, mischievous, and notoriously bad characters in the country ! Surely the man who should be mad or wicked enough to bring together this monstrous family, and to keep up its numbers and character by continual fresh supplies, would be scouted from the society he so outraged,—would be denounced as the author of a diabolical nuisance to his neighbourhood and his country, and would be proclaimed infamous for setting at nought all morality and decency. What is it better, that, instead of a household, it is a whole people we have so brought together, and are so keeping up?— that it is the wide society of the whole world, and not of a single country, against which the nuisance is committed ?

" If then, the question be, What can be done for this colony ? Begin, I should say, by breaking up the system ; begin by removing all the unemancipated convicts. I do not undertake to point out the best mode of disposing of these; but let them be brought home and disposed of in any way rather than remain. There is no chance for the colony until this preliminary step be taken. In the next place I should propose measures, which may be compared to the fumigation of pestilential apartments, or to the careful search made by the Israelites in every recess and corner of their houses, for the purpose of casting away all their old leaven before beginning to make the unleavened loaves for the Passover. There should be a change of place,—a transfer, if possible, of the seat of government to some site within the colony, but as yet untainted with the defiling associations of crime and infamy. *Names* of places, too, should be changed; they make part of the moral atmosphere of a country; witness the successful policy of·the French at the revolution. The name of *Botany Bay*, &c., could not, for generations, become connected in men's minds with honesty, sober industry, and the higher qualities of the British character. Change as much as will admit of change in place and name; and the colonists sent out with authority to effect this may then be selected on the principles which I have recommended for the foundation of an entirely new colony. And it might be worth while to bestow, at first, a labour and expense on this new portion of the colony more than adequate to its *intrinsic* importance; because it would be destined to serve as a nucleus of honest industry, civilization, and general improvement for the rest of the colony,—a scion, as it were, grafted on the wild stock, and designed to become, in time, the whole tree.

" But these measures, if carried into effect at all, must be taken in hand soon. Time,—no distant time, perhaps,—may place this ' foul disnatured' progeny of ours out of our power for good or for harm. Let us count the years that have past since we first scattered emigrants along the coast of America. It is but as yesterday,—and look at the gigantic people that has arisen. Thank Heaven that in morals and in civilization they are at this day what they are. But can we look forward without a shudder, at the appalling spectacle which a few generations hence may be doomed to witness in Australia? Pass by as many years to come as it has taken the United States of America to attain to their present maturity, and here will be another new world with another new people, stretching out its population unchecked; rapid in its increase of wealth, and art, and power, taking its place in the congress of the mightiest nations; rivalling, perhaps, ruling them;—and then think what stuff this people will have been made of; and who it is that posterity will then curse for bringing this mildew on the social intercourse of the world; who it is that will be answerable for the injury done by it to human virtue and human happiness, at a tribunal more distant, but more awful even than posterity."

I would now beg of you, before we proceed to colonization as it is, to read Charles Buller's speech of 1843. A copy of it is enclosed, in the form in which it was published by Mr. Murray at the time, and was soon out of print. As it relates principally to the objects which this country has in colonizing systematically, I think that when you shall have read it, we may deem that part of our subject finally disposed of.*

---

* Since Mr. Buller's death, I have determined to reprint his speech of 1843, in an appendix to this correspondence. It will be found at the end of the volume, with a statement of facts concerning him, explanatory of the circumstances which prevented him from following up his great effort of 1843, by submitting to the public a plan of colonization as complete as his exposition of the objects with which such a plan ought to be framed.

LETTER XIX.

From the Statesman.

THE STATESMAN WONDERS WHY THE NATURAL ATTRAC-
TIVENESS OF COLONIES DOES NOT OCCASION A GREATER
EMIGRATION OF PEOPLE AND CAPITAL; POINTS OUT,
WITH A VIEW TO THE OBJECTS OF THE MOTHER-
COUNTRY, THAT THE EMIGRATION OF PEOPLE AND
CAPITAL MUST BE LARGELY INCREASED; AND ASKS WHAT
IS TO BE DONE IN ORDER THAT ENOUGH PEOPLE AND
CAPITAL MAY EMIGRATE TO RELIEVE THE MOTHER-
COUNTRY FROM THE EVILS OF EXCESSIVE COMPETITION.

YOUR recent letters, the Dean of Carlisle's beautiful
Essay, and Charles Buller's masterly speech, have
made a general impression on me, which I think ought
to be communicated to you now. It will resolve itself
into questions. If you can answer them satisfactorily,
we shall have taken a good step forward.

Admitting, as I already do, that the distinguishing
characteristics of this country and the colonies are a
want of room for all classes here, and plenty of room
for all classes there, I want to know why it is that
people of all classes, and capital, do not emigrate in
sufficient numbers and quantities to reduce competition
in this country within tolerable limits. The competi-

tion must be painful, and the attraction of the colonies great. These forces co-operating, the one in driving and the other in drawing people away, why is it that so few go? why is not more capital sent? But let us note a few particulars. The life of people here who are continually in a state of anxiety with respect to support according to their station, must be disagreeable in the extreme; and I should think that the life of an emigrant colonist, in whatever rank, must be very agreeable. If I were a common labourer, and knew what I know about colonies, I am sure that I would not stay in this country if I could anyhow find the means of emigration to high wages, to the fairest prospect of comfortable independence, and the immediate enjoyment of that importance which belongs to the labouring class in colonies. It strikes me, that men possessing a small or moderate capital should have the same desire to remove from a place where they are pinched and uncomfortable, to one where they would enjoy the (to them I imagine) unspeakable satisfaction of daily counting an increased store. To the poorer gentry even, especially younger sons of men of fortune, and parents whose families of children are as large as their fortunes are small, the colonies must, I fancy, hold out a most agreeable prospect. Indeed, the last of these classes appears to me to be the one that would benefit the most by emigrating. In money they would gain like other people; in feeling more than other people, because they are peculiarly susceptible of such pain as they suffer here and such pleasure as they would enjoy there. They are a class with whom pride, far more than love of money, is the ruling sentiment. I do not mean an improper pride.

What they chiefly suffer here, is the pain of sinking, or seeing their children sink, into a lower station: what they would chiefly enjoy in a colony, is the pleasure of holding themselves the highest position, and seeing their children, the sons by exertion, the daughters by marriage, continue in the first rank. The rank of the colony is doubtless very inferior to that of the mother-country; but of what use is his country's rank to one whose lot is most wounding to his pride? With regard to pride, is not the first position anywhere better than sinking anywhere? I can understand that for a "gentleman," as we say, emigration may be a mortifying acknowledgment to those whom he leaves behind, that he has been forced away by his necessities; but, as a rule, people care very little about what is thought of them by others whom they leave behind for life: the mortification must soon be over: and on the other hand there is the prospect of being received with open arms by the community with which your lot is now cast. If you tell me that there are attachments at home, a love of localities and persons, which indispose all classes to emigrate, I answer that in the class of poor gentry, whether young and unmarried, or of middle age with families, having no good prospect here, it would be troublesome to find one who would refuse a lucrative and honourable appointment for life in any healthy part of the world. For this class, I take it, emigration, as it is going to money and importance, is like a lucrative and honourable appointment for life, and beyond life for the benefit of children as well. Why then do so few of this class emigrate? Cadets of this class swarm in the professions and at the doors of the public offices, beyond all means of providing for them: and there must be thousands, nay, tens of thousands, of families living in what may be termed "genteel colonies" at home and on the continent, for what they call cheapness, but really for the purpose of enjoying more importance than their income would give anywhere else but in a colony. In a colony, their importance would be infinitely greater. Why do they not rather emigrate and prosper, than hide themselves, stagnate, and sink?

Again, supposing that there are circumstances which deter people from emigrating, why is not capital sent? To some extent capital is invested in the colonies with larger returns than could be obtained for it here, and without being accompanied by its owners; but the amount is too small for its abstraction to produce any effect on the money-market of this country. You say that in colonies there is an unlimited field for the productive employment of capital: if so, larger investments of British capital in the colonies are not prevented by want of room there. If A B, remaining in this country, sends out his capital to the colonies and invests it with large returns, why should not C D, and all the rest of the alphabet do the same? I suppose that there must be some limit to the investment of British capital in colonies, though you have not alluded to it, and I cannot exactly perceive what it is.

These questions are pertinent and practical: if the emigration of capital and people has reached its maximum according to the present circumstances of this country and of our colonial empire, it would be idle to think of more extensive colonization as a means of remedying our economical evils and averting our

political dangers. We cannot force either capital or
people to emigrate. The principle of *laissez-faire*
must be strictly observed in this case: and were it
otherwise, I cannot imagine the law or act of government that would have the effect of inducing anybody,
not being so minded at present, to send his capital to
a colony, or go thither himself. If there is no limit
in colonies to the profitable employment of capital
and labour, there must be a limit here to the disposition to take advantage of that circumstance, which no
legislation, that I can think of, would overcome. Let
us beware of indulging in day-dreams. It is plain,
according to your own showing, that the emigration
both of capital and people must be greatly increased
in order to effect the true objects of colonization. It
is to the necessity of this great increase that I would
direct your attention. I acknowledge on the general
principles which you have urged, that the tendency of
colonization is to reduce—to cure and prevent, if you
will—injurious competition at home: but practically
all depends on the amount of the colonization. If in
colonizing we should not reach the indispensable
point, we might as well do nothing as regards the
effect upon this country. By increasing the emigration of people and capital in a less degree than the
whole case demands, we should indeed benefit the
individual emigrants and owners of the exported
capital; and we should likewise, so to speak, enable a
number of people to live here and a quantity of
capital to get employment here, which cannot do so
now: we should do this, according to your theory,
partly by creating a vacuum of people and capital,
which would be instantly filled, partly by enlarging

the home field of employment for capital and labour, as that depends on the extent of the foreign market: but in doing all this, which I admit is not to be despised as an object of national care, we should do nothing in the way of raising either wages or profits at home; we should produce, let me repeat, no effect whatever on the excessive competition for which you present colonization as a remedy.   What is the amount of colonization that would affect wages and profits at home?   The question is not to be answered; but we may be sure that the requisite amount could not be reached without greatly increasing the emigration of people and capital.   I call on you to show how this essential condition of the most effective colonization is to be secured in the face of a limit, in the minds of men, to the emigration of people and capital, over which law and government have no control.   To recapitulate in a single question, I ask, what can we do in order that our colonial territories should have the same effects for us, as the unsettled territory of the United States has for the older portion of that country?

LETTER XX.

From the Colonist.

THE COLONIST BEGS LEAVE TO PREFACE AN ACCOUNT
OF THE IMPEDIMENTS TO COLONIZATION BY A NOTICE
OF ITS CHARMS FOR THE DIFFERENT CLASSES OF
EMIGRANTS.

I ACCEPT your challenge without fear, not boast-
fully, but from confidence in the truth of my
opinion that law or government has control over
the disposition of people and capital to emigrate, and
could, by encouraging that disposition, bring about an
amount of colonization sufficient to affect wages and
profits at home. This opinion has not been hastily
formed, and cannot be very briefly explained; for it is
a deduction from many facts. I will go on to these
after a word of preface.

It is my intention to accept your challenge strictly
in your own sense of it, when I say that the disposition of people and capital to emigrate is limited by
impediments which it is in the power of law or government to remove. Law or government has also the
power to encourage that disposition. In removing
the impediments, and affording the encouragement,
would consist the whole art of national colonization.

It is time for us, therefore, to examine the impediments. But before doing this, I would draw your attention by the present letter to some particulars of the inducements to emigration for various classes of people. These may be termed the charms of colonization. Until you shall be aware of their force, you cannot well understand that of the impediments which counteract them.

Without having witnessed it, you cannot form a just conception of the pleasurable excitement which those enjoy, who engage personally in the business of colonization. The circumstances which produce these lively and pleasant feelings, are doubtless counteracted by others productive of annoyance and pain; but at the worst there is a great deal of enjoyment for all classes of colonists, which the fixed inhabitants of an old country can with difficulty comprehend. The counteracting circumstances are so many impediments to colonization, which we must examine presently: I will now endeavour to describe briefly the encouraging circumstances, which put emigrants into a state of excitement similar to that occasioned by opium, wine, or winning at play, but with benefit instead of fatal injury to the moral and physical man.

When a man of whatever condition has finally determined to emigrate, there is no longer any room in his mind for thought about the circumstances that surround him: his life for some time is an unbroken and happy dream of the imagination. The labourer, whose dream is generally realized, thinks of light work and high wages, good victuals in abundance, beer and tobacco at pleasure, and getting in time to be a master in his trade, or to having a farm of his own. The novelty of the passage would be a delight to him, were it not for the ennui arising from want of occupation. On his arrival in the colony, all goes well with him. He finds himself a person of great value, a sort of personage, and can indulge almost any inclination that seizes him. If he is a brute, as many emigrant labourers are, through being brutally brought up from infancy to manhood, he lives, to use his own expression, "like a fighting cock," till gross enjoyment carries him off the scene: if he is of the better sort by nature and education, he works hard, saves money, and becomes a man of property; perhaps builds himself a nice house; glories with his now grand and happy wife in counting the children, the more the merrier; and cannot find anything on earth to complain of but the exorbitant wages he has to pay. The change for this class of man, being from pauperism, or next door to it, to plenty and property, is indescribably, to our apprehensions almost inconceivably, agreeable.

But the classes who can hardly imagine the pleasant feelings which emigration provides for the well-disposed pauper, have pleasant feelings of their own when they emigrate, which are perhaps more lively in proportion to the greater susceptibility of a more cultivated mind to the sensations of mental pain and pleasure. Emigrants of cultivated mind, from the moment when they determine to be colonists, have their dreams, which though far from being always, or ever fully realized, are, I have been told by hundreds of this class, very delightful indeed. They think with great pleasure of getting away from the disagreeable position of anxiety, perhaps of wearing dependence, in which the universal and excessive competition of this country has placed them. But it is on the future that their imagination exclusively seizes. They can think in earnest about nothing but the colony. I have known a man of this class, who had been too careless of money here, begin, as soon as he had resolved on emigration, to save sixpences, and take care of bits of string, saying, "everything will be of use *there*." There! it is common for people whose thoughts are fixed "there," to break themselves all at once of a confirmed habit; that of reading their favourite newspaper every day. All the newspapers of the old country are now equally uninteresting to them. If one falls in their way, they perhaps turn with alacrity to the shipping-list and advertisements of passenger-ships, or even to the account of a sale of Australian wool or New-Zealand flax: but they cannot see either the Parliamentary debate, or the leading article which used to embody their own opinions, or the reports of accidents and offences of which they used to spell every word. Their reading now is confined to letters and newspapers from the colony, and books relating to it. They can hardly talk about anything that does not relate to "there." Awake and asleep too, their imagination is employed in picturing the colony generally, and in all sorts of particulars. The glorious climate, the beautiful scenery, the noble forests, the wide plains of natural grass interspersed with trees like an English park; the fine harbour, the bright river, the fertile soil; the very property on which they mean to live and die, first, as it is now, a beautiful but useless wilderness, and then as they intend to make it, a delightful residence and profitable domain: all this passes before the greedy eyes of the intending settler, and bewitches him with satisfaction.

This emigrant's dream lasts all through the passage. He has left a country in which the business of the inhabitants is to preserve, use, improve, and multiply the good things they have; he settles in one where everything must be created but the land and some imported capital. He finds that colonizing consists of making all sorts of things not yet in existence. He beholds either nothing but a wilderness, or the first settlers engaged in making roads and bridges, houses and gardens, farms, mills, a dock, a lighthouse, a court-house, a prison, a school-house, and a church. If he goes to a colony already established, still the further construction of civilized society is the sight that meets his eyes in every direction. His individual pursuits consist of a share in the general work of con-struction. A love of building, which is apt to ruin people here, so tempting is the pleasure which its in-dulgence affords, may there be indulged with profit: or rather the building of something is everybody's proper business and inevitable enjoyment: for the principle of human nature which causes the loftiest as well as the meanest minds to take a pleasure in build-ing, is called into exercise, not more in the erection of a palace or cathedral, than in the conversion of a piece of desert into productive farms, in the getting up of a fine breed of cattle or sheep, or in the framing of in-stitutions and laws, suitable from time to time to the peculiarities of a new place, and to the changeful wants of a growing and spreading community. This prin-ciple of human nature is a love of planning for oneself, executing one's own plan, and beholding the results of one's own handiwork. In colonizing, individuals and communities are always planning, executing, and watching the progress, or contemplating the results of their own labours. The results come so quickly and are so strikingly visible! If you had been a colonist, or architect of society, you would feel, as well as Bacon knew by means of his profound insight into human nature, that colonization is heroic work.

Man's love of construction is probably at the bottom of the pleasure which the cultivation of the earth has, in all ages and countries, afforded to the sanest and often the most powerful minds. The healthfulness of the occupation must no doubt count for something; and more, perhaps, should be allowed for the familiar intercourse with nature, which belongs to a pursuit affected by every change of season and weather, and relating to the growth of plants and the production of animal life; but the main charm, I suspect, of the farmer's existence—whether he is a rustic incapable of enjoyment away from his farm, or a retired statesman whose most real enjoyment is his farm—arises from the constructiveness of the pursuit; from the perpetual and visible sequence of cause and effect, designed and watched by the operator. Whatever the proportion to each other, however, that we may assign to the charms of agriculture, they are all felt in a high degree by colonial settlers on land, amongst whom, by the way, must be reckoned nearly all emigrants of the richer and better order. The nature with which a colonial farmer associates, has a great deal of novelty about it as respects the seasons, the weather, the capacities of the soil, the seeds, the

plants, the trees, the wild animals, and even the tame
live-stock, which is affected, often improved, by the
new soil and climate: and all this novelty is so much
pleasant excitement. But, above all, the farm of the
colonial settler has to be wrought into being: the
whole aspect of the place has to be changed by his
own exertions; the forest cleared away, the drainage
and irrigation instituted, the fencing originated, the
house and the other buildings raised from the ground
after careful selection of their site, the garden planned
and planted: the sheep, the cattle, the horses, even
the dogs and poultry, must be introduced into the
solitude; and their multiplication by careful breeding
is a work of design with a view to anticipated results.
The life of a settler, when colonization prospers, is a
perpetual feast of anticipated and realized satisfaction.
The day is always too short for him; the night passed
in profound, invigorating sleep, the consequence of
bodily fatigue in the open air, not to mention the
peace of mind.   Add the inspiriting effect of such a
climate as that of Canada during three parts of the
year, or that of the Southern colonies all the year
round; and you will believe me when I tell you that
most colonial settlers are passionately fond of their
mode of life; you will also perceive why the draw-
backs or impediments to colonization which I am
about to describe, do not quite prevent the better sort
of people from emigrating.

    I ought to have remarked sooner, perhaps, that
when once a colony is founded, emigration to it, of all
classes, depends in a great measure on the reports
which the settlers send to this country of the circumstances in which they are placed in the colony.   If

the emigrants have prospered according to the expectations with which they left home, or if their
anxious hopes have been disappointed, every letter
from the colony makes an impression accordingly upon
a circle of people in this country. All these impressions together gradually merge into a public impression. The colony gets a good or a bad name at
home. Nothing can counteract the force of this
influence. No interest here, such as that of a colonizing company or busy agents of the colony; no
power or influence, such as that of the government;
can puff into popularity a colony which is not prosperous; nor can the utmost efforts of rival colonial
interests in this country, or of the colonial branch of
government, jealous of the prosperity of a colony which
has been founded against its will, run down a prosperous colony in public opinion here, so as to check
emigration to it. Whether or not, and to what extent,
there shall be emigration to it, depends upon the letters
from the colony itself, and the reports made by colonists who return home for some purpose or other. I
am inclined to say, that private letters and reports
alone have this influence; for books, or other publications about a colony, are suspected of having been
written with the intention of puffing or disparaging.
The private letters and reports have more influence
than anything else, because they are believed to contain, as they generally do contain, true information.
It is true information from a colony, therefore, about
the condition of people in the colony; it is the colonial
condition of emigrants which, in a great measure,
regulates emigration, and more especially the emigration of those classes whose ability to emigrate is always
equal to their inclination.

It is not merely because the inclination of the labouring class to emigrate is under the control of their ability, that their emigration is less affected than that of the other classes by reports from the colony. Emigrants of the labouring class very seldom return home to make reports in person; and the writing of letters is not their forte: it is a disagreeable tax upon their attention, almost a painful effort of their feeble skill. The postage deters them, as well as their illiterate state of mind. They receive fewer letters to answer. They have, in comparison with the other classes, an awful conception of the distance which separates them from birthplace, and a vague notion that letters for home may not reach their destination. In comparison with the other classes, emigration severs them from the mother-country completely and for ever.

We may now proceed to the impression made on the different classes at home, by colonization as it is.

LETTER XXI.

From the Colonist.

EMIGRANTS DIVIDED INTO LABOURERS, CAPITALISTS, AND GENTRY.——HOW THE "SHOVELLING OUT OF PAUPERS," AND EMIGRATION AS A PUNISHMENT, INDISPOSE THE POORER CLASSES TO EMIGRATE, AND ESPECIALLY THE BETTER SORT OF THEM.

LAYING aside for the present the subject of the emigration of capital without its owners, there are three classes of people whose inclination to emigrate is variously affected by impeding circumstances. These I shall call the Labourers, the Capitalists, and the Gentry; and it is my intention to notice separately how each class is affected by these circumstances. Let me first, however, say a few words about the gentry class.

This is a class composed of what you call "gentlemen." They may become landowners in the colony, or owners of capital lent at interest, or farmers of their own land, merchants, clergymen, lawyers, or doctors, so that they be respectable people in the sense of being honourable, of cultivated mind, and gifted with the right sort, and right proportion of self-respect. This is what I shall always mean, when calling them "respectable," whether or not they keep a carriage and a butler. The most respectable emigrants, more especially if they have a good deal of property, and are well connected in this country, lead and govern the emigration of the other classes. These are the emigrants whose presence in a colony most beneficially affects its standard of morals and manners, and would supply the most beneficial element of colonial government. If you can induce many of this class to settle in a colony, the other classes, whether capitalists or labourers, are sure to settle there in abundance: for a combination of honour, virtue, intelligence, and property, is respected even by those who do not possess it; and if those emigrate who do possess it, their example has an immense influence in leading others to emigrate, who either do not possess it, or possess it in an inferior degree. This, therefore, is the class, the impediments to whose emigration the thoughtful statesman would be most anxious to remove, whilst he further endeavoured to attract them to the colony by all the means in his power. I shall often call them the higher order, and the most valuable class of emigrants.

The labourers differ from the other classes in this, that however inclined to emigrate, they are not always able to carry their own wish into effect. With them, and especially with the poorest of them, who would be most disposed to emigrate, it is a question of ability as well as inclination. They often cannot pay for their passage. For reasons to be stated hereafter, colonial capitalists will not pay for their passage, how much soever the richer class may long to obtain in the colony the services of the poorer. To some extent, the

cost of passage for very poor emigrants has been de-
frayed by persons wishing to get rid of them, and by
the public funds of colonies wishing to receive them.
It will be my business hereafter to show how easily
the latter kind of emigration-fund might be increased
beyond any assignable limit; but, at present, we must
take the fact as it is, that, even now, more of the
labouring class are disposed to emigrate, than can
find the means of getting to a colony. Supposing,
however, that this difficulty were removed, as I firmly
believe it may be, we should then see that the disposition of the labouring classes to emigrate is limited
by circumstances not relating to their ability.

The first of these is their ignorance of the paradise
which a colony is for the poor. If they only knew
what a colony is for people of their class, they would
prefer emigrating to getting double wages here; and
how glad they would be to get double wages here need
not be stated. I have often thought that if pains
were taken to make the poorest class in this country
really and truly aware of what awaits emigrants
of their class in North America, and if a suitable
machinery were established for enabling them to cross
the Atlantic, and get into employment, by means
of money saved by themselves here, enough of them
would emigrate to cause a rise of wages for those who
remained behind. At present, speaking of the class
generally, they know hardly anything about colonies,
and still less about what they ought to do in order to
reach a colony, if they could save wherewith to pay
for the passage. The colonies are not attractive to
them as a class, have no existence so far as they know,
never occupy their thoughts for a moment. That

they have not much inclination to emigrate should surprise nobody.

But, secondly, they have a disinclination to emigrate occasioned by the " shovelling out of paupers." A parish-union, or landlord, or both together, wishing to diminish the poor's rate by getting rid of some paupers, raise an emigration-fund, and send out a number of their poor to Canada or Australia; probably to Canada, because the cost of passage is so much less. Who are they that go? probably the most useless, the least respectable people in the parish. How are they got to go? probably by means of a little pressure, such as parishes and landlords can easily apply without getting into a scrape with *The Times*. Occasionally they refuse to go after preparation has been made for their departure. Whether they go or stay, the attempt to remove them, not by attraction, but repulsion, makes an impression in the neighbourhood, that emigration is only fit for the refuse of the population, if it is not going to some kind of slavery or destruction. The tendency of these pauper-shovellings is to make the common people think of emigration with dislike and terror.

Thirdly, the punishment of transportation excites amongst the common people a strong prejudice against emigration. The judge, when he sentences a convict to transportation, tells him (and what the judge says, the convict's neighbours learn), that for his crime he is to be punished by being removed from his country and home, separated from his relations and friends, condemned to pass the whole, or a great part, of his life amongst strangers in a distant land. The parson of the parish might, with equal truth, address the very same words to an honest labourer about to emigrate. The judge, indeed, in speaking to the convict, goes on to say, that in addition to the punishment of emigration, he will have to undergo some punishment in the colony; whereas the parson would say to the honest labourer, you as a colonist will be jolly and comfortable. But it so happens, that transported convicts, whether in writing from the colony to their acquaintances here, or talking with them here on their return from transportation, almost invariably report, that they, too, have led a jolly and comfortable colonial life. The assertion is often true: whether true or false, it is insisted upon by the convict, who naturally wishes to persuade others that he has undergone no punishment; that he has cheated the law; that he is not an unhappy wretch, but a favourite of fortune. Now and then, a transported convict may acknowledge to his friends at home, that he is unhappy in the colony; but this is a case of rare exception: in the great majority of cases—in those which make the impression here—the transported convict speaks of his own condition, as a convict, in the very terms which an honest, industrious emigrant uses, when telling of his light work and high wages, his lots of victuals, drink, and tobacco, his frequent amusements, and his contemplated purchase of a hundred acres. Such reports from convicts are being continually received amongst the poor in all parts of this country. They may encourage crime; but they certainly discourage emigration. In the mind of the common people, they confound emigration and punishment, emigration and disgrace, emigration and shame. And the impression is strongest on the best of the common people; on those, that is, who would be preferred by a colony choosing for itself, and whom an imperial legislature would prefer if it really wished to found colonies with the best materials.

LETTER XXII.

From the Colonist.

THE SHAME OF THE HIGHER ORDER OF SETTLERS WHEN
THEY FIRST THINK OF EMIGRATING.——THE JEALOUSY
OF A WIFE.——HOW EMIGRATION, AS THE PUNISHMENT
OF CRIME, AFFECTS OPINION IN THIS COUNTRY WITH
REGARD TO EMIGRATION IN GENERAL.——COLONISTS
AND COLONIES DESPISED IN THE MOTHER-COUNTRY.

IT has been my lot to become acquainted with a considerable number of the gentry class of emigrants; and I declare, in the first place, that I never met with one, who, when he first contemplated emigration, was not ashamed and afraid of his own purpose; and secondly, that I know not of one whose objects in emigrating have been realized. I wish I did not know a great many whose hopes as emigrants have been bitterly disappointed. The causes of the disappointment, as well as the shame and fear, may be easily explained. I will begin with the shame.

You may have a difficulty in believing or understanding it, but much experience has made me confident, that the highest class who think of emigrating, to whom the idea of emigration for themselves ever occurs, associate that idea with the idea of convict transportation, even more painfully than the poorest and meanest class do. This association of ideas is not deliberate, but undesigned, almost unconscious: it is a consequence of the facts, and of the nature of the human mind. A case is within my knowledge, in which a gentleman of good. birth and connexions contemplated emigrating to Australia Felix. He had a small fortune, a large family of children, and a handsome wife, to whom he was tenderly attached, though she was not the wisest of her sex. As the children grew up, the income seemed to grow smaller, though it remained the same; the wants increased whilst the means of supplying them were stationary. The education of the boys was costly; that of the girls inferior to that of other girls in their station. To provide for both, one after another of the parents' luxuries, and of the outward marks of their station, was reluctantly laid down. In order to establish the sons in life, more money was required than could by any means be found; and two of the daughters had already entered on the miserable period between lively girlhood and confirmed old-maidism. The father passed from the state of self-satisfied enjoyment, first into uneasiness, then into impatience, and at last into a discontent at once angry and mournful: the mother fretted continually. They had married very young, and were still in the prime of life. At last, there was added to the mother's troubles, that of jealousy. She had reason to think that her husband's affections were estranged from her. He went to London without telling her for what. He returned without reporting whom he had seen, or what he had done. At home, he took no interest in his usual occupations or amusements. He was absorbed with secret thoughts, absent, inattentive, and unaffectionate, but in apparent good humour with himself, and charmed with the subject of his secret contemplations. He had a key made for the post-bag, which had been without one for years; and instead of leaving all his letters about, as was his wont, he carefully put some of them away, and was caught once or twice in the act of reading them in secret with smiling lips and sparkling eyes. His wife did not complain, but now and then hinted to him that she perceived the change in his demeanour. On these occasions he protested that she was mistaken, and for a while afterwards put a guard upon his behaviour for the evident purpose of averting her suspicions. At last, poor woman, her jealousy exploded; and it turned out that he had been all this time forming a plan of emigration for the family. Whilst he was so engaged, his mind had naturally fixed on the pleasant features of the project; the delightful climate, the fine domain, the pastoral life, the creative business of settling, the full and pleasing occupation, the consequence which a person of his station would enjoy in the colony, the ample room for boys and girls, and the happy change for his harassed wife. This explains his smiling self-satisfaction: his secrecy was deliberate, because he was afraid that if he disclosed his scheme at home before it was irrevocably matured, his wife and her relations, and his own relations as well, would call it a scheme of transportation, and worry him into abandoning it.

They did worry him by talking about Botany Bay. In vain he protested that Australia Felix is not a penal colony: they found out, that though convicts

are not sent to Port Philip to undergo punishment as
convicts, they are sent thither as "exiles;" and that
swarms of emancipated convicts resort thither from
Van Diemen's Land and New South Wales: the lady's
brother, the rector of their parish, explained that Lord
Grey's plan of convict transportation is a plan of emigration for convicts; the very plan contemplated by the
brother-in-law for himself and family. They got hold
of a Hobart-Town newspaper, which contained the
report of a public meeting held for the purpose of
laying before her Majesty's Government a description
of the social horrors inflicted on Tasmania by the plan
of exiling convicts to that island, and starting them
out of the ship on their arrival as free as any other
emigrants, or as thieves in the Strand. The would-be
emigrant so far gave way to this domestic storm, as to
offer, that New Zealand instead of Australia Felix
should be their destination; but then they proved to
him, with the aid of a cousin who is in the Colonial
Office, that convict-boys from Parkhurst prison are
sent to New Zealand, and that Lord Grey contemplates making those islands a receptacle of convict
"exiles." In the end, they taunted him into giving
up his scheme, and settling, poor fellow, at Boulogne,
in order to be somebody there instead of nobody at
home.

I do not pretend that the only argument of the wife
and her supporters consisted of taunts founded on the
late resemblance between emigration and transportation, on their present identity, or on the state of
society in the Southern colonies as it has been affected
by convict colonization. They used other arguments,
but so far of a like kind, that however politely ex-

pressed in words, they consisted of sneers, taunts, and reproaches. Having themselves a lively antipathy to the notion of a gentleman's family emigrating at all, they painted emigration in all its most unfavourable and repulsive colours; and some of the darkest of these are drawn from emigration as the result of burglary, bigamy, or murder, and from the moral and social pestilence inflicted upon colonies by convict emigration. But there are several dark colours besides these, in which emigration for respectable families may be truly described. The next that occurs to me has but an indirect relation to the emigration of convicts.

I would beg of you to exert your imagination for the purpose of conceiving what would be the public state of mind in this country, if the Emperor Nicholas, or President Polk should ask us to let him send the convicts of his nation to inhabit this country as free exiles. Fancy John Bull's fury. His rage would arise partly from his view of the evils to which our country would be subjected, by continually adding to our own criminals a number of Russian or American robbers and assassins; but it would be partly, and I think chiefly, occasioned by the national insult of the proposal for treating his country as fit to be the moral cess-pool of another community. We should feel, that the Russians or Americans as the case might be, most cordially despised us; that as a nation or community we were deemed inferior, low, base, utterly devoid of honourable pride, and virtuous self-respect; that we ought instantly to go to war and thrash the insolence out of the Yankees or the Cossacks. But you can't thoroughly imagine the case, because so gross an insult to so powerful a nation as this, is inconceivable. We put this affront on some of our colonies with as much coolness and complacency as if we thought they liked it. Without the least compunction or hesitation, we degrade and insult a group of our colonies, by sending thither, as to their proper home, our own convicts and those of our other dependencies. In many other ways we treat them as communities so mean and low in character, as to be incapable of feeling an outrage. Our own feeling of contempt for them was capitally expressed long ago by an English Attorney-General under William and Mary. This high officer of the crown was instructed to prepare a charter for establishing a college in Virginia, of which the object was to educate and qualify young men to be ministers of the Gospel. He protested against the grant, declaring he did not see the slightest occasion for such a college in Virginia. A delegate of the colonists begged Mr. Attorney would consider that the people of Virginia had souls to be saved as well as the people of England. " Souls!" said he; " damn your souls!—make tobacco." That was long ago: well, but you will recollect, because it belongs to the history of home politics, that letter which, in Lord Melbourne's time, Mr. O'Connell wrote to one of his " tail," who had got himself banished from decent society in this country, saying in effect, though I can do nothing for you here, if you will retire from Parliament for the sake of the credit of our party, I will get you a place in the colonies. Anything is good enough for the colonies. It would be easy to cite, if they had been published, as Mr. O'Connell's letter was, very many cases in which, and quite of late years too, somebody has obtained a place in the colonies, not only in spite of his having lost his character here, but because he had lost it: somebody wanted to get rid of him, and anything is good enough for the colonies. Some four or five years ago, a young clergyman, wishing to qualify for an appointment in the colonies, was under examination by a bishop's chaplain: the bishop came into the room, and presently observed to his chaplain, that he thought the examination was insufficient as a test of the proper qualities of a clergyman, when the chaplain excused himself by saying, " It is only a gentleman for the colonies:" and the bishop seemed perfectly satisfied with the answer. Contempt for the colonies, a sense of their inferiority or lowness, pervades society here. When it is proposed by a thoughtful statesman to bestow upon those colonies which have none, a considerable portion of local self-government, the vulgar mind of this country is- a little offended, and thinks that a colonial community is rather presumptuous in supposing itself capable of managing its own affairs as well as they can be managed by the Right Honourable Mr. or Lord Somebody, who sits in the great house at the bottom of Downing-street. The vulgar notion is, that, as in the opinion of William and Mary's Attorney-General, the Virginians had not souls to be saved, so colonists in general have not, and have no business to have, political ideas; that the only business for which they are fit, is to send home, for the good of this country, plenty of timber, or flour, or sugar, or wool. As anything is good enough for the colonies, so the colonies are good for nothing but as they humbly serve our purposes.

If we look with care into the causes of the revolt of

the thirteen great English colonies of North America, we find that the leading colonists were made disaffected more by the contemptuous, than by the unjust and tyrannical treatment, which their country received at the hands of its parent. Franklin, the representative in this country of one of the greatest of those colonies, was shied and snubbed in London: the first feeling of disloyalty was probably planted in the breast of Washington by the contemptuous treatment which he received as an officer of the provincial army. The instances of such treatment of colonists are without number.

But that, you may say again, was long ago: well, let us mark the present difference of the reception which we give to foreigners, from that which we give to colonists when they visit England. When a person of any mark in any foreign country comes to London on a visit of curiosity, he has only to make known his arrival, in order to receive all kinds of attentions from the circles whose civilities are most prized; if only a personage in some German principality, or small Italian state, he is sought out, fêted, perhaps lionized, all to his heart's content. When a distinguished colonist comes to London — one even, whose name stands as high in his own community as the names of the leaders of the Government and Opposition do here—he prowls about the streets, and sees sights till he is sick of doing nothing else, and then returns home disgusted with his visit to the old country. Nobody has paid him any attention because he was a colonist. Not very long ago, one of the first men in Canada, the most important of our colonies, came to England on a mission with which he was charged by the colonial House of Commons. He was a Canadian of French origin, of most polite manners, well informed, a person of truth and honour, altogether equal to the best order of people in the most important countries. On account of these qualities, and also because he was rich and public spirited, he enjoyed the marked respect of his fellow-colonists. The delays of the Colonial Office kept him in England for, I believe, more than two years; and during all this time, he resided at a tavern in the city, the London Coffee-House on Ludgate Hill, totally unknowing and unknown out of the coffee-room. He was a Canadian, that is a colonist, and was less cared about here than a load of timber or a barrel of flour coming from the St. Lawrence. This is no solitary instance. Colonists, more especially if they are rich, intelligent, and of importance in their own country, frequently come to England, not merely as foreigners do, to see, but to admire and glory in the wonders of our great little country; and, I repeat, those who come are generally the first people in the colony. Do you ever meet any of them in the houses of your friends? Has ever the name of one of them been upon your own invitation list? Certainly not, unless by some singular accident. But I, in my obscure position, and as having been a colonist myself, see numbers of these neglected visitors of England; and I see how others treat them, or rather neither well nor ill treat them, but take no sort of notice of them, because they despise them as colonists. I am not thinking in the least now of the national impolicy of such inhospitality and bad manners, but exclusively of the fact, that among the gentry rank of this country, colonies and colonists are deemed inferior, low, a baser order of communities and beings; and that in this despicable light we regard them, quite as unaffectedly as William and Mary's Attorney-General did, though we do not express our opinion so emphatically. Is it surprising, then, that an English gentleman should feel somewhat ashamed of himself when he first entertains the idea of becoming a colonist? is not the indisposition of our gentry to emigrate just what might have been expected?

What is worse, speaking generally, colonies and colonists are in fact, as well as in the estimation of the British gentry, inferior, low, unworthy of much respect, properly disliked and despised by people of refinement and honour here, who happen to be acquainted with the state of society in the colonies. But the proof of this must be reserved for another letter.

LETTER XXIII.

From the Colonist.·

LOW STANDARD OF MORALS AND MANNERS IN THE
COLONIES.—COLONIAL " SMARTNESS."—WANT OF IN-
TELLECTUAL CULTIVATION. — MAIN DISTINCTION BE-
TWEEN SAVAGE AND CIVILIZED LIFE.

FROM the sweeping assertion which closed my last
letter, I would except many individuals in every
colony, but only one colonial community. However
marked and numerous the exceptions may be in some
colonies, they are but exceptions from the rule in all;
and in some, the rule has few exceptions. I proceed
to explain and justify the statement.

In all colonies not infected with crime by convict
transportation or banishment, crime is rare in comparison with what it is in this country: it is so, because in a country where the poorest are well off, and
may even grow rich if they please, the temptation to
crime is very weak. In the rural parts of uninfected
colonies, the sorts of crime which fill our gaols at
home, and found some of our colonies, are almost entirely unknown. I have known a considerable district
in French Canada, in which the oldest inhabitant did
not remember a crime to have been committed; and

in the whole of that part of North America, which is some hundred miles long and which contains as many people as·the rural counties of Norfolk and Suffolk, the only buildings in which you can lock up a criminal are two or three jails in towns where British soldiers and shovelled-out paupers are numerous. Crime is rare in Nova Scotia and New Brunswick; so it is in South Africa and West Australia. The colonial soil, in a word, is unsuitable for crime, which grows there slowly and with difficulty. In the convict colonies and their immediate neighbours, it is the imperial government which forces crime to grow abundantly in a soil naturally unfavourable to it.

But the colonial soil everywhere seems highly favourable to the growth of conduct which, without being criminal according to law, is very much objected to by the better sort of people in this country. I mean all those acts which, in Upper Canada and the State of New York, are called "smart" conduct; which consist of taking advantage or overreaching, of forgetting promises, of betraying confidence, of unscrupulously sacrificing all the other numbers to " number one." In colonies, such conduct is commonly termed clever, cute, dexterous; in this country, it is called dishonourable: the honourable colonists who strongly disapprove of such conduct, more especially if they are recent emigrants of the better order, often call it " colonial." For the growth of honour, in a word, the colonies are not a very congenial soil. Neither is knowledge successfully cultivated there. In all the colonies, without exception, it is common to meet with people of the greatest mark in the colony, who are ignorant of everything but the art of getting money.

Brutish ignorance keeps no man down, if he has in a large degree the one quality which is highly prized in the colonies; the quality of knowing how to grow rich. In hardly any colony can you manage, without great difficulty, to give your son what is esteemed a superior education here; and in all colonies, the sons of many of the first people are brought up in a wild unconsciousness of their own intellectual degradation.

Colonial manners are hardly better than morals, being slovenly, coarse, and often far from decent, even in the higher ranks; I mean in comparison with the manners of the higher ranks here. Young gentlemen who go out there, are apt to forget their home manners, or to prefer those of the colony; and one sees continually such cases as that of a young member of a most respectable family here, who soon becomes in the colony, by means of contamination, a thorough-paced blackguard.

If the bad propensities of colonists are not as much as we could wish them under the restraint of either honour, or reason, or usage, neither are they under that of religion. Here, however, I must make one great and signal exception. There is not in the world a more religious people than the great bulk of French Canadians, nor, upon the whole, I believe, anywhere a people so polite, virtuous, and happy. The French Canadians owe their religious sentiments to a peculiar mode of colonization, as respects religion, which is no longer the fashion among the colonizing states either of Europe or America. I speak of quite modern colonies, such as Upper or English Canada, Michigan, South Australia, and New Zealand, when I say that religion does not flourish there. There is in all of them, more or less, a good deal of the observance of religious forms, and the excitement of religious exercises. But in none of them does religion exercise the sort of influence which religion exercises here upon the morals, the intelligence, and the manners of those classes which we consider the best-informed and the best-behaved; that is, the most respectable classes in this country, or those whose conduct, knowledge, and manners constitute the type of those of the nation. Let me endeavour to make my meaning clear by an illustration. Think of some one of your friends who never goes to church except for form's sake, who takes the House-of-Commons oath, " on the faith of a Christian," as Edward Gibbon took it, but who has a nice sense of honour; who is, as the saying goes, as honourable a fellow as ever lived. Where did he get this sense of honour from? He knows nothing about where he got it from; but it really came to him from chivalry; and chivalry came from religion. He would not do to anybody anything, which he thinks he should have a right to complain of, if somebody did it to him : he is almost a Christian without knowing it. Men of this sort are rare indeed in the colonies. Take another case; that of an English matron, whose purity, and delicacy, and charity of mind, you can trace to the operation of religious influences : such beings are as rare in the colonies, as men with that sense of honour which amounts to goodness. In many parts of some colonies, there is, I may say, no religion at all; and wherever this happens the people fall into a state of barbarism.

If you were asked for a summary definition of the contrast between barbarism and civilization, you would not err in saying that civilized men differ from savages in having their natural inclinations restrained by law, honour, and religion. The restraint of law is imposed on individuals by the community; and, as before observed, this sort of restraint, since it only applies to crime, is less needed in colonies than in old countries. But the restraint of honour and religion is a self-restraint; and as it relates only to matters of which the law takes no cognizance—to bad natural inclinations which are equally strong everywhere—it is as much a condition of civilization in the newest colony as in the oldest mother-country. I can only attribute the low standard of honour in colonies to the insignificant proportion which emigrants of the better order bear to the other classes, and to the foul example of the only privileged class in colonies; namely, the public functionaries. These two causes of the want of honour shall be fully noticed ere long. The weakness of religious restraint is owing to the inadequacy of religious provisions for our colonists: and to this topic my next letter will be devoted.

LETTER XXIV.

From the Colonist.

I MUST now beg of you to observe a particular in which colonization differs from nearly every other pursuit that occupies mankind in masses. In trade, navigation, war, and politics—in all business of a public nature except works of benevolence and colonization—the stronger sex alone takes an active part; but in colonization, women have a part so important that all depends on their participation in the work. If only men emigrate, there is no colonization; if only a few women emigrate in proportion to the men, the colonization is slow and most unsatisfactory in other respects: an equal emigration of the sexes is one essential condition of the best colonization. In colonizing, the woman's participation must begin with the man's first, thought about emigrating, and must extend to nearly all the

arrangements he has to make, and the things he has
to do, from the moment of contemplating a departure
from the family home till the domestic party shall be
comfortably housed in the new country. The influence of women in this matter is even greater, one may
say, than that of the men. You may make a colony
agreeable to men, but not to women; you cannot make
it agreeable to women without being agreeable to men.
You may induce some men of the higher classes to
emigrate without inducing the women; but if you
succeed with the women, you are sure not to fail with
the men. A colony that is not attractive to women,
is an unattractive colony: in order to make it attractive to both sexes, you do enough if you take care
to make it attractive to women.

Women are more religious than men; or, at all
events, there are more religious women than religious
men: I need not stop to prove that. There is another
proposition which I think you will adopt as readily:
it is, that in every rank the best sort of women for
colonists are those to whom religion is a rule, a guide,
a stay, and a comfort. You might persuade religious
men to emigrate, and yet in time have a colony of
which the morals and manners would be detestable;
but if you persuade religious women to emigrate, the
whole colony will be comparatively virtuous and
polite. As respects morals and manners, it is of little
importance what colonial fathers are, in comparison
with what the mothers are. It was the matrons
more than the fathers of the New-England pilgrimage,
that stamped the character of Massachussetts and
Connecticut; that made New England, for a long
while, the finest piece of colonization the world has

exhibited. Imagine for a moment, that like Penn or Baltimore, you had undertaken to found a nation. Think of the greatness of the responsibility; figure to yourself how ardent would be your desire to sow the finest seed, to plant the most healthy offsets, to build with the soundest materials. Is there any effort or sacrifice you would be unwilling to make for the purpose of giving to your first emigration a character of honour, virtue, and refinement? Now go on to suppose that in planning your colonization, you had by some strange oversight omitted all provisions for religion in the colony; and that accordingly, as would surely be the case, you found amongst religious people of all classes, but especially amongst the higher classes, and amongst the better sort of women of every class, a strong repugnance to having anything to do with you. If you had made no provisions for religion in your colony, and if people here only cared enough about you to find that out, your scheme would be vituperated by religious men, who are numerous; by religious women, who are very numerous; and by the clergy of all denominations, who are immensely powerful. You would have to take what you could get in the way of emigration. Your labouring class of emigrants would be composed of paupers, vagabonds, and sluts: your middle class, of broken-down trades-men, over-reachers, semi-swindlers, and needy adven-turers, together with a few miserable wives, and a good many mistresses: your higher order of emigrants would be men of desperate fortunes, flying from debt and bedevilment, and young reprobates spurned or coaxed into banishment by relatives wishing them dead. You would sow bad seed, plant sorry offsets, build with rotten materials: your colony would be disgusting.

In former times, before the art of colonization was lost, it was the universal practice in the planting of colonies to take careful heed of religious provisions. Do not be alarmed. I am not going to repeat the sayings that one hears at meetings of the Society for the Propagation of the Gospel, and even in colonization debates in the House of Commons, about the sacred fire of the ancient Greeks transported to their colonies, and the gods of the Romans worshipped in their most distant settlements. Neither would I dwell on the religious zeal which nourished the energy of the Spaniards in their wonderful conquests of Mexico and Peru. But there is a religious feature in the old colonization of England, on which I would gladly fix your attention.

In colonizing North America, the English seem to have thought more about religious provisions than almost anything else. Each settlement was better known by its religion than by any other mark. Virginia, notwithstanding the official reception in England of the proposition that its inhabitants had souls to be saved like other people, was a Church-of-England colony; Maryland was the land of promise for Roman Catholics; Pennsylvania for Quakers; the various settlements of New England for Puritans. History tells us that the founders of the religious English colonies in North America, crossed the Atlantic in order to enjoy liberty of conscience. I fancy that this is one of the many errors which history continues to propagate. I doubt that the founders of any of these colonies went forth in search of a place where they

might be free from religious persecution:* a careful
inspection of their doings, on the contrary, leaves the
impression that their object was, each body of them
respectively, to find a place where its own religion
would be the religion of the place; to form a community the whole of which would be of one religion;
or at least to make its own faith the principal religion
of the new community. The Puritans went further:
within their bounds they would suffer no religion but
their own; they emigrated not so much in order to
escape from persecution, as in order to be able to per-
secute. It was not persecution for its own sake that
they loved; it was the power of making their religion
the religion of their whole community. Being themselves religious in earnest, they disliked the congregation and admixture of differing religions in their settlements, just as now the congregation and admixture of
differing religions in schools and colleges is disliked by
most religious people of all denominations: they wanted
to live, as religious people now send their children to
school, in contact with no religion but their own.
Penn and Baltimore, indeed, or rather Baltimore and
Penn (for the example was set by the Roman Catholic)
made religious toleration a fundamental law of their
settlements; but whilst they paid this formal tribute
of respect to their own history as sufferers from persecution at home, they took care practically, that
Maryland should be especially a Roman-Catholic
colony, and Pennsylvania a colony for Quakers. Therefore, the Roman Catholics of England were attracted
to Maryland; the Quakers to Pennsylvania. New

* See, for an interesting view of this question, *Letters from America*,
by John Robert Godley: John Murray, 1844.

England attracted its own sect of religious people; and so did Virginia.

Altogether, the attraction of these sectarian colonies was very great. The proof is the great number of people of the higher orders who emigrated to those colonies as long as they preserved their sectarianism or religious distinctions. Settled history has made another mistake in leading us to suppose, that the Puritan emigrants belonged chiefly, like the Cameronians in Scotland, to the humbler classes at home: most of the leaders, on the contrary, were of the gentry class, being persons of old family, the best education, and considerable property. It was equally so in Pennsylvania; for in the colonization of that day, there were leaders and followers; and the leading Quakers of that day belonged to the gentry, as respects birth, education, and property. The emigration to Maryland and Virginia was so remarkably aristocratic, that one need not correct history on that point. The emigration to New York, to the Carolinas, to all the colonies, exhibited the same feature, sometimes more, sometimes less, down to the time of the discontents which preceded their independence. All that colonization was more or less a religious colonization: the parts of it that prospered the most, were the most religious parts: the prosperity was chiefly occasioned by the respectability of the emigration: and the respectability of the emigration to each colony had a close relation to the force of the religious attraction.

I am in hopes of being able, when the proper time shall come for that part of my task, to persuade you that it would now be easy for England to plant sectarian colonies; that is, colonies with the strong attraction for superior emigrants, of a peculiar creed in each colony. Meanwhile, let us mark what our present colonization is as respects religious provisions. It is nearly all make-believe or moonshine. The subject of religious provisions for the colonies figures occasionally in speeches at religious meetings, and in Colonial-Office blue-books; but whatever composes the thing itself—the churches, the funds, the clergy, the schools, and colleges—appears nowhere else except on a scale of inadequacy that looks like mockery. If England were twice as large as it is, and ten times as difficult to travel about, then one bishop for all England would be as real a provision for the episcopacy of our church at home as there is in Upper Canada, or indeed in any of our more extensive colonies: it would not be a real, but a sham provision. Let me pursue the example of Upper Canada. If the one bishop is a mockery of episcopacy, still, it may be said, there are clergymen of the Church of England in sufficient abundance. I answer, there are indeed clergymen, but they are not clergymen of the Church of England. They differ from clergymen of the Church of England: they are not supported by endowments which would enable them to be the leaders, rather than the servants of their flocks; they are not otherwise qualified to lead any body, being men of an inferior order as respects accomplishments and wisdom. The ministers of a church, whose system of discipline is based on endowment and dignities, they have no ranks and no endowments. Men of mark or promise in the church at home would not go there: those who do go, are men of neither mark nor promise. Even these are so few in proportion to the great country, as are of course the churches likewise, that out of the towns it is ten to one that a Church-of-England emigrant misses his own church altogether: so he joins some other denomination, or, what is more common perhaps, soon really belongs to none. Thus what is called an extension of the Church of England in Upper Canada, consists of a single bishop for half a dozen Englands as respects the means of episcopal action; of a few dependent, half-starved, makeshift clergy; and of, for the greater part of the colony, nothing at all. The Roman-Catholic Church is not much better off. Mainly dependent for the subsistence of its priesthood on the voluntary contributions of poor Irish emigrants, it is a starved church like the other; whilst, like the other again, it is a church of endowments, but unendowed. What that is, you may judge by the Roman-Catholic Church in Ireland, of which I assure you that both the Roman-Catholic Church and Church of England in Upper Canada have frequently reminded me, by the contrast between their theory of government and their actual position.

The Church of Scotland, by reason of the comparative homeliness and democracy of its theory of government, is in a less false position in the colonies; and it acquires more easily a far greater resemblance to its mother-church. It never indeed leads colonization (with the exception, however, of what the Free Church of Scotland is now doing at Otago in New Zealand); but wherever Scotch settlers abound, the Scottish Church grows after awhile into a position of respectability and usefulness; of very marked respectability and usefulness as compared with that of the great churches of Rome and England. It is, however, behind another church, which alone in the colonies performs the functions of a church; I mean that of the

Wesleyan Methodists. Oh! but this is not a church! Isn't it? At any rate it has all the properties of one. It has a profound and minute system of government, which comprehends the largest and takes care of the smallest objects of a church. It has zeal, talents, energy, funds, order and method, a strict discipline, and a conspicuous success. But our concern with it is only in the colonies. There, it does not wait, as the other churches do, till there is a call for its services, and then only exhibit its inefficiency; but it goes before settlement; it leads colonization; it penetrates into settlements where there is no religion at all, and gathers into its fold many of those whom the other churches utterly neglect. This church alone never acts on the principle that anything is good enough for the colonies. Whether it sends forth its clergy to the backwoods of North America, the solitary plains of South Africa, the wild bush of Tasmania and Australia, or the forests and fern-plains of New Zealand, it sends men of devoted purpose and first-rate ability. It selects its missionaries with as much care as the Propaganda of Rome. It rules them with an authority that is always in full operation; with a far-stretching arm, and a hand of steel. It supplies them with the means of devoting themselves to their calling. Accordingly it succeeds in what it attempts. It does not attempt to supply the higher classes of emigrants with religious observances and teaching. It does this for its own people, who are nearly all of the middle or poorer classes; and, above all, it seeks, and picks up, and cherishes, and humanizes the basest and most brutish of the emigrant population. In the colonies generally, it is the antagonist, frequently the conqueror, of drunkenness, which is the chief bane of low colonial life. It makes war upon idleness, roguery, dirt, obscenity, and debauchery. In the convict colonies, and those which are infected by them, it is the great antagonist of Downing-street, whose polluting emigration it counteracts, by snatching some, and guarding others from the pestilence of convict contamination. If it had the power which the Church of England has in our legislature, it would put a stop to the shame of convict colonization, open and disguised. For it is truly a colonizing church: it knows that in colonization, as you sow, so shall you reap: it acts on this belief with vigour and constancy of purpose that put the other churches to shame, and with a degree of success that is admirable, considering that its first "centenary" was only held the other day.

After the Wesleyans, I should award the first rank in point of efficiency to the two churches of Scotland, but especially to the Free Church, but merely because in the colonies it is becoming the only Church of Scotland. Next come Independents, Baptists, and other Dissenters from the Church of England. Then the Roman Catholics, whose lower position arises from no want of zeal or organization, but solely from the poverty of the great bulk of Catholic emigrants. And last of all figures the Church of England, which, considering the numbers and wealth of her people at home, and her vast influence accordingly, can offer no excuse for neglecting her colonial people; save one only, that in consequence of her connexion with the state, she is, in the colonies, subject to the Colonial Office, and therefore necessarily devoid of energy and enterprise.

I will not meddle here with the causes of the

inadequacy of religious provisions for our colonies; still less with the means of removing them. My only object here has been to show, that the actual state of colonial provisions for religion is well calculated to deter the better order of people, and especially the better order of women, from going to live and die in a colony.

LETTER XXV.

From the Colonist.

COMBINATION AND CONSTANCY OF LABOUR ARE INDISPENSABLE CONDITIONS OF THE PRODUCTIVENESS OF INDUSTRY.—HOW COLONIAL CAPITALISTS SUFFER FROM THE DIVISION AND INCONSTANCY OF LABOUR.

THE condition of a capitalist in a colony is generally well known in the circle which he quitted on emigrating. It is not always a condition envied by them or agreeable to himself: it is often, on the contrary, a state of great unhappiness. Referring to what has been said before about the high rate of colonial profits, I have now to request your special attention to an absolute condition of a high rate of profit anywhere, and, indeed, of any return whatever from capital, which is often wanting or deficient in colonies, though not in old countries.

In this country, for example, it never comes into anybody's head to doubt that capital can be employed in a productive business. There is the capital, and there is the business: put the one into the other, and all will go well. The business, let us suppose, is the farming of 500 acres of fertile land in a high state of cultivation, well found in drainage, fences, and buildings, and rent free: the capital is £5000 worth of the things requisite for carrying on the business of the farm, such as crops in the ground, live stock, fodder, implements, and money at the bank wherewith to pay outgoings till incomings restore the invested capital. Nothing more seems requisite. Now, let us suppose that, by some strange means or other, the farmer were deprived of his horses, and precluded from getting others: his balance, at the end of the year, would probably be on the wrong side. But, now, let us suppose, the number of labourers on this farm being thirty, that two-thirds of them quitted their employer, and that he was totally unable to get others in their place: and suppose, further, that in order to keep the services of the labourers who remained with him, he was obliged to triple their wages. This farmer would soon be ruined. He would be ruined, not by having to pay such high wages, because his whole outlay in wages would not be increased, but by the unproductiveness of the labour of ten men in a business requiring that of thirty. We can hardly bring ourselves to imagine the occurrence of such a case here. It is substantially an every-day case in the colonies. Farmers, or other men of business there, can get and keep horses as many as they please, but they cannot do so with labourers. Labour, which is here a drug, is scarce there. The scarcity of labourers in colonies has effects on the condition of capitalists which require some particular description.

It has long been an axiom with political economists, that the most important improvement in the application of human industry is what they call " the division of labour:" the produce, they show, is great in proportion as the labour is divided. Adam Smith's famous chapter on the subject satisfies the mind on this point. But he fell into an error of words, which has kept out of view until lately, that what he calls the division of labour, is wholly dependent upon something else. It is dependent upon combination amongst the labourers. In his illustrative case of the pin-factory, for example, the separate parts of the whole work of making a pin could not be assigned to different persons —one drawing the wire, another polishing it, a third cutting it in bits, a fourth pointing one end of the bits, a fifth making the heads, a sixth putting them on, and so forth—unless all these persons were brought together under one roof, and induced to co-operate. The bringing together of workmen, and inducing them to co-operate, is a combination of labour: it cannot be properly called by any other name. But how can the same thing be division of labour, and combination of labour? One of the expressions must be wrong. We have seen that what is called combination of labour, is what it is called. Is that really " *division* of labour," which is so called? It is not. The assignment of several parts of a work to different labourers is a division, not of the labour, but of the work or employ- ment. The whole work or employment of making a pin is divided amongst many persons, each of whom takes a distinct part: their labour is not divided, but is on the contrary combined, in order to enable them to divide the employment.

This is not a merely verbal distinction : it is necessary to prevent confusion of ideas, indispensable in order to understand the principal impediment to the emigration of capitalists and gentry. The division of employments, as I cannot help always calling it, increases the produce of industry. But it never can take place without combination of labour. Combination of labour is a condition of all the improvements of industry, and of all the increase of produce in proportion to capital and labour, which are occasioned by division of employments. Combination of labour is further indispensable to the carrying on of works or employments, which are never divided into parts. There are numerous operations of so simple a kind as not to admit of a division into parts, which cannot be performed without the co-operation of many pairs of hands. I would instance the lifting of a large tree on to a wain, keeping down weeds in a large field of growing crop, shearing a large flock of sheep at the right time, gathering a harvest of corn at the time when it is ripe enough and not too ripe, moving any great weight; everything in short, which cannot be done unless a good many pairs of hands help each other in the same undivided employment, and at the same time.

The principle of the combination of labour, which seems more important the more one reflects on it, was not perceived until a colonial inquiry led to its discovery : it was unnoticed by economists, because they have resided in countries where combination of labour takes place, as a matter of course, whenever it is required : it seems in old countries like a natural property of labour. But in colonies the case is totally different. There, the difficulty of inducing a number of people to combine their labour for any purpose, meets the capitalist in every step of his endeavours, and in every line of industry. I shall speak of its consequences presently.

There is another principle of labour which nothing points out to the economical inquirer in old countries, but of which every colonial capitalist has been made conscious in his own person. By far the greater part of the operations of industry, and especially those of which the produce is great in proportion to the capital and labour employed, require a considerable time for their completion. As to most of them, it is not worth while to make a commencement without the certainty of being able to carry them on for several years. A large portion of the capital employed in them is fixed, inconvertible, durable. If anything happens to stop the operation, all this capital is lost. If the harvest cannot be gathered, the whole outlay in making it grow has been thrown away. Like examples, without end, might be cited. They show that constancy is a no less important principle than combination of labour. The importance of the principle of constancy is not seen here, because rarely indeed does it happen, that the labour which carries on a business, is stopped against the will of the capitalist; and it perhaps never happens, that a capitalist is deterred from entering on an undertaking by the fear that in the middle of it he may be left without labourers. But in the colonies, on the contrary, I will not say that this occurs every day, because capitalists are so much afraid of it, that they avoid its occurrence as much as they can, by avoiding, as much as possible, operations which require much time for their completion; but it occurs, more or less, to all who heedlessly engage in such operations, especially to new comers; and the general fear of it—the known difficulty of providing with certainty that operations shall not be stopped or interrupted by the inconstancy of labour—is as serious a colonial impediment to the productiveness of industry as the difficulty of combining labour in masses for only a short time.

Combination and constancy of labour are provided for in old countries, without an effort or a thought on the part of the capitalist, merely by the abundance of labourers for hire. In colonies, labourers for hire are scarce. The scarcity of labourers for hire is the universal complaint of colonies. It is the one cause, both of the high wages which put the colonial labourer at his ease, and of the exorbitant wages which sometimes harass the capitalist. I inclose a letter. The writer was a peasant girl in the parish of Stoke-by-Nayland, Suffolk, whose vicar enabled her to emigrate with her penniless husband to New Zealand. The couple are now worth in land, stock, and money, perhaps seven or eight hundred pounds. She says, " the only cuss of this colony is the exhorburnt wagers one has to pay." She liked the " exhorburnt wagers " whilst her husband received them. I am personally acquainted with a good many cases in which, in West Australia, South Australia, Australia Felix, and New Zealand, the whole property of a capitalist was drawn out of him by exorbitant wages. In those cases, the unfortunate capitalist was a recent emigrant; and he undertook some operation, generally farming on a scale in the English proportion to his capital, which could not be carried on without *constantly combining* a good deal of labour for hire; and he paid away his property in order to induce a number of labourers to continue in his service; in order, that is, to obtain combination and constancy of labour. If he had not obtained it, after placing his capital in an investment that required it, he would have been as effectually ruined as he was by paying exorbitantly for it. Emigrant capitalists are not generally ruined in this way, because they abstain from placing their whole capital in the jeopardy of being dependent for its preservation on combination and constancy of labour. They regulate their proceedings by the supply, and the prospect of a supply, of labour in the colony; and if labour is, or is likely to be, scarce, they abstain from undertaking operations, to the successful completion of which a scarcity of labour is necessarily fatal. But this abstinence is annoying to them; the necessity of observing it, frustrates their plans, and disappoints their hopes. The scarcity of labour forces them into a way of life which they never contemplated, and which they dislike. They are disappointed and uncomfortable. That they are so, becomes known to their friends in England; and the circulation of this knowledge through a number of channels here, gradually forms a public opinion unfavourable to the prospect of capitalists in this or that colony, and becomes a serious impediment to the emigration of people of that class.

LETTER XXVI.

From the Statesman.

THE STATESMAN POINTS OUT AN APPEARANCE OF CON-
TRADICTION BETWEEN THE TWO ASSERTIONS, THAT
LABOUR IN NEW COLONIES IS VERY PRODUCTIVE IN
CONSEQUENCE OF BEING ONLY EMPLOYED ON THE
MOST FERTILE SOILS, AND THAT IT IS UNPRODUC-
TIVE IN CONSEQUENCE OF BEING MUCH DIVIDED AND
INTERRUPTED.

YOUR account of the life of a colonial capitalist
is not very pleasing; and I can well understand
how the circumstances you describe, should operate as
a check to the emigration of people who have the
means of carrying on business here. I fancy that if
the truth, as you conceive it, were fully known in this
country, very few capitalists would be disposed to
emigrate; or that, at all events, but few colonies
would be very attractive to emigrants of that class.
But your view of the matter appears to be at variance
with one of your main propositions as to the attractive-
ness of colonies. You are impressed with a belief
that in colonies generally, the rate of profits is high as
compared with its rate in this country; and in one of
your letters you explained that the high rate of colonial

profits is occasioned, partly by the great productiveness of industry, and partly by the fact that the landlord and the government take but a small share of that large produce. But is the produce large? Is colonial industry so productive as you assert? That they are so is a common belief; but I cannot reconcile the fact with your explanation of the manner in which the scarcity of labour for hire in the colonies impedes combination and constancy of labour. You insist, with every appearance of being in the right, that combination and constancy are essential to a large production in proportion to the capital and labour employed: you say that in colonies, combination and constancy of labour are always difficult, often impossible; that one of the characteristics of colonies is the general separation of labour into single pairs of hands, and the difficulty of retaining even one pair of hands in the service of the capitalist: yet you say that the produce of capital and labour in colonies is greater than in old countries, where the utmost combination of uninterrupted labour by the same hands is general and always facile. Here surely is, if you will pardon me for saying so, the appearance of a monstrous contradiction. I trust that you may be able to explain it away.

LETTER XXVII.

From the Colonist.

THE COLONIST EXPLAINS THAT SCARCITY OF LABOUR IS
COUNTERACTED BY VARIOUS KINDS OF SLAVERY AND
BY THE DRUDGERY OF CAPITALISTS.—EVILS OF THE
PRESENCE OF SLAVE CLASSES IN A COLONY.

THE two propositions are not a contradiction, but
the appearance of one; and the paradox will be
easily explained away.

In spite of the scarcity of labour for hire in colonies
generally, and in all prosperous colonies without
exception, every colony that has prospered, from the
time of Columbus down to this day (nor would I
exclude the colonies of ancient Greece and Rome), has
enjoyed in some measure what I have termed combination and constancy of labour. They enjoyed it by means
of some kind of slavery. In the colonies of ancient
Greece and Rome, all the labourers were slaves. Their
labour was employed as constantly, and as much in
combination, as their masters pleased. It was the
same in the West-India colonies of Spain, England,
France, Holland, and Denmark. The slavery of the
Indians furnished constancy and combination of labour
to the Spanish colonies of Mexico and South America;

that of negroes to the Portuguese colonizers of Brazil. In the greater part of the English colonies of North America, negro slavery counteracted the scarcity of labour for hire. In New South Wales and Van Diemen's Land, there has been convict slavery; in South Africa, the Mauritius, and Bourbon, negro slavery. In the colonies of North America, where negro slavery was not at all, or not largely, established, there has been a virtual slavery in the forms of servants kidnapped in Europe, and "indented" in America, and "redemptioners," or immigrants whom a contract bound to their masters for a term of years, and whom either their utter ignorance of the law and language of America, or the force of opinion and combination amongst the masters, compelled to abide by their contracts for service. There are other ways in which there may be slavery in fact without the name. The freed negroes, and their descendants, of some of the states of North America which either never permitted, or have abolished slavery, are virtually a sort of slaves, by means of their extreme degradation in the midst of the whites; and the hordes of Irish-pauper emigrants who pour into North America, British and American, are, in a considerable proportion, virtually slaves by means of their servile, lazy, reckless habit of mind, and their degradation in the midst of the energetic, accumulating, prideful, domineering Anglo-Saxon race. The slavery of all these different kinds, in these many countries, has constituted an enormous amount of slavery. The negro slaves of the United States must be approaching four millions in number, and worth to sell at market about half the amount of our immense national debt. If we could count the slaves, nominal and virtual—negroes, called slaves, trampled free-negroes, indented servants, redemptioners, convicts, and slavish Irish—who have inhabited modern colonies in various parts of the world since the discovery of America, we should readily understand their importance as an element of colonial society.

Colonial slavery in its various forms has been the principal means of raising that great produce for exportation, for which prosperous colonies are remarkable. Until lately, nearly the whole of the exported produce of the United States, consisting of sugar, rice, tobacco, and cotton, was raised by the combined and constant labour of slaves; and it could not have been raised under the circumstances by any other means. The like cases of the West Indies and Brazil would have occurred to you without being mentioned. The great public works of those states of the American Union that forbid slavery, could not have been attempted without a large supply of slavish Irish labour, by which, indeed, as regards labour, they have been almost entirely executed. Domestic service in those countries depends on the existence of " niggers" called free, and of servile Irish emigration. I could fill a whole letter with bare examples of a like kind, but will confine myself to one more, which will serve for general illustration.

In Tasmania, which is fast losing its ugly name of Van Diemen's Land, there are farms, being single properties, consisting of seven or eight hundred acres each, under cultivation, besides extensive sheep and cattle runs, the farming of which is not inferior to that of Norfolk and the Lothians. A description of one of these farms is before me. The eight hundred acres are divided into fields of from thirty to fifty acres each. The fences are as good as can be. The land is kept thoroughly clear of weeds; a strict course of husbandry is pursued; and the crops, especially of turnips, are very large. The garden and orchards are extensive, kept in apple-pie order, and very productive. The house is of stone, large and commodious. The farm buildings are ample in extent, and built of stone with solid roofs. The implements are all of the best kinds, and kept in perfect order. The live stock, for the most part bred upon the spot, is visited as a show on account of its excellence, and would be admired in the best-farmed parts of England: it consists of 30 cart horses, 50 working bullocks, 100 pigs, 20 brood mares, 1000 head of horned cattle, and 25,000 fine-wooled sheep. On this single establishment, by one master, seventy labourers have been employed at the same time. They were nearly all convicts. By convict labour, and that alone, this fine establishment was founded and maintained. Nothing of the sort could have existed in the island if convicts had not been transmitted thither, and assigned upon their landing to settlers authorized to make slaves of them. In this small island, of which the whole population is under 70,000, there have been at one time fifty establishments much resembling that which I have described. In British North America, there is not one that bears the slightest resemblance to it, in point of scale, perfection of management, or productiveness in proportion to the capital or labour employed: for the slavish Irish labour of a colony is less easily combined, and less surely retained, than convict slave-labour. I doubt whether in all Canada, though many a first-rate English and Scotch farmer have emigrated thither, there is even one farm of 500 acres, the management of which would not be deemed very slovenly in Scotland or England, or of which the produce in proportion to capital and labour amounts to half that of a Tasmanian farm. I rather think, indeed, that in all Canada, there is not a farm of 500 acres in real cultivation, however slovenly and unproductive. The Tasmanian farmer grows rich (or rather did grow rich, for a change of policy at the Colonial Office has put a stop to the supply of useful convict labour): the Canadian farmer vegetates or stagnates: if he and his family do not work hard themselves as labourers, he is very apt to be ruined.

This brings me to another feature of colonial life, which is occasioned by the scarcity of labour for hire. In the colonies where the scarcity of labour for hire is not counteracted by a slavery sharp enough for the purpose, capitalists generally, and especially those of them who cultivate the soil, work a great deal with their own hands: they are labourers as well as capitalists. If a solitary individual cannot without the consent of others enjoy any combination of labour beyond that of his own two hands, he can at any rate make that labour constant: he can depend upon himself for the continuance of the labour which his own hands are capable of performing. The capitalist, therefore, by working himself, secures the constant labour of one pair of hands at any rate. Moreover, when the capitalists generally work with their own hands, they make arrangements among themselves for occasionally combining their labour. Nine of them meet, and help a tenth, A, to build him a house, clear his land, or gather in his crop. Another day, A meets eight of his neighbours, to help B: in turn, C, D, E, F, and the rest get helped. They are all benefited by some combination of labour. Without any kind of slavery, therefore, in a colony, and with the utmost scarcity of labour for hire, there is some constancy and some combination of labour; but the labour which is constant, is that of the capitalist working himself, who is the master of his own pair of hands; and the labour which is combined, is that of more than one capitalist, occasionally agreeing to work together for the benefit of each of them in turn. The farmers of Canada, and of the non-slaveholding states of America, are generally labourers as well as capitalists: it is their drudgery as labourers, not their skill as capitalists, which enables them to produce wheat for exportation.

I have endeavoured to show, that the scarcity of labour for hire in the colonies has been counteracted partly by some kind of slavery, partly, though in a less degree, by the drudgery of the capitalist. If you see this plainly, the paradox must have vanished. The two propositions do not contradict each other. Combination and constancy of labour are essential to a large production. In colonies, combination and constancy of labour are always difficult, often impossible: one of the characteristics of colonies is the general separation of labour into single pairs of hands. But the colonial tendency to separation and inconstancy of labour is counteracted by slavery in various forms, and by the drudgery of the capitalist. The labour of slaves and of capitalists is applied to only the most fertile soils; nearly all the produce is shared by those who raise it, because the share of the land-lord and the government is insignificant: the net pro-duce, over and above rent and taxes, is sufficient to provide for high wages and high profits.

But that which in colonies counteracts the tendency of scarcity of labour for hire, is an obstacle to the emi-gration of capitalists. Capitalists brought up in this country do not like to work with their own hands: they like to direct with their heads the labour of others. The necessity of working with their own hands is apt to disgust the emigrant capitalist, and to send him back to this country a discontented and complaining man. If, in order to avoid the annoyance, and, as he feels it, the degradation, of working with his own hands, and making his children work with theirs, he resorts to some sort of slavery, he is still apt to be very much annoyed. Negro slavery is detestable for the master who was not bred, born, and educated within hearing of the driving-whip. If I could find a stronger word than detestable, I would apply it to the life of a decent Englishman who has become a driver of convicts in Tasmania. "Free nigger" labour, even in domestic service, is not agreeable for the master, because he continually feels that the servant ought to hate him as one of the class which despises and loathes the whole negro race. The careless, lazy, slovenly, dirty, whining, quarrelsome, Saxon-hating, Irish-pauper emigrants are labourers, whom no English or Scotch or American capitalist would be dependent upon for carrying on his business, if he could by any means avoid the trouble and annoyances of such a dependence.

As respects the degraded races and orders of men,

whose presence in colonies counteracts the scarcity of labour for hire, I have thus far alluded only to the individual feelings of capitalists as employers of such labour; but the subject involves another consideration which must not be left unnoticed. The presence of these degraded people in a colony, whether they are negro slaves, " free niggers," convicts in bondage, emancipated convicts, the immediate offspring of convicts, or pauper-Irish emigrants, is a public nuisance, a political danger, a social plague. It is tolerable, indeed, for those who are used to it, and to whom it is, moreover, a convenience in other respects : but the British capitalist is not used to it; it is not yet a nuisance to him, however convenient; he is not forced to put himself into the midst of it; and, in proportion as he is acquainted with its operation in colonies, he is disinclined to emigrate. Something about it is known in this country; enough to create a vague impression that the scarcity of good labour for hire in colonies is a great evil. More and more is likely to be known about it; and I do believe that if the affliction which colonies suffer from the presence of substitutes for good labour for hire, were generally and familiarly known in this country, the emigration of respectable people would nearly cease.

LETTER XXVIII.

From the Statesman.

THE STATESMAN ALMOST DESPAIRS OF COLONIZATION,
AND ASKS FOR A SUGGESTION OF THE MEANS BY
WHICH SCARCITY OF LABOUR MAY BE PREVENTED
WITHOUT SLAVERY.

YOUR explanation has satisfied my judgment
on the point in question, but disappointed my
hopes. I had hoped that we might, at least, colonize
on a much greater scale than at present; but now I
almost despair of it. I saw before how the scarcity of
labour for hire, by injuriously affecting the productiveness of capital and labour, limited the attraction of
colonies for emigrants of the richer class; and I now
perceive how this colonial deficiency is counteracted;
but the remedy strikes me as being worse than the
disease. As an economical remedy, it is but partial
and incomplete, whilst it is itself a political and social
malady. Even if the existence of slave classes in the
colonies were not a political and social evil, how could
we make it correspond in amount with the progress
of colonization? how maintain a supply of slavish
labour in proportion to a great increase of capitalist
emigration? In the British colonies, negro slavery

has ceased, and convict slavery has, I believe, been nearly abolished. Will not the total abolition of convict slavery in Tasmania have the same effect for capitalists there, as the abolition of negro-slavery in the British West Indies? It can have no other effect, if your view of the whole subject is just. Irish-pauper emigration may doubtless be greatly extended; but there are many colonies to which this emigration does not proceed; and in the colonies to which it does, it brings about a state of national antagonism so like that which prevails in Ireland, as to be very disagreeable for Scotch and English emigrants of every class. Upon the whole therefore, it seems to me that we are stopped by a difficulty as formidable, as the scarcity of labour for hire appeared to me before you explained how it was counteracted. I see no use in going on with our inquiry, if you do not see a way of counteracting scarcity of labour for hire in colonies, otherwise than by some kind of slavery. What other impediments to colonization there may be, it matters little to ascertain if the impediment of scarcity of labour for hire, or of the multiform slavery by which it is counteracted, is to continue unabated. I think, therefore, that this is the proper stage in our inquiry for determining what means there may be, besides slavery, of counteracting the scarcity of labour for hire. I am aware that you have a theory on that subject. It is founded of course on a view of the causes of the scarcity of labour for hire, to which I now observe that you have not made any allusion. I understand that you intend to explain them, and to propose a means of removing or counteracting them; but I wish to know at once what your plan is, so that I may determine whether or not it is worth my while to bestow more attention on the whole subject. If your plan for counteracting scarcity of labour for hire without any kind of slavery, should appear sufficient for its purpose theoretically, and practicable as well, let us go on to the other impediments of colonization; if not, let us confess, or I for one shall be under the necessity of confessing, that an increase of colonization corresponding with the wants of the mother-country is out of our reach.

LETTER XXIX.

From the Colonist.

STATE OF COLONIAL POLITICS.—VIOLENT COURSES OF POLITICIANS.—IRISH DISTURBANCES.—MALIGNITY OF PARTY WARFARE.—DESPERATE DIFFERENCES OF CO- LONISTS.—DEMOCRACY AND DEMAGOGUISM IN ALL COLONIES.—BRUTALITY OF THE NEWSPAPERS.

I HAVE deliberately abstained from alluding to the causes of the scarcity of labour. I did so with a view of preserving the order of discussion, which I understood to be a settled point. That order would be greatly disturbed, if I were now to go into the causes of any of the existing impediments to colonization; still more, if I were to pursue the subject of remedies for these impediments. There is, of course, an intimate relation between the causes and the remedies; and in this instance, if I touched upon the causes, I should be led to the subject of remedies, and should almost reverse the settled order of inquiry, by discussing means and plans before the character of the obstacles was defined. It happens, moreover, that the means by which some of the impediments might be removed, would also have the effect of removing others. Before entering on the subject of means, therefore, it seems very expedient to consider all the impediments. I proceed accordingly, taking for granted that on reflection you will approve of it, to notice the remaining impediments to colonization.

I have hitherto spoken of capitalists as a distinct class, because it is as a distinct class that they suffer more than anybody else from the scarcity of labour for hire. But they also suffer along with others from another sort of colonial evils. These evils are all impediments to colonization. They affect the higher order of emigrants. The one to which I propose confining this letter, is the state of colonial politics.

There is nothing perhaps which more offends the tastes and habits of the better class of emigrants, than the state of colonial politics. By the word politics I do not mean government, but what one sex in England supposes that the other talks about when left alone after dinner. Colonial party-politics, then, are remarkable for the factiousness and violence of politicians, the prevalence of demagoguism, the roughness and even brutality of the newspapers, the practice in carrying on public differences of making war to the knife, and always striking at the heart. In a colony with a representative form of government, if the executive, which generally sides with the minority, proposes something disagreeable to the majority, or if the

majority proposes something of which the minority
disapproves, the two parties insult and provoke each
other for a time; and the majority is apt to resort to
impeachment or a stoppage of the supplies. On the
other hand, the minority, not to be behind the majority in resorting to extreme measures, frequently uses
the veto. The last resource of the British constitution,
which we have hardly used at all since we completed
our constitution in 1688, and shall probably never use
again, are ordinary weapons of colonial party warfare.
Rebellions are not very uncommon, and are not common only because, in most colonies, rebellion has no
chance of success. In all our colonies, at all times, a
rebellious spirit may be observed. In saying this, I
do not forget my previous statements about the imperial loyalty of colonists. The rebellious spirit in question does not hate England or the imperial connexion;
it only hates the government of the colony, which is
not England nor the imperial government. What it is,
I shall have the pleasure of explaining soon. Meanwhile you will comprehend, that this hatred of their
government by colonists, and, as a consequence, of
colonists by their government, are disagreeable circumstances in the social state of colonies. It was from
such a state of hatred between subjects and their
government, that the Canadian rebellions sprang, and
that the body of South-African colonists fled, who
settled at Port Natal, and are now fighting with us
there for their independence. It is a state of things
by no means confined, as the last instance shows, to
representative colonies, or caused by representative
institutions. On the contrary, there is less of it in
Canada at this time than in any other colony, because

there representative institutions are becoming a reality,
and regular party-government is taking the place of
what Lord Durham called a " constituted anarchy."
These extremes of violence do not of course break out
very frequently: still, as they are of a character to
insure their being heard of in this country, they happen often enough to make an impression here, that
the peace of colonies is apt to be disturbed by them;
that colonial public life resembles public life in Ireland.
Essentially Irish disturbances of another kind are
by no means rare in some colonies. In Canada, the
Orange and Milesian factions have been effectually
transplanted, and wage a perpetual war. Savage
encounters between them, resulting in bloodshed
amongst the combatants, and producing terror and
disgust for other people, are of frequent occurrence.
Even at the antipodes of Ireland, at Port Philip, in
Australia Felix, a large immigration of Milesian Irish
has produced faction fights and frightful rows, that
could only be suppressed by the armed force of government. But in this respect, Mr. Mothercountry may
say, the colonies only suffer in common with ourselves.
He ought to say, in common with that part of the
kingdom which is called Ireland, and which in candour he should add, is the last place to which the inhabitants of the other parts would think of emigrating.
But there is a violence short of rebellion, faction-
fighting, impeachment, and stopping the supplies, by
which public and also private life in the colonies
generally, more or less, is made uncomfortable for emigrants who have not yet learned to practise it; and
especially if they are emigrants of the most valuable
class. When colonists, I am speaking generally,

and would allow for exceptions, differ upon such
a point, for example, as the amount of a proposed
import duty or the direction of a road, both sides
treat the question as if it were one of life and death;
and instead of compromising their difference, or giving
a quiet victory to the preponderating weight of
votes or influence, they instantly set about tearing
each other to pieces with the tongue and pen, after
the manner of the late Daniel O'Connell. A colonist who meddles with public matters, should have
a skin of impenetrable thickness. Quiet sort of
people who emigrate, though often the best qualified for public business, generally refuse to meddle
with it: they cannot endure the scarification to which
any interference with it would expose them. But it
is not the skin alone that suffers, when thin enough.
Frequent scarification renders most colonial skins so
impenetrably thick, that the utmost vituperation makes
hardly any impression upon them. Recourse therefore is had to something sharper than billingsgate.
It is a general custom in the colonies, when your
antagonist withstands abuse, to hurt him seriously if
you can, and even to do him a mortal injury, either
in order to carry your point, or to punish him for
having carried his. In every walk of colonial life,
everybody strikes at his opponent's heart. If a
governor or high officer refuses to comply with the
wish of some leading colonists, they instantly try to
ruin him by getting him recalled with disgrace: if
two officials disagree, one of them is very likely to be
tripped up and destroyed by the other: if an official
or a colonist offends the official body, they will hunt
him into jail or out of the colony: if two settlers dis-

agree about a road or a watercourse, they will attack each other's credit at the bank, rake up ugly old stories about each other, get two newspapers to be the instruments of their bitter animosity, perhaps ruin each other in a desperate litigation. Disagreement and rivalry are more tiger-like than disagreement and rivalry in this country. Colonists at variance resemble the Kilkenny cats.

Colonial democracy is not pleasant to emigrants of the gentry class : and least of all is it pleasant to them when they happen to be very well qualified by moral and intellectual qualities for taking a useful part in the public affairs of their new country. Colonial democracy is of two distinct kinds. First, in the representative colonies, there is the democracy which arises from a suffrage practically next to universal; and secondly, there is the democracy of the bureaucratic colonies which grows out of arbitrary government. I hope that a few words about each of them may not be unacceptable.

In Canada, as in most of the adjoining States, the best men, as we should consider them,—that is, the wisest and most upright men—are seldom the favourite candidates of the majority of voters, generally not even candidates at all. The favourite candidates are the ablest demagogues; the men who best know how to flatter the prejudices and excite the passions of the ignorant and passionate mass of electors. The result is that not a few of the "representatives of the people," whether in the House of Assembly or the District Councils, are of that order of noisy, low-lived, spouting, half-educated, violent, and unscrupulous politicians, one or two of whom occasionally get into the

British House of Commons. In the Canadian Assembly, there is always a considerable proportion of
Busfield Ferrands and Feargus O'Connors. From
this fact you will infer many more which exhibit the
influence of Canadian democracy. It is an influence
which pervades public life in the colony, and thus to
a great extent keeps the best class of emigrants out of
public life. In saying that the other representative
colonies resemble Canada more or less in this respect,
I must exclude those of the West Indies, in which the
bulk of the people, having been recently slaves, have
not yet acquired the voter's qualification. In those
colonies, however, if the bottom of society is not yet
put at top by a suitable parliamentary suffrage, there
is the prospect of a Black democracy less tolerable for
the higher order of colonists and even for all Whites,
than is, for settlers of the higher order, the actual democracy of colonies inhabited by people of one colour.

The democracy of the representative colonies is
obviously caused by a democratic suffrage : that of the
bureaucratic colonies is occasioned by withholding from
all settlers all part in the government of their country.
In the latter case, the settlers having no political
rights, resort to agitation as the only means of in-
fluencing the governor and his nominated council of
officials. They make use of petitions, remonstrances,
and public meetings. The Opposition of the colony as
distinguished from its Government, is carried on by
means of public meetings. In New South Wales,
Australia Felix, South Australia, and New Zealand,
the common mode of endeavouring to influence the
local government or its masters in Downing-street, is
by getting up a public meeting, and publishing its

proceedings in the newspapers. The calling of a public meeting is an appeal to numbers, to the majority, to the democratic principle. The device of select meetings, such as those from which our anti-corn-law league used to exclude people who disagreed with them, by means of tickets of admission, is not adopted in colonies because it would not work there. It would not work for two reasons; first, because the official party would in some cases snap their fingers at what they might truly call a " hole-and-corner" meeting; and secondly, because, if the majority were excluded from a meeting by means of tickets, and thereby deeply offended, the official party, by the aid of some purchased demagogue, would easily get up a counter meeting more numerous and violent than the one directed against themselves. The system of opposing government by means of public meetings is an irregular democracy for opposition purposes. When the object is, as sometimes happens, to support the government faction, it is more than ever necessary to avoid offending the majority, who therefore enjoy for. the occasion a sort of universal suffrage. None of the factions into which a colony may be divided, has recourse to a public meeting without intending an appeal to numbers. The practice of appealing to numbers becomes habitual. Politicians in the bureaucratic colonies, therefore, not excepting the highest officials when it happens to suit their purpose, naturally resort to the arts of the demagogue; demagogues are the leading politicians. The newspaper press of these bureaucratic colonies is to the full as demagoguish—as coarse, as violent, as unscrupulous, often as brutal—as that of the representative colonies in which the democracy is constituted by law.

Of course, there are exceptions to this as to every other rule. There have been colonial newspapers, though I do not recollect one that lasted long, remarkable for moderation and forbearance. There are one or two colonies, I believe, like West Australia, so stagnant, tame, and torpid, as to have no politics. Even in the most political colonies, there are times, of course, when politics are comparatively asleep. I am speaking generally. As a general rule, colonial politics are like what ours would be, if our suffrage were either made universal, or totally abolished. In either of those cases, I fancy, a colony which had representative government, with a suffrage that gave influence to the wisest and most upright, would attract swarms of the most valuable class of emigrants. At present that is a class of emigrants, which colonial politics repel.

LETTER XXX.

From the Colonist.

YOU may suppose that the democracy of the colonies is accompanied by a perfect equality. It is so with the democracy of the United States, but not with that of our colonies. As in Turkey there is equality without democracy, so in our colonies there is demo- cracy without equality. In the colonies, however, there is but one privileged class which, so to speak, is more privileged than any class in any European country at present, excepting Russia perhaps. This privileged class is as proud, though in a way of its own, as exclusive, as insolent, as deeply convinced of the inferiority or nothingness of the other classes, as was the noblesse of old France. But its privileges are not in any measure the attribute of birth: on the con- trary, those who possess them are seldom high-born, often of the meanest extraction. Neither do the pri- vileges grow out of the possession of wealth: on the contrary, numbers of the privileged class in colonies are generally without property, often in great want of money, not very seldom on the verge of insolvency. The privileged class in colonies is the official class.

I feel at a loss for the means of getting you to understand the nature and extent of the privileges enjoyed by the official class in colonies. It would be easier to make a Frenchman acquainted with the subject. In our colonies, as in France now, office is the only distinction. Of course, whatever is the only distinction in any part of the world, is, in that part of the world, greedily desired and devoutly worshipped by most people. The panting, the dying for office in colonies, is a sight to see. But office in the colonies is so precious, not only because it is the only distinction, but also because it is the only reality of power. The government of our colonies is, for the most part, bureaucratic. In some of the representative colonies, indeed, especially in Canada, the recent adoption of what is called " responsible government" places power in the hands of the parliamentary constituencies and those who can win their confidence; but this is a complete and very modern innovation; and it has by no means been extended to all the representative colonies. As in Canada before this innovation, so now in the representative colonies to which it has not been extended, and in all the bureaucratic colonies without exception, all power originates in and is inherent to office. But there is a distinction between the representative and the bureaucratic colonies which must be noted. In the representative colonies which have not obtained responsible government, as formerly in the two Canadas, the executive and the representative

branches of government are generally at variance:
the executive branch sides with the minority in the
representative branch.　In order to carry on government at all under this curious system, it is indispensable that the executive should have the support of a
party or faction in the colony.　The governor, therefore,
who represents the crown, disposes of offices in favour
of such a faction: indeed, the official faction is really the
government.　It consists of officials and their parti-
sans hoping to be officials.　It is composed, for the
most part, of colonists; that is, natives or fixed resi-
dents of the colony: and it enjoys all the power that
is exercised in the colony; all the power, that is to
say, which is compatible with the existence of a vast
deal of worrying and sometimes impeding opposition
from the majority of the representative body.

　In the bureaucratic colonies, on the other hand, where
constitutionally there is only one branch of government,
where the officials alone legislate as well as execute,
and where accordingly government may be carried on
somehow without the aid of a faction of colonists, the
best offices are filled by appointment from Downing-
street, generally by strangers to the colony, and almost
always without any regard to the wishes of the colonists; and these superior officers appoint to the inferior
offices.　In those colonies, therefore, the power which
the official class enjoys is strictly a privilege, because
it is a power independent of its subjects, inherent, as
I said before, to the possession of office.　But it is not
an unlimited power.　As in representative colonies
not having responsible government, the power of the
official faction is limited by the hindering, worrying
power of the House of Assembly, so in the bureaucratic

colonies, the power of the official class is limited by the superior power of the Colonial Office at home. In the former colonies, an official faction enjoys power limited by a nasty local opposition: in the latter, an official class enjoys power limited by a nastier interference from Downing-street. Still in both cases, the power is immense. In the two Canadas, the official faction, backed by the might of the empire, used to have its own way in spite of the Assembly; and has still, in the representative colonies to which responsible government has not been extended: and in the bureaucratic colonies, the interference of Downing-street is so weakened by distance as to place no very effectual limit on the governing powers of the official class.

Whilst speaking of the official class, I wish to exclude for the present the officers called governors, who represent the crown, are nearly always strangers to the colony, and generally hold their appointment for only a few years, sometimes for only a few months.

The rest of the official body consists of the colonial secretary; the president of the executive council; the treasurer or inspector-general, who is the principal financial officer; the surveyor-general, and commissioner of crown lands, who are a very important people in colonies where there is waste land to be disposed of; the attorney and solicitor general; the judges, and several other judicial officers, such as the sheriff and prothonotary; and some more which it is not worth while to specify. Nor is the above list applicable to all colonies alike, either as respects titles or functions. I give it as a sample, for the mere purpose of indicating the general nature of the functions of the official body in a colony. The subject of those functions and the manner in which they are performed, will be fully considered under the head of colonial government.

In every colony, nearly all the offices are filled by the governor's appointment in form, just as, in form, the crown appoints to most offices in this country. But the manner in which the appointments take place, differs according to certain peculiar circumstances of each of the three classes of colonies before pointed out. In responsible-government colonies, or rather in Canada alone, because there alone has responsible government obtained anything like a firm footing, the governor appoints on the advice of his executive council or cabinet of ministers; and the ministers are from time to time that set of leading colonists who possess the confidence of the representative body. The ministers being, as with us, responsible to parliament, and appointed or removed by the votes of parliament, really carry on the government, and therefore, of course, make the appointments to office, including their own: the governor does not govern, any more than the Queen here; he only reigns, like her Majesty. In Canada, accordingly (though how long this may last, I pretend not to opine; for the new system is far from being thoroughly established), an emigrant colonist may get into office if he takes the proper road. The road to office is open to him as well as to any native. The road to office is popular favour, or the confidence of the constituencies; and there is nothing to prevent any emigrant from winning that, after he gets into the way of winning favour in a country where the suffrage is practically almost universal.

In the representative colonies from which responsible government is still withheld, it is exceedingly difficult for an emigrant to get into office by any means. The colonial faction which governs in spite of a representative assembly, does so by means of holding the governor in leading-strings. This is not the proper place for describing the nature of these strings. Suffice it to say here, that they are most artistically formed and as carefully kept in working order. For the making and preservation of them, time, consecutive effort, and incessant vigilance are indispensable. Those, therefore, who hold the strings are a party of long standing and of permanent organization. They belong to the colony. A stranger arriving there would be incapable of joining them from his ignorance of local politics. Besides, they want all the appointments for themselves and their adherents. Unless the whole, or nearly the whole, patronage of the colony were at their disposal, they could not hold together, and defy the representative body, for a single year. They do hold together so as to be commonly called the family compact. In the course of time, an emigrant who has great talents for intrigue, may penetrate into this close corporation, and become one of it: the thing happens every now and then. But allowing for such rare exceptions, the family compact vigorously excludes emigrants from office. It dislikes and fears emigrants as a class. It dislikes them, more especially if they are rich and clever, as persons who may be willing and able to obtain political influence; as possible rivals, and almost inevitable fault-finders and opponents: it fears them, because they may be able through their connexions at home to get at the governor in some way, and may try to take him out of his leading-strings. They would rejoice if there were no emigration of the better order of people. They do much to prevent it; and they succeed in materially checking it, by variously ill-treating emigrants of that class. The family compact of Upper Canada, before the black day for them which introduced responsible government, used not only to exclude emigrants of that class from distinction and political power in the land of their adoption, but also to affront and injure them by the numerous means which power can employ for such a purpose. This was one of the causes of the rebellion in Upper Canada. Not that the higher class of emigrants, who were then very numerous, were disposed to rebel: their *maladie du pays*, their passionate love of England, prevented that: but those who did rebel, thought that, to be sure, the emigrants who had been so ill-treated by the ruling faction, would be disposed to join in a rebellion; and this expectation, it is now well known, had a considerable share in leading the rebels into action. The case of Upper Canada was not singular, though it is better known than others. I think we may lay it down as a rule, with but very rare exceptions, that in a colony governed by a family compact, emigrants of the better order are a proscribed class as respects the enjoyment of distinction and power. They are mere settlers, snubbed and ill-treated by those who enjoy a monopoly of distinction and power; and they can be nothing else.

LETTER XXXI.

From the Colonist.

HOW OFFICIALS ARE APPOINTED IN THE BUREAUCRATIC COLONIES. — THEY ARE A SORT OF DEMIGODS, BUT VERY MUCH INFERIOR TO THE BETTER ORDER OF SETTLERS IN ABILITY, CHARACTER, CONDUCT, AND MANNERS. — EXAMPLES THEREOF AND THE CAUSES OF IT. — BEHAVIOUR OF THE OFFICIALS TO THE BETTER ORDER OF SETTLERS.

IN a bureaucratic colony, as in others, the governor appoints to office. He is generally in leading-strings like the governor of a family-compact colony; but the strings are pulled by two different sets of hands. As to the great bulk of the higher appointments, he obeys the commands of the Colonial Office at home, which reach him in the form of recommendations delivered by the persons in whose favour they are made. Occasionally, with respect to a higher appointment, and always with respect to a good many of the inferior appointments, especially those of which the salary is small, he takes the advice of " the people about him;" that is, of those among the higher officials who really govern the colony subject to interference from Down-

ing-street. These virtual rulers of the colony do not
hang together with the tenacity of a regular family
compact. Their position does not require that they
should do so. They owe their appointments to Downing-street; and as long as Downing-street supports
one of them he is in no danger of losing his office.
The influence at home which induced Downing-street
to make the appointment, generally contrives to induce
it to support the colonial officer. Such officials,
therefore, are in a great measure independent of the
governor: they may safely, as respects their own
position, neglect the manifold precautions by which
a regular family compact keeps the governor in order.
Neither are they tormented by a house of assembly,
and compelled to guard against its endeavours to take
a part in governing the colony. They are altogether
more at their ease than the members of a regular
family compact, more independent of control, more
free to indulge their personal inclinations and passions.
We find accordingly, that they often quarrel among
themselves, and sometimes with the governor. The
jealousies, and rivalries, and hatreds which belong to
poor human nature, but which in well-ordered societies
are subdued by various restraints, break out uncon-
trolled amongst the officials of a bureaucratic colony.
The official body is sometimes split into hostile factions; individuals have bitter public quarrels; even his
excellency the governor himself is often worried, sometimes upset, by these his nominal subordinates. But
there is one point on which the officials of a bureaucratic colony never differ; one respect in which they
hold together as tenaciously as the best-cemented family
compact. They agree in thinking that colonists or

settlers, people who come out all that way to improve their condition by their own exertions, are an inferior order of beings; and they stick close together in resisting all attempts on the part of settlers to become officials; to get a share in governing the colony. If they were settlers themselves as well as officials, it would be a fair struggle between the ins and the outs, to which no Englishman would think of objecting: but the officials of a bureaucratic colony are hardly ever settlers. They have their salaries to live on, and generally no other property; that is, no property at all in the colony. They consider their salaries a property for life; and the source of it is far away from the colony. They arrive in the colony as utter strangers to it, and in order to exercise the power of governing it: they are, in their own estimation and in that of a good many of the humbler colonists, a sort of demigods, coming from another planet, and gifted by some distant and mysterious authority with the right of governing the settlers. Their dignity would suffer if they became settlers; if they associated with the settlers except on the most unequal terms, or sympathized with them in any way. Like the caste of Brahmins, they hold themselves apart from the rest of the community and immeasurably superior to it: or rather (for this is a truer comparison) they do not belong to the community at all, but resemble the official class in British India, which exclusively governs, but does not settle, and which regards the natives as a race only fit to be governed by a superior race. For natives, read settlers when a bureaucratic colony is in view.

In British India, the natives are what the white

officials deem them: if they were not, they would hardly submit to be ruled by a handful of foreigners. But in the bureaucratic colonies, the officials are, apart from their official position, which is one of exceeding superiority, very much inferior to the better order of settlers. Pray observe that I speak generally, not denying that there are exceptions, and exceptions which it is a pleasure to record. But, speaking generally, the officials of a bureaucratic colony are inferior to the best settlers in property, manners, and character. The most valuable settlers have a good deal of property; some a great deal: the officials hardly ever have any property: it is their poverty at home which induces them to seek a colonial appointment; and they generally spend the whole of their salaries, not unfrequently as much more as they can get into debt. The best settlers are often men of great ability; as is proved by their success as settlers notwithstanding all the hindrances I have enumerated and some which remain to be noticed: most of the officials are persons who, in consequence of their want of ability, have broken down in some career at home, or have had no career but that of being supported in idleness by their relations. It is interest of a kind to be hereafter explained, not suitable ability, which in Downing-street is deemed a qualification for office in the colonies: and those for whom this interest is exerted, are, in point of ability only " good enough for colonies;" that is, persons whose want of ability unfits them for holding office, or otherwise earning their own bread, at home. There are exceptions of more than one kind. It happens sometimes by accident, that a young man of real ability is urged by necessity or led by inclination to prefer an immediate provision in the colonies to waiting for what his talents might obtain for him at home; but generally when a person of real ability gets his friends to solicit Downing-street for a colonial appointment, he either prefers an easy life abroad to hard work at home, or has defects of character, perhaps habitual vices, which disqualify him from getting on where he is known. There are a few men of superior ability in the colonial official class appointed by Downing-street, who are open to no countervailing reproach: and there are more whose ability is allied to defects or vices of character, that render their talent an evil instead of a benefit to the colony: but all the rest, who therefore constitute the great majority, and exemplify rule, are persons who, in consequence of their want of ability, find office in the colonies a refuge from destitution.

What are the conduct, character, and manners of the best class of emigrants, is a point that requires only one remark: those only form the best class of emigrants, whose manners, character, and conduct are unexceptionable. Unexceptionable: I would propose no higher standard by which to measure the conduct, character, and manners of the official class in bureaucratic colonies. Before applying the measure, however, let me again acknowledge that in all colonies probably, certainly in many, there are persons in office who are above the standard; whom we should unjustly disparage by saying that in conduct, character, and manners, they are only unexceptionable. In every class of mankind as numerous as the official class in bureaucratic colonies, there are some people who have been always good, and whom nothing can make bad; "nature's

noblemen," whose duty to their neighbour is prescribed by an inborn conscience, and whose manners
represent an inherent benevolence and delicacy. Such
people may be found at plough, among common sailors,
in the rank and file of desolating armies, in the cor-
ruptest parts of great cities; I had almost said amongst
thieves, the thieving apart.   Such people there are in
bureaucratic-colony official life; duty-doing men, true,
honourable, and public spirited, having generous sym-
pathies, and manners remarkable for gentleness and
refinement.   I am half inclined to mention the names
of some of them.   But all their names would not
occupy much space.   They are a small minority; and
they would be amongst the first to admit the truth of
what I say about the others.   The majority is composed of people, some of whom just come up to the
standard above proposed; some a little below it; some
below it to a degree which you, who have had no personal experience of the colonies, will not readily credit.
Or rather what you will with difficulty believe, is the
large proportion of officials in the bureaucratic colonies
who are below the standard. I mean a large proportion
whether of the whole number of colonial officials, or
in comparison with the proportion of official people in
this country whose manners, character, and conduct,
are worse than unexceptionable.   But how, you will
ask, can this be ascertained?   With respect to conduct at least, I can suggest a means by which your
curiosity might be satisfied. The Colonial Office could
if it pleased, and would if the House of Commons insisted on it, though sorely against the grain, furnish a
return of the number and titles of officials in the bureaucratic colonies, who during the last twenty years

have been dismissed from office for misconduct. It would be needless to specify the nature of the misconduct in each case, because the severe punishment of dismissal from office is only applied in gross and flagrant cases. Indeed, the natural tenderness of officials towards officials induces the Colonial Office, which alone of our public departments is thoroughly bureaucratic in its composition and character, to avoid as much as possible the form of dismissal; and this tenderness equally actuates governors and other colonial officials, when they are under the necessity of removing an erring brother. The usual form of dismissal, therefore, is an intimation to the wrong-doer, that he will only avoid the disgrace of a formal dismissal by tendering his resignation. The form of dismissal is hardly ever used, I think, except when the wrong-doer is also the scape-goat of his official brethren or of his superiors in Downing-street. The common form of real dismissal is resignation. I mention this in order that, if you should try to get such a return, your object may not be defeated by an evasion which might not be discovered, and, if it were, might be defended on the ground of formal accuracy. The return should state under separate heads, whether the officer resigned or was dismissed; if he was dismissed, for what reason; if he resigned, for what known or supposed reason; and whether the expediency of his resignation was intimated to him by superior authority. I have no doubt that there are materials in the Colonial Office for framing such a return, though for most of them a search must be made in the " confidential," " private," and " secret" pigeon-holes of that department; for of course, with the exception always of scape-goat cases, official misconduct in the colonies is carefully kept out of view by those who, if it were mentioned in blue-books, might be held responsible for it.

It would be well in such a return to have a column for cases of pecuniary default, which are very numerous and very important in the amount of money lost, when compared with such cases here. In this column the sum in default should be given, together with the population and annual income of the colony, so as to afford the means of proportionate comparison with this country. Some of the obvious conclusions from this column would startle the British public. Other sorts of misconduct could not be so easily presented in a tabular form: and, at best, many cases of gross misconduct would escape notice, because the wrong-doers were not dismissed in form or in fact, but are still, socially, high above the worthiest of the settlers. Low character and disgusting manners could not be any how set forth in a return. If we could get at ample information on the whole subject of conduct, character, and manners, the disclosures would make honest John Bull's hair stand on end. We should hear of judges deeply in debt, and alone saved by the privilege of their station from being taken to jail by the officers of their own court. We should hear even of governors landing in secret on their arrival, and getting hastily sworn into office in a corner, for the purpose of hindering officers of the sheriff from executing a writ of arrest against his excellency. We should learn that in the single colony of New South Wales, of which the population was at that time under 200,000, many high officials passed through the insolvent court in a single year. It was a year, no doubt, of extraordinary speculation in the colony, occasioned by certain pranks which the government played with the plan of disposing of waste land by sale: but the year 1847 was a year of extraordinary speculation in England without our beholding a considerable proportion of the highest of our public servants relieved from their speculative engagements by our courts of insolvency: and it is right to observe further, that speculation in railways here by people in office is not misconduct, as speculation in the disposal of colonial public land is when the speculators constitute the government which disposes of the land as a trustee for the public. Private speculation by members of the cabinet in a public loan would be more like what took the officials of New South Wales into the insolvent court. In this country, again, bankruptcy or insolvency deprives a member of parliament of his seat; whereas the insolvent officials of New South Wales continued to hold power afterwards as if they had done nothing wrong: a circumstance proper to be noted, as it serves to show the whereabouts of the standard of respectability among the depositories of power in our colonies. But this is an unpleasant topic; and I will dismiss it after mentioning a few more cases, which are taken from a single colony, and occurred at the same time not long ago. The Treasurer—that is, the colonial chancellor of the exchequer—was a defaulter. The Colonial Secretary —that is, the governor's prime minister—was obliged to resign his appointment in consequence of a discovery that a lady who passed as his wife was not married to him; and he afterwards resigned another office in consequence of being accused of forging public documents. An office, the duties of which required very high and peculiar qualities—that of sole judge of a court of law and conscience—was held by a country attorney, whose chief business in England had been the dirty work of elections, and who by that means got the appointment. Another office of still more difficulty and delicacy was given to an awkward half-educated lad of eighteen. Two principal officers of the government fled the colony without waiting to be dismissed, in order to avoid being tried, the one for robbing the pool at cards, the other for a yet more disgraceful crime. And, to conclude, another person, filling an office of great power and importance, was a blackguard in the constant habit of swearing " by the hind leg of the Lamb of God." This last fellow afterwards had the confiding ear of the Colonial Office, in a matter which was decided according to his views, and almost fatally for the colony.

Now for the moral, in pursuit of which I have raked into all this mass of filth. The class amongst whom, to say the least, such people are found in no inconsiderable number, constitutes the only and greatly privileged class in the colonies; the demigods who came from another planet to rule over the settlers. In the colony from which all the latter instances have been taken, there happened to be at the time a number of settlers of the very best sort, gentlemen belonging to some of the best families in England and Scotland; Petres, Cliffords, Dillons, Vavasours, Tytlers, Molesworths, Jerninghams, Sinclairs, Welds, and such like. They went out under the delusion, among others, that they should have some voice in the government of the colony. Instead of that, they were treated by the officials as an inferior sort of people, whose only proper business it was to create a colonial revenue by their industry, and to take off their hats on meeting a public functionary. You doubt: I did myself when first I heard of these things. Pray make inquiry for yourself amongst the families above named. By doing so, you will moreover learn how powerfully the low standard of character amongst the only privileged class in colonies, operates against the emigration of the best class of settlers.

LETTER XXXII.

From the Colonist.

THE COLONIST EXPLAINS THE URGENT NEED OF THE INTERVENTION OF GOVERNMENT IN THE MULTIFA-RIOUS BUSINESS OF CONSTRUCTING SOCIETY, AND DE-SCRIBES THE GENERAL PAUCITY, OFTEN THE TOTAL ABSENCE, OF GOVERNMENT IN THE COLONIES OF BRITAIN.

I HAVE said that the officials govern. How they govern, that is, what sort of laws they make, and how they administer them, and how, to a great extent, they govern without laws according to their own will at the moment; this is an important question to be considered hereafter; but there is another question relating to colonial government which is of even greater importance; namely, how much government British

colonists obtain. You may think that the quality is
of more moment than the quantity. That depends,
however, on the degree in which government is needed.
In this country, we suppose that there is always plenty
of government: we have no idea of a state of things
in which people feel that any government, good, bad,
or indifferent, would be better than not enough of any
sort. In the colonies this is the ordinary state of
things; and the paucity of government is more injurious in the colonies than it would be in an old
country. I will try to explain.

Referring to my letter on the charms of colonization,
I would say that the intervention of government is
more, and more constantly, needed in the multifarious
business of constructing society, than in that of preserving it. The very first operation is to obtain land;
and land, with the essential addition of a good title to
it, can only be obtained by the action of government
in opening the public waste to settlers by extensive
and accurate surveys, and in converting it into private
property according to law. The general drainage of
the new land, and the making of roads and bridges,
require taxation according to law. Magistrates can
only be appointed by authority; and even so simple
and necessary a law as one for putting trespassing
cattle into the pound, cannot exist without the action
of government. A good and well-executed law of
fencing is indispensable to the well-doing, and even to
the peace of a new settlement. Such examples might
be multiplied without end. Without plenty of government, the settlement of a waste country is barbarous
and miserable work: the vain exertions, the desperate
plunges, the stumbles, the heavy falls, the exhaustion

and final faintness of the settlers put one in mind of running, as it is called, in a sack. It is as difficult, as impossible, to colonize well without plenty of government, as to work a steam-engine without fuel, or breathe comfortably without enough air. Ample government, in a word, is the *pabulum vitæ*, the unremitting *sine quâ non* of prosperous colonization. The quality of government, I repeat, is of less moment to colonists than the amount.

Throughout the British colonies, the amount of government is curiously small. In every one of our colonies, the main principle of the government of France has been adopted. Whether the government of the colony is democratic in quality, like that of Canada under the responsible system with a suffrage nearly universal, or despotic like that of South Africa or New Zealand, it is at any rate exceedingly central. Whatever else it may be, every colonial government is of the central kind, just like that of modern France, which resides in Paris, whether it is an emperor Napoleon relying on his army, or a republic based on universal suffrage. In our colonies, government resides at what is called its seat: every colony has its Paris or " seat of government." At this spot there is government; elsewhere little or none. Montreal, for example, is the Paris of Canada. Here, of course, as in the Paris of France, or in London, representatives of the people assemble to make laws, and the executive departments, with the cabinet of ministers, are established. But now mark the difference between England on the one hand, and France or Canada on the other. The laws of England being full of delegation of authority for local purposes, and for special purposes whether local or not, spread government all over the country; those of Canada or France in a great measure confine government to the capital and its immediate neighbourhood. If people want to do something of a public nature in Caithness or Cornwall, there is an authority on the spot which will enable them to accomplish their object without going or writing to a distant place: at Marseilles or Dunkerque you cannot alter a high road, or add a gensd'arme to the police force, without a correspondence with Paris: at Gaspé and Niagara you could not until lately get anything of a public nature done without authority from the seat of government. But what is the meaning in this case of a correspondence with Paris or Montreal? it is doubt, hesitation, and ignorant objection on the part of the distant authority; references backwards and forwards; putting off of decisions; delay without end; and for the applicants a great deal of trouble, alternate hope and fear, much vexation of spirit, and finally either a rough defeat of their object or its evaporation by lapse of time. In France, accordingly, whatever may be the form of the general government, improvement, except at Paris, is imperceptibly slow, whilst in Old, and still more in New England, you can hardly shut your eyes anywhere without opening them on something new and good, produced by the operation of delegated government residing on the spot, or delegated government specially charged with making the improvement. In the colonies, it is much worse than in France. The difficulty there, is even to open a correspondence with the seat of government; to find somebody with whom to correspond. In France, at any rate, there is at the centre a very elaborate bureaucratic machinery, instituted with the design of supplying the whole country with government: the failure arises from the practical inadequacy of a central machinery for the purpose in view: but in our colonies, there is but little machinery at the seat of government for even pretending to operate at a distance. The occupants of the public offices at Montreal scarcely take more heed of Gaspé, which is 500 miles off and very difficult of access, than if that part of Canada were in Newfoundland or Europe. Gaspé therefore, until lately, when on Lord Durham's recommendation some machinery of local government was established in Canada, was almost without government, and one of the most barbarous places on the face of the earth. Every part of Canada not close to the seat of government was more or less like Gaspé. Every colony has numerous Gaspés. South Africa, save at Cape Town, is a Gaspé all over. All Australia Felix, being from 500 to 700 miles distant from its seat of government at Sydney, and without a made road between them, is a great Gaspé. In New Zealand, a country 8 or 900 miles long, without roads, and colonized as Sicily was of old, in many distinct settlements, all the settlements except the one at which the government is seated, are miserable Gaspés as respects paucity of government. In each settlement indeed there is a meagre official establishment, and in one of the settlements there is a sort of lieutenant-governor: but these officers have no legislative functions, no authority to determine anything, no originating or constructive powers: they are mere executive organs of the general government at the capital for administering general laws, and for carrying into effect such arbitrary instructions, which are not laws, as they may receive from the seat of government. The settlers accordingly are always calling out for something which government alone could furnish. Take one example out of thousands. The settlers at Wellington in New Zealand, the principal settlement of the colony, wanted a lighthouse at the entrance of their harbour. To get a lighthouse was an object of the utmost importance to them. The company in England, which had founded the settlement, offered to advance the requisite funds on loan. But the settlement had no constituted authority that could accept the loan and guarantee its repayment. The company therefore asked the Colonial Office, whose authority over New Zealand is supreme, to undertake that the money should be properly laid out and ultimately repaid. But the Colonial Office, charged as it is with the general government of some forty distinct and distant communities, was utterly incapable of deciding whether or not the infant settlement ought to incur such a debt for such a purpose: it therefore proposed to refer the question to the general government of the colony at Auckland. But Auckland is several hundred miles distant from Wellington; and between these distant places there is no road at all: the only way of communication is by sea: and as there is no commercial intercourse between the places, communication by sea is either so costly, when, as has happened, a ship is engaged for the purpose of sending a message, or so rare, that the settlers at Wellington frequently receive later news from England than from the seat of their government: and moreover, the attention of their government was

known to be at the time absorbed with matters relating exclusively to the settlement in which the
government resided. Nothing, therefore, was done:
some ships have been lost for want of a lighthouse;
and the most frequented harbour of New Zealand is
still without one.

Volumes might be filled with cases like this. I do
not mean cases furnished by all the colonies, but that
from each colony cases might be drawn that would
fill volumes. Nay more, each settlement of every
colony would furnish its volumes of cases. For now,
please to observe, that although in such a country as
New Zealand the general government provides an
official establishment, however rude and meagre, for
each distinct settlement, there are parts of every
settlement into which the action of the local official
establishment never penetrates at all. This arises
from the difficulties of communication in a new country. There is a considerable proportion of every
extensive colony—generally the parts most recently
occupied—in which there is no government. But
there are parts of the colony in which construction
or creation is more especially the business of the
settlers, and in which, therefore, government is more
needed than in the other parts. I hope you perceive
now, that there is not an outlying district of any of
our extensive colonies but would furnish its volumes
of cases in which government fails to supply some
urgent want of the settlers. The slow progress, the
rudeness, the semi-barbarism of what are called back-
settlements in Canada and New Brunswick, bush
settlements in Australia and New Zealand, are thus
sufficiently accounted for. The wonder is that they

get on as well as they do. Of this, also, you will probably desire an explanation. It shall be given in due time. Meanwhile, you now, I hope, understand how greatly, not the quality but the paucity of government in our colonies, operates as an impediment to emigration, and more particularly to the emigration of the most valuable class of settlers.

LETTER XXXIII.

From the Statesman.

THE STATESMAN THINKS THAT THE COLONIST HAS EXAGGERATED THE INDISPOSITION OF RESPECTABLE PEOPLE TO EMIGRATE.

PERMIT me to ask you whether you may not be overstating your case. Any one of the impediments to colonization, as you describe them, appears to me by itself sufficient to deter respectable people from emigrating; and I cannot understand how, with such a number of these impediments as you present to my view, there is any respectable emigration whatever. Yet there is some. One hears, every now and then, in society, of some peer's son, or family of good condition, though not large fortune, going out to a colony to settle. I am told that the number who went to Canada shortly before the rebellions was considerable; and the respectability of the emigration to New Zealand was a common topic some few years ago. Mr. Mothercountry assures me, that persons highly con-

nected in this country have gone to Port Philip, and
even to New South Wales, which is altogether a convict colony; not persons, he says, who though belonging to families of consequence were in difficulty or
under a cloud, but persons who took with them an
exemplary character and large capital.   He offered to
give me their names, and to put me in the way of veri-
fying his statement by communication with their
families in England.   He insists that the facts contradict your view of the force of all these obstacles to
colonization.   I do not agree with him to that extent;
but it appears to me, supposing the facts to be as he
represents them, that you over-rate the force of those
obstacles. If your estimate of it were perfectly correct,
nobody would emigrate but the labouring poor and
desperate or needy people of the other classes.   Will
you excuse me for saying that we must be careful to
avoid exaggeration.

LETTER XXXIV.

From the Colonist.

THE COLONIST DEFENDS HIS VIEW OF THE INDISPOSI-
TION OF RESPECTABLE PEOPLE TO EMIGRATE, AND
SUGGESTS FURTHER INQUIRY BY THE STATESMAN.—
TWO MORE IMPEDIMENTS TO COLONIZATION.

I AM glad that you inquire for yourself, in order
to test the soundness of my views. The more
you may do so, the better I shall be pleased. Pray
do take the names of the well-born emigrants, who
carried a high character and good capital to Port
Philip and New South Wales: and ask their relatives
what has become of them. Let me warn you, however, that in putting the question, you must take
some care in order to avoid giving pain. If you find
that half, or a quarter, of these emigrants have
realized the hopes with which they left home—if you
find the family of even one of them pleased with his
position as a colonist—I will acknowledge that I have
exaggerated. You will learn that most of them have
returned to this country, after losing their property
either in the gulf of " exhorburnt wagers," or in some
pit of colonial " smartness" which was dug on purpose
for the unsuspecting emigrant to fall into. You will

not learn that one of them really liked anything but
the climate, and the absence of that uneasiness and
poverty which in this country arises from excessive
competition.   I wish you could fall in with a gentle-
woman who has been induced to emigrate; more
especially if she should be attached to her church and
disposed to enjoy its observances.   Failing such a lady
herself, her correspondents would enlighten you if you
could lead them to tell of her disappointments.   It is
indifferent to me what colony you inquire about.   I
have inquired about many—about some with my own
eyes and ears—and I feel confident that the whole
emigration to Upper Canada and New Zealand, for
example, furnishes no instance of the ultimate settlement of a gentleman's family with satisfaction to
themselves and their friends at home.   There are
families that do not complain; that are induced by
mere pride to conceal their disappointment, or by
pride and common sense to make the best of irre-
mediable ills; to put up even cheerfully with the
painful consequences of an irretrievable step.   But
sift these cases to the bottom, not trusting to generals
but really getting at particulars; and they will sustain
my position even more effectually than cases of sudden
and total failure, for which not circumstances alone
but the individual may have been chiefly to blame.
There is another class of cases, which, though more
numerous, I am afraid, it is not so easy to investigate.
I mean cases in which the emigrant, after being
shocked at the difference between what he expected
and what he finds, gradually learns to like the baser
order of things, takes a pleasure in the coarse licence
and physical excitement of less civilized life, and

becomes a satisfied colonist by imbibing colonial tastes and habits. When this happens, it is difficult for a stranger here to learn the fact; but the relations know and deplore it; and it operates against the emigration of people whose tastes and habits are not colonial, though not so obviously, quite as surely, as cases of loud complaint.

Nevertheless, there are still emigrants of the gentry class: yes, Mr. Mothercountry is right in that; but please to ask him if he knows of any who are going to a colony under the influence of satisfactory reports from other emigrants of that class. At all times there is a certain number of the most valuable class of emigrants; but they go, every one of them, under the influence of some great delusion. One expects to grow rich fast; another, to be of great importance in the colony; a third, to enjoy a great domain as a great domain is enjoyed here; a fourth, to see his wife and daughters, who are fretting here, as happy there as the day is long. All these expectations prove, in ninety-nine cases out of a hundred, mere dreams of the fancy. Those who give way to them, go in spite of the impediments I am describing. If the deluded class was very large, this part of my subject would not exist. The question is, not how many go in spite of the impediments, but how many do the impediments prevent from going? to what extent do the impediments countervail the natural attractions of colonization?

There are two other impediments to colonization, which, as they do not affect all colonies, may be postponed for future consideration; I mean, first, the colonial as distinguished from the home effects of

Convict Transportation, which occur only in the colony of New South Wales and its near neighbours; and, secondly, the presence of Aboriginal Natives; with the revolting process by which their extermination is brought about. The latter set of colonial evils belong chiefly to the colonies of South Africa, Ceylon, and New Zealand. But there remains to be noticed at present one other impediment, the greatest of all, the parent of all the others; and this is our system of colonial government, which will occupy my next letters.

LETTER XXXV.

From the Colonist.

THE COLONIST PURPOSES TO EXAMINE COLONIAL GOVERN-
MENT AS AN IMPEDIMENT TO COLONIZATION, AS THE
PARENT OF OTHER IMPEDIMENTS, AND AS A CAUSE OF
INJURY TO THE MOTHER-COUNTRY; AND TO PROCEED
AT ONCE TO A PLAN FOR ITS REFORM.

HITHERTO in treating of an impediment to colonization, I have attended only to the thing itself and its particular influence on emigration, without noticing any other effect it may have, and without alluding to its causes. A different course will, I think, be found convenient and useful when examining colonial government generally. Our whole system of colonial government is not only by itself an impediment, but also the cause of the other impediments to emigration, which I have barely described: it is also the cause of effects which, though they may help to impede emigration, yet are all something more than that, and different from it; such effects, for example, as the heavy cost which the country incurs in holding its colonies as dependencies, and the disaffection of colonies towards the imperial power.   These are not merely colonial, but also imperial considerations.   Our system of colonial government is a prolific parent of diversified offspring, the whole of which I would, if possible, represent in one picture.   It is also a new system, differing widely from what was formerly the English system of colonial government: I think therefore that in describing it I shall do well to compare it with its predecessor.   And, lastly, as an examination of the subject would be idle save with a view to practical improvement, I purpose, whilst treating of British colonial government as it is and as it was, to collect some materials for a plan of reform, by means of showing how the present system has grown up, and adverting occasionally to the first principles of government and human nature.   In a word, I shall aim at making the view of colonial government as complete, as it is in my power to make it without occupying too much of your time.

LETTER XXXVI.

From the Colonist.

COMPARISON OF MUNICIPAL AND CENTRAL GOVERNMENT.
——CENTRAL BUREAUCRATIC GOVERNMENT OF THE
COLONIES ESTABLISHED BY THE INSTITUTION OF THE
COLONIAL OFFICE. — THE SPOILING OF CENTRAL-
BUREAUCRATIC GOVERNMENT BY GRAFTING IT ON TO
FREE INSTITUTIONS.——FEEBLENESS OF THE COLONIAL
OFFICE.

THERE are two main principles on which, or on a
combination of them, any system of colonial
government must of necessity be founded. The two
principles are of an opposite nature. The first, which
for shortness I shall call the municipal principle, is
that of local self-government; the second, that of
government from the distant centre of the empire,
which may be called the central principle. These, I
say, are the main principles; because whether the
government of a colony is democratic, aristocratic, or
despotic, it must be either municipal or central, or
both combined in some proportion to each other.
The government of Algeria, like that of any department of France, is now democratic, being founded on
representation in the national assembly with a uni-

versal suffrage; but it is eminently central, since the representatives of Algeria have no functions out of Paris, which is the centre of the empire, and no special functions whatever with regard to the colony. Once elected, they are representatives of all France; and the government of all France, Algeria included, is still pre-eminently central and bureaucratic notwithstanding democratic representation. The governments of some of the old English colonies in America were extremely aristocratic, but also municipal, as being authorities identified with their subjects by being formed and fixed on the spot. A colony has been allowed to place itself under the dictatorship of a single colonist: its government was, for the time, despotic but municipal. When a colony submitted itself to the rule of a privileged class, being persons identified with the colony, its government was municipal though aristocratic. These examples suffice to show that in colonial government, the principles of democracy, aristocracy, and despotism are of secondary importance to the municipal and central principles. In colonial government, the grand questions are, which system is to be preferred, the municipal or the central? is it expedient to combine them in one government? and if so combined, which of them should predominate? in what proportion should they be mixed?

In order to solve these questions, it is requisite to compare the two systems in principle and operation.

For the present generation of European statesmen, several things have conspired to place the subject of municipal government in obscurity. Wherever French jacobinism penetrated, it destroyed whatever municipal government it found, and created in its place a system of pure centralization: and that *à priori* philosophy which has been so fashionable in our day, and which treats mankind as a multiplication of the original thinker, has in this country brought views of centralization so much into vogue, that the very subject of municipal government is but little understood by some of the best-informed of our public men. The most common notion of it is, that it is an authority relating exclusively to cities or towns. Yet the municipal institution was but little known to the ancient Greeks, who, with their numerous colonies, chiefly inhabited cities; and a ramification of it appears now throughout the United States, in the "township" government of districts consisting solely of woods and farms. Another common view of the municipal principle is, that it is confined to objects of very minor importance, such as paving and lighting or police in towns, and the management of highways and church-rates in the country. How few remember practically, so to speak, that municipal government was a main cause of the greatness of the greatest of empires. Still fewer ever reflect that the present greatness of England is in no small degree owing to the institution, which colonized English America and formed our Indian empire.

The municipal principle, being that of a delegation of power by the supreme authority, with limits as to locality, or object, or both, may be applied no doubt to the least important matters. It is indeed the principle of that infinite variety of corporations for special or limited purposes (such as our Universities, the Trinity House, the Moneyers of the Mint, and the Bank of England, down to the meanest joint-stock company), which distinguish England and English America from the rest of the world, as they have formed the practical and self-relying character of our race. But whilst the municipal principle embraces the minutest subject, as to which the supreme authority may choose to delegate power, it admits of a delegation of the highest power short of sovereignty or national independence. The custom with those nations which have governed their dependencies municipally, has been a delegation of the maximum of power compatible with allegiance to the empire. Those nations are chiefly the Romans, and the English of the 16th and 17th centuries. But the municipal dependencies of Rome and England were formed by very different processes. If the Romans had colonized like the Greeks, by the creation of independent sovereign states, they would not have invented a system of municipal government for dependencies. The purpose of the invention was to render sovereign states subordinate to Rome, without depriving them locally of the institutions or rights which they possessed before. A city or state, enjoying sovereign power, incurred allegiance to Rome, and became imperially dependent; but it preserved its old laws untouched within its own limits. This mode of acquiring empire by absorption or annexation did not call for the making of municipal constitutions. Nor were the regulations of the Romans for founding military colonies, municipal constitutions, properly speaking: they rather resembled the central authority by which the conquered provinces of Rome were usually governed. Roman history accordingly supplies us with no complete charter of a municipal government. But when England began to enlarge her empire by colonization, our ancestors had to devise a kind of municipality quite different *in form* from that of the Romans. There is ample proof of their having seen the impossibility of governing distant communities well by means of constantly exercising the imperial authority. Besides such evidence on this point as is furnished by the preambles of our old charters of colonial government, it is a remarkable fact, that, until we began to colonize with convicts towards the end of the last century, the imperial power of England never, I believe, in a single instance, attempted to rule locally from a distance a body of its subjects who had gone forth from England and planted a colony. In every such case down to that time, the imperial authority recognised by word and deed the necessity of allowing the colonists themselves to govern locally. Emigrants, however, differed from the inhabitants of such states as became true municipalities of Rome, in already possessing an allegiance which they desired to preserve, and in not possessing a constitution of local government. England therefore reversed the Roman process. The allegiance of the distant community was preserved instead of being created; and the local constitution was created instead of being preserved. But the principle was identical in both cases; namely, delegation, tacit or express, of local powers limited only by general or imperial subordination.

The English mode of giving effect to this principle, being by express delegation, required that municipal constitutions should be framed and written. It has, therefore, furnished us with abundance of models for present use. All of them display one striking feature, though more or less prominently. In every case, the object seems to have been to confer local powers more or less similar in scope to those of a true Roman municipality. Lord Baltimore, the wisest and most successful of English colonizers, was authorized " by and with the advice, assent, and approbation of the freemen of Maryland, or the greater part of them, or their delegates and deputies, to enact *any laws whatsoever* appertaining either unto the public state of the said province, or unto the private utility of particular persons." With regard to powers, Penn merely copied the charter of Baltimore, whose disciple and close imitator he was in many other respects. The Connecticut charter authorized the colonists "from time to time to make, ordain, and establish all manner of wholesome and reasonable laws, statutes, orders, directions, and instructions, as well for settling the forms and ceremonies of government and magistracy, fit and necessary for the said plantation and the inhabitants there, as for naming and styling all sorts of officers, both superior and inferior, which they shall find needful for the government and plantation of the said colony." The first charter of Massachussetts grants power " to make laws and ordinances for the good and welfare of the said company and plantation, and the people inhabiting and to inhabit the same, as to them from time to time shall be thought meet." The colonists of Rhode Island were empowered " to make, ordain, and constitute, or repeal, such laws, statutes, orders and ordinances, forms and ceremonies of government and magistracy, as to them shall seem meet for the good and welfare of the said company, and for the government and ordering of the lands and heredita-

ments, and of the people that do, or at any time hereafter shall, inhabit or be within the same." It is
needless to multiply such examples. Speaking generally, the powers of local government, both legislative
and executive, were granted by a few simple and
comprehensive words. Then came the restrictions,
such as the condition that local laws should not be
repugnant or contrary to the laws of England, and
the reservation by the Crown, in some cases, of the
right to disallow laws, and to appoint certain officers.
These limitations must be carefully examined hereafter. In spite of them, the general characteristic of
England's municipal system of colonial rule, was local
self-government. How well the system worked, notwithstanding a good deal of counteraction, is best
seen by comparing its results with those of the central
system.

This is the system which has been pursued by other
colonizing states of modern Europe. As strangers to
self-government at home, they were incapable of deliberately employing the municipal system. Therefore,
the dependencies of France and Spain, for example,
were ruled from the seat of empire. And what has
this system produced? Communities so feeble, so deficient in the Anglo-municipal quality of self-reliance,
so devoid of " those feelings of pride, and of love and
attachment to liberty, which," says Burke, " belong to
self-government," that some of them have been, and
all probably will be, swallowed up by the self-governed
and energetic English race. It was really the colonists
of New-England who took Canada from France;
Louisiana, which would have been taken if it could
not have been bought, would not have been sold if it

had been worth keeping; and the American colonies of Spain, after a brief exhibition of splendour, occasioned solely by the accident of their abundance in the precious metals, seem destined to be colonized over again by the people whom England's municipal system has planted by their side.

The colonial system of France or Spain exhibits a twofold inferiority when compared with that of England. The old English colonists under the best charters were self-governed in two senses; first, as their government was local, and next, as it was free or popular: whereas the governments of the old colonies of France or Spain were both absolute and distant. Supposing it allowed that an absolute form of government is suitable for new colonies emanating from despotic states, still it is above all things necessary that an absolute government, in order to be tolerable anywhere, should be administered by one who sympathizes with his subjects, whose glory is their prosperity, to whom their misfortunes are at least a discomfort, and whom, if he should be a very bad man, they can at all events check in cases of great need by threaten ing him with the *ultima ratio* of popular despair. But the French or Spanish system placed power in the hands of one who had no sympathy with the colonists, who was not of them, who intended to live amongst them only till he had enriched himself at their expense, and whom even the despair of his subjects did not influence, because he could rely on the support of an overwhelming distant power, whose confidence he possessed, and whose jealousy of its own authority and dignity he could easily excite against the colonists by calling them " disaffected." Nay more, when it happened that a virtuous individual did sympathize with the colonists and generously cultivate their well-being, he was usually recalled by the supreme power, which became jealous of his popularity, or took offence at his disobedience of its ignorant and probably mischievous orders. If the absolute form of government was necessary, then at least sovereign or independent despotism should have been erected. Had this been done, the French and Spaniards might perhaps have shared pretty equally with the English in the ultimate colonization of America; but a combination of the despotic form with distant administration was the worst conceivable government; and the tree has yielded its proper fruit in the degenerate and fading communities resulting from French and Spanish colonization in America.

The first effectual trial of the central system by England was our attempt to deprive the great English colonies in America of their dearest municipal right. It cost us their allegiance. This wound to our national pride seems to have brought the municipal principle into disfavour, when it should have rather produced aversion to the central. Then came convict colonization, to which the municipal system was wholly inapplicable. It was deemed as inapplicable to the helpless communities which came under our dominion by conquest, French Canada alone excepted; and even there, after granting a free form of government to the colonists, we systematically withheld till the other day every proper consequence of representation. By degrees the central system prevailed over the municipal. The establishment of an office in London for the express purpose of adminis-

tering the central system, has finally almost extermi-
nated the old institution; public opinion has nearly
forgotten it; and now every portion of our vast
colonial empire is liable to the most serious injury from an oversight, a misapprehension, a want
of right information, or an error of judgment on
the part of a gentleman sitting in Downing-street, and
called Principal Secretary of State for the Colonies;
not to mention the exhaustion of his mind and body
in the endeavour to do somehow, without neglecting
more urgent calls, what twenty colonial ministers
could not do well, if they had nothing else to do, and
had been brought up to the business.

For the English, having free institutions at home,
had no machinery for administering the central system
abroad. It was impossible that Parliament should
itself legislate for many far-off dependencies; and the
Crown or its Ministry of responsible advisers was as
incapable of performing the executive part of government for the outlying portions of the empire. England,
therefore, once more acknowledged the necessity of a
delegation of power by the supreme authority for
the purpose of governing colonies. But instead of
delegating power to the colonies themselves, as till
then had been the rule, the supreme authority created
an office in London, and upon it bestowed legislative
and executive power over the colonies. Since then it
has been only on rare occasions that Parliament has
meddled with colonial questions; and nearly always
when the interference has been of a legislative character, the enactment was either for the purpose of
authorizing the Colonial Office to legislate by means
of orders or instructions, or for that of adopting

without understanding a suggestion of the Colonial Office. The only real exceptions from the rule of Colonial-Office supremacy have occurred when gross errors of administration, as in Canada and New Zealand, have drawn public attention in this country to a colonial subject. Such exceptions will doubtless be more numerous, if ever the subject of colonization should become popular in this country; but at present, speaking generally, our colonial system of government is thoroughly bureaucratic as well as central.

And hence arises another important consideration. The bureaucratic system is essentially repugnant to our general institutions, and even to our national character. This is shown by its extreme unpopularity as applied to the management of the poor. For the infinitely more difficult task of managing all the public affairs of some forty distant communities, the bureaucratic system in perfection would have been a wretched instrument. But we use it for that purpose in a very imperfect form. In Prussia, where the bureaucratic system worked as well as it ever can, the head of an official department was brought up to the business, commonly died at his post, and was succeeded by one not less intimately acquainted with the subject matter, and habitually versed in the exercise of official authority. The head of our Colonial Office is a Cabinet Minister and a member of either House of Parliament; and if he is a man of any ability, the calls of party, Parliamentary debate, and general legislation, leave him hardly time for sleep, much less for the deliberate and careful exercise of his vast colonial authority. It matters little, therefore, that he enters the Colonial Office with no special aptitude for directing it, and generally leaves it, for a reason totally unconnected with colonial affairs, soon after, or even before, acquiring some knowledge of its business. The Parliamentary Under-Secretary precisely resembles his chief, except in being subordinate to him, and in not bearing the burden of Cabinet discussions and responsibilities. The great bulk, accordingly, of the labours of the office are performed, as the greater portion of its legislative and executive authority is necessarily wielded, by the permanent Under-Secretary and the superior clerks.   These are men of great ability; but it is ability of a peculiar sort.   It is the sort of ability which serves the interests of an office, as such; mere official ability; great diligence, a perfect command over the elements of order, and an intimate knowledge of forms, precedents, and past transactions.   These are not qualifications for law-giving and command. And, moreover, so little is the public aware that the real legislators and rulers of our colonial empire possess even the qualities which I attribute to them, that their very names are hardly known beyond the precincts of Downing-street.   It follows that they are sheltered from all responsibility to public opinion. Where bureaucracy is not a delegated power, but in itself supreme, public opinion which has formed it, and which alone sustains it, likewise watches it and keeps it in order.   Our colonial system of government is the bureaucratic, spoiled by being grafted on to free institutions.

This spoiling is very conspicuous in the weakness of the Colonial Office at home, notwithstanding its despotic authority abroad.   It is a government in the wrong place; a government seated in a foreign country.

Not having been formed by the communities whose government it is, not even breathing the same air with them, it wants the strength which a domestic government derives from its nationality. The nation which surrounds it, scarcely recollects its existence. As a government, therefore, it is like a tree without roots, all stem and branches, apt to be bent any way. As a machine of government, the forces by which it is moved or stayed are quite insignificant when compared with the power they influence. If ever the Colonial Office originates a scheme of policy, it seldom pursues it consistently to the end. It sets off in one direction, and takes another the moment some interest, or clique, or association in this country strongly objects to the first course. At one time, the West-India Body in England suggests what it shall do; at another, the Anti-Slavery Society impels it. To-day its measures originate with some Canada merchants in London; to-morrow it abandons those measures, and pursues others of an opposite tendency at the instance of some London newspaper. At the instigation of a missionary society it all but made New Zealand a convict colony of France; and then yielding to the remonstrances of a joint-stock company, it established the British sovereignty which it had just before loudly repudiated. For awhile the Company led it to favour colonization; but ere long the anti-colonizing views of the Society again prevailed with it; and of late years its policy as to New Zealand has been an alternation of shuttlecock flights between the battledores of Salisbury-Square and Broad-Street-Buildings. It even yields to individual pressure, such as no other department would heed or feel; such as no domestic government would tolerate. Conscious of feebleness arising from the want of a public on the spot to sustain it in doing right and prevent it from doing wrong—fully aware of its own unpopularity as a bureaucratic institution in a free country—well acquainted with the facilities which the free press and the free institutions of this country afford for pressing it disagreeably—the Colonial Office but faintly resists anybody who may choose to make a business of pressing it. A list of the individuals who have made this their business during the last twenty years, would not be very short, and might be given with chapter and verse for what each of them successfully pressed it to do, undo, or leave undone. The whole would form a book of directions for future meddlers in colonial affairs. They would learn from its pages how easy it is for even the most obscure person, if he resides here and sets about the work in earnest, to prompt or thwart the policies of the Colonial Office, to suggest or overturn its decisions, to get its servants appointed or recalled, and to give the great bureaucracy more trouble in a year than it ever spontaneously bestowed on the distant colonies in five. Verily the Colonial Office would be at least more self-impelled if it were seated in Russia or St. Helena.

The spoiling of a bureaucratic institution by seating it in a free country, is more fully seen on examining the defective instruments by which the power of the Colonial Office is administered at a distance. These are, first, officers sent out to the colonies, and, secondly, instructions for their guidance. But it is time to close this letter.

LETTER XXXVII.

From the Colonist.

MODE OF APPOINTING PUBLIC FUNCTIONARIES FOR THE
COLONIES.—GOVERNMENT BY INSTRUCTION.—JESUITI-
CAL CONDUCT OF THE COLONIAL OFFICE.—A COLONIAL
OFFICE CONSCIENCE EXEMPLIFIED BY LORD GREY.—
PROPOSED TABULAR STATISTICS OF DISPATCHES IN THE
COLONIAL OFFICE.

THE officers are not a peculiar class, brought up to
their peculiar business, like members of the various
professions and servants of the East India Company.
Some of them are picked up, one scarcely knows how;
for it is difficult to say by what means they get their
appointments, unless it be that, having broken down in
some regular profession or having taken a dislike to it,
they are in want of a provision and gain it in the colonies
by dint of importunity. Others, and these are a very
numerous class, owe their appointments to Peers and
Members of Parliament, who having poor relations to
provide for, or electioneering obligations to pay off,
seldom think of the colonies but as Mr. O'Connell wrote
about them in that letter which I have already noticed.
The Treasury has a share of the patronage, the Admiralty another, the Horse-Guards a third, and the Board

of Ordnance comes in for pickings.   How would a Prussian bureau have worked with scarcely a voice in the selection of its own instruments?   With the real disposers of colonial patronage, fitness is the last consideration; and, what is still worse, inasmuch as there is no public at home taking an interest in colonial affairs, colonial patronage becomes the refuge for men, whose unfitness for any office whatever forbids their employment by departments which public opinion controls as well as sustains.   Those other departments make a convenience of the Colonial Office: the patronage of the colonies is the receptacle into which they cast their own importunate but very incompetent applicants for public employment.   The great bulk, accordingly, of those whom we send out to the colonies to administer government, even those appointed to the highest offices, are signally unfit for the duties imposed on them.   On this point it is needless to add a word to what has been said before.

But there are exceptions, more especially as to governors, sometimes by design, oftener by accident. Since the rebellions in Canada, the governors of that province have been men of experience and high reputation in public life.   Lord Durham was sacrificed by the Colonial Office, which in its miserable weakness let him fall a victim to party strife at home.   Lord Sydenham, as Governor of Canada, used to speak openly with aversion and contempt of the permanent or bureaucratic part of the Colonial Office, and to boast with justice of his sole reliance for support in England, on his party connexions there, and Lord John Russell's private friendship.   Sir Charles Bagot, who, I fully believe, preserved the colony to England

by a bold and startling measure, seemed to die of
the supposed though unpublished disapproval by the
Colonial Office of a policy which delighted precisely
ten-elevenths of the provincial representative body.
The dauntless self-reliance of the last Governor of
Canada made him careless of support from any quarter,
and even gave him a sort of mastery over the Colonial
Office; but his successors, since there are not two
Lord Metcalfes, may painfully learn that a department,
itself unsupported by public opinion, is always apt to
withhold support from its servants at the very time
when they need it most.

Next as to instructions. These are necessarily
written, on account of the distance. What is the
subject of them? All the public concerns of about
forty distinct communities, scattered over the world,
and comprising an endless diversity of languages,
laws, religions, customs, wants, and economical circumstances. For writing statistically or theoretically,
and but once, on so vast and varied a theme, the
knowledge of the wisest of mankind would be insufficient; a thousand sages would be incapable of
writing upon it continually in the form of useful practical directions. Who it is that writes, I need not
repeat. And what is it that is written? it is legislation and mandate. The commission of every governor
now-a-days enjoins him to rule according to the instructions which he shall receive from Downing-street,
In the bureaucratic colonies, instructions from Downing-
street have the force of Acts of Parliament: in the
representative colonies, the governor, being himself a
branch of the legislature as well as the head of the
executive, is bound to obey them implicitly. Instruc-

tions written in Downing-street really constitute,
therefore, the main instrument of government for our
vast colonial empire. We have subjected a large portion of the world to none of the old forms of government, but to something which differs altogether from
monarchy, aristocracy, democracy, and every combination of these three. Government by instructions!
This institution is so little known except to colonists
and colonizers, that a member of both classes may be
excused for attempting to describe it.

Legislation and mandate must be founded on information of some kind. When these suit the character
and wants of a people, the largest portion of the
business of government consists in the gathering and
sifting of information. In Prussia, the work used to
be done by a vast and well-ordered official establishment: it is done in England, though in some measure
by official means, still chiefly by petitions to Parliament, by debates in Parliament, and above all by
the press, quarterly, monthly, weekly, daily, morning
and evening, and extra-editional: for the colonies, it
purports to be done by the reports of governors. A
governor's reports, and the instructions founded on
information derived from them, form a correspondence
legislative and executive. In this potent interchange
of letters, months elapse, in some cases twelve months,
before an answer can come by return of the post.
Without reverting to the character and position of the
writers on both sides, it is obvious that government
by instructions must be a great make-believe of good
government. Cases indeed happen, but every honest
governor or intelligent colonist would declare them
to be extraordinary cases, in which something useful

is done for a colony by means of instructions from Downing-street. Allowing for these rare exceptions, Colonial-Office instructions are either mischievous or inoperative. When founded on a wrong or imperfect view of things in the colony, as must be the case nine times out of ten, they are mischievous if executed. If mischievous in character, but not executed by a governor of sense and courage, they are still mischievous in effect, by worrying the governor, irritating the colonists, and exposing the supreme authority to little less odium than it incurs when mischievous instructions are executed by a dull or timid governor. The proportion of inoperative instructions is immense. They are inoperative from having been outrun by time and events, or from some other inapplicability to things real in the colony. Why then write at all, except in the few cases where there is a clear necessity for writing, and good assurance that the trouble will not be lost? Because, in fact, the trouble is not lost as respects the writers. Real government of the colonies from London is impossible, but an appearance of governing must be kept up for the sake of the importance and dignity of the Office. The new head of the Office (and the head of the Office is always more or less new*) likes to sign well-written dispatches which may figure in a blue-book; and the writer of them takes a pleasure in giving this satisfaction to his chief. Both classes like the semblance of governing. The writing, therefore, of inoperative despatches is not

* In about twenty years, there have been thirteen Principal Secretaries of State for the Colonies : Bathurst, Huskisson, Murray, Goderich, Stanley, Spring Rice, Aberdeen, Glenelg, Normanby, John Russell, Stanley again, Gladstone, and Grey.

labour lost; but it is mischievous nevertheless. I have seen the House of Assembly in Canada incapable of restraining their mirth, whilst the Speaker was gravely reading instructions to the Governor which his Excellency had been desired to communicate to them: they laughed at the ludicrous inapplicability to Canada of the views expounded in these dispatches, as the dock-yard people at Kingston on Ontario, laughed at the arrival from England of a consignment of water-casks for the use of ships floating on the fresh-water Lake. Considering that these despatches were written in the name of the imperial Sovereign, this disrespectful treatment of them was surely very mischievous.

The official necessity of writing, moreover, combined with the difficulty of writing for practical purposes, has begotten the custom of writing didactically. Long theories of philanthropy and political economy are propounded in despatches. A pamphlet printed in London, and consisting of the opinions of the writer concerning the aborigines of New Zealand, was transcribed, of course without acknowledgment, into the form of a didactic despatch. Certain theories of the Colonial Office *versus* the opinions of the last Committee of the House of Commons on New Zealand, were elaborately set forth in the shape of instructions to Governor Fitzroy, whose own theories were known to be identical with those contained in the despatch. Some twelve years ago, in a circular despatch addressed to the governors of the West-India colonies, I met with a new theory of my own which had been published anonymously not long before. The subject was of vital importance to the West Indies; and the theory pointed to measures which the colonists anxiously desired. Seeing my humble notions dressed up in the ornaments of the best official style, and dignified with the semblance of original thoughts formed in the brain of the Colonial Minister, I innocently concluded that something to be sure would come of it. And something did come of it. The well-written despatch was published here for the credit of the Office; and the colonists soon discovered that all the fine promises it held out to them were nothing but what they disrespectfully called Colonial-Office flummery. How the fact was I cannot know; but I can assure you that in Canada, the despatch of the Colonial Office which led to the British-Canada Corn Act, was originally deemed nothing but a piece of didactic writing. The leading colonists still pride themselves on having converted mere compliment into a valuable reality, by treating it as if it had been a practical suggestion. If this despatch was not written at the instance of the Cabinet at home, with a deliberate view to the admission of American wheat through Canada into England at a fixed duty of four shillings per quarter, it was what the colonists believed it to be; and at any rate, their belief shows that this kind of instructions cannot be very uncommon. The first governor of New Zealand received a body of general instructions, which every reader of them must pronounce admirable in doctrine, tone, and expression. The local government read them by the rule of contraries, having for years pursued a line of conduct just opposite to their particular suggestions and general tenour. Did punishment or censure follow? No, nor complaint, nor even a word of notice. These instructions were of the didactic kind, not intended for effect save in a blue-book.

Figuring there, they had the effect of inducing a superior class of persons to emigrate, with the hope of doing well under a government so admirably taught. I could name several who were led to ruin by their credulous reliance on that didactic dispatch.

Then there is a class of despatches which may be properly termed the obscure. Time will be saved in describing them by first quoting an author who is himself one of the ablest writers of Colonial-Office despatches. In his very clever and entertaining book, called *The Statesman*,* which we are told "treats of topics such as experience rather than inventive meditation suggested to him," he says that the " far greater proportion of the duties which are performed in the office of a minister, are and must be performed under no effective responsibility;" that there are "means and shifts by which the business of the office may be reduced within a very manageable compass without creating public scandal;" and that by these arts the doer of the business "may obtain for himself the most valuable of all reputations in this line of life, that of a ' safe man.' " The means and shifts are " by evading decisions wherever they can be evaded; by shifting them on other departments where by any possibility they can be shifted; by giving decisions upon superficial examinations, categorically, so as not to expose the superficiality in propounding the reasons; by deferring questions till, as Lord Bacon says, ' they ' resolve themselves;' by undertaking nothing for the public good which the public voice does not call for; by conciliating loud and energetic individuals at the expense of such public interests as are dumb or do

* *The Statesman.* By HENRY TAYLOR, Esq. 1836.

not attract attention; and by sacrificing everywhere what is feeble and obscure to what is influential and cognizable." Obscure despatches are commonly written in answer to despatches from governors desirous of escaping responsibility and fixing it on the Office; and their object is to save the Office from responsibility, by fixing it on the governors. The writing of them has begotten a style peculiar to the Colonial Office; a style founded on that view of language which supposes that it was given to us for the purpose of concealing our thoughts; the style which says as little as possible by means of a great quantity of words. I once heard two ex-governors, both of them men of ability, who have since held very high appointments, talk over the subject of Colonial-Office instructions. One of them said, that he had often received long despatches, the meaning of which he could never make out, though he read them over and over again. Well, said the other, and what did you do with them? At length, replied the first, I made a guess at the meaning and acted accordingly. Like you, said the second, I have often striven in vain to find out the meaning of a despatch, and have ended with a guess; but, unlike you, I further conjectured that these obscure directions were intended to get the Office out of a scrape and me into it; wherefore, instead of acting on my guess, I did the reverse. It is only fair to state that he had quarrelled with the Office and resigned his governorship; but in speaking so disrespectfully of his former masters, he differs from most other governors, and resembles colonists in general, only by the frank expression of his contempt and hatred.

Such feelings are indeed excited by two other

classes of instructions. I mean those which are confidential or secret, and those in which words with more than one meaning are studiously employed. They sometimes differ materially from published instructions on the same subject. A flagrant instance of this kind came to light during the New-Zealand controversy; and considering what a large proportion of such cases must necessarily be buried in darkness, the number of them that are known is dismally great. Among " the shifts and means" by the practice of which, says the author of *The Statesman*, " men in office have their understandings abused and debased, their sense of justice corrupted, their public spirit and appreciation of public objects undermined" is the use of words with a double meaning. The object is not, and cannot be, anything but double-dealing: it is the shift of the " safe man," who foresees a future convenience to his office in being able to give to official language an interpretation different from its *primâ facie* meaning. Several tricks of this sort came out in the course of the New-Zealand controversy. They may be uncommon; but enough have become public to create an opinion on the subject even in this country: it was expressed in the House of Commons, when cheers succeeded the proposal that the following words of a New-Zealand savage, addressed to her Majesty's representative in the colony, should be inscribed on the Colonial Office, " Speak your words openly; speak as you mean to act; do not speak one thing, and mean another."

The cheering took place in Lord Stanley's time. Among the loudest in thus denouncing the habitual trickery of the Colonial Office, was the present Colonial Minister; but in his time certainly the department has fully maintained its reputation for being addicted to double-dealing. Indeed, the " smartness" of the *genius loci* is remarkably exemplified by Lord Grey, who notwithstanding the high honour of his father's son, has learned in the great house at the bottom of Downing-street, first, to contend without a blush, that it is perfectly fair and right to quote parts of dispatches, which taken without their context support your own side of a question, and deliberately to suppress other parts which uphold the opposite side; and secondly, to simulate in public, that he is carrying into execution the plans of colonial reform of which out of office he was the zealous advocate, which his subordinates and his own want of practical ability have prevented him from realizing, and of which, therefore, he is in private and in truth as bitter a foe as was ever renegade to the faith he had deserted.

It must be a Colonial-Office conscience that permits recourse to such tricks. In Mr. Taylor's *Statesman*, there is a chapter, which he says that he wrote with " a trembling hand." It consists of an elaborate and very ingenious pleading in favour of allowing statesmen to be guided by two consciences; one for private, and the other for public life; one honest, the other as dishonest as the statesman himself shall think proper. In this chapter he says, " I estimate the consequences of relaxing the law of truth in private life to show a vast balance of evil; and the consequence of relaxing that law in public life to show a serious array of evil certainly; but I hesitate to say a balance." * * * * " Falsehood ceases to be falsehood when it is understood on all hands that the truth is not expected to be spoken." * * * * "A statesman is engaged, certainly, in a field of action which is one of great danger to truthfulness and sincerity. His conscience walks, too, like the ghost of a conscience, in darkness or twilight." * * * * "Upon the whole, therefore, I come to the conclusion, that the cause of public morality will be best served by moralists permitting to statesmen, what statesmen must necessarily take and exercise — a free judgment, namely, though a most responsible one, in the weighing of specific against general evil, and in the perception of perfect and imperfect analogies between public and private transactions, in respect of the moral rules by which they are to be governed." And in another chapter he says, "it will be found to be better for the public interests that a statesman should have some hardihood, than much weak sensibility of conscience." Both freedom of judgment in questions of official morality, and hardihood of conscience too! Bravo, Mr. Taylor! Why should you blush, Lord Grey? Oh, for a Pascal to write *Lettres Provinciales* about Colonial-Office doctrine as given to the world by members of the Colonial Office!

But the greater part of despatches never see the light, without being marked secret or confidential. Whether any despatch, either from the Office to a governor or from a governor to the Office, shall ever be published either here or in the colonies, depends altogether on the pleasure of the Office. The whole correspondence, indeed, remains unseen except by those who write it, and excepting the very small proportion of it for which the Office gives special directions. The colonies, therefore, are ruled by a legislative and executive power, which has an absolute choice between making known and utterly concealing all the grounds of its laws and orders. The portion of them which it does not conceal, is of course very small. If a return were made to the House of Commons of all despatches written and received by the Colonial Office during the last ten years, distinguishing the published from the unpublished, I suspect that not less than nine-tenths would appear in the latter class; and of the remaining tenth it would turn out that a large proportion had not been published till they belonged to the past. The ill results of this part of the system would form a separate and very important chapter.

Another would be the very mischievous uncertainty and delay of legislation by means of despatches whether published or not. The best illustration of this point would be a return for ten years of all despatches received by or sent from the Colonial Office, with the date of each, the date of its receipt, date of the acknowledgment of its receipt, and the date of any substantial answer to it; together with an enumeration of the despatches which have never been substantially answered, and such a brief statement of the topics of the same as would enable the House of Commons to judge whether a substantial answer was required.

But if such a return were deemed too complicated, a statement of the mere number of despatches received by the Colonial Office in one year, would tell a sufficient tale. In the single year 1846, the Colonial Office of Paris received from the single dependency of Algeria, no less than 28,000 despatches, relating to civil, independently of military affairs; 538 a week, or 86 a day, not reckoning Sundays. At what rate do our forty dependencies supply our Colonial Office with despatches? The Algerian rate gives 1,120,000 a year; 3,578 for every working day. Supposing, however, that each of our dependencies produces on the average no more in a year than Algeria does in a week, namely 538 per week, or 28,000 in a year, which must be vastly below the true mark, there are figures enough to assure us that a large proportion of despatches from the colonies cannot by possibility be substantially answered. But the most monstrous return in point of figures, and the most useful in point of instruction, would be one which is indeed impracticable; namely, an account of the number of cases in a year, in which something that ought to have been done in the colonies was left undone because a dispatch was not even written.

And, lastly, with respect to instructions, I have not said a word about the public injury and private wrongs inflicted on the colonists, by the most prompt execution of those which are written in ignorance or on false information. This topic is too large for this place; but its absence for that reason will suggest reflections which may therefore be spared.*

* " Algeria is divided administratively into three zones: the population of the first being chiefly European—this is the civil territory or zone; the second by Arabs and a few Europeans—this is the mixed territory; the third by Arabs only—this is the Arab territory *par excellence.* The administration of the first is the principal and most serious; and is pronounced by all, and especially by the Commission this year (1847) with the examination of affairs in Algeria, to be defective, imperfect in its functions, complicated in its system, slow in its working, making much ado about nothing, doing little, and that little badly. The functionaries of whom it is composed are pronounced ignorant of the language, usages, and history of the country, and unacquainted with the duties imposed upon

them. Their proceedings instead of being rapid and simple, as so necessary in a new colony, are ill-advised, ill-executed, and supereminently slow. The latter defect is chiefly attributable, perhaps, to the fact that from the centralization of affairs in Paris, all the acts must be referred to the head bureau there before the least move of the most trivial nature can be effected. During the last year only, above twenty-four thousand despatches were received from thence by the "Administration civile," and above twenty-eight thousand sent to Paris by this branch in Algiers.

"The immense number of functionaries appertaining to the corps of civil administrators in Algeria is astonishing. At the present period there are above two thousand; yet there is a cry that they are insufficient."

* * * * * * *

"Another and great reason for the slow growth of the colony, is the extreme tardiness with which the administrative forms requisite to the establishment of emigrants are carried out. For instance, though assignments of land are promised, yet a year or eighteen months after application frequently elapses before the grantees are put into possession. The majority of those arriving from the mother-country having but very small capital, it in the intermediate period disappears; they are compelled to devour it to keep body and soul together; and when it is gone their assignment may be allotted to them, with the parental advice, 'There, sit ye down, increase and multiply:' but it comes too late; their only prospect is starvation; and they are fortunate if sufficient remains to them to permit them to shake the dust from off their feet and fly the inhospitable shore, thus preventing others from arriving: for will they not return with outcry and relations of their sufferings ? It is even a fact well known to all, that men of capital, rich French proprietors, arriving in Algeria under the auspices of the Minister of War, have remained as long as five or six years before being able to obtain a promised concession. Others again established provisionally upon a tract of land, the assignment of which has been promised them, have built upon it, cultivated portions of it, and otherwise fulfilled all required conditions; when at last the definite answer is given them—the title to it is *refused !* Being able neither to alienate or to mortgage, they have thus been brought to ruin."

"The generally desolate state of those poor emigrants who do become established in Algeria is painful enough. The villages scattered about the Shael or Massif of Algiers are, with one or two exceptions, the type of desolation. Perched upon the most arid spots, distant from water, there the poor tenants lie sweltering beneath sun and sirocco, wondering, as their haggard eyes rove across vast tracts of inexterminable palmetta and prickly bushes, what there is there 'to increase and multiply' upon, as recommended."—*Narrative of a Campaign against the Kabaïles of Algeria : with the Mission of M. Suchet to the Emir Abd-el-Kader for an exchange of prisoners.* By DAWSON BORRER, F.R.G.S.

LETTER XXXVIII.

From the Colonist.

DISALLOWANCE OF COLONIAL LAWS BY THE COLONIAL OFFICE. — LOT OF COLONIAL GOVERNORS. — EFFECTS OF OUR SYSTEM OF COLONIAL GOVERNMENT.—COUNTERACTION OF THE SYSTEM BY THE *VIS MEDICATRIX NATURÆ.*—PROPOSED ADDITION TO MR. MURRAY'S *COLONIAL LIBRARY.*

WHEN at last a colonial law is made and promulgated, whether by a provincial parliament or a governor with his council of nominees, it is still liable to disallowance by the Colonial Office. Four evils in particular are the result. In the first place, the colonists suffer, during the time necessary for communication with England, from a state of harassing uncertainty and suspense with regard to the ultimate validity of their laws. Secondly, the party or faction in the colony, which has objected to the passing of any law, seeks to thwart the successful party, and to gain its own point, by means of secret influences and intrigues with the Colonial Office. Thirdly, whenever the power of disallowance is exercised, whether honestly by the Colonial Office, or, as sometimes happens, by the Colonial Minister himself, for reasons which appear sufficient to him, the veto is imposed, it must be confessed, by persons much less qualified to judge on the subject than those by whom the law was made, and, in the case of the Colonial Minister himself, by a person fully engaged by matters of far more pressing importance to him. And, lastly, these three effects of the reserved veto necessarily aggravate party animosity in the colony, and tend to destroy that sentiment of loyalty towards the empire which I have described as a passion of British emigrants and their children. The number of colonial laws which have been disallowed during the last ten years, with a brief statement of the nature of each, would form the subject of another incredibly curious return to the House of Commons.

Justice demands that we should rather pity the lot of governors under this system, than blame them for what the system produces. They are frequently punished, and sometimes with the greatest injustice. A governor of more than common ability is the most likely to disregard or disobey instructions drawn up in London, and so to get recalled. The best of governors enters upon office very ignorant of things and persons in the colony. If a representative constitution enables him to discover the bent of the colonial mind on matters which call for decision, he has still to determine whether he will side with the minority or the majority. If he sides with the minority, he sets going that conflict between representative institutions and a despotic administration of them, which is the ordinary state of our representative colonies; and, thenceforth, instead of governing, he only lives in hot water. At length, perhaps, the con-

flict of factions in the colony becomes so violent that
the House of Commons interferes; and then the
governor is recalled by the Colonial Office, which
hitherto, under the influence of some clique, or individual at home, has patted him on the back in his
quarrel with the majority. If he sides with the
majority, between whom and the bureaucracy at home
there is a strong natural aversion, the first good opportunity of recalling him is seldom neglected; or, at all
events, his life is made uncomfortable, and his capacity
for governing much diminished, by the intrigues and
secret influences at home, which the colonial minority
brings to bear against him in Downing-street. In the
non-representative, or bureaucratic colonies, it is still
worse. There, no institution tells the governor what are
the wants and wishes of the colony. The factions which
surely exist among Englishmen wherever government by party has not grown out of free institutions freely administered, have been lying in wait for
him, with nets spread and traps prepared. In his
ignorant helplessness, he almost necessarily falls into
the hands of one or other of them. If he keeps them
off, and judges for himself, he is sure to make
terrible mistakes, partly from ignorance, and partly
because all the factions conspire to mislead and ruin
the governor who sets them all at defiance. This man
causes intolerable trouble to the Colonial Office, and is
soon advised to tender his resignation. A less self-
relying governor has no sooner made up his mind
to which faction he will abandon himself, than all
the others declare war against him; the local press
goads him; the Colonial Office is beset with applications for his removal; some part of the press at home

is induced to attack him; speeches are made against him in Parliament; and if he is not recalled to stop the hubbub, he at best leads a life of care and apprehension. What all governors suffer from the disallowance of their acts by distant, ill-informed, and irresponsible superiors, would form a long chapter. Another might be filled with the troubles of governors, in consequence of having to administer a government without having the patronage of a government at their disposal. Upon the whole, it may be questioned whether the existence of any class of men is much more uncomfortable than that of governors of British colonies. Some few escape the common lot; but they generally do so by the practice of those "means and shifts" which the Colonial Office itself is induced by its weakness to adopt, and because their low ambition is satisfied if they can manage to keep a good salary and the title of Excellency without attempting to govern. It follows, that even if the Colonial Office selected its own servants, men having the spirit and self-respect which accompany capacity for ruling, would be loth to serve the office of governor, except in the few cases where the importance of a colony renders that office important, however uncomfortable.

Turning from particulars to the whole system as displayed by its effects, one is surprised that it should work at all. It produces much trouble here, and endless turmoil in the colonies. It disturbs secretaries of state, worries all governors, and ruins some. It irritates colonial assemblies, deprives them of their just functions, and forces them into violent proceedings, such as political impeachments, the stoppage of supplies, and personal attacks on the local sovereign,

which have been unknown in this country since we
established responsible government for ourselves. It
subjects the bureaucratic colonies to an authority in
all that concerns their welfare, that is ignorantly and
secretly impelled, besides being secret in operation
and arbitrary as well as absolute. It breeds colonial
factions and demagogues. By its injustice and
oppressions, it begets the use of slavish means of self-
defence; hypocrisy, crafty intrigue, and moral assas-
sination of opponents. Thus, and by its false pre-
tences and foul practices, it almost banishes honour
from public life in the colonies, and greatly helps to
bring down the standard of private honour far below
that of the mother-country. It benumbs enterprise,
and forbids creative legislation, in societies whose
natural business is adventure and creation. It is
costly beyond any comparison with the municipal
system, though not burdensome to the colonists in the
same proportion, because, in the bureaucratic colonies to
some extent, this country pays for the misgovernment
which checks the growth of private wealth and public
income. Furthermore, the system, which as to all our
newest colonies we have substituted for the municipal,
in the complete form of the central-bureaucratic-spoiled,
robs the Englishman of what used to be deemed his
birthright. It thus deprives the emigrant, whatever
may be his talents for public business, of all opportunity of exerting himself for the public good, of all the
motives of a laudable ambition, of all pursuits except
the making of money. It places him, whatever may
have been his station here, how much soever he may be
superior in education and property to the highest of
the officials, in a position of mortifying inferiority to

the lowest. To use a heedless expression of the *Quarterly Review*, it renders the colonies " unfit abodes for any but convicts, paupers, and desperate or needy persons." It cures those who emigrate in spite of it, of their *maladie du pays*. It is the one great impediment to the overflow of Britain's excessive capital and labour into waste fields, which, if cultivated into new markets, would increase the home field of employment for capital and labour. It has placed colonization itself amongst the lost arts, and is thus a negative cause of that excessive competition of capital with capital, and labour with labour, in a limited field of employment for both, which is now the condition of England and the difficulty of her statesmen.

But it works somehow. Yes, thanks to the *vis medicatrix naturæ*, which corrects the errors of men by infusing some proportion of good into the greatest of evils. The good principle through which our present system of colonial government is worked at all, is that which Adam Smith had in view, when, contemplating the greatness of English municipal colonization in America, produced as it was by individual exertions without assistance from the government, he exclaimed, *Magna virûm mater!* and attributed all to the country and the institutions which had formed *the men* capable of so great a performance. Englishmen colonize in spite of the Colonial Office and its system. English colonists get on somehow, notwithstanding bad government, or without government. English governors do not quite forget the political lessons which every Englishman that can read learns at home; and their subjects, being English, or of English origin, can bear worse government without fainting; can resist and check it more effectually than the colonists of any other nation. Public opinion here does now and then punish the authors and perpetrators of great colonial wrongs. Even the Colonial-Office bureaucracy, worse though it is in one sense than a Prussian bureau, still, being composed of Englishmen, and breathing the air of England, is not so bad as a bureau of Prussians would be if they were placed in the same false and corrupting position. The system works indeed, but by means of what is contrary to it: it works in spite of its un-English self, by means of the English energy which it depresses, of the self-reliance which it cannot destroy, of the fortitude which resists it; and finally by means of the national institutions and sentiments to which it is wholly antagonist. In a word, it is worked by counteraction.

The contrast between the two systems under comparison, great as it is in every point of view, is in nothing so remarkable as in this; that the one requires counteraction to work at all, whilst the other works well just in proportion as it is not counteracted, but is left to operate by itself; just in proportion, that is, as the municipal principle is adopted without admixture of the central. In the old English colonies of America, the municipal principle was not completely adopted in a single case; in some cases, the central principle was to some extent mixed with it, even in the form of government; and in all, the imperial power, after granting local self-government more or less complete, counteracted its own delegation of authority, sometimes by withdrawing it altogether and governing arbitrarily from the centre of the empire, at others by violating its own grants, and ruling, or attempting to rule, the colonists from a distance notwithstanding their local rights. The history of those colonies, accordingly, is, in a great measure, the history of many struggles between the dependencies and the imperial power. What each side contended for, was the exercise of local authority. The colonists, though they suffered greatly in these contests, still, being armed with their royal charters, assisted by the law of England which at that time deemed self-government the birthright of English colonists, and not a little favoured by distance, obscurity, and civil contests in the mother-country, generally carried their point at last. Practically, therefore, and upon the whole, these colonies enjoyed municipal government. Some of them, for long consecutive periods, and all of them at times, managed their own affairs without any interference from home; and a careful examination of the progress of these communities from the hour of their municipal birth down to that of their sovereign independence, establishes by irresistible evidence two things in particular; first, that whatever sufferings they endured as respects government—that in whatever respects their governments did not work smoothly and beneficially for them as well as for the empire—the sole cause of the evil was some infringement of the municipal principle; and secondly, that an accumulation of such acts on the part of the imperial power, crowned at length by the attempt to tax the colonists without the consent of their local assemblies, was the sole cause of their revolt. These naked positions may have an air of exaggeration or rashness; but I am intimately persuaded of their truth; and I refer you to the principal source of my own convictions. This is a modern work, scarcely known to the public in consequence of its defects of arrangement and style, but containing the best account of England's colonial system of municipal governments; I mean the late Mr. Grahame's *History of the United States*, which, as it ends with the Declaration of Independence, ought to have been entitled a history of English colonization in North America.* This book also contains most valuable proofs of the necessity of combining efficient religious arrangements with good civil government in order to colonize very successfully. The author, a Scotch gentleman by birth, was a zealous Republican, Protestant, and Voluntary, but also a true gentleman at heart in his love of truth, his scrupulous fairness, and his singular tolerance of opinions opposite to his own. He could not theorize. Neither as to government nor religion does he attempt to establish the conclusions which his facts and his laborious accuracy impress upon the speculative reader.

The view here taken of imperial counteractions of the municipal principle, is supported by observing how the *proprietary* charters worked. Mr. Grahame shows very distinctly, that they worked well whenever the grantee, whether an individual or a corporation, resided in the colony, and was identified with the colonists; and that they worked very ill indeed, nearly always when the grantee resided in England. The residence of the grantees in the colony was a carrying out of the municipal principle; their residence here gave effect, so far, to the principle of central or distant government. Baltimore and Penn, and the joint-

---

* With this title, and re-written by a master of style as an abridgment, this most instructive and entertaining work would be a capital addition to Mr. Murray's *Colonial Library;* for it would become a household book in the colonies.

stock company of cabinet ministers who founded Carolina, were kings, in fact, within their colonies. During the periods when Penn or Baltimore resided in his colony, the whole government was local or municipal; whenever he resided in England, and always in the case of Carolina, the kingly authority of the colony was exercised, like that of the present Colonial Office, ignorantly, more or less secretly, and from impulses not colonial. I must repeat, that every dispute between the colonists and their proprietary governments may be traced to the operation of the central principle, through the non-residence of the chief authority in local matters. In whatever point of view the subject is examined, it will be seen that the municipal system suffers, as the central system is modified and improved, in proportion as it is counteracted.

LETTER XXXIX.

From the Statesman.

MR. MOTHERCOUNTRY PROTESTS AGAINST THE ASSERTION, THAT MR. TAYLOR HAS AUTHORIZED THE BELIEF, THAT HIS VIEWS OF STATESMANSHIP WERE DERIVED FROM EXPERIENCE IN THE COLONIAL OFFICE.

IN the early part of our journey, I felt my way carefully, unwilling to take a step without being convinced of the soundness of the footing; but lately I have hurried along without seeing obstacles or rotten places, impelled by a sort of wonder and indig-

nation. Since we got fairly into impediments of colonization, I have not stopped you by uttering an objection or a doubt: and now, I can only say, Lead on;
so bewildered am I by the multiplicity and strangeness
of the objects that have seemed to flit past me during
our last rush through a region of politics whose existence I had not dreamt of before. In plainer English,
I want time for reflection, and am not in the humour
to trouble you with inquiries.

Neither does Mr. Mothercountry make any remarks
on your hideous portrait of his Office. When I showed
him your letters with all sorts of proper apologies, he
did not utter a word about colonial government, but
got angry, and talked of being himself unjustly assailed; of his long and laborious services; and of his
trying position as being the butt of attacks from which
his subordination to others prevents him from defend-
ing himself. In short, he only whined about his own
hard lot, and made pathetic appeals to my compassion.

But he defends Mr. Taylor; and what he says on
this point I must report. He indignantly denies that
we have Mr. Taylor's own authority for asserting that
his opinions, as communicated to the public in *The
Statesman*, are based on his experience in the Colonial
Office. He says that Mr. Taylor himself, in a work
published lately, has contradicted the assertion. Understand, he does not object to your saying that Mr.
Taylor acquired his views of statesmanship in the
Colonial Office, but to your repeating the statement,
after Mr. Taylor, who alone can know how the fact is,
has deliberately contradicted it; he says that it is
shamefully unjust to quote Mr. Taylor's authority for
an assertion which Mr. Taylor declares to be untrue.

LETTER XL.

From the Colonist.

MR. TAYLOR has *not* contradicted the assertion, the repetition of which annoys the whole Colonial Office. In the Preface to his recent work, *Notes from Life*, he says, " In the year 1836; I published a book called the ' Statesman,' a title much found fault with at the time, and in truth not very judiciously chosen. It contained the views and maxims respecting the transaction of public business, which *twelve years of experience* had suggested to me. But *my experience had been confined within the doors of an office;* and the book was wanting in that general interest which might possibly have been felt in the results of a more extensive and varied conversancy with public life. Moreover, the sub-sarcastic vein in which certain parts of it were written, was not very well understood; and what was meant for an exposure of some of the world's ways was, I believe, very generally mistaken for a recommendation of them. I advert, now, to this book and its indifferent fortunes, because whatever may have been its demerits, my present work must be regarded as to some extent comprehended in the same design,—that, namely, of embodying in the form of maxims and reflections the immediate results of an attentive observation of life,—*of official life in the former volume*,—of life at large in this."

This surely is not a contradiction but a confirmation of my statement; fresh testimony by Mr. Taylor himself to the truth of the assertion, that the Colonial Office is the school in which he learned the art of statesmanship. It shows indeed, that he may repent of having communicated his Colonial-Office experience to the public; and that he is now anxious to remove a public impression that he recommended the practices and doctrines which he exposed. And what then? Why, Mr. Taylor only joins others in condemning those practices and doctrines; and in doing so, he repeats his first assurances to the public, that, according to his experience, they are the doctrines and practices of the Colonial Office. I will extract his first assurances from *The Statesman*: you will see that from their very nature they do not admit of being unsaid.

In the Preface to *The Statesman*, he alludes to "the want in our literature of any coherent body of *administrative* doctrine;" and though he modestly disclaims the slightest pretension to supplying the want, he goes on to say, "the topics which I have treated are such as *experience, rather than inventive meditation*, has suggested to me. The engagements which have deprived me of literary leisure and a knowledge of books, have, on the other hand, afforded me an *extensive and diversified conversancy with business:* and I hope, therefore, that I may claim from my readers some indulgence for the little learning and for the desultoriness of these disquisitions, in consideration of the value which they may be disposed to attach to *comments derived from practical observation.*" In his Conclusion, he apologizes for a want of system in his dissertations, and says, "if I had applied myself to devise a system, or even a connected succession, I must necessarily have written more from speculative meditation, less *from knowledge.* What I knew *practically,* or by reflection *flowing from circumstance,* must have been connected by what I might persuade myself that I knew inventively, or by reflection flowing from reflection. I am well aware of the weight and value which is given to a work by a just and harmonious incorporation of its parts. But I may be permitted to say, that there is also a value currently and not unduly attached to what men are prompted to think *concerning matters within their knowledge.* Perceiving that I was not in a condition to undertake such a work as might combine both values, the alternative which I have chosen is that of treating the topics severally, *as they were thrown up by the sundry suggestions of experience.* It is possible, indeed, that by postponing my work to a future period, *a further accumulation of experience* might have enabled me to improve it."

Even if Mr. Taylor had been dishonest and bold enough to unsay these assurances, the retractation would have come too late. Is not that the case with the colouring which he now gives to the contents of his first book? For years he has allowed it to circulate as a body of administrative doctrine which he seriously believed. *The Statesman* has been much read in the colonies, and much used by colonial reformers here, as Pascal turned the books of the jesuits against their corporation, in exposing the political immorality and the anti-colonizing influences of the great corporation which is the government of our colonial empire. Mr. Taylor, his colleagues, and his superiors, have been disturbed and annoyed by the uses made of his book: and his denial now of the accuracy of the sense in which the book has been read, deserves no more weight than a plea of not guilty after confession or boast of guilt has led to accusation. His too-late apology for *The Statesman* almost contradicts itself, by indicating that at the time of its publication— before its publication had troubled himself and his Office—he intended, not an " exposure," but a " recommendation" of the doctrines and practices which colonial Pascals have supposed the book to recommend.

But pray read the book for yourself. In doing so, you will not fail to perceive, that its author's present disclaimer of its title comes also too late, and therefore only confirms the belief to which that title led, that in the Colonial Office, ideas of statesmanship are limited to bureaucratic administration. The book is, in fact, a picture of that sort of government which I have called the central-bureaucratic-spoiled, by one of the shrewdest and most thoughtful of its administrators.

If one official man ought to succeed another because he closely resembles him, your Mr. Mothercountry should be the permanent Under-Secretary for the Colonies after Mr. Stephen, or chief of the tribe of Mothercountry after him by whom the tribe was, if not founded, at least raised to its present importance, as the real arbiter of the destinies of our colonial empire: for he exactly resembles Mr. (now Sir James) Stephen, in treating exposures of the Office as personal attacks on himself, and in complaining that his subordinate position prevents him from repelling them. If anything happened to make our correspondence public, he might probably, by whining about his own services and miseries, induce the present and half-a-dozen ex-Colonial Ministers to bepraise him in Parliament, as by far the most meritorious of mankind. And then, in time perhaps, if our system of colonial government were further brought into public hatred by exposure, his sufferings, under the name of immeasurable public services, might be rewarded by a title and a seat in the Privy Council: for unquestionably, the Right Honourable Sir James Stephen is indebted for his recent honours to the exertions of colonial reformers. How it happens that holders and ex-holders of the Colonial Seals can scarcely avoid ostentatiously patronising a subordinate in equal proportion to his unpopularity, is a question that we may perhaps examine some day: but at any rate, I shall have to explain further on, by again adverting to Sir James Stephen, that the nominal subordinates but real chiefs of the Colonial Office have ample means of addressing the public on their own behalf, and with all the more effect perhaps because they do so anonymously.

LETTER XLI.

From the Statesman.

MR. MOTHERCOUNTRY OBJECTS TO MUNICIPAL GOVERN-
MENT FOR COLONIES, ON THE GROUND OF ITS TEN-
DENCY TO DEMOCRACY, REPUBLICANISM, AND DISMEM-
BERMENT OF THE EMPIRE.

MR. MOTHERCOUNTRY is silent about Mr.
Taylor and *The Statesman;* but he has rallied
in defence of our system of colonial government.
Addressing himself to my conservative predilections,
he says that your doctrines about municipal government for colonies go straight towards democracy,
republicanism, colonial disaffection, and dismember-
ment of the empire. He has not hitherto denied that
municipal government would be best for the colonies;
he seems to admit with Mr. Cornewall Lewis, that a
colony suffers numerous evils by being a dependency;
but he contends, agreeing again with Mr. Lewis, that
a colony municipally governed in your sense of the
words, would be practically independent. If, he
argues, we were to set up this practical independence
throughout our colonial empire, we should soon wish
to pull it down again, because under it the colonies
would nourish democratic and republican ideas, and

be apt to infect the mother-country with them. If we attempted to undo our foolish work, then would occur between the centre of the empire and each of its merely nominal dependencies, a struggle for local power like that which ended in the nominal as well as real independence of the United States. In these struggles, he says, kingly and aristocratic authority would inevitably suffer; republicanism and democracy would get a broader and firmer footing in the world. In short, you are a reckless Destructive.

This objection of Mr. Mothercountry's to local self-government for colonies is so common, that I should like to know at once what you have to say in answer to it.

LETTER XLII.

From the Colonist.

MUNICIPAL GOVERNMENT HAS NO RELATION TO ONE
FORM OF GOVERNMENT MORE THAN ANY OTHER; BUT
IT IS THE SUREST MEANS OF PREVENTING THE DIS-
AFFECTION OF THE OUT-LYING PORTIONS OF AN EX-
TENSIVE EMPIRE, WHICH SURELY RESULTS FROM
CENTRAL-BUREAUCRATIC GOVERNMENT.—THE ORIGINAL
MR. MOTHERCOUNTRY INTRODUCED.

MANY indeed are they who believe, that the municipal system of colonial government has a tendency to promote democracy, republicanism, and colonial disaffection; but this opinion is sincerely held by those alone who have never seriously examined the subject. Between the municipal and republican principles there is no connexion whatever. Is there a country in the world where the monarchical principle is more cherished than in Great Britain? Yet is there no country in the world where the municipal principle, as a delegation of authority for limited purposes, has been so largely carried into effect. What the form of government may be in a municipal dependency, is a matter wholly independent of the municipal character of the government. Municipal, applying the word to colonies, signifies nothing but local. Provided the government of a colony is local, it may be in form either monarchical or republican, aristocratic or democratic, without being more or less municipal. Penn and Baltimore were monarchs in fact within their colonies, though constitutional monarchs enjoined to rule by the help of representative institutions. The municipal governments of Pennsylvania and Maryland were virtually hereditary constitutional monarchies, subordinate to the imperial monarchy. The constitution of Carolina was elaborately aristocratical. In those of Massachusets, Connecticut and Rhode Island, the democratic principle preponderated. In Canada, which is a municipality, though until quite lately very much counteracted, the government is in form a close copy of the imperial government, allowing for the one difference of a very democratic suffrage. If it were made a perfect copy, as it easily might be without in the least diminishing the subordination of the colony, a municipal constitutional monarchy would exist by the side of republics and a republican confederation of them. It is my own deliberate opinion that a vice-monarchy in Canada, precisely resembling the imperial monarchy except in being subordinate to it, might be established with the cordial approbation of the colonists, and with the effect of vastly increasing their prosperity by inducing very many Americans who dislike republican institutions, to bring their wealth into the British province, and become subjects of our Queen. But this is almost a digression. Returning to the question, it will be useful to note that the conversion of American municipal dependencies into republican states, which is often attributed to the repub-

lican tendency of municipal institutions, may with
more reason be ascribed to those counteractions of the
municipal principle in America, by which the sovereigns
of England, acting generally in this respect independently of their parliaments, and even to the last exhibiting a personal animosity to their colonial subjects,
taught the colonists to hate the very name of king.
That this is the more reasonable conclusion of the
two will appear to anybody who, with a view to the
present question, reads over again the Declaration of
American Independence. He would do well at the
same time to remember, that the Spanish colonies of
America have all turned into republics, although—
perhaps because—they were founded and governed on
the central-bureaucratic principle.

With respect to the disaffection of municipal dependencies, facts are still more at variance with the theory.
One seeks in vain for a single instance of disaffection
in a municipal dependency of a great empire, excepting only through the operation of the central principle
in admixture or collision with the municipal. Local
self-government is so precious, that dependent communities enjoying it have invariably reverenced the
imperial power to which they owed the blessing, and
which maintained them in possession of it. This is a
rule without exceptions. Examples of the rule are
furnished in abundance by modern as well as ancient
times. The municipalities of the Roman Empire were
its main stay. Was not the dependence on Rome of
its conquered provinces, the main cause of its down-
fall? The Channel Islands, which govern themselves
locally—which are a capital example of municipal dependency—are devotedly attached to England. The

Tyrolese, with a local parliament, have proved their attachment to the despotic House of Austria by their heroic struggles against the power of Napoleon, and again, lately, by receiving the Emperor with open arms when he was driven from the metropolis of the empire. The Basque provinces of Spain, with their *fueros*, were the last to submit to a revolution which deprived their legitimate sovereign of his throne. The municipal colonies of England in America, notwithstanding the unjust and oppressive infractions of their municipal rights by a series of British monarchs, were at all times prompt to take arms in any quarrel of the mother-country with a foreign state. The Virginians, in their appeals to Charles the Second against his invasions of their municipal constitution, used to boast that of all his subjects, they had been " the last to renounce and the first to resume their allegiance" to the Crown of England. In Canada, just now, disaffection produced by errors of local administration on the part of the central authority, has been converted into loyalty by giving to the colonists the consequences, in addition to the form, of local representation. The disaffection, in some cases the hatred, of the imperial power, which exists in other colonies at present, though their weakness precludes them from manifesting it by acts, is a product of the very reverse of municipal government. Distant government in local matters is so fatal to the interests, and so mortifying to the pride of its subjects, that, in their hearts at least, they can't help being disaffected. Does the present world or history present a single example of a community governed from a distance, whose loyalty to the distant power may not be questioned? The United

Kingdom itself exhibits in Scotland and Ireland the loyalty of one people preserving their own laws, and in practice almost ruled separately after formal incorporation with the empire; and the disaffection of another, which is still in some measure ruled as a dependency stripped by conquest of its local laws. In all times, the main strength of a great empire has consisted of the firmness with which, by means of the municipal principle, it was rooted in the affections of its subjects distant from the seat of empire: a universal cause of weakness in an extensive dominion has been the disaffection of the outlying portions, arising from their misgovernment on the central principle.

But supposing it admitted that the municipal system has no tendency to republicanism, and produces loyalty rather than disaffection — that it is the strongest cement of an empire composed of divers communities—yet the questions may be asked, Would you deprive the imperial power of all local control in the colonies? would you make them wholly independent states within their own bounds, reserving only such allegiance to the empire as would prevent them from being independent, or foreign states? Certainly not. On the contrary, I, for one, am of opinion, that if colonization were systematically conducted with a view to the advantage of the mother-country, the control of the imperial power ought to be much greater, and the connexion between the colonies and the centre far more intimate than either has ever yet been. I regard the waste but partially-occupied territories which this nation has acquired by costly efforts, as a valuable national property, which we have every right in justice, and are bound by every consideration of prudence, to use for the greatest benefit of the people of this country: and instead of leaving colonies to take what form a thousand accidents may determine, and to grow up as cast-aways till they are strong enough to become enemies, I think that the imperial power ought to mould them into the forms most agreeable to itself, and to bind them to this kingdom by indissoluble ties.

And first, as to control. Of real, effective, fruitful control, there never has been half enough: there has been far too much of a control unproductive of any beneficial results to colony or mother-country; productive of the very reverse of the proper objects of control. As to the *amount* of control, I should go beyond the most zealous advocate of the present system: I should wholly differ with him as to the *manner*. He recommends control, arbitrary, undefined, irregular, capricious, and masked; I propose a control according to law; that is, a control definite, orderly, steady, above all seen and understood by the subjects of it. The manner of control appears to me to be of far more consequence than its nature or amount. Very improper limitations of the local powers of a colony, if they were fixed by law so that every colonist should always know exactly what they were, would be far preferable to the most proper limitations imposed from time to time arbitrarily, irregularly, and without warning or other promulgation. The grand point for the colonies, as to government, is that they should always know what they might lawfully do, and what they might not. What the law permitted or forbade them to do, would be a matter of comparatively small importance. If they had a con-

stitutional law, they would accommodate themselves
to it: or, as it would be known at the seat of empire
as well as in the colonies, and its operation would be
visible, they might, if it were hurtful to them, get it
altered by the supreme power which had framed it.
I ask that the colonies should be governed, as a tres-
passer or vagrant is prosecuted in this country, that is
to say, " according to law;" that they should be ruled
even according to the law-martial of a man-of-war
rather than left to the lawlessness of a pirate ship;
that they should be *governed* by the imperial power
instead of being the sport of the chapter of accidents. Government according to law is government: the other manner of government is nothing
but force; and the highest authority on this point—
the greatest incarnation of force that the world has
seen—wondered and lamented at the incapacity of
force to *create* anything. This whine of the mighty
Napoleon should never be forgotten by those who
meddle with the creative business of colonization.

I have now done with the principles of colonial
government. My next will contain the outline of a
plan of colonial government based on the foregoing
principles. But allow me, meanwhile, to suggest that
your careful perusal of the inclosed paper may greatly
serve the object of our correspondence. It contains a
view of that system of colonial government which
I have called the central-bureaucratic-spoiled, by a
hand which the charms of the writer's style will satisfy
you is not mine. I do not send you the little volume
from which it is extracted, entitled *Responsible
Government for Colonies* (which was published in
1840 as a reprint, with some additions, of a series of

articles that first appeared in the *Colonial Gazette*), because that publication has been long out of print, and I have been unable to obtain a copy of it except on loan. The extracts, besides informing and entertaining you, will explain why, in proposing a cognomen for your Downing-street acquaintance, I selected that of " Mr. Mothercountry."*

* It was no secret before Mr. Charles Buller's death, that he wrote the description of " Mr. Mothercountry of the Colonial Office," which many a colonist has got by heart; but the fact is not mentioned in the text, because it was not published till after that was written as it now stands. I assume that now, when the public has lost its favourite among the younger statesmen of our day, no apology is required for reviving here one of the happiest productions of his accomplished pen.

" MR. MOTHERCOUNTRY, OF THE COLONIAL OFFICE.

" In preceding chapters we have endeavoured to show, that that constant reference to the authorities in England, which some persons call " responsibility to the mother-country," is by no means necessary to insure the maintenance of a beneficial colonial connexion. It is not necessary for this purpose that the people or government of England should be constantly interfering in the details of colonial business. It is not desirable that we should regulate these matters according to notions which cannot be half so correct as those of the colonists themselves. But even if it were desirable, and if we were convinced that a colony could never be well governed except by the enlightened opinion, or the responsible ministers of the mother-country, we should still be unconvinced of the possibility of securing an effectual appeal to either. If the public opinion of the British community, and the attention of its legislature and ministry, could indeed be brought to bear on each colonial question as it arises, and to give it the same earnest consideration that it gives to any English question of the same importance, the reference to this country would be productive of no ill, but much good. But the theory of responsibility errs in this, that the mother-country, to which the reference is supposed to be made, never exercises any judgment on the matter; and the decision which is pronounced in its name, is given by the few individuals that think it worth while to usurp its functions for the purpose.

" It is not in the nature of men to feel any very lively interest in the affairs of those, of whom they know so little as the people of this country do of their fellow-subjects in the colonies : and the bitter experience of colonists has taught them how little their condition, and the circumstances which influence it, are appreciated by the people of this country. The social state, and the form of government in the colonies, are both utterly foreign to the notions of Englishmen. We comprehend neither: we know little of the events that have passed in them: and the consequence is, that we understand very nearly as little of what passes in the present day. The newspaper of the morning announces in some out-of-the-way corner, that some ship, which left some unknown spot, in some distant corner of the world, some weeks or months before, has brought perhaps a couple of months' files of colonial papers. We are told that the governor had issued some order, upon a matter of which the nature is utterly incomprehensible to us ; or that the Assembly is " still" occupied with some dispute with him, of the commencement of which we have never heard. If, perchance, there is anything in this news which interests us enough to make us read through the column of the paper, hunt up the geographical and other points which at first puzzle us, and look with impatience for the sequel of the news, the odds are that we get nothing more on the subject for the next month ; and the first time our paper finds room for another set of extracts from the colonial papers, the matter about which we were interested has slipped out of our memory, or some event of importance in home politics absorbs all our attention. This is the normal state of our ignorance on the subject, varied in the case of the most active-minded by the half-information thus picked up, and the prejudices consequently formed. When some event of great importance suddenly rivets public attention on colonial affairs, we come to the consideration of them with this general ignorance and these misconceptions. Nothing but the news of invasion or revolt gives the people at large a real interest in the colonial news of the day. The events that prepare such calamities, have been either unheeded or fostered by the rash decisions which we have given in our inattentive mood.

" As the people judge, so do the representatives act in Parliament. A railway or a turnpike bill ordinarily interests more members than any measure affecting the most vital interests of our most important colonies. Some of them, it is true, attract the notice of two or three members, who think that local knowledge gives them the right to assume airs of great wisdom respecting them. Some ignorant and presumptuous captain in the navy, some still more ignorant and presumptuous colonel in the army, who have passed a year or two in some harbour or garrison of the colony—some retired judge, whose knowledge of a community has been formed on his experience of the criminals and suitors of his court—some ex-official, mixed up with colonial jobs and cliques—some merchant, who urges in the House whatever his partners in the colony tell him is the right thing to promote the interests or importance of the firm—these, with occasionally some gentleman whose more than usually extended tour has carried him to some of our remote possessions, are the only persons, not compelled by the duties of office or opposition, that take what is called an interest in a colony. By some one or other of these, four or five times in a session, questions are addressed to the ministers, or returns required, or motions made. But hardly any one else ever shares in this interest : and such a notice of motion generally insures the House being counted out whenever it comes on ! On some rare occasions the party questions of the day are mixed up in some colonial matter : the opposition come down to fight the battle of the church, or education, or whatever else it may be, on colonial ground ; and the mover is favoured with the unaccustomed honour of an audience and a division. Sometimes the opportunity of wounding a ministry through the side of one of its measures, or of a governor of its own party, occasions similar manifestations of factious force and zeal: and to what mischiefs such conduct gives rise we have had too much experience, in the rejection of the bill for the union of the two Canadas in 1822, and still more recently in the disallowance of Lord Durham's celebrated ordinances. The attention thus given to a colony in these occasional gusts of party feeling, is productive of so much ill, that it is far better for them that

Parliament should preserve its usual apathy, and adopt, as it usually does, whatever legislation the government of the day may recommend.

" There are two modes in which the legislative measures, to which the government wishes to get the sanction of parliament, are framed. Sometimes, though rarely, parliament passes an act after the usual fashion of acts of parliament, settling by positive enactments every detail of the course on which it determines. Except, however, in the case of acts settling the form of government in a colony, this is a labour which is rarely imposed on parliament: and experience shows us how unwise it is to trust the details of such measures to the chances of parliamentary attention. The Canada-Tenures Act is a remarkable instance of this. No act was ever proposed by government with more honest and sound intentions. The purpose was good; and had the bill been passed in the shape in which it was prepared by Mr. James Stuart,* the present chief-justice of Lower Canada, that purpose would have been carried into effect, probably without any concomitant evil. Unfortunately, however, Mr. Stuart quitted England before the bill had passed. During its passage through parliament, one apparently harmless amendment was suggested from one, and another from another quarter; some words were omitted to please one, and others left out to conciliate another. The result was, that this act, which was intended to merely alter tenures, without affecting any existing interest, assailed the vested rights of every married woman and child in the province, gave the seigneurs the most unfair advantage over their tenants, and, in fact, shook every title to land in Lower Canada.

" But parliament in general disposes of the details of colonial questions in a much more summary way. For some time past, the impossibility of determining the details of a colonial measure in the British Parliament has been so much

---

* Who was not an official sent out by the Colonial Office, but a native of Canada, and as thorough a colonist as the province contains. Lord Durham appointed him Chief-Justice of Quebec.

impressed upon the government, that the custom has been to propose that the colonial acts of parliament should be simple *delegations of legislative powers* to some ministerial authority in this country; and they have in consequence simply enabled the crown to legislate for the colonies by order in council. It is thus that for nearly the last twenty years a great part of the legislation of the West-India islands has been carried on ; and the power of making laws has been taken equally from the colonial and imperial legislatures, and transferred to the executive government at home. Nor has parliament taken, in colonial cases, the precautions for retaining a vigilant supervision of the use made of this power, which it has always retained to itself whenever it has delegated similar authority with respect to the mother-country. The poor-law commissioners have the most extensive powers of legislation by means of general rules : the judges of courts of common law have very large powers of regulating the whole administration of the common law by their rules and regulations. Yet in these, as in many other cases of not quite equal importance, the most effectual provisions are made for the utmost publicity ; and it is necessary that all rules made under the delegated authority should, to have permanent effect, be laid on the table of both Houses. But no such precautions are taken with respect to the colonies ; and the powers thus given to orders in council are exercised without any publicity in this country.

" Thus, from the general indifference of Parliament on colonial questions, it exercises, in fact, hardly the slightest efficient control over the administration or the making of laws for the colonies. In nine cases out of ten, it merely registers the edicts of the Colonial Office in Downing-street. It is there, then, that nearly the whole public opinion which influences the conduct of affairs in the colonies, really exists. It is there that the supremacy of the mother-country really resides : and when we speak of that supremacy, and of the responsibility of the colony to the mother-country, you may to all practical intents consider as the mother-country—the

possessor of this supremacy—the centre of this responsibility
—the occupants of the large house that forms the end of that
cul-de-sac so well known by the name of Downing street.
However colonists or others may talk of the Crown, the Parliament, and the public—of the honour of the first, the wisdom
of the second, or the enlightened opinion of the last—nor
Queen, nor Lords, nor Commons, nor the great public itself,
exercise any power, or will, or thought on the greater part
of colonial matters: and the appeal to the mother-country is,
in fact, an appeal to ' the Office.'

" But this does not sufficiently concentrate the mother-
country. It may, indeed, at first sight, be supposed that the
power of ' the Office' must be wielded by its head: that in
him at any rate we have generally one of the most eminent of
our public men, whose views on the various matters which
come under his cognizance, are shared by the cabinet of which
he is a member. We may fancy, therefore, that here, at least,
concentrated in a somewhat despotic, but at any rate in a very
responsible and dignified form, we have the real governing
power of the colonies, under the system which boasts of
making their governments responsible to the mother-country.
But this is a very erroneous supposition. This great officer
holds the most constantly shifting position on the shifting
scene of official life. Since April, 1827, ten different Secretaries of State have held the seals of the colonial department.
Each was brought into that office from business of a perfectly
different nature, and probably with hardly any experience in
colonial affairs. The new minister is at once called on to
enter on the consideration of questions of the greatest magnitude, and at the same time of some hundreds of questions of
mere detail, of no public interest, of unintelligible technicality,
involving local considerations with which he is wholly unacquainted, but at the same time requiring decision, and decision
at which it is not possible to arrive without considerable
labour. Perplexed with the vast variety of subjects thus
presented to him—alike appalled by the important and unimportant matters forced on his attention—every Secretary of

State is obliged at the outset to rely on the aid of some better informed member of his office. His Parliamentary Under-Secretary is generally as new to the business as himself: and even if they had not been brought in together, the tenure of office by the Under-Secretary having on the average been quite as short as that of the Secretary of State, he has never during the period of his official career obtained sufficient information, to make him independent of the aid on which he must have been thrown at the outset. Thus we find both these marked and responsible functionaries dependent on the advice or guidance of another; and that other person must of course be one of the permanent members of the office. We do not pretend to say which of these persons it is, that in fact directs the colonial policy of Britain. It may be, as a great many persons think, the permanent Under-Secretary; it may be the chief, it may be some very subordinate clerk; it may be one of them that has most influence at one time, and another at another; it may be this gentleman as to one, and that as to another question or set of questions : for here we get beyond the region of real responsibility, and are involved in the clouds of official mystery. That mother-country which has been narrowed from the British isles into the Parliament, from the Parliament into the executive government, from the executive government into the Colonial Office, is not to be sought in the apartments of the Secretary of State, or his Parliamentary Under-Secretary. Where you are to look for it, it is impossible to say. In some back room —whether in the attic, or in what story we know not—you will find all the mother-country which really exercises supremacy, and really maintains connexion with the vast and widely-scattered colonies of Britain. We know not the name, the history, or the functions of the individual, into the narrow limits of whose person we find the mother-country shrunk. Indeed, we may call him by the name, of which we have thus shown him to be the rightful bearer; and when we speak of Mr. Mothercountry, the colonist will form a much more accurate notion than heretofore of the authority by which he is in reality ruled.

" Of the individual thus bodily existing, but thus dimly seen, we can of course give our readers none but the most general description. We will not flatter the pride of our colonial readers, by depicting this real arbiter of their destinies as a person of lofty rank or of the first class among what we call statesmen. He is probably a person who owes his present position entirely to his own merits and long exertions. He has worked his way through a long and laborious career of official exertions; and his ambition is limited to the office that he holds, or to some higher grade of the permanent offices under government. Probably married at an early age, he has to support and educate a large family out of his scanty though sure income. Once or twice a year he dines with his principal; perhaps as often with some friend in parliament or high office. But the greater part of his days are passed out of all reach of aristocratic society; he has a modest home in the outskirts of London, with an equally modest establishment: and the colonist who is on his road to ' the Office,' little imagines that it is the real ruler of the colonies that he sees walking over one of the bridges, or driving his one-horse chay, or riding cheek by jowl with him on the top of the short coach, as he comes into town of a morning.

" Mr. Mothercountry's whole heart is in the business of his office. Not insensible to the knowledge or the charms of the power which he possesses, habit and a sense of duty are perhaps often the real motives of the unremitting exertions, by which alone he retains it. For this is the real secret of his influence. Long experience has made him thoroughly conversant with every detail of his business; and long habit has made his business the main, perhaps with the exception of his family, the sole source of his interest and enjoyment. By day and by night, at office or at home, his labour is constant. No pile of despatches, with their multifarious enclosures, no red taped heap of colonial grievances or squabbles, can scare his practised eye. He handles with unfaltering hand the papers at which his superiors quail: and ere they have waded through one half of them, he suggests the course, which the previous measures dictated by himself compel the government to adopt. He alone knows on what principles the predecessors of the noble or right honourable Secretary acted before : he alone, therefore, can point out the step which in pursuance of the previous policy it is incumbent to take : and the very advice, which it is thus rendered incumbent on the present Secretary of State to take, produces results that will give him as sure a hold on the next Secretary of State.

" But with all this real power, Mr. Mothercountry never assumes the airs of dictation to his principal. Every change of the head of the department, though really consolidating his power, gives occasion for a kind of mutiny against it. The new Secretary enters with some purpose of independence : he has heard of Mr. Mothercountry's influence ; and he is determined that he will act on his own head. He goes on for a while on this plan ; but it is sure to be no long time ere something comes before him for which he is obliged to refer to Mr. Mothercountry : he is pleased with his ready, shrewd, and unobtrusive advice : he applies to him on the next occasion with more confidence : he finds that Mr. Mothercountry takes a great deal of trouble off his hands ; and great men are sure at last to fall under the dominion of any man that will save them trouble.   By degrees, he begins to think that there are some things which it is better to leave altogether to Mr. Mothercountry ; and as to all he soon finds it prudent to take no step until he has heard what Mr. Mothercountry has to say about it.   If things go smooth, his confidence in Mr. Mothercountry rises : if they go ill, his dependence on him is only the more riveted, because it is Mr. Mothercountry alone who can get him through the colonial contest or Parliamentary scrape in which he has involved himself.   The more independent he has been at first, the more of these scrapes he has probably got himself into ; and the more dependent he consequently becomes in the long run. The power of Mr. Mothercountry goes on increasing from secretary to secretary, and from month to month of each secretary's tenure of office ; and the more difficult the government of the colonies becomes, the more entirely it falls into the hands of the only men in the public service who really know anything about colonial affairs.

" This is perhaps the best result of such a system : and our experience of the follies and presumption of the only Secretary of State that ever undertook to act for himself, is a proof that, under the present system, Mr. Mothercountry's management is better than that of the gentlemen whom he generally gets put over his head. But the system of intrusting absolute power (for such it is) to one wholly irresponsible, is obviously most faulty. Thus, however, are our colonies ruled : and such is the authority to which is committed that last appeal from the colonies themselves, which is dignified with all these vague phrases about the power, the honour, the supremacy, and the wisdom of the mother-country.

" We have described the secret and irresponsible, but steady rule of Mr. Mothercountry, in whom we have personified the permanent and unknown officials of the Colonial Office in Downing-street, as very much better for our colonies than that to which they would be subjected, were the perpetually-shifting secretaries and under-secretaries of state really to pretend to conduct affairs of which they understand nothing. It must not be inferred from this, that we think it a really good system. It has all the faults of an essentially arbitrary government, in the hands of persons who have little personal interest in the welfare of those over whom they rule—who reside at a distance from them—who never have ocular experience of their condition—who are obliged to trust to second-hand and one-sided information—and who are exposed to the operation of all those sinister influences, which prevail wherever publicity and freedom are not established. In intelligence, activity, and regard for the public interests, the permanent functionaries of " the Office" may be superior to the temporary head that the vicissitudes of party politics give them ; but they must necessarily be inferior to those persons in the colony, in whose hands the adoption of the true practice of responsible government would vest the management of local affairs.

" A thorough knowledge of the internal economy of this vast number of different communities, situated at the most distant points of the globe, having the most diverse climates, races, productions, forms of government, and degrees of wealth and civilization, is necessarily one which the best-employed experience of the longest life can never be supposed to give. From his entrance into his office, the necessary labours of the day have occupied almost the whole of Mr. Mothercountry's time and thoughts ; and though we will give him credit for having picked up such information as elementary books can give, it cannot very well be imagined that he has learnt from books, newspapers, and oral information, all that mass of particulars respecting manners, things, and persons, that is requisite for forming in the mind a complete picture of the social and political, the physical as well as the moral condition of those numerous countries. It is in the very nature of duties so laborious as his, that Mr. Mothercountry should be able to attend to little except to the questions presented for his decision by the parties contending in the colonies, and should form his notion of their condition from these rather than from more extended reading and observation. Compelled to examine the complaints and answers of the various parties, he gradually imbibes the idea that the whole state of affairs is set forth in these statements and counter-statements. He fixes his eye on the grievances and squabbles that occupy the addresses of Assemblies, the despatches of governors, and the disputes of officials ; and gets to fancy, naturally enough, that these are the matters on which the mind of the colony is intent, and on which its welfare depends. Hence the result is, that since, in colonies as elsewhere, the real interests of the community are over-looked in such disputes, Mr. Mothercountry has at his fingers' ends, after a long devotion to the subject, nothing better than a very complete knowledge of very immaterial incidents ; and that when he fancies he knows all about a colony, he has, in fact, only been diverting his attention from everything that is worth knowing respecting it. Thus, while the question of

contending races was gradually breaking up the whole social
system of Lower Canada, Mr. Mothercountry, unconscious of
the mischief, thought that he was restoring order and satisfaction by well-reasoned despatches on points of prerogative and
precedent. Experience may give Mr. Mothercountry more
information respecting the whole mass of our colonies than
any other individual probably possesses. But it is, after all, a
very incomplete information, and one which does not prevent
his continually committing those gross blunders of which our
colonial history is the record.

"This is the necessary consequence of the variety and distance of Mr. Mothercountry's dominions. He has, in addition,
the faults of that permanent and irresponsible power, combined with subordinate position, which we always perceive in
a government of bureaus and offices. It is a position which
engenders not a little conceit; and in whatever form Mr.
Mothercountry appears—even in that of the humblest clerk—
you always find out that he thinks, that he and his associates
in 'the Office' are the only people in the world who understand anything about the colonies. He knows his power too,
and is excessively jealous of any encroachment on or resistance
to it. It is a power, he well knows, which has its origin in the
indolence and ignorance of others : he fancies, therefore, that
it is assailed by any one who understands anything of the
colonies, or takes any interest in them; and to all such people,
therefore, he has a mortal dislike.

"And though Mr. Mothercountry has none of a fine gentleman's aversion to work, but on the contrary devotes his
whole energies to his business, he likes to get over his work
with as little trouble as possible. It is his tendency, therefore,
to reduce his work as much as he can to a mere routine; to
act on general rules, and to avoid every possible deviation
from them; and thus to render the details of his daily task as
much a matter of habit as he well can. A hatred of innovation is a distinguishing feature of his, as of the general official
character. Everything new gives trouble : to enter upon a
new course with respect to distant communities, is always

matter of danger and doubt, unless the step is founded upon a more complete knowledge of the state of things than Mr. Mothercountry can afford time to acquire. He is very much afraid of being attacked in Parliament or the newspapers ; and as it is almost always a sufficient answer for the great mass of men, that you have done in any particular instance what had usually been done hitherto, he likes always to have this answer to give. Nor do the common motives to exertion act on him to induce him to labour in the work of improvement. He well knows that he shall have none of the glory of improvements in which the public take an interest. The credit of these is sure to be ascribed to the chief Secretary. It is but human nature, then, that he should hate innovation, and discourage every project of improvement. Those who have suggested any improvement in the system existing in our colonies, or proposed to found new colonies on a new principle, know to what a complete science the officials of the colonial department have brought their mode of repelling all such invasions of their domain.

"But the worst of all Mr. Mothercountry's faults is his necessary subjection to sinister interests and cabals. Whereever the public cease to take an interest in what is going on, the reign of cliques and cabals is sure to extend : and whenever the actions of the government are not guided by public opinion, they inevitably fall under the influence of some sinister interest. Every one of our colonies has its own jobs, its own monopolies, and its own little knots of bustling and intriguing jobbers. These spare no pains to get the ear of Mr. Mothercountry. Backed by some strong mercantile, or official, or parliamentary connexion, they press their views on him ; relying partly on their better knowledge of the peculiar subject on which they have so deep an interest, partly on the fear they can inspire by the threat of an appeal to Parliament or the press. Then, again, there are persons whose past official position and party connexions enable them to bring a strong party influence to bear on him. On one or two points there has been excited a powerful interest, which has organized itself into associations, represented by constituted bodies and accredited officers, always ready to push their own views, and able to excite a strong public feeling on their particular point, if their representations should be neglected. While these narrow views and partial interests have these active organs, the colonial public and the interests of the colony have rarely any, never equally efficient representatives. A long experience has taught Mr. Mothercountry, that without conciliating these various juntas, he never can hope to govern quietly, but that if he manage to get their concurrence, he runs little risk of effectual opposition from either the British or colonial public. His whole aim, therefore, necessarily is to conciliate all of these bodies, or when their interests happen to run counter, either to give each its turn, or to conciliate the most powerful. One day, accordingly, we find him conciliating the knot of merchants that enjoy the existing monopoly; another day, those who are exerting themselves for a freer trade; at one time he is holding out his hand to the West-India interest; another time he seems to be entirely under the influence of the abolitionists. These are the sectional influences under which such a government is sure to fall, owing to its freedom from responsibility to a wide public opinion.

"The worst instance of the operation of these secret influences on Mr. Mothercountry is to be found in the colonial appointments. If he were left to himself, and could appoint as he chose, he might doubtless job a little, but, on the whole, he would probably pay some regard to competence in some of his appointments. But the patronage of the Colonial Office is the prey of every hungry department of our government. On it the Horse Guards quarters its worn-out general officers as governors: the Admiralty cribs its share; and jobs which even parliamentary rapacity would blush to ask from the Treasury, are perpetrated with impunity in the silent realm of Mr. Mothercountry. O'Connell, we are told, after very bluntly informing Mr. Ruthven that he had committed a fraud which would for ever unfit him for the society of gentlemen at home, added, in perfect simplicity and kindness of heart, that if he would comply with his wishes and cease to contest Kildare, he might probably be able to get some appointment for him in the colonies.

"It is, however, not only of the cliques and interests at home that Mr. Mothercountry is thus placed under the influence. The same causes that render the action of small knots of men operative on him in England, place him under the same necessity of courting the good opinion and disarming the hostility of every well-organized interest in the colonies. Now, the strongest and most active interest in a colony is always that of the little knot that governs it—the family compact, which Lord Durham has described as being the necessary result of the irresponsible government of our colonies. Creatures of the Colonial Office, as these compacts are, they nevertheless manage to acquire a strength which renders them very formidable to Mr. Mothercountry. Even when he gets on bad terms with them, he never abandons the hope of reconciliation with them, or the demeanour necessary to insure it. But you will rarely find him quarrelling with them. A despotic and irresponsible authority is always obliged to govern by a small knot of men ; and these colonial compacts are the natural agents of the compact at home. Thus the mischiefs produced by irresponsibility in the colony, are augmented and perpetuated by the responsibility to Mr. Mothercountry.

"The working of the appeal to Mr. Mothercountry in fact only adds to the amount of colonial misgovernment ; and instead of obviating the mischiefs of the system pursued in the colonies themselves, it only adds another element of delay, obstruction, and inconsistency. Bad as is the government of Turkish Pachas, the Porte never interferes except to make matters worse ; and ill as the colonial compacts manage, the appeal from them to Mr. Mothercountry only adds fresh fuel to colonial irritation and individual grievance. His ignorance of the real state of affairs in the colony, his habits of routine, his dependence on the secret cliques and interests at home, produce an invariable tendency on his part to stave off the decision of every question referred to him. Every matter referred to him is sure to be referred back to the colony ; and every successive answer to every fresh reference only serves him to raise some new pretext for postponing his decision. He is engaged in a perpetual struggle with the colonial compacts, in which he and they have no object but that of throwing on each other the responsibility of deciding. With this view, he has perfected a complete art of irrelevant and apparently purposeless correspondence, by which he manages to spin out an affair until it either evaporates into something absolutely insignificant, or until at any rate the patience and interest of all parties concerned are completely worn out. For this purpose, he has invented and brought to considerable perfection a style peculiar to colonial despatches ; a style in which the words of the English language are used with a very admirable grace and facility, but at the same time with an utter absence of meaning. In this singular style we hope some day to give our readers a lesson ; but we need now only observe that it is of great utility in enabling Mr. Mothercountry to keep up hopes of a decision, while he is leading his reader further and further away from it. If any decision is got, it is generally on some point that virtually leaves the question at issue undecided. But sometimes even the semblance of decision is omitted ; and the systematic postponement merges into the neglect of absolute oblivion. Thus it has been known, that even reserved acts of colonial parliaments have been poked away in one of Mr. Mothercountry's pigeon-holes, and never brought out of it till the period in which they could receive the necessary sanction had passed : and in another instance, a colonist who inquired for a private act, on which his whole property depended, was told that instead of having received her Majesty's assent, it was nowhere to be found.

"But the appeal to Mr. Mothercountry in individual cases is even more mischievous to the parties concerned. It is a mere device in general for prolonging the tortures of the unhappy victim, who, bandied about from colony to England, from Secretary to Secretary, from Under-Secretary to Under-Secretary, from clerk to clerk, wastes away hope and existence, as a subject of Mr. Mothercountry's systematic procrastination.

" There are rooms in the Colonial Office, with old and meagre furniture, book-cases crammed with colonial gazettes and newspapers, tables covered with baize, and some old and crazy chairs scattered about, in which those who have personal applications to make, are doomed to wait until the interview can be obtained. Here, if perchance you should some day be forced to tarry, you will find strange, anxious-looking beings, who pace to and fro in feverish impatience, or sit dejected at the table, unable in the agitation of their thoughts to find any occupation to while away their hours, and starting every time that the door opens, in hopes that the messenger is come to announce that their turn is arrived. These are men with colonial grievances. The very messengers know them, their business, and its hopelessness, and eye them with pity as they bid them wait their long and habitual period of attendance. No experienced eye can mistake their faces, once expressive of health, and confidence, and energy, now worn by hopes deferred, and the listlessness of prolonged dependence. One is a recalled governor, boiling over with a sense of mortified pride, and frustrated policy; another, a judge, recalled for daring to resist the compact of his colony; another, a merchant, whose whole property has been destroyed by some job or oversight; another, the organ of the remonstrances of some colonial parliament; another, a widow struggling for some pension, on which her hopes of existence hang; and perhaps another is a man whose project is under consideration. Every one of these has passed hours in that dull but anxious attendance, and knows every nook and corner of this scene of his sufferings. The grievance originated probably long years ago, and bandied about between colony and home, by letter or by interview, has dragged on its existence thus far. One comes to have an interview with the Chief Secretary; one, who has tried Chief and Under Secretaries in their turn, is now doomed to waste his remonstrances on some clerk. One has been waiting days to have his first interview ; another, weeks to have his answer to his memorial ; another, months in expectation of the result of a reference to the colony ; and some reckon the period of their suffering by years. Some are silent; some utter aloud their hopes or fears, and pour out their tale on their fellow-sufferers ; some endeavour to conciliate by their meekness ; some give vent to their rage, when, after hours of attendance, the messenger summons in their stead some sleek contented-looking visitor, who has sent up his name only the moment before, but whose importance as a Member of Parliament, or of some powerful interest or society, obtains him an instant interview. And if by chance you should see one of them at last receive the long-desired summons, you will be struck at the nervous reluctance with which he avails himself of the permission. After a short conference, you will generally see him return with disappointment stamped on his brow, and, quitting the office, wend his lonely way home to despair, or perhaps to return to his colony and rebel. These chambers of woe are called *the Sighing Rooms :* and those who recoil from the sight of human suffering, should shun the ill-omened precincts."—*Responsible Government for Colonies.* London : James Ridgway. 1840.

LETTER XLIII.

From the Colonist.

SKETCH OF A PLAN OF MUNICIPAL-FEDERATIVE GOVERN-
MENT FOR COLONIES; WITH AN EPISODE CONCERNING
SIR JAMES STEPHEN AND THE BIRTHRIGHT OF
ENGLISHMEN.

SINCE it is the constitutional law of a colony, whatever it may be, which necessarily forms the ties by which the dependency is bound to the empire, the subject of the imperial connexion is involved in the question of what the constitutional law should be.

I assume that the municipal is the right principle on which to frame a colonial constitution. The colonists themselves should be authorized by express delegation, to do within the colony whatever the imperial power has no object in preventing, or in regulating according to its own views. They should be empowered, in the words of one of the old charters (2nd Grant to Virginia, by James I., 1609), " to make, ordain, and establish all manner of orders, laws, directions, instructions, forms, and ceremonies of government and magistracy, fit and necessary, for and concerning the government of the said colony and plantation; and the same at all times hereafter, to abrogate, revoke, or change, as they in their good discretion shall think to be fittest for the good of the adventurers and inhabitants there." But these words, standing alone, would give unlimited local power. The grant of power, therefore, should be accompanied by conditions or restrictions concerning the matters intended to be at all times subject to direct imperial control.

Whilst reflecting on the frame-work of a colonial constitution, I once imagined that it might be possible to write down with precision, in two distinct classes, the empowering and the conditional or restrictive provisions of a charter, so that whatever the colonists might do, and whatever they might not do, should be fully expressed. But an attempt to proceed in this way soon convinced me of its futility. It soon became obvious, that volumes might be filled with a bare statement of the things which the colonists might do, and would after all be a very imperfect permissive code. In beginning that idle attempt, I forgot the suggestions of all experience. All experience as well as reason suggests, that the empowering part of a colonial charter should consist of a few plain, general, and all-comprehensive terms. On the other hand, reason and experience alike point out, that an opposite course should be pursued in framing the restrictive and regulating clauses of a charter. Whatever the imperial power chooses that the colonists shall not do, and whatever mode of doing any thing it chooses to insist upon, should be very fully and particularly expressed. The best of the old charters was most imperfect in this respect. All the charters, for example, provided that local legislation should not be " contrary" or " repugnant" to the laws of England. What this meant, nobody has ever yet been able to find out. If it was intended that the local laws should not be different from those of England, the limitation utterly contradicted the grant; and it was, besides, a very absurd provision, since the grant gave power to " make any laws whatsoever," because the colonists, from the great difference of their circumstances, were sure to need laws materially different from those which suited the people of England. We may conclude, therefore, that this was not the purpose of the condition. Whatever its purpose was, the condition itself was always inoperative from vagueness. But that same vagueness gave it fatal effect as a subject of dispute between the Crown and colonists. The unavoidable disregard of this provision by the colonists, furnished the Crown with pretexts for accusing them of violating their charters, and with pretexts for violating them itself. Any degree of vagueness or obscurity in a restrictive provision would necessarily be a source of discord, not only between the Crown and the colonists, but between parties in the colony who would inevitably put different interpretations on words open to more than one. And besides the discord, the whole subject matter of the indefinite provision would be in a state of uncertainty and precariousness; the very state which is not according to law. In drawing a municipal charter, therefore, it should be a rule admitting of no exception, to express restrictive provisions with such fulness and particularity as to prevent all mistake or doubt as to the nature and extent of the intended limitation. For the same reason, the same rule should be strictly observed in defining the *modus operandi* of local powers delegated to the colonists subject to the condition of being exercised in a particular way.

The manner of granting comprises substance as well as form; but the amount and character, or subject, of limitations and special directions is a consideration perfectly distinct from the manner of imposing them. What are the proper subjects of limitations and special directions? They may be divided into matters of substance and matters of form. As an example of the first, I would mention the disposal of waste lands; a function in the right exercise of which the imperial power has the deepest interest. Of the second, the form of the colonial legislature is a good example; for it is an object of the highest importance to the imperial power, both as a means of promoting the emigration of valuable colonists, fit leaders and employers of the poorer class of emigrants, and as a means of harmonizing as far as possible the national character of the colonists with that of the people of the mother-country, that the creative institutions of the colony should resemble those of the metropolis. If these examples suffice for exhibiting the nature of the subjects as to which control by the imperial power should be embodied in a colonial charter, this rule may be deduced from them; that the subjects of imperial control should be those only, as to which the imperial power has some object of its own to accomplish by means of the control.

But for the application of this rule I pretend to lay down no supplementary rule. This is a point upon which opinions will necessarily differ. There are not perhaps a dozen people who hold, or could be brought to hold speculatively, the very same opinion with regard to the matters as to which the imperial power has objects of its own to serve by locally controlling a colony. Practically most people would agree on this question, if the question were made practical by a Ministry having decided opinions on the question, and proposing a measure founded upon them. Till that shall happen (the supposed event, now more than ever, appears far distant), any full definition of these particulars would only be a butt for the tribe of Mother-country to shoot at. Instead, therefore, of attempting to define completely what should be the subjects of imperial control, I will only mention in general terms a few that have occurred to myself.

The most important of them, of course, is the form of the colonial legislature. In order to make it harmonize with that of the mother-country, it should be representative, aristocratic, and monarchical.

If I could please myself in this particular, the electoral franchise should be so limited by a property qualification, as to deprive the poorest immigrants and settlers, which is another expression for the most ignorant, of the superior influence in the legislature which universal suffrage bestows on the most numerous class: for besides the ordinary objections to universal suffrage for a people most of whom are very ignorant, there are two others peculiarly applicable to new countries; namely, the constant influx of strangers, and the roving disposition of fresh colonists.

These reasons were urgently pressed upon Lord Grey's notice whilst he was framing a constitution for New Zealand. I inclose the copy of a letter which some colonists who were in England addressed to him at the time, and in which the objections to the universal suffrage that he adopted, are fully set forth.*   Of this letter Lord Grey took no notice; probably because its objections to a universal suffrage tallied with some contained in that letter of mine to Mr. Gladstone which had blistered his jealous temper.   But, however this may be, other efforts were made to save New Zealand from the evils, which it was known that he intended to inflict on the colony by making universal suffrage the basis of its constitutional law.   Amongst these one is so instructive, that I must trouble you with a brief account of it.

After Lord Grey had been for some time engaged by himself in attempting to make a constitution for New Zealand, it became known that he had given up the task, and handed it over to Mr. (now Sir James) Stephen, who really framed the constitution that was promulgated by Lord Grey, and destroyed by him before it could get into operation.   The colonists, therefore, who had in vain protested against the suffrage by letter to Lord Grey, now induced a Director of the New-Zealand Company, Mr. Aglionby, who fully agreed with them upon this point, to obtain an official interview with Mr. Stephen, and repeat their objections.   At first, the usually grave old chief of the tribe of Mothercountry playfully quizzed Mr. Aglionby, the English Radical, for objecting to an unlimited suffrage: but when the objector, in the simplicity of his honest heart, explained, that though he approved of household suffrage for this country, there are peculiar objections to it for a new colony—viz., the

---

* This letter, which very completely exposed, by anticipation, the defects and vices of the last constitution bestowed by imperial Britain on a colony, will be found in an Appendix.

constant influx of strangers and the roving disposition
of fresh colonists—Mr. Stephen ceased joking, and declared with remarkable earnestness and solemnity, that
his conscience would not allow him to have a hand in
depriving any of her Majesty's colonial subjects of their
birthright! So a constitution was framed and promulgated, under which the party-character of a general
election in the colony might have been determined by
the arrival of a few shipfulls of Dorsetshire paupers
or Milesian-Irish peasants. This provision, however,
insured the early overthrow of the constitution by
Lord Grey himself. Of course Mr. Stephen had not
the slightest view to that result in standing up on this
occasion for that birthright of Englishmen, which has
been smothered almost out of memory by his long
administration of colonial affairs in the name of a
succession of Principal Secretaries of State. Nevertheless, it may be as well to note that Mr. Taylor
dedicates his exposure of the jesuitical statesmanship
of the Colonial Office to Mr. Stephen, in the following
words: "To James Stephen, Esq., Under Secretary
of State for the colonies, as to the man within the
author's knowledge in whom the active and contem-
plative faculties most strongly meet, are inscribed
these disquisitions concerning the attributes of a
statesman."

This episode is by way of answer to some questions
in your second letter. A property qualification in
land, its amount in extent or value being such that
few could possess it except permanent settlers having
a deep interest in the future well-being of the colony,
would yet, from the facility of obtaining landed property in a new country by means only of industry
and steadiness, render the franchise attainable by the

steadier and more intelligent portion of the working
class : and I think it desirable that if there were any
property qualification for representatives, it should
not exceed that of voters, so that morally-qualified
members of the working class might take a direct part
in legislation.

With respect to a second legislative body, resembling the British House of Lords, I think that the
resemblance should be real, not a mere sham of
resemblance as in Canada and others of the present
representative colonies.   A second chamber composed
of mere nominees of the executive, holding their seats
for life, is an absurd and mischievous institution.   It
provides, not for more legislative deliberation, but for
conflicts and impediments instead of legislation.   As
far as I am aware, no feasible substitute for it has ever
been proposed.   People who have never seriously
reflected for a moment on the founding or creative
attributes of colonization, laugh if one proposes that
the second chamber in a colony should be hereditary;
yet many a one of them would give his ears to be a
hereditary legislator himself. When the late Lord Grey
was expected to advise a great increase of the peerage,
three hundred persons are said to have applied to him
for the distinction. Men do not forfeit their love of distinction by becoming colonists.   It appears to me that
the progress of colonization would be vastly accelerated,
and the colonization itself immeasurably improved, if
the colonies, instead of affording no distinctions but
those which belong to bureaucracy and free-masonry,
held out to valuable immigrants the prospect of such
distinction as every young lawyer in this country, every
merchant and manufacturer when he sets out in trade,
every young officer in the army or navy, fancies that

the sovereign may perchance bestow upon him some day or other as the reward of great success in his career. Those who smile at the suggestion, are perhaps moved by the contrast between their own sentiment of little respect for colonies, and of great respect for the dignity which it is proposed to establish in those despised portions of the empire. But be this as it may, that " provident circumspection," which the preamble of Baltimore's charter attributes to the great colonizer, and which is the first quality of a colonizing authority, would not reject my proposal because it is most ridiculed by those who are least acquainted with the whole subject. I propose, then, that the second legislative body shall be hereditary, but with a condition. The condition is, that an inheriting member of the council should possess the same property qualification as his predecessor. This property qualification should be very high; such a permanent landed property as would, upon the whole, render the council a fair type of the class of settlers having the greatest property interest in the well-being of the colony. If a member of the council got rid of his qualification, he should forfeit his seat. A good system of registration would at all times make known whether or not he continued to possess the qualification.

The members of council should be appointed by the chief executive magistrate of the colony, but only on the advice of persons responsible, like cabinet ministers here, to the representative body. For in order to complete the resemblance of the provincial to the imperial constitution—in order to constitute a harmonious government, legislative and executive, instead of subjecting the colonists to the miseries of a " constituted anarchy "—it is indispensably requisite that the head of the executive, being himself a third branch of the legislature, with a veto upon all legislative acts, and with every other attribute of the sovereign at home, should be himself irresponsible to the colonists by means of being surrounded by responsible advisers. The British constitution, having grown up by slow degrees, and never having been written, contains no express provision to this effect; but the custom is the hinge upon which our whole system of government turns, the oil which gives smoothness to the working of the whole machine. This is the part of our constitution, which at the worst renders monarchy a cheap and excellent substitute for the Presidential Election, and which foreigners, notwithstanding their numerous imitations of our fundamental law, are still, and in but a few cases, only beginning to understand. In order to give a colony the immediate benefit of it, we cannot wait to let it grow from the seed as it has grown here, but we must transplant a perfect offshoot: we must write the provision down in the colonial charter. I propose, therefore, to insert in the charter two clauses, providing, first, that no act of the head of the executive shall be valid unless performed on the advice of an executive council; and secondly, that members of the executive council shall be removeable, or rather removed *ipso facto*, by an address to the head of the executive from the representative branch of the legislature praying for their removal.

The chief magistracy, or head of the executive and third branch of the legislature, remains to be provided: and here it is, I think, necessary to establish a wide difference between the colonial and imperial constitutions. The imperial sovereign is a person as well as an institution, and we reverence the one as much as we value the other. To transplant a complete off-shoot of the whole is, therefore, simply impossible. The nearest approach to doing so would be by the erection of Canada, for example, into an independent monarchy, and filling its throne with a child of the British Sovereign. But the colonies are intended to be subordinate to the empire; and though it would, I think, be wise to make the younger branches of our royal family, whose social position here is anything but agreeable, subordinate sovereigns of the more important colonies, yet subordination requires that the colonial chief magistrate should be appointed and removeable by the imperial. I am sure, however, that he ought to be appointed like an English judge, *quam diû bene gesserit,* so as not to be removable except for proved misconduct. If he were removeable by address to the Crown from both Houses of Parliament, imperial objects would be sufficiently guarded; and in order to guard the colony against such unconstitutional violences and follies on the part of the chief magistrate as provoke rovolutionary proceedings by the people—in order to give the colonists an equivalent for the memory of expulsion from the throne and of a royal scaffold—in order that the head of the executive in the colony should not violate with impunity the provision binding him to act according to the advice of a responsible executive council—a petition to the Crown from both branches of the colonial legislature for the removal of the local chief-magistrate, should be declared in the charter to be of the same force as addresses from both Houses of Parliament. And it appears by no means incompatible with colonial subordination, that the colonies should be allowed some voice in even the selection of their governors.

As the circumstances of a colony are open to greater, more frequent, and more sudden fluctuations than those of an old country, frequent elections of the representative body should be guaranteed by the charter.

I omit minor provisions, such as a guarantee for frequent meetings of the legislature, the numbers of such legislative bodies, and the modes of proroguing and dissolving the provincial parliament. But there remains to be stated a provision of the highest importance.

In order to retain for the imperial power the most complete general control over the colony, the colonial constitution, instead of being granted immutably and in perpetuity, as our old municipal charters were, should, in the charter itself, be declared liable to revocation or alteration by the Crown upon address from both Houses of Parliament.

But in order to guard against the unavoidable indifference of Parliament to colonial questions, and their proneness to adopt any colonial suggestion of the Ministry of the day; which body again is always disposed to adopt without examining any suggestion of the Colonial Minister; who, lastly, must generally take his ideas from the nameless members of his Office —in order, that is, to prevent Mr. Mothercountry from meddling with colonial constitutions—I think it would be most useful to erect some tribunal open to the public, presided over by a high legal functionary, and moved by barristers-at-law, to which should be submitted the grounds on which the Ministry of the day proposed to revoke or alter a colonial constitution: and unless such tribunal decided that the grounds were sufficient, the question should not be submitted at all to the decision of Parliament. This tribunal would be an improvement on the Supreme Court of the United States, which determines questions of difference between the State and Federal governments; for however a change in the American constitution may at any time be required, it can only be brought about by the operation of a cumbrous elective machinery which has never yet been called into action. To the proposed English tribunal, other questions between the colony and the mother-country might be submitted, before being submitted to Parliament, besides that of an alteration in the fundamental law of the colony: and thus all such questions, instead of being determined arbitrarily and in secret, or left unsettled, by the irresponsible clerks of the Colonial Office, would be brought by the parties to it—the Crown on one side, the Colony on the other, either having the right to initiate a cause—before an open court, where it would be argued by practised advocates, viewed by the judge in all its aspects, and finally decided in the face of the public according to law.

Colonists and colonial reformers at home have proposed that every colony should have a representative in the British House of Commons. The object of the suggestion is most desirable, but, I think, not attainable by that means. The object is to bestow on every colony the great advantage of being able to hold legitimate communication with the imperial public and government. It is not supposed that the vote of a colonial member of the House of Commons would serve any good purpose, but that if he were a member of the imperial legislature, the imperial public and government would listen to him as the special representative of the colony; would never come to a decision concerning the colony without hearing what he had to say about it; and would give their attention to suggestions originating with himself. And all this is probably true. But might he not be quite as effectually the representative of the colony at home, without being in Parliament? If he might, the whole advantage for the colony would be secured, without having recourse to a measure, which really is open to very serious objections, and still more opposed to some of John Bull's probably unconquerable prejudices.

By recurring to the colonizing wisdom of our ancestors, we shall discover a simple, effectual, and unobjectionable means of attaining the object in view. Under the municipal authority vested in them by our old colonial charters, the old colonies used to appoint "Agents" to reside in England, and to serve as a medium of communication between the colonial and imperial governments. Benjamin Franklin was agent for Pennsylvania, Mr. Roebuck for the House of Assembly of Lower Canada, and the late Mr. Burge for Jamaica. What a cost in money, trouble, and shame, the empire might have saved, if the imperial government had lent a favourable ear to these distinguished representatives of colonies! But the valuable institution of colonial representatives at home, has gradually fallen into discredit and practical disuse since the Colonial Office was instituted; and it exists now, for the most part, with no effect but that of adding a few sinecures to the patronage of the Colonial Office.   For the Colonial Office, having got to be the real government of the colonies, virtually appoints the colonial agents who purport to be accredited to it by the colonies!

Supposing the government of the colony to be really municipal, it would itself appoint its Agent.   If it were the organ of the portion of the colonists having the greatest interest in the colony's well-doing, it would select for Agent or Resident in England one of the most respectable and capable of the colonists. Such a person, so accredited to the imperial government, would be a personage here, and would have weight accordingly with our government and public. He would keep the colony informed of matters at home, with which it behoved the colonists to be acquainted; and he might powerfully forward the interests of both colony and mother-country, by helping to promote the emigration of capital and labour: for in this branch of colonization, there is no more urgent want than some authority residing in the mother-country, but identified with and responsible to the colonists.

The Agents (Representatives seems a better title) would, of course, be appointed and removeable by the governor of the colony on the advice of his responsible council of ministers, and paid by the colony.

If the ancient institution of colonial agency at home were thus revived and improved, as it might easily be, the effect would be to add another powerful tie to the connexion between the colony and the mother-country. To some extent a Representative would have the functions of the representatives of the States of America in the United-States Congress.   Our system of colonial government, viewed as a whole, would be federative as well as municipal.

Recurring to the charter of colonial government, this should declare that the legislative and executive government prescribed by it should have unlimited power within the colony, " excepting only, as is by these presents otherwise provided and directed." The old charters generally, after giving the local government power to make any laws whatsoever, with some specified exceptions, went on to grant certain other powers, such as that of erecting judicatories, or employing a militia. After the main grant, such provisions would be mere surplusage and encumbrance, as they obviously are in the old charters. The deliberate omission, however, of all particulars from the granting portion of the charter, renders it the more necessary to be very careful in setting down the exceptions.

The exceptions which occur to me at present, are,

I. Whatever relates to the employment, command, and discipline of her Majesty's forces, by land and sea, within the colony at all times; and, during war time, in case of any attack upon the colony, the command of the local militia and marine.

II. Whatever relates to intercourse on public matters with the servants of any foreign power within the colony, such as a consul or the captain of a man-of-war, for the management of which the Governor alone should have a special commission from the Crown.

III. The functions of the post-office, so far as relates to the transmission of letters to and from the colony, which should be conducted by the British

Postmaster-General. The publication of two reports on the post-office of Canada from a commission appointed by Lord Sydenham, which were transmitted to the Colonial Office by Sir Charles Bagot, would, by itself, satisfy public opinion here, that the internal post-office of a colony ought to be a business of the local government, as it was under the old charters. Indeed, the abuses of the local post-office in every colony under pretended imperial management, are perfectly monstrous; and it seems impossible to prevent abuses, when distance, and the necessary indifference of the British public with respect to post-office management in a colony, put responsibility out of the question. Moreover, the patronage of the local post-office, the best that exists in a new country, is an essential means to the well-working of a local constitutional government.

IV. The most important exception is that of directions in the charter for the disposal of waste land, and of the proceeds of its purchase-money, by the local government. But this last subject, which is that of colonization independently of government, will have our exclusive attention after a few reflections, in my next letter, on the probable operation of the proposed system of municipal-federative government for colonies, as a substitute for the central-bureaucratic-spoiled.

LETTER XLIV.

From the Colonist.

SOME REFLECTIONS ON THE PROBABLE OPERATION OF
MUNICIPAL-FEDERATIVE GOVERNMENT FOR COLONIES,
AS A SUBSTITUTE FOR THE CENTRAL-BUREAUCRATIC-
SPOILED.—A GRAND REFORM OF THE COLONIAL OFFICE.

ALLOW me to begin this letter with a request and
a warning.

I beg of you to understand, that the plan of
colonial government set forth in my last is intended
for a mere outline, and that I am conscious of its
being very imperfect as such. A complete plan, with
all the reasons for each provision, would be the proper
subject of a Report by a Parliamentary Commission
expressly charged with the framing of a plan. The
framing of a complete plan is not the proper business
of any individual: it is the duty of a Ministry,
supposing always that a British Ministry could be
induced to form definite ideas with respect to the
true principles of colonial government. Be pleased,
therefore, to consider my rough skeleton of a plan as
designed to be little more than an illustration of my
own view of those principles.

In the next place, I venture urgently to recommend,

that you abstain from propounding to the House of Commons anything like a plan intended to be complete. The time for doing that is yet far off, and may perhaps never come. If you did it prematurely, you would make enemies but no friends; you would incur the hostility of the whole tribe of Mothercountry, without having brought public opinion up to the mark of enabling you to brush aside their selfish objections and malicious cavils. You would besides, startle the ignorant whose name is Legion, *bore* the indifferent who are still more numerous, and perhaps see the House counted out in an early stage of your intended exposition. There is a time for all things; and I repeat, the time for action in this matter has not yet arrived, except as regards the agitation of principles and the promotion of inquiry.

Recurring to the principles which my sketch of a plan is intended to illustrate, I would now beg of you to consider how some such plan would operate in removing the political impediments and affording encouragement to colonization.

The office of governor would be so much more respectable, its tenure so much more secure (for generally it would be a life-tenure, and often, if the colonists had a voice in the selection of governors, practically a tenure descending from father to son), and the position of reigning, but not ruling, so much more comfortable, than the lot of governors can be under the present system, that men of consequence and perhaps high reputation would be candidates for the office of subordinate sovereign. The provisions for meeting cases of extreme misconduct on the part of governors, are rather provisions against their occurrence; for assuredly, without some such means as those suggested for making the governor irresponsible, but his advisers responsible to the colonists, it is hardly possible that a resemblance of the British constitution should be for any long time administered, in a colony less formidable than Canada is now, without producing discord. I conclude, therefore, that British colonial governors, besides possessing such personal importance and character, as would induce the colonists cheerfully to treat them as subordinate sovereigns, would be under the necessity, as the imperial sovereign is, of either reigning constitutionally or ceasing to reign. What a change!

The governors not attempting to govern any more than her Majesty does, and the Colonial Office not meddling with local affairs except in matters reserved for imperial administration, the great bulk of the public functionaries in the colony would be colonists, settlers, people not without any interest, but with the greatest interest in the welfare of the colony; and offices in the colony, as well as seats in the colonial legislature, would generally be filled by colonists of some distinction and known aptitude. The colony would be governed with a view to its advantage. The colonists themselves would have the power to spread government into even the remotest settlements, by means of instituting a system of municipalities subordinate to their own. The whole field of colonial ambition would be open to colonists. So surely, I cannot help thinking, a very superior class of people would be induced to emigrate. If this last effect of a good colonial constitution took place, most of the enumerated impediments to colonization would disappear. There would be an end of the low standard of colonial morals and manners. The self-restraints which belong to civilization, would be substituted for the barbarous licence of colonial life: for the sense of honour may be transplanted like the habit of crime; and even without a specific plan of religious provisions, the supposed change in the character of our emigration would by itself make some provision for the restraints of religion as well as for those of honour. And lastly, colonial party-politics would no longer revolt emigrants of the better class, because free government by party, with a suffrage not democratic, would take the place of constituted democracy in some colonies, and constituted anarchy in the others.

But there would still be hostile parties in a colony: yes, parties instead of factions: for every colony would have its " ins" and its " outs," and would be governed as we are—as every free community must be in the present state of the human mind—by the emulation and rivalries, the bidding against each other for public favour, of the party in power and the party in opposition. Government by party, with all its passions and corruptions, is the price that a free country pays for freedom. But the colonies would be free communities: their internal differences, their very blunders, and their methods of correcting them, would be all their own: and the colonists who possessed capacity for public business—the Pitts and Foxes, the Broughams and Lyndhursts, the Peels and Russells of a colony, with their respective adherents —would govern by turns far better on the whole, we may be sure, than it would be possible for any other set of beings on earth to govern that particular community.

But let us suppose that the colonies were worse governed by their own leading men than by the Mothercountry tribe: even then, though the present impediments to colonization would not be removed but somewhat aggravated, still the imperial government and people would be gainers. Judging from ample experience and from a moment's reflection on the nature of the British race, the government of colonists by themselves, however bad it might seem to us, would not seem bad to them: they would like it and be very proud of it, just as on the whole we Britons at home like and are proud of our government, though it is often very bad in the eyes of philosophers and other nations. The colonists, making their own laws, imposing their own taxes, and appointing their own functionaries, would be pleased with their government, as every man is pleased with his own horse that he bought or bred according to his own judgment: for colonists would not be human, still less of the British temper, if they were not always pretty well satisfied with themselves and their own doings. Thus the mother-country would, at the worst, be spared the annoyance and shame of colonial discontent, and complaint, and disaffection. The Canadian rebellions and the present state of government or rather rebellion-at-heart in many of our colonies, could not have occurred under the proposed system. And finally, we should be spared the whole cost of colonial government as distinguished from colonial empire: for, of course, if the colonists governed themselves locally as respects legislation, taxation, and appointing to office, they must themselves pay for their local establishments. Nor would they object to this:

on the contrary, they would prefer it. I see that Lord Grey has recently proposed, that the salary of governors which is now paid by the colony, shall be paid by England: for what purpose? with what effect but that of increasing the power of the tribe of Mothercountry. Under our old municipal system, the colonists deemed it a privilege to raise the money for their own government, because they found that it enabled them to object with more reason to a meddling with their local affairs by officials in England. So, in our day, the obligation on colonies to defray the whole cost of their internal government, would be one security for the preservation of their municipal independence, and would therefore be considered rather a benefit than a burthen. Nor would any pecuniary burthen be imposed upon them: on the contrary, they would have less to pay than at present: for by nothing is municipal more distinguished from central government, than by its superior cheapness. Under the old English municipal system, thirteen important colonies obtained more government in each of them, than is bestowed on all our present colonies together. Their population nearly equalled that of all our present colonies. Their thirteen very complete and satisfying governments cost altogether about one hundred thousand pounds a year! a memorable proof, says Adam Smith, of the little cost at which colonies may be not only governed but well governed.

But what would become of the Colonial Office, if all the colonies were placed on a footing of government like that which makes the Channel Islands as devotedly attached to the Crown of England as we are here at home? It might remain to misgovern the dependencies, which are not colonies: only in that case, we should have to change its name. But even its name might be preserved, if its functions, as respects the true colonies, were defined to be the administration of those colonial matters only, which our system of municipal government specifically reserved for imperial administration. In the exercise of these functions, as they would be such as concerned the imperial government and public only, it would be made responsible like our own government, through being watched and kept in order by the public opinion of this country. Obviously, moreover, it would be a separate department of the imperial government, for administering executively the federative relations between the mother-country and the colonies, which, on behalf of the colonies, would be administered by the proposed colonial Representatives at home. But its legislative power over the colonies would, of course, be wholly abolished. Downing-street would undergo a grand reform. Is there anybody not belonging to the Office, and not being one of its interested hangers-on, who thinks that it ought to be preserved as it is? If I had room and it were worth while, I would place before you the views of the question of reforming the Colonial Office, which were eagerly expressed by its present Parliamentary organs, just before they were trapped and tamed by the original Mr. Mothercountry.

It seems almost needless to mention, that under the proposed reform of colonial government, or anything like it, the practice of colonizing with convicts wearing chains on their legs, and still more that of pouring criminals into our colonies with pardons in their pockets, would altogether cease, and would only be

remembered by us with a blush for having ever permitted such abominations.

But even if, by these or any other and better means
(and I am far from clinging to my own plan as the
best), we succeeded in making the colonies not only
habitable for the better order of emigrants, but
places in which that class might enjoy, in addition
to the natural charms of colonization, both those
which arise from the gratification of pride and ambition, and those which belong to the creative
business of legislating for new communities, there
would still remain the economical impediment of
scarcity of labour for hire. We must now proceed, therefore, to the causes of that impediment,
and the means of removing them. I am in hopes of
being able to satisfy you, that measures which would
put an end to scarcity of labour for hire in the colonies, would also give a great impulse to the progress
of colonization. If it should prove so, the mother-
country is deeply interested, politically and socially,
in this question of colonial economy.

LETTER XLV.

From the Colonist.

THE COLONIST, BY A SKETCH OF THE HISTORY OF SLAVERY, TRACES SCARCITY OF LABOUR IN NEW COUNTRIES TO ITS SOURCE IN THE CHEAPNESS OF LAND.

IT is strange that it should never have come into the head of philosopher or philanthropist to ascertain the causes of the revival of slavery by all the nations of modern Europe which have engaged in colonization. Political economists were bound to make this inquiry; for without it their science is incomplete at the very foundation: for slavery is a question of labour, "the original purchase of all things."

Philanthropists, however, have treated it as a moral and religious question, attributing slavery at all times and places, but especially in modern times and in America, to the wickedness of the human heart. So universal, indeed, is the doctrine, that we find it in the most improbable of places; in the latest and wisest of treatises on political economy, whose author speaks of "the infernal spirit of the slave-master." The infernal spirit of Abraham and Joshua; of Socrates and Plato; of Cicero and Seneca; of Alfred the Great; of Las Casas, who laid the foundation of negro slavery in America; of Baltimore, Penn, and Washington! These names alone show that the spirit of the slave-master is not that love of oppression and cruelty, which the exercise of unlimited power over his fellow-creatures is apt to beget in man: that infernal spirit is, and not universally, a mere effect of keeping slaves. The universal spirit of the slave-master is his motive; the state of mind that induces him to keep slaves; the spirit which, operating on individuals and communities, has ever been the immediate cause of slavery. It is not a wicked or infernal spirit. Neither communities nor individuals keep slaves in order to indulge in oppression and cruelty. Those British colonies — and they are many — which would get slaves to-morrow if we would let them, are not more wicked than we are: they are only placed in circumstances which induce us to long for the possession of slaves notwithstanding the objections to it. These circumstances, by producing the state of mind in which slavery becomes desirable for masters, have ever been the originating cause of slavery.

They are not moral, but economical circumstances: they relate not to vice and virtue, but to production. They are the circumstances, in which one man finds it difficult or impossible to get other men to work under his direction for wages. They are the circumstances, referring to a former letter, which stand in the way of combination and constancy of labour, and which all civilized nations, in a certain stage of their advance from barbarism, have endeavoured to counteract, and have in some measure counteracted, by means of some kind of slavery. Hitherto in this world, labour has never been employed on any considerable scale, with constancy and in combination, except by one or other of two means; either by hiring, or by slavery of some kind. What the principle of association may do in the production of wealth, and for the labouring classes, without either slavery or hiring, remains to be seen; but at present we cannot rely upon it. Recurring, therefore, to hiring and slavery as the only known means of rendering industry very productive, let us now consider what relation these two social arrangements bear to each other.

Slavery is evidently a make-shift for hiring; a proceeding to which recourse is had, only when hiring is impossible or difficult. Slave labour is on the whole much more costly than the labour of hired freemen; and slavery is also full of moral and political evils, from which the method of hired labour is exempt. Slavery, therefore, is not preferred to the method of hiring: the method of hiring would be preferred if there were a choice: but when slavery is adopted, there is no choice: it is adopted because at the time and under the circumstances there is no other way of getting labourers to work with constancy and in combination. What, then, are the circumstances under which this happens?

It happens wherever population is scanty in proportion to land. Slavery, except in some mild form, as the fading continuation of a habit, and with some advantage to the nominal slaves but real dependents, whom at least it sheltered from the evils of competition, has been confined to countries of a scanty population, has never existed in very populous countries, and has gradually ceased in the countries whose population gradually increased to the point of density. And the reason is plain enough. Property in land is the object of one of the strongest and most general of human desires. Excluding the owners of land, in whom the desire is gratified, few indeed are those who do not long to call a piece of the earth their own. Landowners and persons who would be glad to be landowners, comprise the bulk of mankind. In populous countries, the desire to own land is not easily gratified, because the land is scarce and dear: the plentifulness and cheapness of land in thinly-peopled countries enables almost everybody who wishes it to become a landowner. In thinly-peopled countries, accordingly, the great majority of free people are landowners who cultivate their own land; and labour for hire is necessarily scarce: in densely-peopled countries, on the contrary, the great majority of the people cannot obtain land, and there is plenty of labour for hire. Of plentifulness of labour for hire, the cause is dearness of land: cheapness of land is the cause of scarcity of labour for hire.

Test these conclusions by reference to universal history. Abraham, the slave-master, said unto Lot, who was another, "is not the whole land before thee?" The ancient Greeks were themselves colonists, the occupiers of a new territory, in which for a time every freeman could obtain as much land as he desired: for a time they needed slaves; and the custom of slavery was established. They sent forth colonies, which consisted in part of slaves, removed to a waste territory for the express purpose of cultivating it with constancy and combination of labour. The Romans, in the earlier stages of their history, were robbers of land, and had more than they could cultivate without slaves: it was partly by means of slavery, that they at last grew to be so populous at Rome as no longer to need slavery, but to ask for an agrarian law. The Roman world was indeed so devastated by wars, that except at the seat of empire, population never perhaps attained the proportion to land in which real slavery naturally disappears. The serfdom of the middle-ages was for all Europe, what it is for Poland and Russia still, a kind of slavery required by the small proportion of people to land; a substitute for hired labour, which gradually expired with the increase of population, as it will expire in Poland and Russia when land shall, in those countries, become as scarce and dear as it became in England some time after the Conquest. Next comes the institution of slavery in America by the colonies of nations which had abolished serfdom at home; colonies in whose history, whether we read it in Raynal, or Edwards, or Grahame, we find the effect and the cause invariably close together; the slavery in various forms of bondage, growing out of superabundance of land.

The operation of superabundance of land in causing a scarcity of free labour and a desire for slaves, is very distinctly seen in a process by which modern colonists always have endeavoured to obtain free labour. Free labour, when it can be got and kept in a colony, is so much more productive than forced, that the colonial capitalist is always ready to pay for it, in the form of wages, more than slave labour would cost, and far more than the usual rate of wages in an old country. It is perfectly worth his while to pay, besides these high wages, the cost of the passage of free labour from the old country to the colony. Innumerable are the cases in which a colonial capitalist has done this, confident of the prudence of the outlay. It was commonly done by the founders of our early colonies in America, and has been done by many capitalists in Canada, South Africa, the Australias, and New Zealand. To do this appears such a natural, suitable, easy way of obtaining labour for hire, that every emigrant capitalist thinks of doing it; and thousands (I speak within compass) have tried the experiment. It is an experiment which always fails: if it always or generally succeeded, scarcity of labour for hire would not be a colonial evil. I have never missed the opportunity of tracing one of these experiments to its results; and I assure you that I have never been able to discover a single case of success. The invariable failure is produced by the impossibility of keeping the labour, for the passage of which to the colony the capitalist has paid: and it happens as follows.

Under this voluntary method of importing labour, all capitalists do not pay alike: some pay; some do not. Those who do not pay for the importation of labour, can afford to pay for the use of it more than those who pay for the importation. These non-importing capitalists, therefore, offer to the newly-arrived labourers higher wages than the employer who imported them has engaged or can afford to pay. The offer of higher wages is a temptation which poor emigrants are incapable of resisting. When the non-importing capitalist is not rogue enough to make the offer to the labourers whom his neighbour has imported, still the labourers know that such higher wages can be obtained from persons who have not imported labourers: they quit the service of their importer, and, being now out of employment, are engaged by somebody who can afford to pay the higher wages. The importer, I repeat, never keeps the labour which he has imported.

Nor does the non-importing capitalist keep it long. With these high wages, the imported labourers soon save the means of acquiring and cultivating land. In every colony, land is so cheap that emigrant labourers who save at all, are soon able to establish themselves as landowners, working on their own account; and this, most of them do as soon as possible. If the land of the colony were of limited extent, a great importation of people would raise its price, and compel some people to work for wages; but the land of colonies is practically of unlimited extent. The immigration of labour, therefore, has no effect on the supply in the market: yes, it has an effect; it increases the demand without increasing the supply, and therefore renders the demand more intense: for the great bulk of imported labourers become landowners anxious to obtain labour for hire. The more labourers are imported, the greater becomes, after a while, the scarcity of labour in proportion to the demand: and at the bottom of the whole mischief is the cheapness of land.

It was cheapness of land that caused Las Casas (the Clarkson or Wilberforce of his time as respects the Red Indians of America) to invent the African slave trade. It was the cheapness of land that brought African slaves to Antigua and Barbadoes; and it is a comparative dearness of land, arising from the increase of population in those small islands,

which has made them an exception from the general
rule of West-Indian impoverishment in consequence of
the abolition of slavery before land was made dear.
It was cheapness of land that caused the introduction
of negro slaves into Virginia, and produced the
various forms of bondage practised by all the old
English colonies in America. It is cheapness of land
in Brazil, Porto Rico, and Cuba, which causes our
African squadron, and not only prevents it from
serving its purpose, but causes it to be a means of
aggravating the horrors of the African slave trade.

The cause is always the same, in form as well as in
substance : the effect takes various forms. Amongst
the effects, there is the prodigious importance of Irish
labour to the United States—the extreme " convenience of the nuisance" of an immigration of people
whose position as aliens, and whose want of ambition
and thrift, commonly prevent them from acquiring
land, however cheap it may be; there is the oft-
repeated prayer of our West-India planters (not
residing in Barbadoes or Antigua) to the imperial
government, for some plan for establishing a great
emigration of free labour from Africa to the West
Indies; there is the regret of New South Wales at
the stoppage of convict emigration to that colony;
there are the petitions which several colonies have
addressed to the home government, praying for convict emigration : and, lastly, there is the whole batch
of economical colonial evils, which I have before described under the head of scarcity of labour for hire,
and which operate as one of the most formidable impediments to the emigration of the most valuable class
of settlers.

If all the political impediments to colonization were removed, this economical one would still be sufficient to prevent the emigration of capitalists or capital on any great scale. Indeed, so long as it shall last, no considerable capitalists will emigrate, hoping to prosper, except under a delusion which will be dissipated by six months' experience in the colony: and this delusion, in consequence of the increasing spread of true information about colonial life, is likely to have fewer victims than heretofore. I am looking forward to almost a stoppage of emigration as respects all but the very needy or desperate classes; provided always, however, that the cause of scarcity of labour in the colonies cannot by any means be removed, and prevented from returning. My own notion of the means by which the scarcity of labour might be effectually removed and prevented from returning, must now be explained.

LETTER XLVI.

From the Colonist.

THE COLONIST SUGGESTS THE MEANS BY WHICH LAND MIGHT BE MADE DEAR ENOUGH TO PREVENT A SCARCITY OF LABOUR FOR HIRE.

SOME land in colonies is as dear as the dearest land in old countries. In Wall Street, and the lower part of Broadway, New York, land is even dearer than in Lombard-street and Cornhill, London; the reason being that the part of New York which has become the centre of the commerce of that great city, is a narrow point of land hemmed in on three sides by water, so that although commerce in New York is less, the competition for room at the centre of commerce is greater than in London. So in various parts of every colony, there is land which fetches a high price, because it is of limited extent. In new countries, nearly as in old, land in the centre of a city, in every part of a town, or in the immediate vicinity of towns, or of good roads, is of limited extent. It is land enjoying certain advantages of position; and as such land is no more unlimited in America or Australia than in England, it is, as in England, the subject of competition, and fetches a price measured by the degree of competition for it. But this land is not that of which the cheapness produces scarcity of labour in new countries: it is land so dear as to be either out of the reach of the working-classes, or for them less desirable at its price than land for which there is little or no competition. This last is the land by means of obtaining which labourers become land-owners: it may be called indifferently the lowest-priced land, the cheapest land, or land of the mini-mum price. I beg you to bear in mind, that only the cheapest land in a colony, is that whose price affects the labour market.

The price of this land, as of all bare land, and of everything else which it costs nothing to produce, depends of course on the relation between the demand and the supply. In colonies, where wages are so high that everybody may soon acquire the means of pur-chasing land, the demand is according to population; the supply consists of the quantity of the cheapest land open to purchasers. By augmenting the popu-lation or diminishing the quantity of land, the price would be raised: it would be lowered by augmenting the quantity of land or diminishing the population. Now, over the proportion which these two shall bear to each other, the state or government possesses an absolute control. The amount of population indeed does not depend on the government; but the quantity of land does; and thus the government has control over the proportion which land bears to population, or population to land. In the very beginning of a colony, all the land necessarily belongs to the govern-ment or is under its jurisdiction; and it is the govern-ment, which suddenly or by degrees makes all the land private property, by disposing of it to individuals. The government may employ a profuse or a niggard hand; that is, it may bestow much or little on the colonists in proportion to their numbers. In West Australia, for example, the government allowed the first 2000 settlers to appropriate about 3,000,000 acres; whilst in South Australia, with a population now amounting to 40,000, less, I believe, than 500,000 acres have become private property: in one case, 2000 people got as much land as the counties of Middlesex, Essex, Suffolk, Hertford, and Cambridge; in the other, 40,000 people got only as much land as the county of Cambridge: the bestowing disposition of the government was a hundred and nineteen times stronger, and the proportion of private land to people a hundred and nineteen times greater, in the one case than in the other. The history of colonization abounds with like examples of the control exercised by government over the proportion between land and people.

It has been said above, that government may dispose of land with a niggard hand. Do not suppose that any colonizing government has ever done so. All colonizing governments have done just the reverse, by disposing of land with a profuse hand. The greediness of colonists has been equal to the profusion of the governments. The colonists, full of the ideas about land which possess people in old countries— emigrating indeed because at home the cheapest land had got or was getting to be scarce and precious— could never obtain too much land for the satisfaction of their desires: and the governments, universally down to the other day, seemed to have looked upon waste land as a useless property of the state, only fit to be squandered in satisfying the greedy desires of colonists. Throughout what may be termed the colonial world, therefore, allowing however for a few exceptions in which a colony has grown to be as densely peopled as an old country, there has at all times existed a proportion between land and people, which almost prevented competition for the cheapest land, and enabled every colonist to obtain some land either for nothing or for a price little more than nominal. Whatever may have been the price of the dearest land in a colony, the price of the cheapest has never, with the above exceptions, been sufficient to prevent labourers from turning into landowners after a very brief term of hired service.

There are two modes in which the government disposes of waste land; either by gift or sale. Gift, or grant, as it is called, has been the most common mode. Until lately, the British government always disposed of land by grant. The United States, soon after they became independent, adopted the plan of selling, to which, with the exception of some extensive grants, they have since adhered. About seventeen years ago, our government substituted throughout the colonies the plan of selling for that of granting.

The plan of granting may be said to involve unavoidably an extreme profusion in the disposal of land. When the land can be got for nothing, everybody wants as much of it as he can possibly get; and the government, of course deeming the land of no value, or it would not part with it for nothing, is prone to indulge the greedy desires of individuals by a process so very easy to the government as that of saying " take what you please." Under this plan, therefore, the quantity of land granted has always been so very abundant in proportion to population, that it may be said to have been supplied, like air or water, in unlimited quantities; that is, not in any proportion to the market-demand for land, but so as to prevent such a demand. In many cases, the government made a practice of giving land to people of the labouring class, when of course there was no market-demand for land except in advantageous positions, and the cheapest land was so cheap as to bear no price at all. Even when grants were not made directly to the class of labourers, the profusion with which they were made to other classes, caused the cheapest land to be " dirt cheap," and indirectly bestowed land upon labourers for almost nothing: practically, under this system of profusion, the government exercised no control over the proportion between land and people.

Even if the government should intend to carry out the plan in such a manner as to prevent scarcity of labour by making the cheapest land somewhat dear, or difficult of acquisition, it would not be able to accomplish the object by that means. The purpose of the government would be defeated by the nature of things. So long as land was to be obtained for nothing, the greediness of individuals to obtain it would be irresistible by the government, even for a single year. Supposing that the government resisted for a while, and so made the cheapest land comparatively dear, the greediness to obtain for nothing land bearing a price (for in the supposed case all land would have a market value) would overcome the resistance of the

firmest government, and again knock down the price
of the cheapest land. But further, supposing that the
government did resist the importunity for grants of
valuable land, by what means could it regulate the
supply so as to maintain the most beneficial proportion between land and people? How would it know
from time to time what quantities of land ought to be
granted? How could it estimate the different effects
on the markets of land and labour of granting this or
that quantity? These questions show that the plan
of granting is devoid of regulating power; that it is
incompatible with the indispensable employment of a
measure of supply. And lastly, there is an objection
to the plan of granting, which is very strong without
an effectual restriction of the quantity, but would be
stronger with it. However profusely land may be
granted, some of it acquires in time a value depending
on advantages of position: and this consideration explains why people are so greedy to obtain land for
nothing, even though at the time of being obtained it
has no market value. This consideration also shows
that under the plan of granting, however profusely,
the government has the opportunity, and the strongest
temptation, to favour its friends, to practise favouritism and official jobbing in the disposal of land.
There is no instance of a colonizing government that
was able to resist this temptation. Official favouritism
and jobbing in the disposal of land by grant, constitute one of the most prominent and ugliest features
of colonial history: and they have been one of the
most effectual impediments to colonization, by producing an immense crop of disappointments, jealousies,
envies, and irritations. But if favouritism and jobbing

in the disposal of waste land made the colonists hate each other and their government when the quantity granted was practically without limit, what would happen if the quantity were so restricted as to render all the land granted immediately valuable? The government would be more than ever tempted to favour its friends; the officials more than ever tempted to favour themselves and their connexions; the friends of government and the connexions of officials greedier of land than was ever known; and the whole colony in an uproar of disaffection to its government. This is the last objection to the plan of granting. It was by placing all these objections before Lord Howick in 1831, that the colonizing theorists of 1830 put an end to the plan of granting waste land throughout our colonies.

LETTER XLVII.

From the Colonist.

IN ORDER THAT THE PRICE OF WASTE LAND SHOULD
ACCOMPLISH ITS OBJECTS, IT MUST BE SUFFICIENT
FOR THE PURPOSE. HITHERTO THE PRICE HAS BEEN
EVERYWHERE INSUFFICIENT.

THE plan of selling contains within itself an effectual regulator of the quantity disposed of. This
is the price which the government requires for new land.
This price may indeed be so low, as not to operate as
a restriction at all. This happened in Canada when
the plan of selling was first adopted there, and when
the price required by the government hardly amounted
to more, or may even have amounted to less, upon
small purchases, than the fees of office previously
required for grants. The first price of public land in
Tasmania was 5s. an acre : the cost of a Tasmanian
grant in two cases with which I happen to be acquainted, was 58l. for 50 acres, and nearly 100l. for
70 acres. In the colonies generally, I believe, excepting as to large purchases, a grant used to cost
more than the price which was afterwards required
by the government when it substituted selling for
granting. So low a price as this has no influence on

the market-value of the cheapest land, no effect on the supply of labour for hire. The mere putting of a price, therefore, on all new land may accomplish none of the objects in view. In order to accomplish them, the price must be sufficient for that purpose. But the price may be low or high as the government pleases: it is a variable force, completely under the control of government. In founding a colony, the price might be so low as to render the quantity of land appropriated by settlers practically unlimited: it might be high enough to occasion a proportion between land and people similar to that of old countries, in which case, if this very high price did not prevent emigration, the cheapest land in the colony might be as dear, and the superabundance of labourers as deplorable as in England: or it might be a just medium between the two, occasioning neither superabundance of people nor superabundance of land, but so limiting the quantity of land, as to give the cheapest land a market value that would have the effect of compelling labourers to work some considerable time for wages before they could become landowners. A price that did less than this, would be insufficient; one that did more, would be excessive: the price that would do this and no more, is the proper price. I am used to call it the sufficient price.

The sufficient price has never yet been adopted by a colonizing government. The government of the United States, whose sole object in disposing of new land by sale instead of grant, was to hinder official favouritism and jobbing, has never required a higher price than two dollars an acre; and for a long while past, its price has been only one dollar and a quarter

an acre.   In our colonies, the price has varied from five
to forty shillings.   That these prices are insufficient for
the purpose in view, is shown by facts, and may be
made plainer by a supposed case.

The facts consist of the economical impediments to
colonization which I have described before, and which
have been as vigorous under the plan of selling as
under that of granting.   The substitution by the
United States of selling for granting has not in the
least diminished the value of negro slaves, or the
necessity in the free states of relying for the conduct
of works requiring much constancy and combination
of labour, on a vast immigration of such natural slaves
as the poorest Irish.   The scarcity of labour in our
colonies has been as great and injurious since, as it
was before, the imposition of a price on new land.   In
all our colonies, notwithstanding the price put on new
land, the cheapest land has been so cheap that the
poorest class (for in a colony nobody is quite poor)
could readily obtain land of their own: in all the
colonies they have done this; and everywhere accordingly labour for hire has been so scarce, that it was
dangerous, often fatal, for the capitalist to engage in
any work requiring the constant employment of many
pairs of hands.

I must here explain, however, that in most of our
colonies, the price would have been inoperative if it
had been ten times as high as it was.   In Canada and
New South Wales, for example, land had been granted
with such reckless profusion before the plan of selling
was adopted, that if this plan had even, by means of
an enormous price, put an end to the acquisition of
new land, it would still have had no effect on the land

and labour markets. The quantity of land in proportion to people was already so great as to occasion practically an unlimited supply, whilst the demand could only increase by the slow progress of births and immigration. In these two colonies, therefore, as in others where the plan of granting was once profusely carried into effect, the cheapest land has been as cheap since, as it was before the imposition of a price on new land; and in each of these colonies, a price on new land, however high it might be, would remain inoperative for ages to come. In such colonies, the mere putting of a price on new land only operates as a restriction on the use of newly-discovered spots highly favourable for settlement, and as a tax upon colonization; the very last sort of tax that a colonizing government would think of imposing.

How a price on new land might be rendered beneficially operative in colonies where the quantity of private land is already excessive, is a point to be considered presently. Here I would remark, that there are but three places in which the price of new land has had the least chance of operating beneficially. These are South Australia, Australia Felix, and New Zealand. In none of these cases did the plan of granting with profusion precede that of selling; but in none of them did the price required prevent the cheapest land from being cheap enough to inflict on the colony all the evils of an extreme scarcity of labour for hire. In these cases, moreover, a large portion of the purchase-money of waste land was expended in conveying labourers from the mother-country to the colony. If this money had not been so spent, the proportion of land to people would have been very much greater than it was, and the price of new land still more completely inoperative.

More facts might be cited to show the insufficiency of the highest price yet required for new land; but I proceed to the supposed case, which I think serves to illustrate this subject better than the small stock of not very conclusive facts, which are furnished by the brief and bungling trial in practice of the plan of imposing a price on waste land with a view to the greatest productiveness of colonial industry. Suppose, then, that Liebig should discover a process by which the water of the sea might be converted into fertile land, at a cost of, let us say forty shillings an acre. Suppose, further, that the state did not monopolize the exercise of this art, but allowed a free trade in it. Immense capitals would be invested in this trade. The quantity of sea converted into land would be as much as there was a prospect of being able to sell for the cost of production and a profit besides. A remunerating price would not exceed fifty shillings an acre; that is, forty to cover outlay, and ten for profit. At this price, fertile land might be obtained in unlimited quantities. In this country, including the new territory, the price of the cheapest land would not exceed fifty shillings an acre. Population might increase as fast as it could, but the price of the cheapest land would not rise. Some of the cheapest would become dear, and even the dearest, in consequence of competition for it when the progress of settlement had conferred on it certain advantages of position: but there would always be plenty of land on sale at the price of fifty shillings. Call on your imagination to conceive what would happen. Is it

not clear that pauperism, as that arises f
abundance of people in proportion to ⌐
entirely disappear? The demand for labour ⌐
cultivation of the new land would draw away all
superfluous hands from the old parts of the country;
and we should be no more troubled with pauperism
in England than they are in colonies. Wages in
England would be as high as in America. But these
blessings would be accompanied, or rather succeeded,
by a set of curses. The passion for owning land,
which belongs to human nature, which is latent when
there is no opportunity of gratifying it, but surely
breaks out in the majority of people whenever it can
be easily gratified, would become as active here as it
is in America and other colonial parts of the world:
for with a colonial rate of wages, and with fertile land
always on sale at the price of fifty shillings an acre,
every man who desired it might easily gratify the
longing to become a landowner. The utmost effect
of such a price as fifty shillings an acre, would be to
compel the labourer to work for wages a little longer
than if he could get land for nothing. But this
would not prevent a scarcity of labour for hire nearly
as great as that which takes place in America. It
follows that not instantly, but very soon after getting
rid of pauperism, and seeing our labouring classes as
well off as those classes are in America, we should
begin to complain of scarcity of labour for hire. How
quickly and perfectly we should find out the value of
combination and constancy of labour! In a little
while, how glad we should be to divert the stream of
poor Irish emigration from America to England: that
is, provided the Irish, being able to get new land for

fifty shillings an acre close at home, would come to England as aliens and natural slaves; which they would not. We should, ere long, I suspect, unless our climate were an objection to it, begin to hanker after negro slavery. We should certainly, in order to get large public works performed at all, keep our own convicts at home. We should be, as it were, colonists, continually suffering all sorts of inconvenience and discomfort from the scarcity of labour for hire. But we should find out quickly enough, in the case supposed, that scarcity of labour for hire is caused by cheapness of land. With the exception of the small proportion of the people who in the case supposed would be labourers for hire, every man would be palpably interested in making land dearer: even the labourers would have the same interest, though it would be a little more remote, and therefore, perhaps, much less obvious. In all probability, therefore, we should pass a law for making land dearer. This would be the easiest thing in the world to do. It would be done by putting a price upon new land over and above the cost of production. This price would be a mere tax, a useless, and therefore hurtful impediment to the acquisition of new land, unless, along with the cost of production, it were high enough for its only legitimate purpose. In the colonies, there is no cost of production. There, the whole good effect must be produced by a price imposed by government, or not produced at all. The supposed case, as I have stated it, must contain some grave errors of reasoning, if fifty shillings would be a sufficient price to require for new land in the colonies.

LETTER XLVIII.

From the Statesman.

MR. MOTHERCOUNTRY TAUNTS THE COLONIST WITH
BEING UNABLE TO SAY WHAT WOULD BE THE SUF-
FICIENT PRICE FOR NEW LAND.

I AM beginning to understand your plan of colonization as respects the disposal of land; but a
difficulty has been suggested to me by my Mr. Mother-
country, which I hasten to communicate to you. He
says, that though you have been preaching for years
about the sufficient price, you have never ventured to
say what it ought to be. He says, that you have been
frequently asked to mention what you deem the sufficient price, but that you have carefully avoided
answering the question. He says that you fight shy
of the question; that it puzzles you; that in truth you
know not how to answer it; and that your silence
on this point shows (I beg your pardon for even communicating the offensive inference), that you know
your theory to be impracticable: for, he adds, what
becomes of all the fine arguments for a sufficient
price, if nobody, not even the author of the theory,
can tell us what is the sufficient price? He referred
me to an article in the *Edinburgh Review* for July,

1840, for proof that your theory is wanting in the scientific precision which you attribute to it.

I dare say you have heard all this before; but even so, the repetition of it now will recal the subject to your mind at the fittest stage of our inquiry: for, obviously, our next step is to determine the sufficient price. I am curious to see how you will reply to Mr. Mothercountry's *argumentum ad hominem.*

LETTER XLIX.

From the Colonist.

THE COLONIST REPLIES TO MR. MOTHERCOUNTRY'S TAUNT, INDICATES THE ELEMENTS OF A CALCULATION FOR GETTING AT THE SUFFICIENT PRICE, AND REFERS TO MR. STEPHEN AND THE EDINBURGH REVIEW.

IT is quite true that I have been frequently and tauntingly required to mention what I deem the sufficient price. But I have hitherto avoided falling into the trap, which that demand upon me really is. I might have named a price, and stuck to it without giving reasons: in other words, I might have practised a Colonial-Office "shift" by "deciding categorically, so as not to expose the superficiality in propounding the reasons": or I might have named a price, and attempted to justify the decision by reasons: but in the one case, your Mr. Mothercountry would have been entitled to call me a charlatan, and in the other a goose. For there is no price that would be suitable for the colonies generally : the price must needs vary according to peculiar natural and other circumstances in each colony: and in order to determine the price for any colony, practical proceedings of a tentative or experimental nature are indispensable. If so, what a mess I should have got into, had I responded to the taunting call of Mr. Mothercountry and his allies!

That it is so becomes very plain, when one considers what are the elements of a calculation made with a view of determining the sufficient price for any colony. There is but one object of a price; and about that there can be no mistake. The sole object of a price is to prevent labourers from turning into landowners too soon: the price must be sufficient for that one purpose and no other. The question is, what price would have that one effect? That must depend, first, on what is meant by " too soon"; or on the proper duration of the term of the labourer's employment for hire; which again must depend on the rate of the increase of population in the colony, especially by means of immigration, which would determine when the place of a labourer, turning into a landowner, would be filled by another labourer: and the rate of labour-emigration again must depend on the popularity of the colony at home, and on the distance between the mother-country and the colony, or the cost of passage for labouring people. Secondly, what price would have the desired effect, must depend on the rate of wages and cost of living in the colony; since according to these would be the labourer's power of saving the requisite capital for turning into a landowner: in proportion to the rate of wages and the cost of living, would the requisite capital be saved in a longer or a shorter time. It depends, thirdly, on the soil and climate of the colony, which would determine the quantity of land required (on the average) by a labourer in order to set himself up as a landowner: if the soil and climate were unfavourable to production, he would require more acres; if it were favourable, fewer acres would serve his purpose: in Trinidad, for example, 10 acres would support him well; in South Africa or New South Wales, he might require 50 or 100 acres. But the variability in our wide colonial empire, not only of soil and climate, but of all the circumstances on which a sufficient price would depend, is so obvious, that no examples of it are needed. It follows of course that different colonies, and sometimes different groups of similar colonies, would require different prices. To name a price for all the colonies, would be as absurd as to fix the size of a coat for mankind.

" But at least," I hear your Mr. Mothercountry say, "name a price for some particular colony; a price founded on the elements of calculation which you have stated." I could do that certainly for some colony with which I happen to be particularly well acquainted; but I should do it doubtingly and with hesitation: for in truth the elements of calculation are so many and so complicated in their various relations to each other, that in depending on them exclusively there would be the utmost liability to error. A very complete and familiar knowledge of them in each case would be a useful general guide, would throw valuable light on the question, would serve to inform the legislator how far his theory and his practice were consistent or otherwise: but in the main he must rely, and if he had common sagacity he might solely and safely rely, upon no very elaborate calculation, but on experience, or the facts before his face. He could always tell whether or not labour for hire was too scarce or too plentiful in the colony. If it were too plentiful, he would know that the price of new land was too high; that is, more than sufficient: if it were hurtfully scarce, he would know that the price was too low, or not sufficient. About which the labour was—whether too plentiful or too scarce—no legislature, hardly any individual, could be in doubt; so plain to the dullest eye would be the facts by which to determine that question. If the lawgiver saw that the labour was scarce and the price too low, he would raise the price: if he saw that labour was superabundant and the price too high, he would lower the price: if he saw that labour was neither scarce nor superabundant, he would not alter the price, because he would see that it was neither too high nor too low, but sufficient. Recurring to the supposed discovery of Liebig, the legislature of this country would always be able to judge whether new land was supplied too fast, or not fast enough, or at the rate of a happy medium between excess and deficiency. The evidence on which the legislature would form its judgment, would be all the facts which show whether labour is scarce, or superabundant, or neither one nor the other. Whether here or in a colony, these facts are so very manifest, and so unerring as indications, that a wrong conclusion from them would be hardly possible. Only, of course, I am supposing that the legislature of the colony would possess an intimate knowledge of the colony, and would be deeply interested in coming to à right judgment: a Downing-street legislature judging for the distant colonies, or a distant colonial legislature judging for us, would indeed, notwithstanding the patent nature of the guiding facts, be apt to make terrible mistakes.

The raising or lowering of the price according to the evidence of a necessity for either step, is what I called just now a tentative or experimental proceeding. In either case, the legislature would have to wait and see whether the alteration produced the desired effect. But there is an objection to lowering the price, which makes it desirable, that the legislature, in trying its experiments, should begin with a price obviously too low, and should raise the price by careful degrees so as to run little risk of ever making it too high. The objection to ever lowering the price is, that whenever this was done, some of those who had purchased at the higher price, would complain that they had been made to pay more than their successors, and more than was necessary. It would be by no means certain that they really had paid more than was necessary at the time of their purchase: for the circumstances of the colony at that time might have required that price, for the greatest good of those purchasers as well as of the whole colony. Nor, if new circumstances required a lower price—such a circumstance, for example, as a great spontaneous and unexpected immigration of labour into the colony, which suddenly and greatly increased the proportion of people to appropriated land—would these earlier purchasers at the higher price suffer any injustice from a lowering of the price. They might suffer hardship, but no injustice. If the higher price had been

kept up so long after it became too high, as to confer
on land the monopoly value which arises from scarcity,
then, when the price of new land was lowered, the
general value of appropriated land would decline;
and the amount of its fall would be so much loss
to all landowners. This would be a hardship: but,
for two reasons, it would not be an injustice. All
landowners would have purchased with a full knowledge of the wish and intention of the legislature to
lower the price whenever population should be superabundant, or if, after a trial, it should appear too high:
nobody would have been deceived or misled: and
secondly, the monopoly value of land which had been
created by keeping up too high a price, though a
benefit to the landowner, would be a benefit, which as
accruing to him against the will of the legislature
and contrary to his own expectations when he purchased, and as being a wrong to the community
at large, ought justly to be taken from him as soon
as possible.   Injustice, therefore, there would be
none in lowering the price.   I have said, that the
scarcity-value conferred on land by too high a
price, would be a benefit to the landowner; but this
was only said for argument's sake: for in truth, a
colony in which appropriated land was kept at a scarcity value, would be a most unpopular colony in the
mother-country; and its landowners would miss the
benefits enjoyed by the landowners of a colony into
which there pours a constant stream of capital as well
as people.   The landowners, in the supposed case,
would obtain a scarcity-value for their land, similar to
that which takes place in Tipperary; but they would
miss a position-value, so to speak, like that which

occurs in Lancashire : they would lose more than they would gain. Upon the whole, therefore, it appears to me, that purchasers at a higher price would suffer neither injustice nor hardship by a lowering of the price when this step became expedient for the good of the whole colony.   But in consideration of our proneness to be jealous and envious of our neighbours, I would guard, if possible, against even the appearance of giving an advantage to the later purchaser.   I think, therefore, that the colonizing legislature ought to begin with a price clearly too low, and to raise the price by degrees with a cautious but resolute hand.

If your Mr. Mothercountry should say that a system which requires, in at least one of its processes, the exercise of much caution and resolution, is not a self-adjusting system, but one liable to be deranged by human infirmity, and therefore one not to be relied upon, I would answer, nobody has ever attributed to it that magical property of being able to work itself without legislative or administrative care, which its official opponents, in order to decry it, have represented that its advocates claimed for it.   The article in the *Edinburgh Review* was written by a gentleman, then a clerk in the Colonial Office, and a friend of Mr. Stephen's, the permanent Under-Secretary.   Mr. Stephen's influence with that eminent journal has been used to prevent the circulation of favourable views of the theory, as well as to circulate hostile views.   Two habitual contributors to the *Review* offered to its editor, the late Professor Napier, at different times, and without each other's knowledge or mine, two articles, of which the object was to explain and recommend the theory; but he declined to insert either, on the ground, in the one case, of having pledged the *Review* to the opinions of Mr. Stephen's friend; and, in the other, of his unwillingness to displease Mr. Stephen. To save trouble, in case you should mention this to your Mr. Mother-country, I add that though Professor Napier is no more, the two gentlemen in question are alive, and in full recollection of the facts.

Thus, you see, the whining of colonial Downing-street, about being debarred from communication with the public, is not founded in fact. No other public department has better, nay equal, means of using the anonymous press for defence and attack. I almost wish now, that this peculiarity of the Colonial Office had been described under the head of government.

LETTER L.

From the Colonist.

SELLING WASTE LAND BY AUCTION WITH A VIEW TO OBTAINING THE SUFFICIENT PRICE BY MEANS OF COMPETITION, IS EITHER A FOOLISH CONCEIT OR A FALSE PRETENCE.

IT has been imagined that the sufficient price might be obtained by means of competition, if new land were offered for sale by auction at a low upset price. I am at a loss to conceive how this notion could be entertained by a reasonable mind. If the quantity of land were practically unlimited, there would be no competition, except for spots possessing some advantage of position; and spots of land for which there

would be competition, are just those for which the
poorest class of buyers, or the labourers, would not
bid: they would buy only that land for which there
was no competition, and which, therefore, they would
obtain at the upset price. It follows, that unless the
quantity of land offered for sale were limited, it would
be necessary, under a system of sales by auction, to
make the upset price a sufficient price: the necessity
of determining a sufficient price would be just the
same as if the land were sold at a fixed uniform price
without auction. Unquestionably, if the quantity of
land offered for sale were sufficiently limited, there
would be competition for all new land; and the lowest
price obtained would exceed the upset price in proportion to the degree of limitation. But in order to
obtain this result, the government must needs determine what degree of limitation would produce enough
competition to make the lowest selling price a sufficient price. The sufficient price would still be determined by the government, but by means of a sufficient limitation of the quantity offered for sale. By
limiting the quantity, as has been shown before, the
government might determine the price of the cheapest
land in the colony, without putting any price on new
land, or under the plan of granting. The government, that is, might do this provided limitation of
quantity were practically susceptible of being made a
regulator of price. But practically, as has been explained before, limitation of quantity could not be
used by the government as an efficient regulator of
price; and again, if it were so used, its operation
would be wholly independent of selling by auction,
since if there were no auction, but the land given for

nothing, the lowest price of land in the colony would be sufficient if the limitation of the quantity of granted land were sufficient. Selling by auction, indeed, may serve other purposes than that of determining the sufficient price by means of competition; but when employed for this purpose, which it cannot serve, it is a self-delusion or a cheat; a fancied means of doing what it cannot do, or a make-believe of doing what is not done. In the United States, they sell by auction; but the quantity offered for sale being practically unlimited, the upset price is the usual selling price. In our colonies, very great prices have been obtained by means of selling at auction certain spots, which were supposed likely to enjoy, ere long, great advantages of position: but the obtaining of these great prices for some land had not the slightest effect on the lowest price of land in the colony: that did not exceed the lowest price at which land could be obtained at the auction sales; namely, the upset price. I must not omit, however, to mention that one or two cases have happened in which the lowest price obtained by auction considerably exceeded the upset price. The result was brought about by offering for sale less land than was wanted by buyers at that time and place: some competition for all the land was really produced, but solely by means of limiting the quantity offered for sale. In these cases, however, great evils arose from the attempt of the government to determine prices by limitation of quantity. The accidental or arbitrary limitation was not, and could not have been, continued; and when a less limitation took place—when more land was afterwards offered for sale than was wanted by intending buyers at the time and place—the lowest price of land fell; and the buyers at the first sales discovered that the government had induced them to pay a price higher than that which others now paid, or for which they could now sell their land. These cases, in which auction did produce competition for all the land put up to sale, exemplify the inadequacy and unsuitableness of competition produced by limitation of quantity as a means of getting at the sufficient price. The experience furnished by the United States and our colonies, agrees with the reasoning which shows, that selling by auction for the alleged purpose of obtaining the sufficient price, is either a foolish conceit or a false pretence.

By looking to the papers that your Mr. Mothercountry sent to you at an early stage of our correspondence, with the passages marked which exhibit colonial hostility to what he called *my* " scheme," you will find that the colonists, especially in New South Wales, bitterly complain of the plan of selling public land by auction. Their objections to it are identical with mine, as you will see by my next letter.

LETTER LI.

From the Colonist.

FURTHER OBJECTIONS TO THE PLAN OF SELLING WASTE
LAND BY AUCTION.——ADVANTAGES OF A FIXED UNI-
FORM PRICE.

THERE are seven other and very grave objections
to the plan of selling by auction.

1. Auction fails altogether in its object unless, by
means of competition, it produces for some land a
higher price than the upset price. Supposing the
upset price to be a sufficient price as regards scarcity
of labour, then all that auction produces above that
price, is so much capital unnecessarily taken from the
settlers. If, by means of the upset price, care is taken
that nobody obtains land for less than the sufficient
price, then all excess above that price is a useless and
mischievous tax on colonization. More than the sufficient price, the government never ought to obtain by
any means. When, further, the government does obtain by means of competition at auction more than
the sufficient price, the excess is the profit on his investment which the settler would have made if he had
bought at the upset price: and the government, instead of letting this profit go into the pocket of the

settler sooner or later after the sale, puts it into its own pocket at the time of the sale. Now, one of the greatest encouragements of colonization is the prospect which the settler has of making a profit by his investment in the purchase of land. First, then, by unnecessarily diminishing the capital of the settler even before he begins to settle, and, secondly, by depriving him of the prospect of enjoying himself the benefit of future competition for his land, the government, when it effectually sells by auction, very effectually discourages the emigration of capitalists and impedes the progress of colonization.

2. In order that auction should be effectual, time must be given for the growth of competition : a sale by auction, whether in this country or in a colony, would be absurd without ample notice by advertisement. Intending purchasers, therefore, must wait some time for the announced day ·of sale. But for settlers, and especially for new emigrants, all waiting is full of mischief, being the parent of idleness, inertness, and despondency; often of hard-drinking, to drown the care of suspense and hope delayed. No tongue can tell what injury this waiting for a sale by auction has inflicted on settlers in our newest colonies.

3. As well before as after the government has declared its intention of laying a district open to purchase, intending purchasers take great pains, and incur no little trouble and cost, in selecting the spots of land, which, for some reason or other, generally on account of their peculiar suitableness to the settlers' purpose, they prefer to other spots. When the sale takes place, therefore, many an intending purchaser is bent on obtaining a particular lot or lots. This at

least would always happen if the land were not sold by auction. For when it is sold by auction, the intending purchaser of a particular lot is apt to be outbid beyond his means. When this happens (and nothing is more common), the settler does not realize his choice at all: the time, and exertion, and money which he has spent on selection, are thrown away: and he has to repeat the process, with very likely the same result over again. At last, perhaps, the settler is deprived of all freedom of choice, being compelled to take land which he does not prefer, or to which he has strong objections. I suspect that this occurs in even a majority of cases. How the probability, or only the risk of it, must discourage the attendance of intending purchasers at auction sales, is sufficiently obvious.

4. In his anxiety to obtain the land on which his heart is set, the settler is apt to bid beyond his means; and when the lot is knocked down to him, he is incapable of using it. The impoverishment of the settler by means of obtaining the lot which he has selected, is a common occurrence: the utter ruin of settlers by this means is not very uncommon.

5. Under the auction plan, the honest industrious settler is liable to be plundered by jobbing and roguery of various sorts. The official surveyors, by means of information obtained whilst they were making the survey, have it in their power to job; and under our system of colonial government, official surveyors are capable of jobbing in the very souls of their parents and children. Officials of all sorts who can obtain from the surveyors' reports superior information as to the varying qualities of the land, can job if they please, and do job most wofully. The speculating capitalist can job, by means

of his command of money. The *bonâ fide* settler, the man ready and anxious to lay out his money in land and improvements upon it, has to buy off these harpies. Often, when his means are insufficient for that purpose, they sell him the land on credit at an exorbitant price, and ruin him by means of the heavy interest. In America, the inherent evils of mere jobbing at the auction sales are moderated by an occasional administration of Lynch law: a speculator who attends the sale for the mere purpose of harassing and so robbing the good settler, runs some risk of being shot; besides, in America, where the great quantity of land always offered for sale prevents competition save for peculiarly eligible spots, the inherent evils of jobbing at auction sales are less than in our colonies. There, the quantity having been generally limited with an express view to competition, and the auction plan not having lasted long enough to suggest the employment of Lynch law, mere jobbing in public land at the auction sales has been a cruel oppression of the settler class.

6. Competition at auction-sales gives rise to unneighbourly and vindictive feelings among the settlers. The man who is partially ruined by a neighbour's running him up at a sale, never forgets the injury, and his children inherit the rancour so occasioned. The auction sales in our colonies have produced a large stock of envious and revengeful passions in many a neighbourhood, where, colonization being the business of the people, feelings of kindness and a disposition to help one's neighbour would be sedulously encouraged by a really colonizing government.

7. And lastly, the plan of auction is very unpopular in the colonies, excepting of course amongst the harpy

class, who by means of it prey on the class of true colonists. To the class of true colonists it is invariably and grievously hurtful. They continually and loudly complain of it; and the maintenance of it in spite of their complaints is a most offensive and tyrannical exercise of the despotic authority by which our colonies are governed.

Continually for years, these reasons against auction have been pressed on the notice of the Colonial Office, and especially of the present Colonial Minister, but without the least effect; or rather, I should say, with only a bad effect. For Lord Grey, who is the parent of the auction nuisance in our colonies, loves it as a mother does her rickety child, all the more when its deformities are pointed out. His affection for it has at length become so strong, that arguments against it put him into a rage; and to all such arguments he virtually replies, never by counter-arguments, if any such there are, but by expressions of sulky obstinacy which remind one of the American help's answer to the bell—" the more you ring, the more I won't come." And such things can be, because, unavoidably, there is no public in this country that cares about the colonies.

The mode of selling to which auction has been preferred, is that of allowing settlers to take land at pleasure on paying a fixed uniform price, which should of course be the sufficient price. The price being sufficient, fixed, and uniform, the settler would pay to the government the purchase money of as many acres as he wanted, and would take the land without further ado. He would pay the sufficient price, but no more. He would retain for use the whole of his capital, except the indispensable price of his land. Whatever increased value future competition might put upon his land, would belong to him. Land-buying—in other words emigration and settlement—would thus be greatly promoted. The settler would not be kept waiting an hour for anything, after having chosen the spot of land he would best like to acquire. He would realize his own choice, without being injured or harassed, or even frightened by jobbing speculators. Nothing would happen to disturb his kindly feelings towards his neighbour; and he would not, for anything in the mode of selling public land, hate his government. The plan of a fixed and uniform price, is free from all the objections to auction.

You will ask how, with a fixed and uniform price, competition between two or more settlers for the same piece of land, would be determined. By letting first come be first served. The man who first paid his purchase-money into the land-office and designated the spot of his choice, would get that spot, though a hundred men should afterwards apply for it. The hundred would be told that it was already sold. But two or more men might apply for the same spot at the same time: yes, possibly in the abstract, but really almost never, if, as clearly ought to be the case, the quantity of land always open to purchasers were so ample as to be practically unlimited. Now and then, however, such a thing might happen as two or more men entering the land-office at the same moment and applying for the same spot. On the occurrence of this rare event, the competition would be determined by letting the applicants draw lots for the preference. This mode of determining the competition is so simple and so perfectly fair, that nobody could mistake its operation, or feel that it had done him the least injustice. But there are objectors, official advocates of auction, with Lord Grey at their head, who say that drawing lots for the preference would be a lottery, and would promote a spirit of gambling amongst purchasers. The reply is, first, that the occasion for drawing lots would scarcely ever happen; secondly, that even if it happened frequently, it would not operate like a lottery, because the necessity of having recourse to it would occur accidentally, without design on the part of the competitors, and the competition would not last five minutes; thirdly, that if a gambling spirit were promoted by the frequent drawing of lots among competitors for the same piece of land at the same moment, the evil would be incalculably less than that of all the villanies and cruelties of the auction, which is the only possible alternative of the fixed price. But in practice, I repeat, the drawing of lots would hardly ever occur; and when it did, it would be wanting in those properties of a lottery which cultivate the gambling spirit. The lottery argument against a fixed price is of that class, which Single-speech Hamilton advises us to employ when we want to give an odious appearance to the proposal of our adversary.

I must point out, however, that although, as a rule, two people would hardly ever apply for the same bit of land at the same moment, exceptional occasions do arise in which the drawing of lots does partake in some measure of the gambling character of a lottery. This happens when a considerable number of people are about to emigrate for the purpose of planting a new settlement, and when they pay here a fixed price

per acre for land that they have not seen.   They pay
not for land, but for a right to take land when they
reach the colony.   In the exercise of this right, it
would be impossible to adopt the principle of first
come first served; because all the purchasers have
already come; they are all present together; and
every one of them wishes to have first choice in the
selection of land.   An order of choice, therefore, must
be determined somehow.   For the right to choose
pieces of land, out of a quantity which the purchaser
has not yet seen, experience has proved, as a moment's
reflection would suggest, that people cannot be induced to bid against each other at auction: either
they will not buy at all, or they will only pay a price
not exceeding what they believe will be the value of
the least valuable spot of the land to be hereafter distributed amongst them.   This must necessarily be a
known, fixed, and uniform price.   When they have
paid this price, the question arises, who is to choose
first, who second, and so on?   If anybody knows how
this question can be determined with perfect fairness
to all parties, except by letting the purchasers draw
lots for priority of choice, he has discovered what has
escaped the earnest research of many ingenious minds.
According to our present knowledge, we must either
use this method of determining priority of choice, or
we must renounce the practice—a practice which has
founded South Australia and four Settlements in New
Zealand—of founding settlements by means of selling
land in this country to the first body of intending
colonists.   That in such case the drawing of lots is a
kind of lottery, is obvious; but it is a lottery without
blanks, however high the prizes may be; and finally,

so far as there is evil in it, it is like many other cases in which priorities are determined by lot, or, like most of the steps which man takes with a view to good results, an imperfect means of doing what could not be done with as little admixture of evil, or perhaps at all, by any other means. This, I suppose is the view of the subject taken by the Archbishop of Canterbury, who, as president of the new Association for founding a settlement in New Zealand, has given his high moral sanction to the plan of drawing lots in cases of necessity.

LETTER LII.

From the Colonist.

LORD GREY'S CONFUSION OF IDEAS RESPECTING THE OBJECTS WITH WHICH A PRICE SHOULD BE REQUIRED FOR NEW LAND.—ANOTHER OBJECTION TO A UNIFORM PRICE FOR WASTE LAND, WITH THE COLONIST'S ANSWER TO IT.

THE uniformity of a fixed price has been objected to, on several grounds.

First, says Lord Grey, as land is of different qualities with respect to fertility and the probability of future advantages of position, it ought to fetch different prices. Why " ought"? The only reason given is the "woman's reason"—" Because it ought." What does " ought" mean in this case? Do we owe any duty to the land, that commands us to make it fetch different prices because it varies in quality? Is there any person to whom we owe this duty? Verily, if we were selling land in this country—either our own land for ourselves, or somebody else's land for him, or crown land for the public—we should be bound to obtain the highest possible price, and of course to require a higher price for the more valuable portions. But that is because in this country, all the land being appropriated, the sole object in selling always is to get the highest price: whereas in a colony, under the circumstances in question, the object would be only to get the sufficient price; and it would be an important object to avoid taking more than that out of any buyer's pocket. Confusion of ideas is at the bottom of all these notions about the expediency of auction, or some other way of getting a price for colonial waste land in proportion to its present or probable value. The totally different circumstances of the colony and the old country—the totally different objects with which landed property is sold here and would be sold there—are so confounded in Lord Grey's mind, that he unconsciously applies old-country rules to the colonial question. His "ought" really means that selling land for its market value is the only mode of selling land, as respects both objects and means, to which his mind is accustomed, and which he is able to comprehend. With equal truth, a predecessor of his might have written to the Governor of Upper Canada, " I send you water casks for the fleet on Ontario, because my familiar ideas on the subjects of fleets and water assure me that all water which bears a fleet must be salt." On further reflection, it is rather to ignorance about the colonies—to the absence of colonial ideas at the Colonial Office—than to official confusion of colonial and old-country ideas, that such unhappy mistakes would be most justly attributed.

The second objection to a uniform price is, that if the price were sufficient, land of very inferior quality, as respects either fertility or position, would not be bought at all. Certainly it would not be bought if it were so inferior as to be, according to the market value of the cheapest land in the colony, worth less than the sufficient price. But the inferiority of position would not last long. The progress of settlement around and beyond such neglected spots, would soon confer advantages of position upon them. Roads would be made near or through them. Population and the average value of land would increase around them. In time, unless they were so sterile by nature as to be what we term here land not worth reclaiming, new facilities of improving them—of conveying all sorts of things between them and the town—and the increased value of all land in their neighbourhood, would make them worth the sufficient price; and then they would be bought. Meanwhile, they would be used for pasturage : for, as I shall explain presently, it is contrary to the principle of a sufficient price for freehold land, to put any price upon the use of land for pasturage only. But if these spots were so sterile and so out of the way, like the barren tops of mountains, as not to be worth cultivating under any circumstances, they would never be sold, but always used, if fit even for that, as runs for cattle and sheep during the time of year when some grass will grow almost everywhere except on bare rock. If they were not even fit for that, they would never be used at all. And what then? Why, these barren, out-of-the-way spots would only resemble similar spots in old countries, which nature has condemned to uselessness for ages. To perpetual uselessness, nature has probably not condemned a morsel of the earth's surface. But now, observe that the time at which land of inferior fertility and position increased in value, would come very much sooner, and the degree of increased value for the worst of such land would be much greater, under a plan of colonization which made labour plentiful, than under the usual scarcity of labour. Roads would come sooner and be more numerous; the cost of reclaiming waste land would be less, not in consequence of lower wages (for wages might be higher with than without the more productive employment of labour), but in consequence of the greater power of combined and constant labour; and the proportion of non-agricultural classes to the agricultural class— or, in other words, the number of local customers for the sellers of landed produce — would be very much greater than it is now in any colony. Upon the whole, then, it seems probable that if no land could be got for less than the sufficient price, inferior land would become worth that price sooner than, with scarcity of labour, it becomes worth cultivating at all. If so, this objection to a uniform price is converted into a recommendation: and if not, it is still not a valid objection to the uniform price as part of a system, except on the unreasonable supposition that inferior land would probably be cultivated sooner under a system which makes the cheapest land worth at market hardly anything, than under one which would make all appropriated land worth at least the sufficient price.

LETTER LIII.

From the Colonist.

SOME probable effects of the sufficient price must be briefly noticed, before I come to two of them which demand particular explanation.

At first sight, it appears that wages would be lower and profits higher than when land was superabundant and labour scarce, because, of the whole produce of capital and labour, the capitalist would pay less to the labourer and keep more for himself: a greater competition for employment amongst the labourers, no longer able to acquire land with great facility, would bring down wages and raise profits. And this would really happen if the productiveness of industry remained unaltered. But, really, inasmuch as the productiveness of industry would be increased (to what extent one cannot tell, because what the energetic and intelligent, as well as combined and constant labour of freemen can do with the virgin soils of a new country has never yet been tried); inasmuch as the produce to be divided between the capitalist and the labourer would be greater, both parties might obtain more than when that produce was less. At all events, there would be far more to divide. If the competition of labourers for employment enabled the capitalist to keep the whole increase for himself, the labourers would be dissatisfied, and the colony would become unpopular with the labouring class at home; when it would be seen that the competition of labourers in this colony was too great, and the price of new land more than sufficient. The produce being greater, it would always be for the advantage of capitalists and the whole colony, that such a share of the increase should go to the labourer, as would keep the colony popular with the labouring class at home; and this would always be secured, by taking care that the competition of labourers for employment was never too great; in other words, that the price of new land was never more than sufficient.

The produce of industry being greater in consequence of the new facilities for combining labour, dividing employments, and carrying on works which require long time for their completion, everybody in the colony would be richer: and the colony being able to export and import more, would be a better customer of the mother-country.

Nevertheless, I suppose you to ask, although the sufficient price prevented labourers from too soon turning into landowners, how would enough labourers be obtained? The sufficient price does not provide for immigration of labour. If the colony could depend for labour upon nothing but the increase of people by births on the spot, it would be requisite to make the sufficient price of land high enough to keep wages down to an old-country rate, and to prevent most labourers from ever becoming landowners. A colony so near to England as Canada, might obtain labourers by the immigration of poor people at their own cost; but what would become of the more distant colonies, South Africa, the four Australias, Tasmania, and New Zealand? In the latter places, the colonization, or gradual settlement of the waste, would be of a good sort, but would be extremely slow. The sufficient price alone, provides only for civilized, not for rapid colonization.

I answer, that the sufficient price, by itself, would provide for a more rapid colonization than has ever been seen in the world. So bold an assertion requires careful proof. This rapidity of colonization in consequence of the sufficient price is the first of those effects of the sufficient price which demand particular explanation. I must, however, reserve it for another letter.

LETTER LIV.

From the Colonist.

WITH A SUFFICIENT PRICE FOR WASTE LAND, CAPI-
TALISTS WOULD OBTAIN LABOUR BY MEANS OF
PAYING FOR THE EMIGRATION OF POOR PEOPLE.

THE price being sufficient to prevent labourers
from turning into landowners too soon, it
would now be worth the while of capitalists to procure labour from the mother-country at their own cost;
it would "pay" emigrating capitalists to take out
labourers along with them. And why? Because,
now, all labourers being under the necessity of remaining labourers for some years, it would be possible,
and not difficult, for capitalists to enforce contracts
for labour made in the mother-country. Referring
to a former letter, the temptation of the labourer to
quit the employer who had brought him to the colony,
would be no longer irresistible. With the very high
rate of wages that the importing employer of labour
could afford to pay, provided he could keep the labour
he imported, the cost of the labourer's passage would
be, as the saying is, a mere flea-bite; an entity hardly
worth taking into the calculation of his outgoings and
incomings. The difference between the wages that

the importing and the non-importing capitalist could afford to pay, would be so slight as to be without practical effect. The importing capitalist would be able, without feeling it, to pay the same wages as the non-importing capitalist, and would be better able to keep the labourers he imported, by treating them with kindness and consideration for their human pride as well as their physical wants, than the other would be to entice them away by the promise of such treatment. In most cases, therefore, the non-importing capitalist would become an importing one: when it had become easy to keep imported labour, the motives for importing labour, instead of enticing it away from one's neighbour who had imported it, would be strong enough, in the great majority of instances, to abolish the temptation to this kind of robbery: and if some would-be robbers remained, they would be prevented by the frowns of society from doing so great a wrong to their neighbour for so small a gain to themselves. Upon the whole, therefore, I think that the inducements to the importation of labour by capitalists would be as great as they are in Brazil and Cuba; perhaps greater, if we consider the superiority of free to slave labour, as respects the power of production. At the least, there would be a great deal of inducement of the same kind, in regard to the paying by capitalists for the passage of labourers, as that which, if no impediments were put in the way of its operations, would probably, land continuing dirt cheap and labour for hire almost unknown in America, convey a million of negro slaves from Africa to America in the course of every year. If free imported labour could be kept in our colonies, I can see no limit to the

probable amount of labour-emigration by means of
the payment of the labourer's passage by his future
employer. For the importers of labour, in the case
supposed, would be not only capitalists within the
colony, but capitalists emigrating to the colony, who,
feeling that they should be able to enforce in the
colony a contract for labour made at home, would
take along with them the labour which they expected
to require, and would send for more if more should
be required: and assuredly, the economical attraction of being able to keep labour for hire in the colonies, would (provided always the political evils were
removed) lead to an emigration of capitalists and
capital, to the extent of which it would be difficult to
assign a probable limit. If labourers and capitalists
poured into the colony at the rate which seems
probable under the circumstances supposed, colonization would be very rapid as well as good in kind, or
civilized: and the sole cause of the whole improvement would be the sufficient price.

LETTER LV.

From the Colonist.

THE SUFFICIENT PRICE PRODUCES MONEY INCIDENTALLY. —WHAT SHOULD BE DONE WITH THE PURCHASE-MONEY OF NEW LAND?—SEVERAL EFFECTS OF USING THE PURCHASE-MONEY AS A FUND FOR DEFRAYING THE COST OF EMIGRATION.

I PROCEED to the second effect of the sufficient price, which requires particular explanation.

The sufficient price would bring money into the colonial exchequer. If it were in full operation throughout our colonies, it would produce a vast deal of money; for the sale of waste land in the United States at a price little more than nominal (4s. 7½d. an acre) produces about a million sterling a year, and has produced, in one year of unusual speculation, as much as four millions, or more than the whole annual expenditure of the federal government at that time. The question arises then, what should be done with the money produced by the sufficient price? And in the whole art of colonization, there is no question of more importance.

The putting of money into the colonial exchequer would not have been designed by the government.

The getting of money by the government would be a result of selling land instead of giving it away: but as the only object of selling instead of giving is one totally distinct from that of producing revenue—namely, to prevent labourers from turning into land-owners too soon—the pecuniary result would be un-intended, one might almost say unexpected. So com-pletely is production of revenue a mere incident of the price of land, that the price ought to be imposed, if it ought to be imposed under any circumstances, even though the purchase-money were thrown away. This last proposition is the sharpest test to which the theory of a sufficient price can be submitted; but if it will not stand this test—if the proposition is not true—the theory is false. Assuming it not to be false, the money arising from the sale of land is a fund raised without a purpose, unavoidably, incidentally, almost accidentally. It is a fund, therefore, without a desti-nation. There would be no undertaking, no tacit obligation even, on the part of the government to dispose of the fund in any particular way. It is an unappropriated fund, which the state or government may dispose of as it pleases without injustice to any-body. If the fund were applied to paying off the public debt of the empire, nobody could complain of injustice, because every colony as a whole, and the buyers of land in particular, would still enjoy all the intended and expected benefits of the imposition of a sufficient price upon new land: if the fund were thrown into the sea as it accrued, there would still be no injustice, and no reason against producing the fund in that way.

If this reasoning is correct, the government would

be at liberty to cast about for the most beneficial mode of disposing of the fund. Upon that point, I do not pretend to offer an opinion: but if the object were the utmost possible increase of the population, wealth, and greatness of our empire, then I can have no doubt that the revenue accruing from the sale of waste land, would be called an emigration-fund, and be expended in conveying poor people of the labouring class from the mother-country to the colonies. Let us see what would be the principal effects of that disposition of the purchase-money of waste land.

1. It would no longer be desirable for colonial or emigrating capitalists to lay out money directly in taking labour. to the colony; but they would do so indirectly when, by purchasing land, they contributed to the emigration-fund. They would see, more distinctly than if the purchase-money of land were not an emigration fund, that in paying the sufficient price for land they purchased labour as well as land; they would pay the sufficient price more cheerfully; and the working of the plan of colonization would be better understood, and the plan itself more popular, both in the colonies and in the mother-country: points of great importance with a view to getting into quick and full operation a system so novel, and so much at variance with common ideas about the disposal of waste land in colonies.

2. If the price were sufficient, even though the purchase-money should be thrown away, there would always be in the colony a supply of labour corresponding with the demand; but if the immigration of labour were only spontaneous, the progress of colonization how much soever faster than if new land were too cheap

and the capitalist had no motive for directly importing labour, would be slower than if every purchase
of land *necessarily* brought labour into the colony.
Colonization would be improved both in kind and pace
by imposing the sufficient price; but its pace would be
prodigiously accelerated by using the purchase-money
as an emigration-fund. If the emigration-fund were
judiciously expended, emigrating capitalists would be
allowed to take out with them, free of cost, such
labourers as they might expect to require in the
colony. They would have indeed, when they bought
waste land in the colony, to contribute to the emigration-fund; but as their land would bear a market
value equal at least to what they paid for it, they
would really get the labour for nothing. This, and
the opportunity of selecting the labour here, would
induce many a capitalist to emigrate who might not
otherwise think of doing so. I am speaking now, as
much from experience as from reason, having been
convinced, even by very imperfect and much-impeded
experiments in the founding of South Australia and
New Zealand, that the class of emigrating capitalists
set a high value on the opportunity of engaging
labourers here and taking them out free of cost. In
this way, then, both capitalists and labourers would
go to the colony, in greater numbers than if the purchase-money were not used as an emigration-fund;
but in how much greater numbers, experience telleth
not, and would only tell when the whole system was
in real and full operation after the political impediments to colonization had been removed.

3. But some notion of what would then be the rate
of colonization, may be formed by observing another

effect of turning purchase-money into emigration-fund. Every sale of land would produce a corresponding amount of immigration. Emigrants would pour into the colony at a rate of which there has been no example in the settlement of new countries. Some idea of what that rate would be when the plan was in full operation, may be formed by comparing what took place in South Australia, Australia Felix, and the New-Zealand Company's Settlements, with what has happened when colonies were founded without an emigration-fund. Although in the cases mentioned, the price of land was by no means sufficient, the amount of immigration in proportion to appropriated land was, to speak much within compass, twenty times greater than in any case where spontaneous emigration was alone relied upon for peopling the colony. I should not wonder to see it fifty times greater under the whole plan, not thwarted, but sustained by authority.

4. But whatever might be the amount of emigration caused by using the purchase-money of land as a fund for taking poor people to the colony, it would cause a different proportion between land and people from that which would take place if the purchase-money were any otherwise employed : the proportion of population to appropriated land would be very much greater in the one case than in the other. From this it follows, that the price of waste land, which would be only sufficient if the purchase-money were not used for emigration, would be excessive if it were so used. Suppose that without an emigration-fund, 5*l.* per acre proved the sufficient price; that is, neither too much nor too little. But that means neither too much nor too little for a certain proportion of people

to land, emigration not being promoted by a public
fund. Now apply the emigration-fund. So many
more people go to the colony, that the proportion
of people to land is greatly increased. The price
of 5*l.* was just sufficient for the old proportion: it is
excessive under the new proportion. If under the
old proportion, it just prevented labourers from becoming landowners too soon, under the new one it
would prevent them from doing so soon enough. By
causing an excessive proportion of people to land, it
would bring down wages, do a wrong to the labouring
emigrants, and render the colony unpopular with that
class at home. Then would be seen a necessity for
altering the price; for lowering it from what just
sufficed without an emigration-fund, to what would
just suffice with one. The general conclusion is, that
a less price would be sufficient if the purchase-money
were, than if it were not devoted to emigration.

With an emigration-fund, therefore, the new land
would be cheaper; and the cheaper waste land is in
a colony, provided it is dear enough to prevent a mischievous scarcity of labour, the more are people of all
classes at home induced to select that colony for their
future home. The emigration-fund, besides enabling
poor people to go to the colony, and attracting capitalists by enabling them to take labourers along with
them, would provide for all classes the attraction of
cheaper land than if there were no emigration-fund.
Altogether, the effect of devoting the purchase-money
of land to emigration, would be to accelerate immensely the rate of colonization, and to augment
more quickly than by any other disposition of the fund,
the population, wealth, and greatness of the empire.

5. A particular effect of devoting the purchase-money to emigration remains to be noticed; and a very pleasing effect it would be. The term of the labourer's service for hire would be shorter; the time when he might turn into a landowner with advantage to the whole colony, would come sooner. Suppose 5*l.* were the sufficient price without an emigration-fund, and 2*l.* with one. With new land at 5*l.* an acre, the emigrant labourers might, always on the average, have to work ten years for wages before they could buy enough land to set up upon as masters : with new land at 2*l.* an acre, they could become landowners and masters at the end of four years. These figures are entirely hypothetical; and what the real difference would prove to be I do not pretend to say; but manifestly it would be very considerable. It is a difference which should be strongly impressed on the mind of the colonizing legislator; for a perception of it teaches that the devotion of the purchase-money to emigration, besides being the disposition of the land-fund most conducive to the increase of population and imperial wealth and greatness, would powerfully tend to render the whole system popular with the working classes, and, in particular, to prevent them from objecting to the groundwork of the system, which is the sufficient price.

LETTER LVI.

From the Statesman.

MR. MOTHERCOUNTRY OBJECTS TO THE SUFFICIENT PRICE,
THAT IT WOULD PUT A STOP TO THE SALE OF WASTE
LAND.

I HAVE a pleasure in being able to inform you,
that your plan of land-selling and emigration is
now as clear to me, as it was lately involved in a sort
of mysterious obscurity. Now, at least, I understand
it. I see too, that my Mr. Mothercountry, upon whom
I can make no impression by repeating your exposition
of the plan, has never understood it. And no wonder; for it is plain that he has never tried to understand it, and is still unwilling to be taught. On this
subject, he is a striking example of the proverb about
wilful deafness.

However, amongst the foolish objections which he
makes to the plan, and which I was able to dispose of
myself, there is one which I was incapable of meeting.
You shall have it in his own words, so far at least as
I am now able to avoid falling into your manner of
writing on this subject. He said: " Admitting, as I
am far from doing, that the plan would work in a
colony founded according to it, it is wholly inappli-

cable to the present colonies; and after the turmoil occasioned by these amateur colonizers in the South-Australian and New-Zealand affairs, we are not likely to let them get up any more colonies. In a colony already established, the plan could not work, because the only effect of the 'sufficient price' would be to put a complete stop to the sale of waste land. It would have this effect, because in all these colonies, for years and years to come, land already appropriated will be extremely cheap. My own opinion is (and I hold the faith in common with Adam Smith, and all other economists who wrote before this new light broke upon the world), that land in a colony ought to be extremely cheap; the cheaper the better: but be that as it may, to sell dear land in a colony where there is plenty of cheap land, would be simply impossible. An effect of the old plan of colonizing (which I think a good effect produced by a good plan) is to make it impossible, that the new plan should have any effect but that of completely preventing further colonization. In most of the colonies, not an acre would be sold for ages at this nonsensical sufficient price. This scheme of a sufficient price, take it at the best, is an impracticable theory. Allow me to say, that I am surprised to see a person of your understanding waste his time on such a whimsey."

LETTER LVII.

From the Colonist.

THE COLONIST EXAMINES MR. MOTHERCOUNTRY'S PRO-
POSITION, THAT THE SUFFICIENT PRICE WOULD PUT
A STOP TO SALES OF LAND.——SUGGESTION OF LOANS
FOR EMIGRATION TO BE RAISED ON THE SECURITY
OF FUTURE SALES.

YOUR Mr. Mothercountry's objection would show,
that he understands the sufficient price better
than you have been led to suppose. I could explain
the state of his mind on the subject; but it is not
worth while. On one point I quite agree with him.
The Colonial Office will easily prevent the foundation
of any more colonies. Amongst those who, of late
years, have tormented the Colonial Office by founding colonies, there is not one that could be persuaded
to take part in another enterprise of the kind; so
effectually has the Colonial Office, by tormenting
them in its turn, disgusted them with such work.
As most of them are public men of more or less
mark, or topping London merchants, their dread of
having anything to do with the Colonial Office has so
far become a general feeling, that I can only wonder
at the recent formation of a society for planting a

fresh settlement in New Zealand. The time, however, is not distant when these latest amateurs of colonization will be as sick of the pursuit as the others have long been. But this is becoming a digression.

In his objection to the sufficient price, your Mr. Mothercountry is both right and wrong in supposing, that no public land at all would be sold in the case which he puts. No public land would be sold to people of the labouring class; none to anybody whose object was to get land as cheap as possible. But however high the price of public land, and however great the excess of appropriated land, there would be spots in the unappropriated territory enjoying, or likely to enjoy, peculiar advantages of position, which speculators would buy with a view to selling their land again. I allude to such spots as the mouths of rivers, the shores of harbours, and other good natural sites of towns, which it might " pay" to buy, even though the district surrounding them were only used for pasturage or lumbering, and remained for some time unappropriated. By degrees, a certain town population growing in these spots, the land in their immediate vicinity would acquire a position-value above the sufficient price, and would be sold accordingly. In a like manner, if a good road were made through the wilderness, between a harbour and one of these spots in the interior, much of the land on both sides of the road would acquire a position-value above the sufficient price, and would then be sold. Again, in various spots throughout an unappropriated pastoral district, sheep and cattle farmers would be glad to buy, at almost any price, enough ground for a homestead and some cultivation around it. I perceive many other cases in which public land would be sold, notwithstanding that its price was higher than the price of the cheapest appropriated land; but these examples suffice for exhibiting the principle of such sales. The principle is, that position-value would not be affected by the sufficient price, but would be just the same, wherever it occurred, whether the sufficient price were high or low. This value would generally exceed the highest conceivable sufficient price; and whenever it did, the land would be bought at the sufficient price, whatever that might be. I am inclined to think, that although the sufficient price was high enough to prevent the sale of any land not enjoying a value of position, position-value would continually spread into and along the nearest boundaries of unappropriated districts; and that thus considerable sales of public land would take place, and a considerable emigration-fund would be obtained, notwithstanding the great cheapness of the cheapest appropriated land. In some colonies, such as New Zealand, where the quantity of appropriated land is not yet monstrously excessive, an emigration-fund would soon accrue; and the outlay of the emigration-fund, by pouring people into the colony, would soon raise the value of the cheapest private land to an equality with the price of public land. So far, then, I think Mr. Mothercountry in the wrong.

On the other hand, I fully agree with him, that where private land is monstrously superabundant, the sufficient price would, for a long while, stop the sale of all public land not possessing or acquiring a position-value. But, as he ought to have told you, I have always been aware of this difficulty, and have suggested various means of overcoming it.

The first suggestion is, that future sales should be anticipated, by the raising of loans on the security of such sales; and that the money should be laid out on emigration. This would be useful in the case of a new settlement, because the first emigrants might be loath to pay the sufficient price until the spot was in some measure peopled: it is indispensable, with the view of bestowing the advantages of the whole plan on a colony, where the old practice of granting land with profusion has made the cheapest land extremely cheap. In the case of a new settlement, if the government peopled its land first, and sold it afterwards, it would sell it more readily than if it sold it first and peopled it afterwards. In the case of an old colony, where private land was extremely superabundant, the anticipation of future sales of public land, by raising money for emigration on that security, would alter the proportion of people to land in the appropriated territory, according to the scale on which this mode of proceeding was adopted. If enough people were thus conveyed to the appropriated territory to raise the price of the cheapest land there up to the price of public land, this part of the colony would be as well supplied with labour for hire, as it would have been originally if it had been founded on the plan of a sufficient price employed as an emigration-fund. But then, objectors have said, future sales of public land being anticipated, when these sales took place, the purchase-money, instead of being devoted to emigration, must be employed in paying off the loans; and for this part of the colony there would be no emigration-fund. Truly; but, in that case, either an emigration-fund would not then be needed, or there would be a perfect equivalent for one as respects the goodness at least of the colonization. At a certain stage in the course of colonizing a waste country, and long before all the waste land is disposed of, it becomes most inexpedient to introduce more people from the mother-country; quite necessary to keep the remaining waste for the purposes of the colonial population, now very numerous and always rapidly increasing by births and spontaneous emigration. From that time forth, of course, the purchase-money of public land would first go to pay off the previous loans for emigration, and then form part of the general colonial revenue. But if this stage were not yet reached—if an emigration-fund were needed, but could not be got—then it would be necessary, from that time forth, to go on settling the wilderness without an emigration-fund, and to raise the price of public land up to what would be sufficient, the purchase-money *not* being devoted to emigration. In either case, the principle of the sufficient price would be maintained; scarcity of labour would be prevented.

This result, however, would not be obtained in the earlier stage of colonization, unless the scale of borrowing for emigration, on the security of future sales, were sufficient to supply in the appropriated territory whatever might be the demand for labour. On private land, the sufficient price would not be imposed by law. Therefore, until emigration raised the price of the cheapest private land up to that of public land, emigrant labourers would be able to obtain land for less than the sufficient price: and in this case, there might be a scarcity of labour, but not if emigration were on a great enough scale to put a labourer in the place of him who had become a landowner too soon. With emigration, indeed, proceeding and promised as to the future on this scale, few would be the owners of land who would be induced to part with an acre of their property for less than the price of public land. The future sales of public land being sufficiently anticipated, the future value of private land would be, as it were, sufficiently anticipated likewise, by the unwillingness of the owners to sell for less than a price which at no distant day they would feel sure of obtaining. If so (but all, I repeat, would depend on the scale of emigration, actual and provided for), there would never be a vacuum in the labour-market for emigration to fill up: the evil would be prevented by the certainty of a remedy being at hand in case of need.

LETTER LVIII.

From the Colonist.

SUGGESTION OF A FURTHER MEANS FOR ENABLING THE
SUFFICIENT PRICE OF PUBLIC LAND TO WORK WELL
IN COLONIES WHERE PRIVATE LAND IS GREATLY
SUPERABUNDANT AND VERY CHEAP.

BUT now let us suppose the case (which is that
put by Mr. Mothercountry) of a colony in which
land was greatly superabundant, but nothing at all
was done to remedy the past profusion of the government in granting land. In this case, the putting of
a price on new land would do good to nobody. The
price whatever its amount, would not be " sufficient"
for the only legitimate end of putting any price on
mere waste. In this case, then, the putting of a pretended sufficient price on new land is a useless impediment to the further appropriation of land in peculiarly eligible spots as these are discovered, a foolish
check to colonizing enterprise, and a mischievous
deduction from the capital of the pioneers of settlement. But this, which has been here supposed, is
exactly what we do in New South Wales and some
other colonies. In these actual cases, the price of
public land, as an alleged means of doing some good,

is a pretence or a delusion: the design of it is a pretence; the result of it is a delusion; the reality is nothing but a taxing of colonization for revenue. Do me the favour to ask Mr. Mothercountry if he knows of a worse species of taxation for colonies.

But it is easy to conceive another case, in which the government should be really desirous of giving full effect to the whole plan, but want means to pour into the colony enough people to raise the price of the cheapest private land up to the price of public land. The inability would consist of the want of a sufficient emigration-fund. The future sales of public land would not be deemed by capitalists a security valuable enough to warrant the advance on loan of all the money required. In this case, the cheapest private land being too cheap, labourers taken to the colony would too soon turn into landowners; and their place in the labour market would not be immediately filled by other emigrants. There might exist all the evils of scarcity of labour, notwithstanding a high price for public land, and some emigration by means of loans raised on the security of future sales.

If I have made the nature of the evil clear, you will readily perceive what kind of remedy would be appropriate. The object is to raise the price of the cheapest private, up to that of public land. With this view, numerous modes of proceeding have been suggested. Amongst these is, what they call in America, a " wild-land tax." This is a tax upon private land because it remains waste; a species of fine imposed on the owner for being a dog in the manger; for neither using his land nor selling it to somebody who would use it. This tax makes effectual war upon the nuisance of unoccupied, in the midst of occupied private land; but it tends to lower instead of raising the price of land, by forbidding landowners to wait before they sell for an expected time of higher prices. This tax, therefore, is most inapplicable to the object now in view.

Another tax proposed with a view to that object, is one intended to have the effect of preventing owners of private land from selling at less than the price of public land. This would be a tax upon private sales below the public price, sufficient in amount, in each case respectively, to raise the buying price up to the public price. If, for example, the public price were 2*l.* an acre, and the land were sold at 1*l.*, the buyer would have to pay 1*l.* more to the government, paying in all 2*l.*; that is, the public price. In two different ways, this tax would conduce to the end contemplated. First, it would prevent emigrant labourers from getting land too soon : secondly, it would provide an additional security on which to raise loans for emigration. In theory, this tax is unobjectionable: the effect of it would be to apply to private land *after* mischievously excessive appropriation, the whole principle of a sufficient price and loans for emigration as applied to waste land *before* appropriation. But I fear that this tax would not work in practice : it would, I think, be too easily evaded; for though government can prevent people from putting a value on something, less than the real one, by taking the thing off their hands at their own false valuation (as is done with respect to imported goods liable to *ad valorem* duty on importation), still I do not see how, in the supposed case, the buyer and the seller could be hindered from conspiring to pretend, that the price at which they dealt was equal to the price of public land though really far below it: and whenever they succeeded in making this pretence pass as a reality, they would evade the tax. The facility of evasion would be great; the temptation strong; not to mention the roguery which the practice of evasion would involve and render customary.

We are driven, therefore, to a kind of taxation which would neither be liable to evasion, nor so perfectly fitted to the object in view. This is a tax on all sales of private land acquired before the institution of the sufficient price for public land; and the devotion of the proceeds of the tax to emigration, either directly in defraying the cost of passage for labouring people, or indirectly as an additional security on which to raise emigration-loans. The tax might be either *ad valorem;* so much per cent., that is, upon the purchase-money of every sale: or it might be, what would much better agree with the object of the tax, a uniform sum per acre equal to the acreable price of public land. Thus if the price of public land were 2*l.*, the purchaser of 100 acres of private land, at whatever price, would have to pay 200*l.* to the government as a contribution to the emigration-fund. It would be requisite to make the purchaser liable, because the seller, having got his money, might evade the tax; whereas the purchaser could be made to pay the tax or forfeit the land. Or rather, probably, the best mode of levying the tax would be a good system of registration, under which payment of the tax would be a condition of valid title. Whatever the mode, however, of preventing evasion of the tax, when due, the imposition of this tax on the first sale of any land after the law came into force (but of course not on any subsequent sale of that land) would be to put the sufficient price upon all the land of the colony, with this only difference between public and private land, that in one case the price would be paid before, and in the other, sooner or later, after appropriation.

I see one way, and only one, in which this tax could be evaded. Labourers wishing to get land, but unable or unwilling to pay the tax in addition to the purchase-money, might induce proprietors to let land to them on so long a lease as to make the tenure equal in value to freehold, or at all events on such a tenure as would serve the labourer's purpose. It would therefore be requisite to impose the tax upon lettings as well as sales. When, after a day fixed by the law, land was let, the lessee, or landlord, or rather the land, would become liable for the tax. A provision in the registration for invalidating lettings in respect of which the tax was not paid, would prevent evasion of this part of the measure.

I have called this measure a tax on sales and lettings, but have done so only for the sake of facility of exposition. It would not really be a tax, because one effect of the whole plan of colonization, an essential part of which this measure is, would be, supposing the payments on sales and lettings of private land to be an additional security for emigration-loans, to increase the value of all private land by at least as much as the amount of the tax. Indeed, ere long, the rapid pouring of people into the colony which would be possible with the double security for emigration-loans, must render the tax a mere trifle in comparison with

the new value which it would help to confer immediately on private land.   But, there is one case of
hardship which might happen in the meanwhile, and
which should be guarded against.   The whole system
being in operation, most owners would not be sellers
or letters, but tenacious holders of their landed property; waiters for the great and general rise in the value
of land, which they would see to be approaching. But
some few would be unable to wait : their circumstances
would command, and yet the tax might forbid them
to sell or let.   In order comprehensively and effectually to guard against such cases of hardship, the
government might give notice before the whole law of
colonization came into force, that it would purchase at
a valuation any land which anybody wished to sell in
that way.   A time must of course be fixed, after
which the government would no longer do this. As
the valuation in every case would be according to the
very low value of the land at the time, excluding all
allowance for prospective value, no landowners, I
repeat, except those who at that particular time were
under a necessity of selling, would offer their land to
the government.   These, I am persuaded, would be
very few.   Whatever land came into the hands of
government under this part of the law, would be resold
as soon as a price was offered for it equal to a sum
composed of the price which the government had paid,
of all the expenses incurred, and of the tax on sales.
Such a price would be offered before long.   If it were
deemed unadvisable or impossible that the government
should be out of its money so long, then the law
might provide that the government, instead of paying
for the land at the time of buying it, should engage to

pay interest on the price till the land should be sold again, and then to pay the principal. This engagement of the government would be as valuable to the seller, if it were made transferable like an Exchequer Bill, as the purchase-money in hand.

I am much afraid that you must be growing tired of these doctrinal particulars.

LETTER LIX.

From the Statesman.

THE STATESMAN TELLS OF MR. MOTHERCOUNTRY'S INTENTION TO MAKE THE COMMISSIONERS OF COLONIAL LAND AND EMIGRATION WRITE OBJECTIONS TO THE SUFFICIENT PRICE FOR WASTE LAND.

AS decidedly as common prudence will allow me to express an opinion on a question so new to me, I think you have shown that the extreme cheapness of private land in some colonies is not, even as respects those colonies only, a valid objection to the sufficient price for public land. But Mr. Mothercountry still objects to it. He does not offer specific objections to your plan for remedying the evils of superabundant private land, but merely says that it is absurd. When I pressed for his reasons, he proposed to write to me on the subject; and I have accepted his offer. I gathered, that his intention is to set the Colonial Land and Emigration Commissioners the task of objecting to the latter part of your scheme; and as they ought to be masters of a subject which it is their especial function to understand thoroughly, I wish to keep my own opinions on it unsettled till after seeing what they may have to say. If I get anything from them that appears worth sending to you, you shall have it without delay.

Do not suppose that I am tired of your " doctrina₁ particulars." On the contrary, I feel obliged to you for taking the trouble to furnish me with them; for I wish to understand the subject thoroughly, not to get a superficial smattering of it. I imagine, however, that we are near the end.

LETTER LX.

From the Colonist.

THE COLONIST ANTICIPATES THE PROBABLE WRITING OF THE COMMISSIONERS.

THEORETICALLY, indeed, it is the especial function of the Colonial Land and Emigration Commissioners to be masters of the subject which their title expresses; but practically they have very different functions. Of these, one which the Colonial Office frequently imposes on them, is that of picking holes in a suggestion about colonization, which the Office dislikes *per se*, or dislikes being troubled with. By much practice they have become skilful in this sort of official business, and really do it very well. You may expect, therefore, some cleverish special-pleading against " saddling colonies with debt," " taxing the feeble resources of young societies," and " giving an

unhealthy stimulus to emigration." As these gentlemen always have an eye to their chief's predilections
and antipathies, they may also throw in an argument
for " spontaneous" emigration, of which Lord Grey has
been very fond ever since certain elaborate and impracticable schemes of his own for promoting what he
now calls " forced" emigration, all broke down. But
they will not, partly because they dare not, examine
the question candidly with a view of throwing light
upon it. They dare not, because, in the first place,
though their office is in Park-street, they are, from the
very nature of the commission, mere clerks of colonial
Downing-street; and secondly, because, whilst the
" good hater," whose helpless subordinates these Commissioners are at present, hates nothing more than a
suggestion of mine, his irascible and vindictive temper
makes those who are at his mercy, and who know
him, tremble at the thought of his displeasure.

I hope indeed that we are not far from the end;
but several matters remain to be explained, because
they are really essential conditions of the well-working
of the plan of colonization as here laid down. Nay,
as such, they are rather parts of the plan.

LETTER LXI.

From the Colonist.

AT the sufficient price, there should be the most complete liberty of acquiring private property in public land: for any restriction of this liberty would be tantamount to a restriction of the quantity of land open to purchase, and would be a difficulty, over and above the sufficient price, placed in the way of a labourer desirous to become a landowner. If the price were really sufficient, any further restriction would be an oppression of the labouring class. Though not so oppressive to the other classes, it would be very unjust and very impolitic as respects them also; since if the government professed to allow the utmost liberty of appropriation on the one condition of paying the sufficient price, any further restriction, not absolutely unavoidable, would be a wrong, and the completion of a fraud, towards every purchaser. If the further restriction were irregular and uncertain in its force, every man would be put out in his calculations;

nobody would be able to regulate his proceedings by his knowledge of the law: the system, instead of being administered according to law, would be subject to arbitrary and perhaps mysterious derangement, like our present political government of the colonies.

A price which would be sufficient with perfect liberty of appropriation, must be both excessive and insufficient without that liberty. If the price by itself were restriction enough, then a restriction of the quantity besides would be like adding to the price for some purchasers and diminishing it for others. If the quantity were so restricted as to occasion competition, one with another among intending purchasers, there would be a scramble for the land; and though nobody would pay more than the fixed price, those who were not so fortunate as to get land from the government, would have to buy from the others at an enhanced price; or they would have to go without land: and in either case, the lucky or perhaps favoured purchasers from the government would really obtain land possessing at the time a competition-value over and above its cost, which would be the same thing for them as getting land for less than the price of public land. The price, therefore, at which people obtained public land, would virtually be, in some cases more, in some less, than the price required by the government as being neither more nor less than sufficient. This counteraction of the principle of the sufficient price would be a serious evil, but not the only one. In addition to it, in the case supposed of competition produced by a restriction of quantity, there would be a frequent selection of the same spot by many purchasers, and a drawing of lots for the preference; much merely speculative investment; plenty of waiting; and plenty of bad blood amongst neighbours. There would be, in short, though in a mitigated degree, all the evils which attend upon restricting the quantity of land with a view to competition, and then selling by auction.

It seems at first sight, that nothing would be easier than to establish a perfect liberty of appropriation. The government, apparently, would only have to tell every purchaser to go and pick the land he liked best, as soon as the purchase-money was paid. But what is it that he would have to pick out of? A great wilderness, about which, until it was duly surveyed, nobody could possess the requisite knowledge for picking well. Suppose, however, though it must be merely for the sake of illustration, that purchasers generally could find out without a proper survey, where the best land was; where this or that natural circumstance existed that suited their respective objects; where the land was most heavily timbered, where clear of timber, where alluvial, where light; where water abounded, and was scarce; what was the course of streams; where mill-sites and fords occurred; the probable line of future roads; and so forth *ad infinitum*: suppose all this, if you can conceive what is manifestly impossible, and even then what would happen? The explorer, having chosen his spot, could not describe its boundaries to the government; in most cases, he could not even tell the government where the spot was; for without a map, he could not say it is here or there. Without a map, all he could say is, it is somewhere where I have been, but whereabouts the spot is I cannot tell, except that it is near a river, and not far from some hills.

On looking twice, therefore, at this subject, it becomes plain that in order to let the purchaser choose his land with a sufficient knowledge of the country, and further in order to let him point out his choice to the government and obtain a properly descriptive title, a good map, the result of a careful survey, is indispensable. Waste land not surveyed, is not land open to purchasers, any more than unpicked cotton or unthrashed corn is fit for market.

It follows, that if the sufficient price were intended to be the only restriction as to quantity, and that, as to choice within the quantity open to purchasers, there was to be no restriction, the whole plan could not work even decently without ample surveys. The surveys should, at least, be so extensive as to prevent any one from being compelled to take inferior land when there was superior land within reach. Except in countries of immense extent, the surveys should extend over the whole colony: and at any rate, for all colonies, a very large extent of the waste adjoining every settlement should at all times be kept surveyed, in order that so wide a liberty of choice should at all times exist.

I hardly know which is of the most consequence; extent, or completeness and accuracy of survey. Whatever the extent, the whole affair would be in a mess without completeness and accuracy. Without completeness—that is, unless all the natural features of the country, and all sorts of information about its varied soils and natural productions, were laid down on the map—purchasers would choose in ignorance, would often make bad selections, and would justly reproach the government with having misled them. Without accuracy, all kinds of confusion would arise

in settling, or rather in pretending to settle, the
boundaries of selections; and as the land increased in
value (which under the operation of the whole system
it would do almost as soon as it was bought), there
would be boundless and endless litigation amongst
purchasers, and between purchasers and the government.

The evils above described as being sure to arise
from insufficiency, incompleteness, and inaccuracy of
survey, though presented to you hypothetically, are
wretched facts in all our colonies more or less; and in
some of the colonies, the whole mischief is so great as
to be hardly credible by those who have not witnessed
it. For an ample description of it in one case, I would
refer you to Lord Durham's Report, and the evidence,
in one of its appendices (B), on which his picture of
surveys in Canada was founded. If you should take
the trouble to examine it, you will agree with me that
the whole system, or rather slovenly practice, of
public surveying in Canada was at that time really
abominable. It is not much better now. In several
other colonies, it is as bad as it ever was in Canada.
In hardly any colony is it better than very mistaken
in theory, defective in practice, and most extravagant
in cost. In the United States alone, the government
has seriously thought about this matter, and done
what it conceived to be best and cheapest. But the
plan of that government is unsuited to open countries,
where artificial marks on the ground are soon ob-
literated; and it also has the effect of circumscribing
freedom of choice within limits that would be too
narrow if public land cost the sufficient price. In
the one or two of our colonies where public surveying

has been best managed, it is far behind that of the
United States in efficiency and accuracy; and in no
one British colony has a system been adopted, that
would allow a sufficient price to work half as well as
if the surveys were sufficient in extent, complete,
accurate, and cheap.   How they might be made all
this, is a question upon which I am ready to enter if
you please; though I think you may as well spare
yourself the trouble of examining it whilst our system
of colonial government shall remain as it is, and those
who administer it be jealously adverse to every proposal of improvement.   If, however, you do not investigate this subject now, I must beg of you to take
for granted, that a vast improvement of colonial surveying would not be difficult, and to remember that
without it the plan of a sufficient price with its appen-
dages cannot work well.

LETTER LXII.

From the Colonist.

PROPOSED SELECTION OF EMIGRANTS, WITH A VIEW OF MAKING THE EMIGRATION-FUND AS POTENT AS POSSIBLE.—MORAL ADVANTAGES OF SUCH A SELECTION.

WHEN it was first proposed to sell waste land instead of granting it, and to use the purchase-money as an emigration-fund, the further proposal was made, that the money should be expended in paying for the passage of labouring people only, and that in the selection of such people for a passage wholly or partially cost free, a preference should always be given to young married couples, or to young people of the marriageable age in an equal proportion of the sexes. The latter suggestion was founded on certain considerations which I will now mention.

1. The emigration-fund ought to be laid out so as to take away from the old country, and introduce into the colonies, the greatest possible amount of population and labour; in such a manner that, as an emigration-fund, it should have the maximum of effect both on the colonies and the mother-country.

2. If the object were to procure at the least cost

the greatest amount of labour for immediate employment in the colonies, it would appear at first sight that the emigrants ought to be, all of them, in the prime of life.   But it is only at first sight that this can appear; because on reflection it is seen, that two men having to perform, each for himself, all the offices that women of the labouring class usually perform for men—to cook their own victuals, to mend their own clothes, to make their own beds, to play the woman's part at home as well as the man's part in the field or workshop—to divide their labour between household cares and the work of production—would produce less than one man giving the whole of his time to the work of production.   This is a case which illustrates the advantages of combination of labour for division of employments.   If the two men combined their labour, and so divided their employments—one occupying himself solely with household cares for both, and the other with earning wages for both—then might the produce of their united labour be equal to that of one married man; but, speaking generally, it would not be more.   In new colonies, men have often made this unnatural arrangement; and to some extent they do so now in colonies where there are many more men than women.   We need not stop to look at the moral evils of an excess of males.   In an economical view only, it seems plain that poor emigrants taken to a colony by the purchase-money of waste land, ought to be men and women in equal numbers; and, if married, so much the better.

3. If they were old people, their labour would be of little value to the colony; not only because it would soon be at an end, but also because it would

be weak, and because after middle age few workmen can readily turn their hands to employments different from those to which they are accustomed. In order that poor emigrants taken to a colony should be as valuable as possible, they ought to be young people, whose powers of labour would last as long as possible, and who could readily turn their hands to new employments.

4. But are there any objections to a mixture of children? To this there are four principal objections, besides others. First, if the children were the offspring of grown-up emigrants, it follows that those parents could not be of the best age; that if old enough to have children, they would be too old to come under the description of the most valuable labourers. Secondly, children are less fit than old people to undergo the confinement and other troubles of a long sea voyage. Of this you may convince yourself by visiting a ship full of emigrants at Gravesend, bound to New York. You will find those who are parents, and especially the mothers, troubled and anxious, fearful of accidents to their children, restless, starting at every noise; if paupers, glad to see their little ones stuffing themselves with the ship's rations, dainties to them, poor things! who have plenty to eat for the first time in their lives; if paupers, looking back without affection, and to the future with gladsome hope, but, being parents, with apprehension lest, in the distant land of promise, the children should suffer more than they have endured at home. You will see the children, if of the pauper class, delighted at meal-times, smiling with greasy lips, their eyes sparkling over the butcher's meat, but at other times

sick of the confinement, tired of having nothing to do, wanting a play-place, always in the way, driven from pillar to post, and exposed to serious accidents. Those poor emigrants, on the contrary, who are neither parents nor children—young men and women without any incumbrance—you will find quite at their ease, enjoying the luxury of idleness, pleased with the novelty of their situation, in a state of pleasurable excitement, glorying in the prospect of independence, thanking God that they are still without children, and, if you should know how to make them speak out, delighted to talk about the new country, in which, as they have heard, children are not a burthen but a blessing. Thirdly, when children first reach a colony, they necessarily encumber somebody. They cannot for some time be of any use as labourers: they cannot produce wealth wherewith to attract, convey, and employ other labourers. To whatever extent, then, the emigration-fund should be laid out in removing children instead of grown-up people, the value received by mother-country and colony would be less than might be. By taking none but very young grown-up persons, the maximum of value would be obtained for any given outlay.

5. The greatest quantity of labour would be obtained more easily than a less quantity. The natural time of marriage is a time of change, when two persons, just united for life, must nearly all seek a new home. The natural time of marriage, too, is one when the mind is most disposed to hope, to ambition, to engaging in undertakings which require decision and energy of purpose. Marriage, besides, produces greater anxiety for the future, and a very strong desire to be

better off in the world for the sake of expected offspring. Of what class are composed those numerous
streams of emigrants, which flow continually from
the Eastern to the outside of the Western states of
America, by channels, until lately rougher and
longer than the sea-way from England to America?
Neither of single men, nor of old people, nor of middle-
aged people dragging children along with them, but, for
the most part, of young couples, seeking a new home,
fondly encouraging each other, strong in health and
spirits, not driven from birth-place by the fear of
want, but attracted to a new place by motives of
ambition for themselves and for children to come.
This then is the class of people, that could be most
easily attracted to a colony by high wages and better
prospects. The class which it is most expedient to
select, would be the most easily persuaded to avail
themselves of a preference in their favour.

6. A preference in favour of the best class is all
that the law should declare. For there might not
exist in the old country a sufficient number of the
most valuable class of labouring emigrants to supply
the colonial demand for labour. Suppose, for example,
that the United States determined to lay out the
annual proceeds of their waste-land fund, which on
the average exceeds 1,000,000*l.*, in providing a passage
for poor young couples from Ireland to America. This
outlay, the passage of each person costing 4*l.*, would
provide for the annual emigration of 125,000 couples.
But in Ireland there are not so many as 125,000
couples, or 250,000 individuals, born in the same year
and grown up. As the constant emigration of all, or
may be half, the couples who every year reach the age

of marriage, must very soon depopulate any country, we may be sure that a portion only of this class will ever be disposed to emigrate. Whenever a number sufficient to meet the colonial demand for labour should not be disposed to emigrate, it would be necessary to offer a passage to couples older or younger by one, two, or three years, but always giving a preference to those who were nearest to the marriageable age. At all times, in short, the administrators of the emigration-fund could only give a preference to the most eligible applicants at the time.

7. Supposing all the people taken to a colony with the purchase-money of waste land, to be young men and women in equal numbers, let us see what the effect would be on the colonial population. At the end of twenty years after the foundation of Virginia, the number of colonists was about 1800, though the number of emigrants had been nearly 20,000. This rapid decrease of population was owing in some measure to the miserable state of things that existed in Virginia before the colony was enriched by the introduction of slave-labour; but it was in no small degree owing to this; that of the 20,000 emigrants, only a very few were females. As there was hardly any increase of people by births in the colony, the local population would at all events have been less at the end of twenty years, than the number of emigrants during that period. In New South Wales, it has never been difficult for the poorest class to maintain a family: yet until young couples were for the first time taken to that colony about sixteen years ago, its population was nothing like as great as the number of emigrants. Of those emigrants (they were mostly

convicts), by far the greater number were men; and of the handful of women, many were past the age of child-bearing. Had they consisted of men and women in equal proportions, but of the middle age, the number of emigrants might still have exceeded the colonial population; but if they had consisted of young couples just arrived at the age of marriage, the population of the colony would have advanced with surprising rapidity. I once reckoned that at the time in question, the population of the colony would have been 500,000 instead of its actual amount, 50,000; that the increase of people, and, we may add, the rate of colonization, would have been ten times greater than they were, with the same outlay in emigration. At that time, the proportion of young people in New South Wales was very small: in the supposed case, it would have been much greater than it has ever been in any human society. According, of course, to this large proportion of young people would have been the prospect of future increase. If all the people who have removed from Europe and Africa to America, had been young couples just arrived at the marriageable age, slavery in North America must have long since died a natural death: no part of North America, perhaps no part of South America, would now be open to colonization.

8. In any colony, the immediate effect of selecting young couples for emigration, would be to diminish in a curious degree the cost of adding to the colonial population. The passage of young couples would not cost more than that of all classes mixed; but the young couples would take to the colony the greatest possible germ of future increase. In fact, the settlers of New South Wales who in a few years made that

colony swarm with sheep, did not import lambs or
old sheep; still less did they import a large proportion of rams.   They imported altogether a very small
number of sheep, compared with the vast number
they soon possessed.   Their object was the production
in the colony of the greatest number of sheep by the
importation of the smallest number, or, in other
words, at the least cost: and this object they accomplished by selecting for importation those animals
only, which, on account of their sex and age, were fit
to produce the greatest number of young in the
shortest time.   If emigrants were selected on the
same principle, the appropriated land, it is evident,
would become as valuable as it could ever be, much
sooner than if the emigrants were a mixture of
people of all ages.   In the former case, not only would
all the emigrants be of the most valuable class as
labourers, but they would be of the class fit to produce the most rapid increase of people in the colony,
and so to confer on new land as soon as possible
the value that depends on position.   The buyer of
new land, therefore, would have his purchase-money
laid out for him in the way most conducive to a demand for accommodation-land and building-ground;
in the way that would serve him most.   And something else would flow from this selection of emigrants,
which it is very needful to observe.   The emigration-
fund being so much more potent in its operation,
any given outlay would have a greater effect on the
colonial proportion of land to people.   With the selection, the labour-market would be more largely supplied than without it: a shorter term of labour for
hire by the emigrants would suffice for the greatest

productiveness of industry: a lower price of public land would be sufficient. And yet both of the proposed securities on which to borrow money for emigration, would be more valuable: notwithstanding the lower price for public land and the lower tax on private sales and lettings, the means of paying off the emigration-loans would be obtained much sooner than without this selection of emigrants. With the selection, it would be more easy, as well as in many ways more advantageous, to get the whole plan into full work, even in colonies where land is the most superabundant.

9. The moral advantages of such a selection of emigrants would not be few. If the emigrants were married (as they all ought to be, and as by rejecting unmarried applicants, it would be easy to take care that they should be), each female would have a special protector from the moment of her departure from home. No man would have an excuse for dissolute habits. All the evils which in colonization have so often sprung from a disproportion between the sexes, and which are still very serious in several colonies, would be completely averted. Every pair of emigrants would have the strongest motives for industry, steadiness, and thrift. In a colony thus peopled, there would be hardly any single men or single women: nearly the whole population would consist of married men and women, boys and girls, and children. For many years the proportion of children to grown-up people would be greater than ever took place since Shem, Ham, and Japhet were surrounded by their little ones. The colony would be an immense nursery, and, all being at ease, would present a finer opportunity than has ever occurred for trying what may

be done for society by really educating the common people.

The selection and conveyance of poor emigrants obtaining a passage to the colonies by means of the purchase-money of waste land, is the part of the plan of the theorists of 1830, which in practice has been attended with the least disappointment. The example of something like a careful administration of this part of the theory was set by the South Australian Commissioners, who were zealously assisted by two of the framers of the theory in starting this new kind of emigration. By following the example thus set, the New-Zealand Company and the Colonial Office Commissioners in Park-street have brought about a revolution in the character, at least, of long-sea emigration for the poorer classes. A voyage of 16,000 miles is now made by a shipful of poor emigrants, with a lower rate of mortality amongst them during the voyage, than the average rate of mortality in the class formed by the families of our peerage. In most of the ships, the number of passengers is greater at the end than at the beginning of the voyage. The Southern colonies have received by this means, a class of labouring emigrants incomparably superior in point of usefulness to the old-fashioned ship-loads of shovelled-out paupers. The nearer equality of the sexes in this emigration has produced the good moral results that were expected from it, or rather averted the very bad moral results that had flowed from inequality between the sexes in all previous emigration: and the colonies to which this selected emigration has been directed, have received an amount of the germ of increased population, of which, in proportion to the number of emigrants, there has been no previous example. Altogether, what has been done, establishes the infinite superiority of systematic emigration to that " spontaneous" scramble which Lord Grey now applauds, and which, often afflicting Canada with malignant fever, necessitates a lazaretto on the St. Lawrence, as if, says Lord Durham, British emigrants came from the home of the plague.

But the administration of the emigration-fund of colonies is still, I believe, open to great improvements. The selection of emigrants has never been as good as it might be. The South-Australian Commissioners were new to their work, and neither personally interested in it nor responsible to anybody. The New-Zealand Company was for years rather a company for disturbing the Colonial Office and usefully agitating colonial questions of principle, than for colonizing; and now it is only a company for trying in vain to colonize. The Commissioners in Park-street have not been of a class, to whom much personal intercourse with poor emigrants could be agreeable (and without close personal intercourse between the poorest emigrants and the highest executive authority in this matter, it is impossible that the business should be very well done); they have been in no measure responsible to the colonies whose funds they expended, and which were alone much interested in watching their proceedings; their official house, in Westminster, seems poked as if on purpose out of the way of shipping business and emigrant resort; and they have naturally fallen into a practice, which must be extremely convenient to them, of getting their emigration business done by contract and by men of busi-

ness.   But the main business of the contractors is to
make as much as they can by their contracts.   So we
hear of emigrant ships bound to Adelaide or Port
Philip, receiving a few English passengers in London,
and filling up with the most wretched Irish at Plymouth, whom the contractor finds it " pay" to bring
from Cork on purpose to fill up with, because, as
respects food and accommodation during the voyage,
there are no passengers that cost so little as the Irish
poor, or are so easily imposed upon by the captain who
represents the contractor.   This case of defrauding
the colonies by sending them inferior labour for their
money which pays for superior, indicates that it does
not stand alone as to mismanagement.   In all parts of
this administration, all the administrators have mis-
managed a little.   There has been a little waste of precious funds, a little neglect here and there, a little
overlooked deviation from rules, a little imposition of
" false character" upon the examiners of applications
for a passage, and, I rather think, not a little jobbing
in accommodating friends or persons of influence with
a free passage to the colonies for emigrants whom
they wanted to shovel out.   The sum of mismanagement is considerable.   It would have been greater
but for a sort of rivalry between companies and commissioners, which led them to watch each other, but
which has now ceased; and it can only be surely
guarded against in future, by a plain, unmistakeable,
immutable law of emigration, with provisions for rendering its administrators in some measure responsible
to the colonies, which alone can be sufficiently interested in the good administration of the law to
furnish the safeguard of a vigilant public opinion constantly attending to particulars.

LETTER LXIII.

From the Statesman.

AN IMPORTANT OBJECTION TO THE COLONIST'S WHOLE
PLAN OF COLONIZATION APART FROM GOVERNMENT.

AFTER a long conversation yesterday with my Mr.
Mothercountry, I am under the necessity of reporting two objections of his, the force of which I
could not help admitting at the time: but as you have
before enabled me to recall similar admissions, so I
trust that you may now put me in the way of silencing
the objector. It would be satisfactory to stop his
mouth this time; for these two, he says, are his last
objections; and to me they certainly appear rather
formidable. You shall have them one at a time.

The first of them, however, relates only to those
countries which are not covered with a dense forest
like Canada, but in which there is abundance of open
land, covered with natural pasturage for sheep and
cattle, such as New South Wales. Here, says my
prompter, the sufficient price would have a most
injurious effect: it would prevent the use of the
natural pasturage. In open countries, where food for
animals is produced in abundance without cost, pastoral occupations are the principal source of individual

and public wealth. What nature produces in these countries, the inhabitants find it worth while to use, by keeping vast numbers of cattle, horses, and sheep: but if you compelled every one, before he could use natural pasturage, to pay for it a " sufficient price " per acre, you would, in fact, forbid him to use it: for the use of pasturage, when it costs nothing, only just remunerates the capitalist; and if you added to his outlay a considerable price for every acre used, he could not carry on his business without loss. By imposing the sufficient price on all land in pastoral countries, you would destroy their principal branch of industry and source of wealth. You might as well propose to make the fishermen of Newfoundland pay a sufficient price per acre for the use of their cod banks.

LETTER LXIV.

From the Colonist.

THE COLONIST FIRST ADMITS, AND THEN ANSWERS THE OBJECTION.

I AGREE with every syllable of the objection to a sufficient price for the use of natural pasturage. Indeed, I claim the argument as my own; for it has been taken, almost verbatim, from some anonymous writing of mine. But then, your prompter and I direct the argument against totally different objects. He directs it against me as the proposer of a price for natural pasturage, which I am not; I direct it against his Office, which really is the imposer of a price on natural pasturage, notwithstanding this conclusive argument against the proceeding. The theorists of 1830 never thought of compelling settlers to pay for the use of natural pasturage. According to their theory, it is the extreme cheapness, not of natural pasturage, but of land for cultivation, which occasions scarcity of labour for hire. Labourers could not become landowners by using natural pasturage. The use of it requires, in order to be profitable, the employment of a considerable capital, of numerous servants, and of very superior skill: it is a business requiring from the outset much combination of labour for division of employments, and the unremitting constancy of the combined labour: it is a business altogether unsuitable to the common labourer or small capitalist. Whether, therefore, the use of natural pasturage were cheap or dear, the labourer would either sooner or later cease to work for wages; the term of his working for wages would in either case depend, not at all on the cost of natural pasturage, but wholly on the price of freehold land. It is for this alone — for the sort of property in land which a labourer would require in order to cease working for hire, and to set up for himself as a competitor with his former employers in the labour-market —that the theorists of 1830 have ever proposed a sufficient price. According to their view of the matter, the words " a *sufficient* price for the use of natural pasturage" are unmeaning or nonsensical.

Nevertheless, between abundance of natural pasturage and the sufficient price for freehold land, there is a close and important relation. The abundance of

natural pasturage in a colony is, like the existence of
valuable mines or prolific fishing-banks, a source of
wealth supplied by nature, but which can only be
turned to great account by means of placing com-
binable and constant labour at the disposal of the
capitalist.   In colonies, therefore, to which nature has
given this advantage, it is more than usually desirable
that the property in land which converts the hired
labourer into a landowner, should be dear enough to
prevent a great scarcity of labour for hire; and that
all those measures for promoting labour-emigration, of
which the sufficient price is the basis, should receive
their utmost development.   But if the abundance of
natural pasturage thus furnishes an additional reason
for working out completely, and on the greatest possible
scale, the principle of a sufficient price for freehold
land, what shall we say of the policy of the Colonial
Office and its official instruments in the colonies,
who put a price upon the use of natural pasturage
for no purpose but that of getting money out
of the settlers?   The prosperity of New South
Wales, for example, is wholly dependent on the use
of vast tracts of natural pasturage.   With labour as
dear, and as scarce at whatever price, as it is in New
South Wales, the production of fine wool at a cost
not involving loss, would be utterly impossible without the aid of nature in supplying the sheep with
food.   The wool-growers of New South Wales, therefore, who formerly got the use of pasturage for nothing, must still get it or be ruined.   As they have
no choice between getting it and being ruined, their
government, being despotic, can make them pay for
it as much as they can afford to pay.   Short of paying

more than they can afford—more, that is, than their occupation would leave after replacing capital with some profit—they cannot help paying whatever their government chooses to require. This absolute necessity of paying in order to preserve the staple business of the colony, renders the putting of a price on the use of natural pasturage a remarkably facile and pleasant sort of taxation: facile and pleasant, that is, for the officials of a government which has no sympathy with its subjects. As regards the subjects, this is a most unwise and oppressive tax; unwise, as it is a tax on the article of primest necessity in New-South-Wales life; oppressive, as it was imposed and is maintained in spite of every kind of complaint and opposition from the colonists. And this is what Lord Grey calls, perhaps believes to be, carrying out the plan of the theorists of 1830.

According to the principles of their theory, the natural pasturages of a colony, which nature has freely given, the colonists should use without let or hindrance of any kind from their government: and, moreover, their government ought to afford them every facility in its power for making the most of that natural advantage. It behoves the government, therefore, to frame a set of laws for the disposal of the natural pasturage in New South Wales or New Zealand; laws which should provide facilities instead of obstacles. Such laws would establish a perfect liberty of choice by the flockmasters themselves, together with certainty and stability in the whole proceeding. The laws of our pastoral colonies on this subject (if laws those " Regulations" may be termed, which have been framed by the passions of Lord Grey, or by the joint wisdom of some fine gentleman in Park-street, and some "Excellency" captains on the spot), would almost seem to have been designed to check colonial prosperity by means of direct obstacles, and of giving to the whole process a character of uncertainty and instability. This, of course, was not really the aim of these bureaucratic labours: but such is the result of ignorance and carelessness in the mode of imposing on the pastoral colonies the most objectionable of taxes.

Lest all this should not enable you to silence your Mr. Mothercountry as respects his baseless *pasturage* objection to the sufficient price, I will place a fact at your disposal for that purpose. When Lord Grey, soon after he became Colonial Minister, was framing some regulations for the disposal of about 180,000,000 acres of pasturage in New South Wales (the area is more than three times that of Great Britain), he consulted on the question of the best mode of proceeding, two gentlemen, who, in my opinion, possess between them more completely than any other two men I could name, the theoretical knowledge and the practical Australian experience for giving useful advice on the subject. Before telling him their opinion, they consulted me; and we three perfectly agreed, I think, on all the main points. He took their advice by the rigid rule of contraries! As they are both known friends of mine, this may be another of the cases in which Lord Grey's fear of being prompted by me has been the motive of his legislation for the colonies. But if so (and if you can find any other reasonable explanation of his conduct in this matter, I withdraw my supposition), to what strange influences does our system of colonial government subject the destiny of the most important of our colonies!

LETTER LXV.

From the Statesman.

THE STATESMAN'S MR. MOTHERCOUNTRY MAKES HIS LAST
OBJECTION.

I SEND the second of my Mr. Mothercountry's last
objections, without waiting for your answer to
the first.

Supposing (I will state the objection as if it were
my own) that the whole plan were established by law
—the sufficient price, with perfect liberty of appropriation as to locality, and, wherever they were needed,
the two securities for emigration-loans—still the plan
would not work: or rather, the more completely it
was established by law, the more surely would the
law be evaded, and the plan break down in practice.
In proportion as all private land was made dear, by
means of the sufficient price for public land and of
the operation of the emigration-loans in filling the
colony with people, would be the desire of the poorest
class to evade the law. Seeing the market-value of
all private land greatly increased for a time at least,
their desire for owning land would be stronger than
ever; and as the gratification of that desire would be
impeded by the price of public land, and the tax for

emigration on private land, they would endeavour to obtain cheap land in spite of the law. By "squatting"—that is, settling on public land without a title —they could obtain land for nothing: there would be a lawless appropriation of the public land on the old terms virtually of a free grant. If the government attempted to enforce the law by ousting squatters from their locations, there would be a struggle between the government and the squatters; and in this contest, the squatters would beat the government. No colonial government has been able to prevent squatting. What is called "the squatting interest" in a colony, becomes so strong after a time, that it always triumphs over a colonial government. More stringent laws, increased penalties, even British regiments, might be applied without effect. But if, even as things are now, the squatter invariably beats the government, he would do so more easily and surely under the proposed system, because, under it, people would be more tempted to squat, squatters more numerous, the squatters' outcry against the law louder, the disturbance of the colony greater, the trouble of the Colonial Office more intolerable, and the final concession by the government of a good title to the squatters, more than ever probable: the motives for squatting, and the probability of the ultimate victory of squatters over the law, would be so much stronger than these are now, that the law would inevitably be set aside: your plan contains within itself a sure cause of failure.

Since the above was written, your answer to the pasturage objection has come to hand, and been con-

veyed to our partner in these discussions. I will not
tell you how he received it, except by saying, that if
you wish to oblige me, you will send just such another
to his squatting objection.

LETTER LXVI.

From the Colonist.

MR. MOTHERCOUNTRY'S LAST OBJECTION ANSWERED.

THE second answer must necessarily resemble the
first, in at least taking the form of an endeavour
to turn the tables upon my critic: for he leaves me
no choice but to do that or succumb. This is an
irresistible mode of assailing when you are in the
right, but dangerous when you have no case. I suspect that our Mr. Mothercountry is less cautious than
most of the tribe.

It is all true, what he says about squatting in
times past; quite true, also, that if a higher market
value were conferred on all private land in colonies,
and a sufficient price were required for all public
land, one motive for squatting would be stronger:
but both these propositions together express only
part of the truth. I will endeavour to supply that
part of it which has been withheld.

So far as my knowledge extends, no colonial government ever seriously attempted to prevent squatting
by discouraging it: all colonial governments have
encouraged it in various ways. A very effectual way

of encouraging it was by readily letting every body
of squatters gain their point; for, of course, the gaining of their point by one body greatly encouraged
other bodies to attempt a similar victory over the law.
In most colonies, it got to be a common and sound
opinion, that somehow or other, by hook or by crook,
sooner or later, the man who occupied some public
land without leave from the government, would obtain possession of it by a good title.   One can hardly
conceive a greater encouragement to the practice.
The practice was thus encouraged by colonial governments, because they have all deemed waste land a
public property not worth taking any heed about,
because it was the least troublesome course for them,
and because public opinion in the colonies has approved of the course which the governments found
most pleasant for themselves.   Public opinion was in
favour of letting the squatter conquer the law, because
the expense, and trouble, and delay of obtaining a
legal grant were practically so great, except for a
favoured few, that squatting was another word for
colonization; and of that, naturally, colonial opinion
was in favour.   I would refer you for information on
this point to the appendix to Lord Durham's Report,
marked B.   When you shall have read the evidence
it contains about the difficulties of obtaining a legal
grant in Canada, and the squatting occasioned by
those difficulties, you will more readily understand
why public opinion in colonies should be in favour of
the squatter.   But colonial public opinion favours
the squatter for other reasons.   Whenever a colonial
government, either from idleness, or caprice, or want
of surveys, withholds a fertile district from would-be

settlers upon it, whether as cultivators or stock-holders, it induces public opinion to approve of that district being occupied by squatters rather than not occupied at all. At this moment, for example, a large portion of New Zealand is in the course of being occupied by squatters, because, by all sorts of mismanagement and neglect, the land is withheld from occupation according to law. The greater part of New Zealand must be either colonized in this way or not colonized at all; and thus even the warmest friends of systematic colonization, including the sufficient-price theorists, can neither blame these occupiers of land without leave from the government, nor wish that their proceedings should be stopped. It is better to subdue and replenish the earth by squatting, than to leave it a desert. Considering the operation of our present colonial policy, if policy it may be termed, as regards getting legal possession of waste land in the colonies, it is well for us that our colonial people have the hardihood and enterprise to colonize independently of their government. For my part, I heartily wish them success, for the reasons which induced Lord Durham to befriend the squatters in Canada on an enormous scale, and which will be found in the aforesaid Appendix to his Report.

But we are supposing thus far the continuance of the present slovenly and neglectful practices with regard to the disposal of waste land. Let us now suppose that there were a good law of colonization, including perfect liberty of appropriation at the sufficient price, together with the best provisions for the due administration of the law. All the motives of the squatter would be gone, save one. The poorer settler might still wish, might wish more strongly than before, to obtain waste land for nothing: but this mere money motive, is, I believe, the weakest of the squatter's motives, under present circumstances; and in the supposed case, it would be effectually outweighed by a new set of counter motives. The waste land of the colony would be deemed a most valuable public property, and would be cared for accordingly by the government: thus the contemplating squatter, instead of hoping to overcome the law, would expect the defeat of an attempt against it. Land in unlimited quantities, and with perfect liberty of choice as to the locality, would be obtainable with perfect ease at the sufficient price: thus the inducements to squatting now furnished by the great difficulty of obtaining a legal title to land in the most eligible spots, would be at an end: and public opinion, instead of encouraging the squatter, would help the law in deterring or punishing him. The public property would be guarded from invasion like that of individuals; and in pastoral countries, moreover, the whole of it, long before it was sold at the sufficient price, would be legally occupied by individuals who would help to defend it against the squatter. On the whole, I am persuaded, after much inquiry and reflection on the subject, that under a good and responsibly-administered law of colonization, colonial squatting would be as rare as the invasion of private estates is in this country.

LETTER LXVII.

From the Statesman.

MR. MOTHERCOUNTRY is furious, and objects
again, but " positively" for the last time.
He says that your sufficient price would have the
effect of " concentrating" the settlers injuriously, or
preventing their useful " dispersion" over the waste
as owners of the most fertile spots. He contends that
you want to produce a density of colonial population
by squeezing the colonists into a narrow space; and
that though it might be for the advantage of the colonists if they were less dispersed, your plan of preventing them, by means of a high price for new land, from
appropriating the most fertile spots where they like
best, would be a mischievous restriction on the exercise of their own judgment in a matter of which they
must be the best judges. He calls the sufficient price
an iron boundary of settlement, which is intended to
prevent colonists from using land outside of a district
not yet appropriated and used. He argues, with, I
must say, an appearance of being in the right, that

the productiveness of industry would be mischievously affected, if settlers were compelled to use land of inferior quality inside a given district, when there was land outside the boundary of a superior quality: and he has proved to me by ample evidence, that in several colonies, loud complaint is made of the restrictive operation on the choice of the best spots for settlement, of the mode of selling waste land instead of granting it. I am wholly unable to answer this objection. You are doubtless aware of it. Yet, looking back to your letters, I find that you have never once used the words " concentration" and " dispersion." When I mentioned this to Mr. Mothercountry, he chuckled, and said that he was not surprised at your avoiding the weakest point of your scheme. Pray enable me to confound him if you can.

LETTER LXVIII.

From the Colonist.

THE COLONIST ANSWERS MR. MOTHERCOUNTRY ON THE SUBJECT OF " CONCENTRATION " AND " DISPERSION " OF SETTLERS.

I DELIBERATELY avoided using the words " concentration" and " dispersion." I did so in order to avoid leading you into a misconception, into which the too unguarded use of those words by me on former occasions has led many colonists and some people at home. But I had no intention of wholly avoiding the subject as a weak point. I only wished,

by postponing all notice of it till the theory of the
sufficient price was developed, to be able to enter on
this question of concentration and dispersion with the
least possible risk of being misunderstood.

I entirely admit so much of Mr. Mothercountry's
objection as alleges, that, with respect to the choice of
land for settlement, the settlers must be the best
judges. Not only must they be the best judges in a
matter that so deeply concerns their own interests,
but it is impossible that anybody should be able to
judge for them in this matter without falling into
great mistakes and doing them great injury. New
land is wanted for an infinite variety of purposes,
amongst which let us note agriculture, pasturage,
lumbering, mining, quarrying, the erection of mills,
and the formation of villages and towns. These
various purposes are contemplated by an equal variety
of settlers or companies of settlers. There is no
business more entirely a man's own business, than that
of a settler picking new land for his own purpose;
and the truism of our time, that in matters of private
business the parties interested are sure to judge better
than any government can judge for them, is an error,
if the best of governments could determine as well as
the settler himself the quality and position of land
the most suitable to his objects. He is deeply interested in making the best possible choice. He alone
can know precisely what the objects are for which he
wants the land. The government choosing for him,
either a particular lot of land, or the district in which
he should be allowed to choose for himself, would
have no private interest in choosing well; and the
private interest of the officials employed by the

government would be to save themselves trouble by choosing carelessly. In most cases, they would be utterly ignorant of the purposes for which new land was in demand. Their highest object as officials (except in those rare instances where love of duty is as strong a motive as self-interest), would be to perform their duty so as to avoid reproach; and this motive is notoriously weak in comparison with self-interest. But indeed they could not by any means avoid reproach. For supposing (though but for argument's sake) that the surveyor-general of a colony, in marking out districts to be opened to purchasers, made an absolutely perfect selection with a view to the purchasers' interest, the intending purchasers would not think so. Every man is fond of his own judgment, especially in matters which deeply concern himself. If the government said to intending purchasers, Take your land hereabouts, they would reply, No, we wish to take it thereabouts : they would reproach the surveyor-general with having opened a bad district to settlers, and left a good one closed against them. And again, even if they were not dissatisfied at the moment of taking their land, it is certain that if they failed as settlers, and from whatever cause, they would lay the blame of their failure upon the government, complaining that if they had been allowed to take land where they liked best, their undertaking would undoubtedly have prospered. For all these reasons (and more might be urged), I would if possible open the whole of the waste land of a colony to intending purchasers : and I hereby declare, that as perfect a liberty of choice for settlers as the nature of things in each case would allow, is an essential condition of the well-working of the sufficient price.

To such practically unlimited liberty of choice, the objection has been urged, that the settlers would disperse themselves too much. They would, it has been said, wander about the waste portions of the colony, and plant themselves here and there in out-of-the-way spots, where, being distant from a market, and from all that pertains to civilization, they would fall into a state of barbarism: instead of acquiring wealth as all colonists ought to do, the settlers would only raise enough produce for their own rude subsistence; and the colony, instead of exporting and importing largely, would be poor and stagnant, like West Australia, for example, where the first settlers were allowed to plant themselves as they liked best, and did, being under 2,000 in number, spread themselves over an extent of land as great as two or three counties of Norfolk: in a word, there would be mischievous dispersion.

But mischievous to whom? Mischievous, if at all, to the settlers themselves. The supposition then is, that the settlers would injure themselves in consequence of not knowing what was for their own advantage. Would the government be likely to know that better than the settlers? But let us see how the facts stand. There are plenty of cases in which mischievous dispersion has taken place, but not one, to my knowledge, in which the great bulk of settlers had a choice between dispersion and concentration. In the founding of West Australia, there was no choice. In disposing of the waste land, the government began by granting 500,000 acres (nearly half as much as the great county of Norfolk) to one person. Then came the governor and a few other persons, with grants of immense extent. The first grantee took his principality at the landing-place; and the second, of course, could only choose his, outside of this vast property. Then the property of the second grantee compelled the third to go further off for land; and the fourth, again, was driven still further into the wilderness. At length, though by a very brief process, an immense territory was appropriated by a few settlers, who were so effectually dispersed, that, as there were no roads or maps, scarcely one of them knew where he was. Each of them knew, indeed, that he was where he was positively; but his relative position, not to his neighbours, for he was alone in the wilderness, but to other settlers, to the seat of government, and even to the landing-place of the colony, was totally concealed from him. This is, I believe, the most extreme case of dispersion on record. In the founding of South Africa by the Dutch, the dispersion of the first settlers, though superficially or *acreably* less, was as mischievous as at Swan River. The mischief shows itself in the fact, that two of the finest countries in the world are still poor and stagnant colonies. But in all colonies without exception, there has been impoverishing dispersion, arising from one and the same cause.

The cause appears at first sight to have been the unlimited liberty of the settlers' choice in the selection of their land. But a second glance at the subject shows the first impression to have been erroneous. When the dog was in the manger, the cow had to go without hay, or pick up what rubbish she could elsewhere. Only the first grantee at Swan River had a real liberty of choice as to locality: the second had less liberty, the third still less, and so on. At last, when a dozen people had appropriated enough land for the support of millions, nobody else had any liberty at all: the whole of the land suitable for settlers at the time was gone, and held by a handful of people, veritable dogs in the manger, who could not use their property, and yet would not part with it, because, coming from an old country where land has both a scarcity and position value, they deemed it worth more than anybody would think of paying for it under the circumstance of the vast extent of private land in proportion to population. The same thing has occurred everywhere more or less. In Canada, I am sure it is speaking within compass to say, the great bulk of private land was first obtained by people who could not use it on account of its extent, and yet would not part with it to real settlers: and I think it probable that in that colony at this time, more than half the private property in land is thus placed as the hay was by the dog in the manger. Ample evidence on this point, with respect to all the British American colonies, will be found in Lord Durham's Report and its appendices, especially in Appendix B. But if an inquiry concerning the disposal of waste land, like that which Lord Durham instituted in Canada, New Brunswick, and Nova Scotia, had been extended to our other colonies, we should have ample proof that in all of them, a small proportion of the settlers have been allowed to act the part of the dog in the manger towards the others, towards fresh emigrants, and towards posterity. The placing of immense quantities of waste land in such a state of private property as prevents it from being used—as keeps it always *waste* land—has been the universal vice of colonial governments acting under instructions from Downing-street. The result occurs, whether the land is granted in quantities exceeding the grantees' means of using the land, or is sold at a price so low as to encourage absentee ownership: but of course when the price is more than nominal, the evil of a great excess of private land beyond colonial means of reclaiming it from a state of waste, is very much mitigated. In those colonies, therefore, where land has only been obtainable by purchase, which are only South Australia, Australia Felix, and the New-Zealand Company's Settlements, the proportion of *dog-in-the-mangered* land is comparatively small.

But hitherto I have alluded only to individuals or private companies, whom an error of government constitutes dogs in the manger. Besides these, there is in all the colonies, as well when land is granted as when it is sold, a great dog in the manger, which does more mischief than all the little ones put together. This is the government itself. Everywhere in the colonies, the government makes " reserves " of waste land. It marks out places in the wilderness, sometimes small sections, sometimes great districts, generally both, and proclaims that *there* the acquisition of land is not permitted, and settlement is forbidden. Such were the Clergy Reserves in Canada, being sections of a hundred acres each, marked out in all parts of the province wherever land was obtainable by grant, and in the proportion to private grants of one in eleven. To these were added, in the same proportion, Crown Reserves, being sections of a hundred acres each, which the government condemned to perpetual waste. As the clergy could not use their land and were not permitted to sell it, their reserves, like those of the crown, were permanent deserts inter-spersed amongst the settlers, in the proportion, reckon-ing both kinds of reserve, of one desert for five and a half occupied sections. But these reserves, mis-chievous as they were, had a less dispersing effect, than has the reservation by government of large tracts of waste land, which is a common practice in all the colonies. The land is " reserved " from grant or sale—that is, from occupation and settlement—at the mere pleasure of the officials, who are wholly irre-sponsible to the colonists, from a variety of motives, sometimes really public, but oftener capricious, fan-tastical, or corrupt, never justifiable. The governor, a naval captain whose only knowledge of colonies has been acquired by visiting their harbours in a man-of-war, fancies that this or that spot will make a fine township " by and by;" so it is reserved " for the present." The Colonial Secretary or the Private Secre-tary thinks that in such a settlement, the colonists ought to be " discouraged" from spreading to the east or west, because it will be more for their advantage to spread northward or southward: so individual judgment is controlled, and colonization forcibly diverted from its natural course, by a great " reserve" in the "improper" direction. The officials of the Land Office have friends, or perhaps secret partners, who would like to acquire this or that spot by purchase, but not at pre-sent: either their funds are not ready, or they would like to keep their money for use at colonial interest till the spread of colonization beyond the coveted spot shall have given it a position-value, when by means of the rogueries of the auction system, or some other

mode of benefiting by official favour, they hope to
get it for less than its value: so it is "reserved" for
their convenience and profit. The only real public
motive for reserving land is the deficiency of surveys.
But this is rather an excuse than a motive. In the
name of this excuse, immense "reserves" by the
government condemn a large proportion of the waste
in every colony to long-continued barrenness, and
cruelly interfere with the settler's liberty of choice as
to locality. Reserves from the want of surveys are
perhaps the most mischievous of all, because the area
over which they operate is greater than that of all the
other reserves combined.

The evils occasioned by all these modes of circumscribing the choice of settlers as to locality, ought to
have been mentioned under the head of impediments
to colonization; for of these impediments, they constitute perhaps the most effectual. The dispersion of
the settlers which they forcibly occasion, is the main
cause of the difficulties of communication for which
colonies are remarkable, and of the many barbarizing
circumstances, economical, social, and political, which
these difficulties occasion. For one representation of
the whole mischief, I would again refer you to Lord
Durham's Report and its Appendix B.

But even here, enough of the case has been exhibited, to furnish us with the means of confounding
our Mr. Mothercountry. According to the whole
plan of· colonization which I am developing, there
would indeed be no liberty of appropriation for the
dogs, small or great; but there would be absolute
liberty for the cows, and because all the dogs would
be effectually kept out of the manger. Dispersion or

concentration is a question of locality alone. As to locality, all the restrictions on the choice of *bonâ fide* settlers, which occur through the operations of private dogs in the manger, would be prevented by the sufficient price, because that would deter every man from acquiring more land than he could use; and the restrictions now imposed by government would be removed, by abolishing all sorts of " reserves," including those occurring from deficiency of surveys. The only restriction on liberty of choice would be the sufficient price; but that would apply to quantity alone, not at all to locality: and that restriction as to quantity, not to dwell here on its other merits, would itself be a means of promoting the utmost liberty as to locality.

LETTER LXIX.

From the Colonist.

BY WHAT AUTHORITY SHOULD BE ADMINISTERED AN IMPERIAL POLICY OF COLONIZATION APART FROM GOVERNMENT?

THE time has now come for settling, if we can agree about it, to what authority the administration of a good law of colonization ought to be entrusted. My own opinion is, that the colony would perform this function better than the mother-country could. If that is not your opinion likewise, pray let me know what meaning you on this occasion attach to the words " the mother-country." On the assumption that, as respects the administration of colonial authority, "the mother-country" signifies the Mr. Mothercountry of the *Colonial Gazette*, I propose, that if ever the imperial legislature should see fit to frame a good law of colonization, the administration of such law should be confided to the local governments of the colonies.   Such a law would lay down general rules for the disposal of waste land and the promotion of emigration.   These general rules would be embodied in the colonial charters of government before proposed, in the form of stipulations or directions by which the local government would be bound in carrying on the work of colonization.   Thus, in a matter which is of great general moment to the empire, the imperial government would establish an imperial policy; but instead of attempting, what it could not perform well, the particular execution of this policy in every colony, it would confide that task of executive details to the parties most deeply, immediately, and unremittingly interested in its best possible performance: that is, for each colony separately, to the responsible municipal government of that colony alone.

It may seem to you, that there is part of such a policy which a colonial government could not administer well; namely, the selection of poor emigrants in this country.   I once inclined to that opinion myself, but have changed my mind by attending to the suggestions of experience.   If the colonial government pledged itself from time to time to pay a sufficient amount of passage-money for each of a certain number of labouring emigrants landed in the colony in good health, and approved of by the colonial governments as respects age, sex, previous occupation, and established character at home, the selection and carrying out of labouring emigrants would become an important business amongst the shipowners of this country, and could be conducted by means of contracts between the local governments and such shipowners, in the framing of which absolute securities might be taken, on the principle of " no cure no pay," that every object of the colony should be accomplished. The proposed colonial Representatives at home might afford valuable assistance in this part of the work of colonization. But I must not be led into details here; for the meeting of Parliament approaches. I will therefore close this part of our subject with two general propositions: 1st, if the imperial government bestowed good municipal constitutions on the colonies, but did not care to form a good law of colonization apart from government, the colonies and the empire would gain by handing over to the colonies the whole business, both legislative and executive, of disposing of waste land and promoting emigration: 2nd, if there were no good law of colonization, nor any municipal system of government for the colonies either, then, since the whole of colonization *as it is* would continue, neither colonies nor empire need care by whose hands the economical part of it was administered.

LETTER LXX.

From the Statesman.

THE STATESMAN DESCRIBES A SCENE WITH MR. MOTHER-
COUNTRY, AND ANNOUNCES THAT THE PROJECT OF
ACTION IN PARLIAMENT ON THE SUBJECT OF COLO-
NIZATION IS ABANDONED.

CONSIDERING our Mr. Mothercountry's disposition to construe arguments which he dislikes,
into attacks upon himself or the Office that he reveres,
I have not thought it worth while to repeat to him
your answer to his very last objection; though I must
confess that the temptation was strong upon me to
humble him a little. I longed to do so the more perhaps, because, having exhausted his stock of criticism
on your proposals, he has now taken to boasting of
the grandness of our present colonization under the
management of Downing-street. Yesterday, he came
here to dinner, and met two of those friends of mine,
who, I informed you at the opening of our correspondence, induced me to study the subject of it with
your assistance, and who lately joined a party of
visitors congregated here for the purpose of talking
over the prospects of the coming session. Addressing
himself to these colonial reformers, who had however

excited him by uttering some of their opinions, he ridiculed the notion that colonization is one of the *artes perditæ*, and even claimed for our own time a great superiority to the sixteenth and seventeenth centuries. He contrasted Australia as it is, with North America as it was before the war of independence. At that time, said he, no city in the American colonies, after two centuries of colonization, had a population equal to that of Sydney at present; that is, sixty years after its foundation. The imports and exports of the Australasian group, after only sixty years colonization, exceed those of all English North America at the time of the tea-riots at Boston. Within the last sixteen or seventeen years, we have sent out 120,000 emigrants to Australasia. Between 1837 and 1847, we actually doubled the population of New South Wales. And all this has been accomplished without cost to the mother-country; for the passage of this great number of poor emigrants was paid for with funds derived from carrying into effect a new principle of colonization, according to which waste land in the colonies is sold instead of being given away, and the purchase-money is used as an emigration-fund.

Here, one of my friends could bear it no longer, but interposed by telling him, that he was only repeating a speech which Lord Grey delivered at the close of last session in the House of Lords, and which has just been published as a pamphlet by Ridgway. The pamphlet was produced; for my friend had brought a copy with him amongst other papers relating to our contemplated movement in the House of Commons. What passed further it would be useless to report, with two exceptions.

First, Mr. Mothercountry's vaunting about colonization in Australasia under the Colonial Office, was
changed into whining about himself and his poor
Office, when we pointed out to him that the population of the whole Australasian group, after sixty years
from the foundation of Sydney, amounts, as you have
observed, to no more than that of the town of Glasgow;
that his grand town of Sydney was created by convict
labour conveyed to the antipodes at an enormous cost
to the mother-country, and by a vast expenditure of
British money in maintaining convict, including military, establishments on the spot; and that the greatness
of the Australasian export and import trade is due, in
no measure to the superiority of modern colonization
under bureaucratic management, but principally to
the beneficence of nature in providing our colonists at
the antipodes with natural pasturages, which the
Colonial Office taxes as if it deemed the advantage
too great for colonists to enjoy undiminished.

Secondly, I reminded him of his statement to me
soon after he came to reside in this neighbourhood,
that Lord Grey gives *you* credit for having invented
the "new principle" of colonization of whose effects
he had just been boasting; and then I begged him to
observe that Lord Grey, in his pamphlet speech, which
mainly consists of bragging about the great effects of
that principle in Australasia, claims all the merit to
the Colonial Office and himself, just as if the principle
had been discovered by them, and nobody but they
had had any part in giving effect to it.   The resemblance between what he had just been doing himself
and Lord Grey's proceeding, evidently struck him:
perhaps he heard one of my friends whisper to me

whilst he looked at him, *mutato nomine de te fabula narratur:* at all events, I thought he would have wept with vexation, such strange grimaces did he make, and gulping noises in his throat.   But let us change the theme.

I wish that the one which must now be presented to you, were as pleasant as it is truly disagreeable to me, not to say painful.   After much consultation with my friends, after showing them our correspondence, after using every argument that I can think of to induce them to fulfil their purpose of bringing the whole subject of colonization before the House of Commons early in the ensuing session, I have now the mortification of being told by them (for in fact it comes to this), that they see insuperable obstacles to the contemplated proceeding.   It would be idle to tell you all that has past between us; but I must just indicate the nature of the " difficulties" which they consider insurmountable.   One of these would-be reformers of our colonial system thinks, that public opinion is not yet ripe enough for action in Parliament.   " But action in Parliament," said I, " is the best way of ripening public opinion."   The reply was, that the state of parties is unfavourable to the movement: some party collision might ensue, when a fusion or amalgamation of parties resulting in a strong government composed of the best men in all the now broken-up parties, is the object of sensible politicians.   Another objector hinted at family connexions, and a personal friendship, that indisposed him to join in any course at which Lord Grey was likely to take offence. Then somebody remarked, that a real exposition in the House of Commons of our system of colonial government, if it did not speedily bring about a thorough reform, would probably produce great commotion in the colonies, and entail on the mother-country an increase of expense for military and naval purposes, at the very moment when the tide of popular opinion has just strongly set in for economy. There were more objections; but I may state them all under one description; that of " lions in the path;" little lions and big; in some paths several. My friends " admitted," and " perceived," and " wished" with me; thought the object excellent; and deemed success probable, because, whilst great benefit to this nation and the empire must result from colonial reform, no " interest" would be opposed to it except only the despotic-helpless Colonial Office. But with all this clear seeing and positive opinion, my friends would not stir a step: anything but action. Thus all my trouble is lost, and, what vexes me far more, all yours.

I have thought about moving by myself; but in this path, I, too, see one lion very distinctly, and several looming in the distance. The thought of a probable disagreement with my friends, in consequence of separating from them and leaving them behind in this matter, is very discouraging. Neither can I fearlessly incur the risk of engaging alone in a contest with general prejudice based on ignorance, and the still more formidable indifference of public men and the great public itself to every sort of colonial question. Oh, that I had the self-reliance which something appears to have banished from public life since 1846! I almost long for a good stock of vulgar impudence. Just now, at any rate, I wish I were out of Parliament.

LETTER LXXI.

From the Colonist.

I AM less annoyed than you seem to have expected; for practice makes perfect even in bearing disappointments. And, as another proverb says, good cometh out of evil: our correspondence has exhausted me, and I am glad to rest.

If your friends had persevered in their intention, I should have wished to trouble you with some further observations on points which, though hitherto left unnoticed because I wished to pursue with as little disturbance as possible the order of inquiry laid down by yourself, would yet be of practical importance if Parliament took up our subject in earnest. As a better time may come, it seems well that I should just mention the topics, which would have occupied several letters if our correspondence had continued. They shall be stated briefly; and in the mere notes of them which I intend to follow, no care will be taken either to observe order or to *explain* anything. If ever our correspondence should be renewed at your instance, you may expect to receive letters containing :—

I.

A plan of colonization (not emigration) exclusively applicable to that portion of Ireland, in which the bulk of the people is still Irish and Roman Catholic; a plan expressly framed with a view to the political condition, the social peculiarities, and the fervent nationality, of the Milesian-Irish race in Ireland. With respect to this scheme, however, upon which great pains have been bestowed in the hope of making it a real, practicable, and effectual, because radical, measure, for serving the most miserable nation on the face of the earth, there exists what you may deem a lion in *my* path. "Circumstances" would prevent me, even if our correspondence proceeded now, from communicating this plan to you at present; perhaps from ever communicating it to you at all: and I am " not at liberty" now to say more on the subject.*

II.

Some notions of a plan, both for securing ample religious and educational provisions in British colonies,

* Amongst these circumstances are the facts, that the plan of Irish colonization in question was framed conjointly by Mr. Charles Buller, another gentleman, and myself; and that during a visit which Mr. Buller paid me in France shortly before his death, for the purpose of re-considering and perfecting the scheme, we determined that no particulars of it should be mentioned in this book, which was then nearly ready for the press, but that, if the state of politics favoured the attempt, he should endeavour to make what we hoped might prove a better use of the plan in another way. In the Appendix No. I., will be found a further statement concerning the purpose which was frustrated by his death.

and for causing religious differences, which are at present as inevitable as the return of daylight in the morning, to aid in promoting colonization, as they indubitably promoted it in the early settlement of North America by England. In this scheme, the principle of "religious equality before the law" is strictly adhered to; but for that very reason, and also because colonization is the business in hand, the Church of England would spread faster and on a greater scale than the others, in proportion to the greater number and greater wealth of her members, instead of lagging behind them as she does now. I am bound to add, that my notions on this subject were not originally formed in my own mind, but, for the most part, suggested to me by Dr. Hinds.

III.

A plan of colonization for the West Indies. In this scheme, the economical principles of colonization set forth in our correspondence are observed with respect to public land, private land, and emigration-fund; but Africa is the country from which it is proposed that the emigration of labour should be attracted: and there are some provisions for causing the civilization of negroes in the West Indies to have some good effect on the barbarism of Africa. If this scheme answered its purpose, free-labour in the West Indies would produce intertropical commodities at less cost than slave-labour anywhere, and would of course, free trade prevailing, drive slave-grown produce out of the markets of the world. It is a scheme for wounding slavery and the African slave-trade at their roots.

IV.

A brief history of convict colonization by England.

Under this head, I should endeavour to show how convict emigration, besides making honest people in all ranks ashamed to emigrate, operates as an impediment to the emigration of valuable settlers, by giving, in one group of our colonies, a base jail-like character to colonial society, and a brutal jailer-like character to colonial government.

A curious branch of this subject, though not strictly pertaining to colonization, would be the successful counteraction of our missions to the heathen in Polynesia, by the " Devil's Missionaries" whom we spread all over that part of the world.

V.

Some suggestions, the aim of which is, to make colonizing companies seated in the mother-country, very effective instruments of the state in promoting the emigration of capital and labour, because properly-empowered and properly-restrained instruments.

VI.

A suggestion, the object of which is, to enable any " gentleman" father wishing to make his son a colonist, to prepare him, by suitable teaching and discipline, for succeeding in a colonial career, instead of, as now commonly happens, sending him away so well qualified for failure, as to run great risk of losing his money, his principles, his character, and his peace of mind.

VII.

A particular account (but this would be written at leisure for amusement) of Mr. Taylor's experience of the Colonial Office during twelve years.

VIII.

Some account of my own experience of the Colonial Office during twenty years.

THE END.

APPENDIX.

No. I.

[As time passed on after Mr. Charles Buller's speech on colonization in 1843, he was reproached, as well by friends as by persons who differed from him in party politics (for he had no enemies), with being inconsistent, and with neglecting a self-imposed task, by disappointing that public hope of his future usefulness as a colonizing statesman, to which his successful effort in 1843 had given occasion. If he had lived another year, his own conduct would probably have vindicated his reputation from this censure. But as he is gone, the duty now devolves upon his friends. None of them, as it happens, possesses so good means as myself of performing this duty; and therefore I undertake it.

To some extent, his premature death from mere delicacy of physical organization accounts for his apparent neglect of a public question which he had appropriated, and of his own fame. He was not really indifferent to either; but he was ever incapable of exerting his rare intellectual faculties without injury to his bodily health, and was often, for months together, incapacitated by bodily weakness from greatly exerting them at all. Thus, from 1843 to 1846, his physical strength was often over-tasked by his labours in the New-Zealand controversy: but his exertions during that period were far from being fruitless; for he was the life and soul of the discussions upon colonial policy which grew out of the New-Zealand case, and which mainly produced the actual disposition of the public mind towards a reform of our whole colonial system. All this took place when his party was in opposition.

In 1846, he accepted the nearly sinecure office of Judge Advocate General, but only on a distinct understanding with Lord Grey, that his duty in the House of Commons should be to follow up there, in co-operation with Mr. Hawes, the exertions for colonial reform and improved colonization, which they three had made together in opposition. But this arrangement, which was semi-officially announced, and in the reality of which Mr. Buller firmly believed, was totally disregarded by Lord Grey. The new minister was not in office a month, before he embraced views of colonial policy opposite to those which he had previously entertained, and which Mr. Buller continued to hold. By this most unexpected turn of events, Mr. Buller was placed in a position of extreme irksomeness. Precluded by his subordinate position in the Government from taking a course of his own in Parliament, and supposed to be in close agreement with Lord Grey, he was held responsible for measures, and for neglect, of which he cordially disapproved. From this thraldom he only escaped by becoming President of the Poor Law Commission, at the close of 1847. Soon after that event, I received a letter from him, from which an extract follows:—

"London, 15th December, 1847.

"I am much delighted, my dear Wakefield, by once more seeing your handwriting, and by your friendly congratulations on an appointment at which many of my friends look blank. Anything, as you say, was better than a sinecure, with a pretence of work in which I had no share. And my firm belief is, that the administration of the Poor-Law is a matter in which good is to be done, and honour acquired. Circumstances favour a reasonable administration of the law : and there is a general disposition to let any one who will undertake it in a proper spirit, succeed. And if I do succeed, no one will ever again say I am a mere talker with no qualities for business. I incur responsibility, I know : but sweat and risk are the purchase-money of every palm worth wearing. * * * * * * ; and I feel rejoiced to find your judgment in favour of the step I have taken.

" Nothing pleases me so much as your seeing in this an opening for a renewal of our colonizing co-operation."

The colonizing co-operation was renewed. In April, 1848, Mr. Buller came to see me at Reigate, for the purpose of discussing the question, whether anything could be attempted, with a fair prospect of success, for reviving the public interest in colonization which had died away during the previous two years. He was the more anxious that we should determine this question in the affirmative, because his brief experience of Poor-Law administration had impressed him with a fear, that unless colonization (not shovelling out of paupers by mere emigration) were undertaken systematically, the poor-rates would ere long attain under the new law, their maximum under the old; an anticipation that is now all but realized. But we decided the question in the negative. One of the grounds of this decision was the expediency, in our united opinion, of waiting till after the publication of the present volume.

On the 3rd of October last, however, when I was in France, engaged in completing the preparation of this volume for the press, I received a letter from Mr. Buller, in which he proposed to pay me a visit, and

said, " Not only do I want to see you on general
politics, but I have a particular project to discuss with
you; and I am anxious to do so, because you can lend
me the most valuable assistance, and, I think, realize
a great idea." The " particular project" and the
" great idea" were the project of a set of remedial
measures for Ireland, with some views as to the means
of inducing Parliament to adopt them. One of this
set of measures was to be a plan of colonization for
the Irish part of Ireland, or for the special use and
benefit of the Milesian-Irish race, who never colonize,
but only emigrate miserably.

The subject of such a plan had been matter of frequent discussion before, between Mr. Buller and me;
and our opinions upon it agreed. But since those
discussions, I had had the advantage of frequently
discussing the subject with a gentleman intimately
acquainted with Ireland, with Irish emigration, with
the state of Irish emigrants in the countries to which
they resort, and with the principles of colonization
and colonial government set forth in this volume:
and with his most valuable assistance, I had formed
notions about colonization for Milesian Ireland, which,
when Mr. Buller came to see me, were already put in
writing for insertion amongst the foregoing pages.
This new plan, Mr. Buller fully examined with me,
and in the end adopted its leading features. But we
then agreed further, that the plan would stand a
better chance of being soon adopted by Parliament,
if it were not published in my book: and we parted
on the understanding, that as soon as the book was
published, after passing through his hands for critical
revision on its way to the printer, he should make

such use of the plan as we might then deem most expedient. His sudden death frustrated our whole purpose: but as I resolved to make no change in the book in consequence of that event, the plan is still in my desk.

More might be said about Mr. Buller's lively and practical interest, after he ceased to be Judge Advocate General, in the subject which he had previously illustrated with such admirable ability; but the above explanation suffices for establishing the fact, and doing justice to his fame as a colonizing statesman.]

SPEECH OF CHARLES BULLER, ESQ., M.P.

IN THE HOUSE OF COMMONS,

On Tuesday, April 6, 1843,

ON SYSTEMATIC COLONIZATION.

SIR,—I cannot enter upon the subject which I have undertaken to bring before the House to-night, without asking its indulgence on the ground of the unfeignedly painful consciousness which I have of my very small personal claim to attention, and of my utter inability to do justice to the magnitude of my subject. It would be most unjust to the House were I to allow it to be supposed that the grave and difficult nature of the question which I propose to bring before it, and its want of connexion with party feelings and party interests, will at all indispose it to yield me its kind and patient attention. I must say, in justice to the present House of Commons, with the majority of which I have seldom the happiness of voting, that, however I may deplore the violence of party spirit to which we occasionally give way, I never sat in any parliament which has shown itself so conscious of the deteriorating character of our party strifes, and so desirous to make amends for its indulgence in them by every now and then giving a calm attention to matters of public concern, beyond and above the low domain of party. If it were not so, indeed, we should be culpable beyond our predecessors. For these, in truth, are times in which the most thoughtless can hardly fail, every now and then, to have a suspicion that the events that are passing around us, and in which we bear a part, involve consequences of wider scope and greater moment than the interests of political rivalry. Amid the very clash and tumult of party strife in which we, like those who have gone before us, are too apt to concentrate our energies and thoughts, we cannot help being, every now and then, conscious of such heavings of the soil on which we tread as to compel us to believe that around us are fearful agencies at work that threaten the solidity of the very framework of society. We have of late had warning enough of the necessity of looking to the material condition of the country, from the existence of distress of an unusual extent, duration, and severity. Owing, too, to inquiries which we never had the wisdom or the boldness to make before, we are now in possession of a fearful knowledge of the moral and intellectual state of the great masses of our people. And from such events as the disturbances of last year, we know well what effects physical distress and moral neglect have combined to produce in the temper of the masses, and how terrible is the risk to which we are exposed from this settled, though happily as yet undisciplined disaffection? With such matters as these fresh in our memories, and reflected in our apprehensions, we should, indeed, be possessed by some judicial madness were we to take no thought of the condition of the people, or to dismiss from our consideration any scheme suggested with a view of bettering it, until we had proved their insufficiency, or exhausted their efficacy.

I do not believe, however, that there ever took place in the house a debate calculated to fill the public mind with such despair as that which was raised by my noble friend the member for Sunderland, when he brought forward his motion on the distress of the country, in a speech showing so accurate and comprehensive a knowledge of the state of the country, and so wise an appreciation of the immediate remedy, that I cannot but regret that he has left me anything to do which might legitimately have been made a part of his remedial plan. For what was the result of that debate? An universal agreement as to the existence, and even the intensity of the mischief—an entire disagreement as to the remedies proposed. No one ventured on that occasion to deny the fact of very severe distress ; but, at the same time, whatever measure was proposed for the relief of it was nega-tived by a majority which proposed no remedy of its own.

The view which I take of the existing evil, and of the appropriate remedy, would so much more be obscured than strengthened by any exaggeration, that I must guard myself against being supposed to represent the difficulties of the country as either unparalleled or desperate. It admits of no doubt, that even after so long and severe a distress as that which has for some years hung over every class and interest in the empire, we are actually a richer people, with more of accumulated wealth, more of the capital of future commerce, than we ever possessed at a former period. But still, without any exaggeration—without believing that our resources are less than they used to be—without desponding for the future, it cannot be denied that this is a period in which wealth, though actually greater, is growing at a less rapid rate than before—that it is a period of depression and stagnation—that a smaller amount of useful and profitable enterprises are being carried on now than five or six years ago—that there is less employment for capital, and that business brings in smaller profits—that there are more people out of employment, and that the wages of those who are employed are less than they used to be. The great increase of poor-rates within the last year or two, owing to no disposition to relax the administration of the law, is an unequivocal proof of suffering in the labouring class; and the falling off of the revenue from customs, excise, stamps, and taxes, furnishes as undeniable evidence of a diminution of the comforts of the people; and though there is not the slightest ground for fearing ruin as a nation, there is evidently an amount of individual suffering, so wide and so severe, that we cannot contemplate its existence without pain, nor its prolonged duration without alarm. There is no denying that the present distress is not that of any simple class interest, or branch of industry. It can therefore be the result of no partial cause. And it has lasted so long, that there is no ground for attributing it to temporary causes, or hoping that it may cease when they shall have ceased to operate.

I do not deny the influence of temporary causes in producing the present very severe distress. I admit, with gentlemen opposite, that successive bad harvests, wars, unsettled commercial relations, the monetary and commercial derangements of other countries, particularly the United States, and an undue impulse to speculation, together with the consequent disastrous reaction, have undoubtedly combined to disturb our commerce; and I think it impossible to deny that, had these causes not been in operation, the distress which we lament would have been different in character and in intensity. But, on the other hand, I do not think that it has been shown that the operation of these temporary causes can be taken as a satisfactory solution of the whole of our distress. I think it clear that, besides these, there have been at work more permanent causes of distress; and that, in fact, the temporary causes are but forms in which the permanent evils of our state have exhibited themselves.

For instance, much of the distress has been ascribed to over-production. It has been asserted that during the entire period of distress, with falling prices and markets becoming, day by day, flatter and flatter, this insane energy of over-production went on building more mills, multiplying fresh powers of machinery, and adding fresh heaps to the pre-existing accumulations of unsaleable wares. To a certain extent there is, I fear, too much reason to admit this account of the history of our trade, and to believe that even after the long period of distress which we have gone through, it is too probable that—instead of relief being afforded in the most obvious manner—namely, by low prices having diminished production, and the supply of our goods having, therefore, been reduced to an equality with the demand,— production having, in fact, gone on under the pressure of low prices, the supply of many kinds of goods is now almost, if not quite, as redundant as ever. But I cannot understand how this can be regarded as a full explanation of the origin of the distress. The alleged over-production may have laid the foundation for a greater future distress; but I cannot conceive how it can be made out, under the circumstances in which it occurred, that distress would have been avoided, had over-production not taken place. Can it be alleged that, during this period of over-production, capital or labour were withdrawn from their ordinary occupations? Did any trade or enterprise of any kind suffer from the diversion of capital into channels in which more than ordinary profits were expected? Was the over-production carried on by means of capital borrowed from foreigners? Were the labourers taken from the fields, or the ordinary business of trade, to work in the cotton-mills? Or were foreign labourers imported into this country to supply the scarcity of English hands? Why, it is notorious that, during the last two or three years, we were lending money to the foreigner; that there has been a considerable emigration of labourers; that after all this, and all the over-production of which you speak, there never was so much money lying idle; and that our workhouses were getting crowded with able-bodied men, who could not get employment. If the mills, of which so much complaint is made, had not been kept in activity, the money which was required to work them would have been brought into a previously over-crowded money market; and the labourers whom they employed would have been so many more inmates of the workhouses. Is it not clear, then, that the over-production which is spoken of, however it may possibly aggravate future distress, has, in fact, only given a precarious, may be, ultimately, a mischievous employment; but still an employment which would not otherwise have been afforded to English capital and labour? If there had been no over-production, there would have been distress— different, perhaps, in form and in results—but still distress; for there would have been an additional amount of capital and labour unemployed. Your temporary cause, in this instance, instead of solving the whole problem, points us merely to permanent causes, which must be comprehended and removed ere we can hope to remove the sufferings of the people.

That you cannot explain the existing distress by temporary causes alone, is evident from the state of things in another country, in which these causes have operated in an even greater degree than here, without producing anything like the suffering which has been felt here. Whatever shocks our trade has experienced during the last few years, no one can compare them for severity with those which have been felt in the United States. Since 1836, the history of the trade of the United States has consisted of a series of crises, with intervals of stagnation. " I doubt," says Mr. Everett, in the wise and feeling answer which he recently made to a deputation of holders of Slave Stock; " I doubt if, in the history of the world, in so short a period, such a transition has been made from a state of high prosperity to one of general distress, as in the United States, within the last six years." And yet, has there been there any of what we should call distress among the quiet traders and artisans? of any inability to employ capital with ordinary profit? Or any general want of employment for labour? Of any great depression of wages? Or anything which we should call the extreme of destitution. Have even the unscrupulous demagogues of their hustings or their press ventured to describe such sad scenes as those which official inspection has shown to have been but too frequent at Bolton and Stockport? Have you heard in that country of human beings living huddled together in defiance of comfort, of shame, and of health, in garrets and in cellars, and in the same hovels with their pigs? Have you heard of large and sudden calls on the bounty of individuals, of parishes, or of the government? Of workhouses crowded? Of even the gaol resorted to for shelter and maintenance? Of human beings prevented from actually dying of starvation in the open streets, or of others allowed to expire from inanition in the obscurity of their own dwelling-places? The plain fact is, that though hundreds of enterprises have failed, and enormous amounts of capital have been sacrificed, and credit has been paralysed, and hundreds that were wealthy at sunrise have been beggars ere the same sun was set, and thousands have been suddenly deprived of the work and wages of the day before, yet capital and labour have never failed to find immediate employment in that boundless field. That fearful storm has passed over the United States, leaving marks of tremendous havoc on its credit and wealth and progress; but the condition of the masses has never been substantially affected. How comes it that these temporary causes, which produce so frightful an amount of distress in England, do not, when acting with double and treble violence in the United States, produce a tithe of the suffering? Does it not show that in this country the real mischief lies deep, and is ever at work? And that the temporary causes to which you ascribe temporary distress are of such fearful efficacy only because they aggravate the effects of causes permanently depressing the condition of the people.

I think, Sir, that we cannot contemplate the condition of this country without coming to the conclusion that there is a permanent cause of suffering in the constant accumulation of capital, and the constant increase of population within the same restricted field of employment. Every year adds its profits to the amount of capital previously accumulated; and certainly leaves the population considerably larger at its close than it was at its commencement. This fresh amount both of capital and population have to be employed; and if no further space for their employment be provided, they must compete for a share of the previous amount of profits and wages. The tendency of this cause to reduce both profits and wages is undoubtedly counteracted by what has fortunately been the still greater tendency of increased demand from foreign countries, of discoveries of fresh products of nature, and of improvements in various processes of art, especially in agriculture, to enlarge the field of

employment; so that, in fact, the condition of the great mass
of our countrymen has, as regards mere physical circumstances, indisputably gone on improving from century to
century since the Norman conquest. But it is as indisputable
that this enlargement of the field of employment, though in
the long run greater, is not so steady as the growth of capital
and population; and that during the intervals that elapse
ere fresh employment is found, competition, in a restricted
field, oftentimes reduces both wages and profits, and occasions periods of distress.

In this country, since the peace, there has been an immense
accumulation of capital, of which great part has, no doubt,
been turned to excellent account in extending our trade and
manufactures; in improving our agriculture; in covering the
country with public works and private dwellings; and in
bringing within reach of the humblest of our people comforts
which formerly only the wealthy could command. But, over
and above this, there has been a further accumulation of
capital for which no profitable employment could be found;
and which has consequently been thrown away in the most
unsafe investments—lent to every government that chose to
ask us for loans—sunk in South American mines, or fooled
away in the bubble speculations of the day. In loans to
foreign countries, I have heard that a sum so large has been
sunk that I fear to repeat it; and of this a great part may be
regarded as absolutely lost, owing to the dishonesty of the
debtor states. Such speculations are the inevitable result
of an accumulation of capital, which there are no means of
investing with profit; and of course the failure of such
speculations narrows the field of employment still more, by
producing a general unwillingness to embark even in safe
enterprises. We are now in one of those periods of stagnation of trade, while millions by which it could be profitably
carried on are lying idle in the coffers of our capitalists.
The general complaint is, that no man can find a safe, and
at the same time profitable investment for money; that the
rate of interest on private security is lower than it was ever
known; that the price of public securities keeps rising—not
because the country is prosperous—but because the universal
stagnation and want of confidence prevent men from investing their savings in any other way; that the profits of
business also are very low; and that every kind of business
is more and more passing into the hands of great capitalists,
because they can afford, on their large amounts, to be content with a rate of profit, at which the smaller capital would

not produce a livelihood. This state of things is the result of having more capital than you can employ with profit; and the cry of distress to which it gives rise will continue as long as capital continues to accumulate in a restricted field.

No one will question the fact that there is a most severe competition among labourers: that from the highest to the lowest occupation of human industry, almost every one is habitually overstocked; that in all there is the utmost difficulty of getting employment; and that the gains of some, if not all of every class, are diminished by the competition of redundant labour. The liberal professions are more overstocked than any others. Gentlemen of the first station and fortune find a difficulty in knowing what to do with their younger sons; and you hear every day of the sons of gentlemen entering into occupations from which their pride in former times debarred. Among the middle classes you hear the same complaints. There is the same intense competition amongst tradesmen, and notoriously a most severe competition amongst farmers. And the competition of educated men is nothing in comparison with the severity of that competition which exists amongst educated women, who are, unhappily, compelled to maintain themselves by their own exertions in that very limited range of employments in which our manners allow them to engage.

The extent of the competition for employment among those who have nothing to depend upon but mere manual labour unhappily admits of easy and certain proof, by a reference to the broad and indisputable conclusions forced on us by statistical accounts. Since 1810 more than six millions have been added to the population of Great Britain; and for all this additional population agriculture has not supplied any, or hardly any, additional employment. Yet the condition of our agricultural labourers is anything but such as we could wish. In the course of the violent recrimination which anti-corn-law lecturers and farmers' friends have been lately carrying on, we have heard fearful accounts of the deplorable physical condition of the agricultural labourers—their low wages, their wretched habitations, their scanty food, bad clothing, and want of fuel. On the other hand, we have had held up to us the habitual privations to which the labourers in various trades and manufactures are subject. The perpetual strikes in various trades— the long-continued misery of such a class as the hand-loom weavers —then the dreadful facts laid open by the inquiries put in motion by the Poor Law Commissioners and by the noble lord the member for Dorsetshire (Lord Ashley), respecting the unremitting and unwholesome labour carried on in many trades—the wretched poverty, precarious existence, and mental abasement of vast bodies of our artisans—above all, the miserable and degrading occupations to which a large portion of our population is condemned to resort, are proofs of a constant pressure of the population employed in trades and manufactures upon the means of subsistence which they afford. Look at the accounts of thousands of men, women, and children congregated together without any regard to decency or comfort in noisome sites and wretched hovels— of those who wear out their lives in the darkness of coal and iron mines, doing what is commonly considered the work of brutes, in a moral and intellectual state hardly raised above that of the mere animal—of the shirt-makers, who get ten-pence for making a dozen shirts; and of the 15,000 milliners in this metropolis, habitually working for the scantiest wages, in close rooms, always for 13 or 14 hours a day, sometimes for days and nights together, 9 out of 10 losing their health in the occupation, and scores of them falling victims to con-sumption, or rendered incurably blind whenever a court mourning, or any festivity of particular magnitude tasks their powers more than usual. These are all consequences of the one leading fact, that every year that rolls over our heads brings an addition of 300,000 to the population of Great Britain, and that unless in proportion to the increase of population there is a simultaneous increase of employment —unless fresh work be found for as many pair of hands as there are fresh mouths to feed, the condition of our popula-tion must sink, and there must be acute suffering. In Ireland the condition of the people is at all times more uneasy ; in any crisis, their sufferings infinitely more horrible. Can this be wondered at, when we know, on the highest official authority, that in that part of the United Kingdom there are more than 2,000,000 of persons always in distress for 30 weeks in the year from want of employment ?

It is this constant swelling of population and capital up to the very brim of the cup that is the permanent cause of uneasiness and danger in this country : and this that makes the ordinary vicissitudes of commerce fraught with such in-tense misery to our population. When our condition in ordinary times is that of just having employed sufficient for our capital and population, any check to the necessary in-crease of employment, much more any defalcation of the ordinary sources, must be attended with absolute destitution to that large proportion of our people who can save nothing from their daily earnings, and who, if they chance to lose their present occupation, can find no other to turn to. Contrast this with the state of America. I dare say some gentlemen may smile when I remind them of Mr. Dickens's account of the factory girls at Lowell, and their joint-stock pianoforte, and their circulating library, and the " Lowell Offering" to which they contributed the effusions of their fancy. But he must be heartless indeed who would feel no other emotions than those of ridicule, when he contrasts with the condition of our poor operatives the degree of education, the leisure, and the pecuniary means which are indicated by the possibility of having such amusements. Why, of all these Lowell girls there is hardly one that, besides all her actual comforts, has not saved more or less of money, and who, if the factory were to fail and be broken up to-morrow, and its 20,000 workpeople discharged at an hour's notice, would not be able to fall back on those savings, and would not either find immediate employment, or, as they are generally daughters of respectable farmers, or rather yeomen, be able to return to a comfortable home, from which her parents had very reluctantly spared her assistance in domestic labours. But when such failures happen in this country, the blow must, from the necessity of the case, fall for the most part on labourers, who have saved little or nothing, find no new employment open to them, and, if they return home, do so only to share want with their families, or to bring that family with themselves on the parish. Hence that extreme misery which follows in this country on any sudden cessation of a particular employment; for instance, the horrible destitution in the highlands, to which our attention was called two or three years since by the honourable member for Inverness-shire, and which arose from the substitution of barilla for kelp in our manufactures, and the sudden stoppage of the herring fishery. Hence comes that intense suffering which presses on particular localities when the course of events changes the sites of particular trades, as when the silk manufacture moved from Spitalfields to the north, or the woollen manufactures passed from Wiltshire and Somersetshire to Yorkshire. Hence the temporary sufferings that ensue to large classes of labourers and artisans when some change of fashion, or other accident, deprives them even for awhile of the usual demand for their labour; and hence the more permanent and entire distress envelopes those whose particular employment is every now and then superseded by some invention of machinery most useful to the public at large, but utterly ruinous to those whom it displaces. And hence it is that causes which hardly exercise a visible effect on the labouring population of the United States, involve large bodies of ours in the most intense suffering. There the labour and capital which are displaced from one employment find every other deficient in both, and are immediately absorbed in them, to the great advantage of the community. Here they are thrown back upon other employments all previously overstocked, and hang dead weights on the productive industry of the country. And the same considerations will enable us to account for the perplexing and contradictory phenomena of our present condition, and show us how it happens that we hear a cry of stagnation of business, of want of employment, and extreme destitution throughout the industrious classes, at the same time that we see around us the most incontestable evidences of vast wealth rapidly augmenting: how it is that in this country there are seen side by side, in fearful and unnatural contrast, the greatest amount of opulence, and the most appalling mass of misery—how it is that the people of this country appear, when contemplated at one and the same time, from different points of view, to be the richest and the neediest people in the world.

When I speak of distress and suffering among the industrious classes of this country, I must guard against being supposed to mean that I regard their physical condition as worse than it used to be. Taking the condition of the whole people of Great Britain for periods of eight or ten years at a time, I feel little doubt that, as far as external causes go, they are, on the whole, better off than they used to be. But even these assertions of a general improvement in the external condition of the people must be qualified by the admission, that there appears to be a class positively more, though comparatively less, numerous, which suffers fearfully, and that the rear of the community, in the present day, seems to lag further behind, both morally and physically, than it used to do of old. I doubt whether there ever before was in this country such a mass of such intense physical suffering and moral degradation as is to be found in this metropolis, in the cellars and garrets of Liverpool and Manchester, and in the yet more wretched alleys of Glasgow; and I have very little doubt that there never before prevailed, in any portion of our population, vice so habitual and so gross as is there to be found. The general comfort of the great body is increased ; but so also is the misery of the most wretched. We witness constantly more of the extreme of suffering ; we have a positively larger number of the dangerous classes in the country. I cannot but think, too, that the condition of the productive classes is more precarious than it used to be, and that great bodies of them run more frequent risk of sudden and total destitution than they used to do. It is obvious that this must be a consequence of that extreme subdivision of employment which is one of the results of increasing civilization. The more you confine the workman to one particular process or occupation, the more exposed you are to the sudden and complete displacement of the persons so employed by some improvement or change of fashion, or other cause that dispenses with their services.

But it is a perfectly different kind of change in our working people which induces me to regard the occurrence of periods of extreme distress as both far more afflicting to themselves and dangerous to others, than it used to be. What matters it that the scourge be no heavier, or even that it be somewhat lighter, if the back of the sufferer be more sensitive ? and what avails it that the external condition of our people is somewhat improved, if they feel the less evils which they have to bear now more acutely than they used to feel the greater which they submitted to once ? That they do so is obvious to any one who listens to them ; that they must do so is in the very nature of things. For, whatever may be the increase of enjoyments among our people, it is obvious that the standard of comfort has increased much more rapidly. Every class, when in full employment, commands a far greater amount of enjoyments than it used, and consequently every member of that class is accustomed to regard as necessary to a comfortable existence—to consider as a kind of rights, what his predecessor would have looked upon as luxuries, which nothing but singular good luck could place in his way. Each class is now cognizant of the habits of those which are above it, and the appetites of the poor are constantly sharpened by seeing the enjoyments of the rich paraded before them. And, as the enjoyments of the prosperous, so are the sufferings of the distressed, better known to all than they used to be. The horrible details given in the reports to which I have had occasion to refer reveal certainly no worse state of things than has for ages been going on in crowded cities, in poor villages, in unwholesome factories, and in the bowels of the earth. On the contrary, it seems clear, from the unvarying testimony of all witnesses, that, in

almost every particular, bad as these things are, they were
worse formerly. But then, formerly no one knew of them.
Now, zealous humanity, now statesman-like courage, that
does not shrink from investigating and exposing the full
extent of our social ills, in order to ascertain the extent of
the remedy that must be provided, searches out the unknown
misery, drags suffering and degradation from their hiding-
places, and harrows up the public mind with a knowledge of
the disorders to which we used to shut our eyes. Thus, the
very improvements that have taken place make lesser distresses more intolerable than greater used to be ; the general
elevation of the standard of comfort makes each man feel
privations to which he would have been insensible before.
The increase of information respecting passing events
diffuses over the entire mass a sense of sufferings which
were formerly felt by few but the actual sufferers; and the
irritation thus created is heightened by the contrast of
luxuries, which wealth never could command before, and by
a disparity between the ease of the rich and the want of the
poor, such as no previous state of things ever presented.

It is idle, then, when we are discussing distress to make
it a matter of statistical comparison between the present and
other days, and to think we disprove the reasonableness of
complaint, by showing that men used to complain less, when
they had less of the external means of enjoyment. Men do
not regulate their feelings by such comparisons. It is by
what they feel that you must measure the extent of their
suffering; and if they now feel more acutely than they did
the pressure of such occasional distress as has always been
their lot, we must be more than ever on our guard to better
the general condition of the people, and to prevent the
occurrence of these periods of extreme suffering. If humanity did not induce us to do our utmost for this object, a
mere politic view of our own interests would compel us: for
depend upon it that the people of this country will not bear
what they used; and that every one of these periods of distress is fraught with increasingly dangerous effects on the
popular temper, and with increasing peril to the interests of
property and order. And if you mean to keep government
or society together in this country, you must do something
to render the condition of the people less uneasy and precarious than it now is.

I speak plainly, because nothing but harm seems to me
to result from the habit which we have of concealing the
apprehensions, which no man of reflection can contemplate

the future without entertaining. We are beginning to know something of our own people; and can we contemplate the state of things laid open to us, without wonder that we have stood so long with safety on this volcanic soil? Does any one suppose that we can tread it safely for ever? I need not detail to you the dangerous doctrines that circulate among the people, or the wild visions of political and social change which form the creed of millions. Such creeds are ever engendered by partial knowledge acting on general ignorance. Circulating undisturbed among the masses, they start forth into action only when distress arrays those masses in disaffection to the law. It should be the business of a wise and benevolent government to dispel such evil dispositions by enlightening its people, and diffusing among them the influence of religion and knowledge; but it should also be its care to prevent the existence of that distress, which irritates the existing ignorance of the people. While, therefore, I go heartily along with the noble lord, the member for Dorsetshire, and others, who grapple with the general ignorance as the giant evil that oppresses the country; while I feel convinced that never again can the government of this country rest securely on any other support than that afforded by the general diffusion of sound instruction among the subjects; and while I look to education as the great remedy on which we must rely for removing the evils of our condition, I still say that simultaneous with our efforts for this purpose must be some efforts to better the physical condition of the people. Without relieving them from the pressure of want and the undue toil, which is now often required from them, you will in vain proffer the blessings of a higher moral state to those who can give no thought to anything but the supply of their physical wants. You will always be liable to have your most benevolent and sagacious plans thwarted by some outbreak, of which the watchword shall be, like the simple and expressive cry of the insurgents of last summer—" A fair day's wages for a fair day's work." This must be secured to honest industry ere there can be contentment among the people, or any basis for operations directed to their moral good. This you must secure for them, let me tell you, if you wish to retain your own great advantages of position and property: if you mean to uphold and transmit to your children those institutions through which you have enjoyed at once the blessings of freedom and order: if you hope to escape the tremendous wrath of a people whom force will vainly attempt to restrain, when they have utterly lost all reliance on your power or inclination to care for their well-being. Some improvement of their condition you must secure for the people, and you must secure it before long. But that you will never do until, by laying open a wider field of employment, you can succeed in diminishing that terrible competition of capital with capital and labour with labour, which is the permanent cause of distress.

It is with this view that I propose that you should investigate the efficacy of colonization, as a remedy against the distress of the country. I say as a remedy, because I do not bring it forward as a panacea—as the only, as an infallible remedy for every ill—but as one among many remedies, which would be valuable, even if they could not go the length of entirely removing distress, provided they enable us to render its recurrence less frequent, its operation less intense, and its pressure less severe. I say distinctly, that you will not effect your purpose of permanently and fully bettering the condition of the people, unless you apply a variety of remedies directed to the various disorders of their present state. But confining myself to the economical evil that arises solely from that one cause, of which I have laboured to describe the operation, namely, the competition both of capital and labour in a restrictive field, I propose colonization as a means of remedying that evil, by enlarging the field of employment. With other remedies of an economical nature, that have many advocates in this house and in the country, I come into no collision; because the mode in which they propose to attack the evil is not that of enlarging the field of employment. Some gentlemen urge the relaxation of the new poor law as a measure of justice to the labouring class; while others, with the same view, insist on a rigid execution of its provisions. But the question of the administration of the poor law is obviously a question relating merely to the distribution of the existing produce of the country, and can have no direct connexion with that of increasing its amount. Another remedy was proposed, the other night, which is certainly more akin in character to the one that I urge—namely, the allotment of small pieces of land among the labouring class. But this I shall not now discuss, because the matter was disposed of the other night by an apparently general concurrence in what I regard as the sound view of the allotment system; and that is, that it may be made of great utility to a large portion of the labouring class, if had recourse to only as a

means of supplying additional comforts and occasional independence to labourers, whose main reliance is on wages;
but that it would entail the greatest curse on our labouring
population, if they were ever brought to regard the cultivation of small allotments as their principal means of subsistence.

There is, however, one remedy suggested for the relief of
distress, which proposes to effect its end in the same manner
as that which I advocate—namely, by opening a wider field
of employment to the labour and capital of the country.
This it is proposd to do by freely admitting the produce of
foreign countries; supporting our labourers by all the additional supplies of food which we can draw from abroad; and
exchanging for that food and other produce the manufactures
wrought by the labourers who subsist on that imported food.
Sir, in the principles and objects of the friends of free trade
I fully concur. I not only think that we ought to do what
they propose, but I am ready to admit that the first and
most simple and most effectual mode of enlarging the field
of employment is by trading on the freest terms with all the
existing markets in the world. I propose colonization as
subsidiary to free trade; as an additional mode of carrying
out the same principles, and attaining the same object. You
advocates of free trade wish to bring food to the people.
I suggest to you at the same time to take your people to the
food. You wish to get fresh markets by removing the
barriers which now keep you from those that exist throughout the world. I call upon you, in addition, to get fresh
markets, by calling them into existence in parts of the world
which might be made to teem with valuable customers.
You represent free trade as no merely temporary relief for
the distresses of our actual population, but as furnishing
outlets of continually extending commerce to the labour of
our population, whatever its increase may be. In these
anticipations I fully concur; and I would carry out the same
principle, and attempt to make yet more use of these blessed
results, by also planting population and capital in the vast
untenanted regions of our colonies; and calling into existence markets, which, like those now in being, would go on
continually extending the means of employing an increasing
population at home.

I must not, therefore, be understood to propose colonization as a substitute for free trade. I do not vaunt its
efficacy as superior; indeed I admit that its effect in extending employment must be slower. But, on the other

hand, it will probably be surer; and will be liable to no such interruptions from the caprice of others, as trade with foreign nations must always be subject to. I grant that the restrictive policy of other nations is, in great measure, to be ascribed to the influence of our example; and I am inclined to concur in the hope that the relaxation of our commercial system will be the signal for freedom of trade in many other countries. But still we are not sure how soon this effect may be produced; how long an experience may be required to convince our neighbours of the injurious operation of monopoly; or how soon or how often the policy of protection may reappear in some shape or other, whether finding favour with the fantastic minds of statesmen, or the capricious feelings of nations, or dictated by political views totally independent of merely economical considerations. But of the legislation of your own colonies—of the fiscal policy of the different portions of your own empire—you can always make sure, and may rely upon being met by no hostile tariffs on their part. The commerce of the world is narrowed now not only by our own legislation, but by that of other powers; the influence of restrictive views is extending and acquiring strength among them. Within the last few years no less than eight hostile tariffs have been passed against us, more or less narrowing the demand for our manufactures. I say, then, that in the present day the restrictive policy of other nations must enter into our consideration as an element, and no unimportant element, of commercial policy; and, though I advise you to set the example of free trade to others, and extend your intercourse with them to the very utmost, still at the same time take care to be continually creating and enlarging those markets which are under the control of no legislation but your own. Show the world that, if the game of restriction is to be played, no country can play it with such effect and such impunity as Great Britain, which, from the outlying portions of her mighty empire, can command the riches of every zone, and every soil, and every sea, that the earth contains; and can draw, with unstinted measure, the means of every luxury and the material of every manufacture that the combined extent of other realms can supply. This we have done, or can do, by placing our own people in different portions of our own dominions; secure that, while they remain subjects of the same empire, no hostile tariff can by possibility exclude us from their markets; and equally secure that, whenever they shall have outgrown the state of colonial dependence, and nominally or practically asserted, as they will do, a right to legislate for themselves, our hold on their markets will be retained by that taste for our manufactures which must result from long habit, and by that similarity of customs and wants which kindred nations are sure to have. Under these impressions I direct your attention to colonization as a means, I should say not merely of relieving distress, but of preventing its recurrence, by augmenting the resources of the empire and the employment of the people. The suggestion of this remedy appears to be the simple result of the view of the evil, which I have described as the permanent cause of distress in this country. Here we have capital that can obtain no profitable employment; labour equally kept out from employment by the competition of labour sufficient for the existing demand; and an utter inability to find any fresh employment in which that unemployed capital can be turned to account by setting that unemployed labour in motion. In your colonies, on the other hand, you have vast tracts of the most fertile land wanting only capital and labour to cover them with abundant harvests; and, from want of that capital and labour, wasting their productive energies in nourishing weeds, or, at best, in giving shelter and sustenance to beasts. When I ask you to colonize, what do I ask you to do but to carry the superfluity of one part of our country to repair the deficiency of the other: to cultivate the desert by applying to it the means that lie idle here: in one simple word, to convey the plough to the field, the workman to his work, the hungry to his food?

This, Sir, is the view that common sense suggests of the primary benefits of colonization. When Abraham found that the land could not support both him and Lot, " because their substance was so great," his simple proposal was that they should separate, and one take the right hand and the other the left. The same view, as well as the sad necessities of civil strife, prompted the Greeks and Phœnicians to colonize. When the youth of the city could find no land to cultivate in the narrow precincts of its territory, they banded together, crossed the sea, established themselves in some vacant haven, and thus at length studded the shores of the Mediterranean with cities and civilization. And in later times this has been the simple and obvious view that the pressure of population on the means of subsistence has suggested to the advocates of emigration in this country. A vast number of persons capable of working can find no employment here. Their competition beats down wages; but, when wages have been reduced to the utmost, there are still superfluous labourers, who can get no employment, and who must either starve or depend on charity. A number of the latter are induced to emigrate, and are established in Canada or Australia, at the cost, at the outside, of one year's subsistence in the workhouse. By their absence, the poor-rate is immediately relieved: if the emigration be sufficiently extensive, the due relation between employment and labour is restored, and the wages of those who remain at home are raised, while at the same time the emigrant exchanges a life of precarious dependence and squalid misery for plenty and ease in his new home. If this were all the good that could result from the change, it would still be a great gain. I know that it would require a great effort to remove so large a proportion of our population as materially to affect the labour-market. At the end of every year, the population of Great Britain is at least 300,000 more than it was at the beginning. With the best imaginable selection of emigrants, you would have to take out at least 200,000 persons every year, in order to keep your population stationary; and even such an emigration would not be sufficient, because the momentary withdrawal of labour would give an impulse to population, and ere long supply the vacuum thus created. Still, even with these limited results in view, I should say it would be most desirable that emigration should be carried on, on a large scale, were it only that we might at any rate turn a large number of our people from wretched paupers into thriving colonists; that we might enable them to transmit those blessings to a posterity which they could not rear at home; and that the mere temporary relief—which is, I admit, all that could result from a sudden reduction of numbers—might be made use of for a breathing-time, in which other remedies for the condition of the people might be applied with better chance of success than it would be possible to expect under the actual pressure of redundant numbers.

But the whole, nay the main advantage of colonization, is not secured by that mere removal of the labourer from the crowded mother country, which is all that has been generally implied by the term emigration. His absence is only the first relief which he affords you. You take him hence to place him on a fertile soil, from which a very small amount of his labour will suffice to raise the food which he wants. He soon finds that by applying his spare time and energies to raising additional food, or some article of trade or material of manufacture, he can obtain that which he can

exchange for luxuries of which he never dreamed at home.
He raises some article of export, and appears in your market
as a customer.   He who a few years ago added nothing to
the wealth of the country, but, receiving all from charity,
simply deducted the amount of food and clothing necessary
for existence and decency from the general stock of the
community—he, by being conveyed to a new country, not
only ceases to trench upon the labour of others, but comes,
after providing his own food, to purchase from you a better
quality and larger quantity of the clothing and other manufactures which he used to take as a dole, and to give employment and offer food to those on whose energies he was a
burden before.   Imagine in some village a couple of young
married men, of whom one has been brought up as a weaver,
and the other as a farm-labourer, but both of whom are unable to get work.   Both are in the workhouse; and the
spade of the one and the loom of the other, are equally idle.
For the maintenance of these two men and their families,
the parish is probably taxed to the amount of 40*l.* a year.
The farm-labourer and his family get a passage to Australia
or Canada ; perhaps the other farm-labourers of the parish
were immediately able to make a better bargain with their
master, and get somewhat better wages ; but, at any rate,
the parish gains 20*l.* a year by being relieved from one of
the two pauper families.   The emigrant gets good employment; after providing himself with food in abundance, he
finds that he has therewithal to buy him a good coat, instead
of the smock-frock he used to wear, and to supply his children with decent clothing, instead of letting them run about
in rags.   He sends home an order for a good quantity of
broad cloth ; and this order actually sets the loom of his
fellow-pauper to work, and takes him, or helps to take him,
out of the workhouse.   Thus the emigration of one man re-
lieves the parish of two paupers, and furnishes employment
not only for one man, but for two men.
    It seems a paradox to assert that removing a portion of
your population enables a country to support more inhabitants than it could before; and that the place of every
man who quits his country because he cannot get a subsistence, may speedily be filled up by another whom that very
removal will enable to subsist there in comfort.   But the
assertion is as true as it is strange.   Nay, the history of
colonies will show that this theoretical inference suggests
results which fall inconceivably short of the wonders which
have been realized in fact; and that we may fairly say that

the emigration of Englishmen to our colonies has, in the course of time, enabled hundreds to exist in comfort for every one who was formerly compelled to quit his country.

The settlement of the United States was originally effected by a few handsful of Europeans. Deducting those who perished in the hardships of early settlement, and those who were not of an age or kind to add to the population, the original stock of European emigrants, from whom the present population of the United States are derived, must have been a very small number. This fraction has now swelled to no less a number than thirteen or fourteen millions of white people. If the United States had never been settled, and our emigrants had stayed at home, do you think it possible that the population of the United Kingdom would have been larger by thirteen or fourteen millions than it now is? —that we should have had and maintained in as good a state as now forty millions of people within these islands? Is there any reason for supposing that we should now have had any additional means of supporting the addition of the original emigrants? Nay, is it not absolutely certain that without colonizing the United States, we should not at this moment have been able to maintain anything like the population which at present finds subsistence within the limits of the United Kingdom? How large a portion of that population depends on the trade with the United States, which constitutes one-sixth of our whole external trade? Without that trade, what would have been the size, and wealth, and population of Manchester, and Liverpool, and Glasgow, and Sheffield, and Leeds, and Birmingham, and Wolverhampton —in fact, of all our great manufacturing districts? What would have been the relative condition of those agricultural districts, whose industry is kept in employment by the demand of that manufacturing population? What that of this metropolis, so much of the expenditure of which may indirectly be traced to the wealth created by the American trade? In fact, what would have been the wealth and population of this country had the United States never been peopled? Considering all the circumstances to which I have adverted, I think it will be admitted that it is no exaggeration to say that, taking the United Kingdom and the United States alone, the fact of colonizing that single country has at least doubled the numbers and wealth of the English race. And can it be doubted that if, at the various periods in which the colonization of the United States was effected, an equal number of persons had gone to some other

vacant territory, as extensive as the peopled portion of the
United States—and many more than such a number, be it
observed, perished in abortive attempts at settlement in
America—I say if such a number had so settled elsewhere,
is there any reason to doubt that another great nation of our
race, as populous, as wealthy as the United States, might
have been in existence, might have added another eight
millions to our export trade, and might have supported a
second Lancashire in full activity and prosperity in our
island ?

See, then, what colonization has done even when carried
on without vigour, purpose, system, or constancy on the
part of the mother-country ; and judge what would be its
results, and with what rapidity they might be attained, if
you were to colonize with system and vigour.   They are
results not to be measured by the relief given to the labour-
market or the poor-rate ; but vast as the consequences implied in the founding of great commercial empires, capable
of maintaining millions of our population by creating a
demand for their labour.   When I propose colonization, I
think it wholly unnecessary to enter into nice calculations of
the exact number of persons whom it is necessary to withdraw annually, in order, as they say, to keep down population ; because, as I have attempted to show, the numbers
withdrawn from us measure but a very small portion of the
good of colonization, which mainly consists in the demand
created for our labour and capital by the people in our
colonies ; and which benefits us not in those merely whom
it takes away, but in those whom it enables to exist here in
comfort.   I look to the great, the perfectly incalculable
extension of trade which colonization has produced, and
which, with all the certainty of calculation from experience,
it may be expected to produce again.   And such ground for
expecting such results will surely justify my regarding it as
that remedy for the present causes of our distress which is at
once the most efficacious, and the most completely at our
command.

I have directed your attention to the United States alone
—the greatest colony, it is true, the world ever saw, but by
no means the only proof of my assertion of the immense extension given to trade by planting settlers on new and
ample fields.   Compare the trade which we have with the
countries of the Old World with that which we have with the
colonial countries, and see how vast is the proportion which
we carry on with the latter.   I hold in my hand some calcu-

lations from the returns laid before the house respecting the trade and shipping of this country. The first is a statement of the declared value of British and Irish produce and manufactures exported from the United Kingdom in 1840, distinguishing the exports to old countries from those to our own possessions, and countries that have been colonies. I find that the total amount of these exports is—to foreign countries 22,026,341*l.* while that to our own possessions, and to countries which still belong to other powers, or have recently been colonies, amounts to no less than 28,680,089*l.*, or nearly as four to three. Take the employment given to our shipping, and you will find the results very remarkable ; for while the amount of British tonnage employed in the trade with foreign countries appears, from a similarly constructed table which I hold in my hand, to be 1,584,512 tons, that employed in trade with our foreign possessions and the colonial countries amounts to 1,709,319 tons. With respect to shipping, indeed, the result is more remarkable if we confine ourselves merely to our own colonies, for it appears that the trade of the three great groups of colonies alone—those of North America, the West Indies, and Australia—employed in 1840, 1,031,837 tons, or nearly one-third of the whole British tonnage cleared outwards.

I mention these results merely to show the great positive amount of our present dependence on colonial trade. I know that I must be careful what inferences I draw from these facts. I am liable to be met by the answer, that all this difference between our intercourse with the two kinds of countries arises, not from any greater capacity of demand in colonial countries, but from the artificial restrictions that misdirected legislation has placed on the natural course of trade ; that we have excluded foreign goods, and foreign countries have excluded our manufactures ; while our colonies, on the contrary, have been compelled to take our manufactures and use our shipping. To a certain degree, no doubt, there is truth in this reply ; and it cannot be doubted that our own folly has been the main cause of restricting the demand for our manufactures among foreign countries. But I think when you come to look more minutely into the details of the two kinds of trade, you will find that there is more than even legislative tricks can account for.

I will take two great classes of countries, the first being the whole of the independent nations of Europe, and the second those which can properly be called colonial countries.

From the latter class I exclude altogether the East Indies, and Java and Sumatra, because, in fact, they are old settled countries, under European dominion—the Channel and Ionian Islands, because, although British possessions, they are not colonies—Mexico and Guatemala, because the greater part of their population is the old Indian population —Western Africa, which forms an important head in the returns, because, in fact, it relates to a trade, not with European colonists, but with the Negro nations of Africa— and Texas, and New Zealand, simply because no return of the exports to those countries is to be got. I have taken down the population of the different countries of each class which enter into my list, the amount of export of British produce to each, and the amount of that produce which falls to the share of each inhabitant of each country. I find that the following European nations—Russia, France, Austria, Prussia, the rest of Germany, Cracow, Denmark, Sweden, Norway, Spain, Portugal, Italy, Switzerland, Belgium, Holland, and Greece, contain altogether a population of 211,130,000; and annually import of our goods to the value of 21,000,000l. On the other hand, our own colonies of St. Helena, the Cape, Mauritius, Australia, the West Indies, and British North America—the emancipated colonies, including the United States, Hayti, Brazil, Peru, Chili, and those on the La Plata, together with the nominal colony, but really independent island of Cuba, contain a total population of rather more than 36,000,000; and the exports of them amount to rather more than the exports to all the European states specified above, with their population of about six times as many. The average consumption of each inhabitant of the colonial countries is no less than 12s. a head, while that of the European countries is only 2s. a head. I grant that this proportion is very much swelled by our own colonies, of whose trade there is a kind of monopoly. Still, putting our own possessions out of the question, I find that the average consumption of our produce throughout what I have classed as colonial countries is not less than 7s. 3d. per head, being more than three and a half times as great as the average consumption of the European states, which is, as I said, 2s. a head. The greatest consumption of our goods in the whole world is that of no less than 10l. 10s. a head in the Australian colonies—the part of our empire in which the greatest amount of fertile land is open to the settler; in which there has of late been, in proportion to its population, the greatest fund derived from the sale of public lands; and into which there has been the greatest proportional immigration. This trade, which took less than 400,000*l.* worth of our goods in 1831, took more than two millions' worth in 1840, being increased fivefold in nine years; and it disposes of more of our goods than does the whole of our trade with Russia, with its population of 56,000,000, consuming only per head seven pennyworth of our goods. The comparison is curious in some other respects. Spain takes of our goods 9*d.* per head for her population; our worst customer among her old colonies, Columbia, takes four times as large a proportion; whilst her colony of Cuba takes no less than 1*l.* 4*s.* 4*d.* per head, being at the rate of more than thirty times as much as Spain. Our civilized neighbours in France take to the amount of 1*s.* 4½*d.* per head; while Hayti, composed of the liberated negro slaves of that same France— Hayti, which it is the fashion to represent as become a wilderness of Negro barbarism and sloth, takes 5*s.* 4*d.* per head, being four times the rate of consumption in France.

But I think, Sir, that I may spare myself and the House the trouble of any further proof of the advantage of colonies —an advantage secured by no jealous and selfish monopoly of their trade, but resulting from mere freedom of intercourse with nations whose kindred origin makes them desire, whose fertile soil enables them to purchase, our commodities. I think I need use no further argument to show that when the cause of mischief here is the confinement of capital and labour within the narrow limits of the present field of employment, the most obvious and easy remedy is to let both flow over and fertilize the rich unoccupied soil of our dominions. Had our colonies been joined to the United Kingdom,—had it happened that instead of our conquering or discovering Canada or Australia, when we did, continents as vast and as rich had risen out of the sea close to the Land's End, or the west coast of Ireland—who can doubt that we should have taken no great time to discuss the theory of colonization; but that the unemployed capital and labour would speedily and roughly have settled the question by taking possession of the unoccupied soil? Suppose that instead of actually touching our island, this imaginary region had been separated from it by a strait as wide as the Menai Strait; who can doubt that, in order to facilitate its cultivation, government would have undertaken to bridge over that strait at various points? Instead of such a strait, the Atlantic and Pacific roll between us and our colonies; and the question is, as you cannot bridge over the ocean, will

you think it worth your while to secure the great blessings
of colonization by making arrangements for providing capital
and labour with a free, cheap, and ready access to the fields
in which they can be productively employed? This is the
practical question to be solved. Few will dispute that colonization, when once effected, produces such benefits as I
have described. But the real question is, what outlay will
be requisite in order to put us in the way of receiving these
benefits? And is the object, good as no one will deny it to
be, worth the price we shall have to pay for it?

With the estimate I have formed of the almost boundless
extent of good to be anticipated from the foundation of
colonies, I should be prepared to say that it would be well
worth while, if necessary, to devote large funds to the promotion of extensive and systematic colonization. I should
not hesitate to propose a large grant of public money for the
purpose, did I not think that the most efficient mode of
colonization is that which can be carried on without any
expense to the mother-country. Capital and labour are
both redundant here, and both wanted in the colonies.
Labour, without capital, would effect but little in the colony;
and capital can effect nothing unless it carries out labour
with it. In the United States, where there is a general
diffusion of moderate means, capital is found in conjunction
with labour; and the simple process of emigration is, that
the labourer moves off to the Far West, carrying with him
the means of stocking his farm. Here, where the labouring
class possesses no property, few of the labourers who desire
to emigrate can pay for their own passage; or if they can
scrape together enough for that purpose, they arrive in the
colony paupers, without the means of cultivating and stocking farms. The capitalist would willingly pay for their
conveyance, did they, in the first place, consist of the kind
of persons who would be useful in a colony; and, secondly,
had he any security for their labour when he had got them
to the colony. But those whom distress urges to offer
themselves as emigrants are oftentimes men past their full
work, often men debilitated by disease, and still more, often
men so worn to one particular process as to be totally unfit
to exercise, and unable to learn the employments suited to
their life in a colony; and all generally want to carry with
them a still greater number of women and children, of all
ages, requiring care, instead of adding to the stock of
labourers. And then the system that used to prevail in

our colonies was fatal to all working for wages. Land was to be obtained so easily, that no one would think of tilling the land of another when he could get as much as he chose for himself. Labourers, as fast as they arrive in the colony, were enabled to acquire farms for themselves; and the consequence was, that the capitalist, having no security either for the services of the man whom he might carry out, or for a supply of labour from the general body of labourers in the colony, would do nothing at all in the way of taking out emigrants.

By the operation of these causes, emigration used to go on in a most unsatisfactory manner; and the great purposes of colonization were in no respect attained. Numbers, it is true, emigrated; some who went to the United States, where they could get work for wages, did well. But the emigration produced no effect on the labour-market; it notoriously did not even relieve the poor-rates; comparatively little of it went to our colonies; very much of that little was of a kind to be of little service in colonial labour; and being unaccompanied by capital, often produced only extreme suffering to the emigrants, and a great dislike to emigration here. I think it may be truly said that this emigration, large in amount as it was, did very little for the colonies, and little indeed for any body, except in as far as it added to the wealth of the United States, whom the influx of Irish labourers enabled to construct those great public works which have given so amazing a stimulus to their prosperity. On the whole, emigration promised to be of little service until Mr. Wakefield promulgated the theory of colonization which goes by his name; and suggested two simple expedients which would at once counteract all the evils which I have been describing, by attracting capital as well as carrying labour to the colonies. These suggestions consisted in putting a stop to the gratuitous disposal of the waste lands of the colonies, and selling them at a certain uniform price, of which the proceeds were to be expended in carrying out emigrants, and in making a selection of young persons of both sexes out of those who were desirous of being so assisted to emigrate. It was quite obvious that such selection of emigrants would relieve this country of the greatest amount of actual competition in the labour-market, and also of those most likely to contribute to the increase of population; while it would remove to the colonies, at the least possible expense, the persons whose labour would be most likely to be useful, and who would be most likely to

make continual addition to their deficient population. It
was equally obvious, that, under the system of selling lands,
the labourers thus arriving in the colony would be unable
to get land of their own until they had acquired the means
of purchasing it; that they would have, therefore, to work
for wages; that, therefore, the capitalist, if he paid for their
passage out, might count on their labour, and they as confidently on employment; that capitalists would, therefore,
be tempted to purchase, being sure that their purchase-
money would provide them with that labour which is their
first necessary; and that thus you might count on getting
from the sale of lands the means of carrying on a large and
constant emigration in the mode adapted to confer the
greatest amount of benefit on the colonies.

I may now speak of Mr. Wakefield's system of emigration
as one of which the great principles— the sale of colonial
land, the expenditure of the proceeds in carrying out labourers, and the selection of the labourers from the young
of both sexes, have received the sanction of the best, as well
as the most general opinion. This was not done, certainly,
until after a long and uphill fight, in which it was a hard
matter to conquer the apathy, the ignorance, and the prejudices of the public; and harder still to make any impression on the unimpressionable minds of men in office. But,
fortunately, the system in question found, from the first,
most able advocates among some of the most distinguished
writers out-of-doors, as well as among some of the ablest
members of this House; among whom I must name with
particular respect my honourable friend the member for
Sheffield (Mr. Henry George Ward), who, four years ago,
brought this question before the house, in a speech which I
could wish to have been heard by no one who has now to
put up with mine as a substitute; my honourable friend the
member for Limerick (Mr. Smith O'Brien), who has since
been the advocate of the same views; my noble friend the
Secretary for Ireland (Lord Eliot), who gave them his
powerful aid when chairman of the committee of this house
on New Zealand; together with my honourable friend the
member for Gateshead (Mr. William Hutt), and another
friend of mine, whom I am sorry to be able to mention by
name—I mean Mr. Francis Baring. I should trespass too
much on the time of the house were I to take this public
occasion of enumerating all who have at different times
given these views their valuable aid, but I must not omit the
name of my lamented friend Lord Durham, who in this as

in other cases, showed his thorough grasp of every colonial question; who was an early friend of a sound system of colonization; who had the opportunity of giving official sanction to these principles in his important mission to Canada; and from whom we expected still more when this, with other hopes, was buried in his untimely grave. But it is necessary to a due understanding of the history of the question that I should acknowledge how much we owe to others, who had the opportunity, when in office, of giving executive effect to improved principles. Among·these, the first place is due to my noble friend the member for Sunderland (Lord Howick), who, in February, 1832, when he had been about a year in office, took the first great step that the government has taken in the right direction, by promulgating the regulations whereby the sale of land was substituted for the old irregular habit of gratuitous grants, and the application of the proceeds to the conveyance of selected emigrants was commenced. My noble friend the member for London (Lord John Russell) made the next great step when he organized the machinery of public emigration, by constituting the Land and Emigration Commissioners, and prescribed the nature of their duties in instructions which contain an admirable view of the general duties of a government with respect to colonization. My noble friend must have the satisfaction of knowing that he has left behind him a colonial reputation confined to no party; and that, among those who are interested in the well-being of our colonies and colonial trade, many of the most eager opponents of his general politics were the first to regret that their efforts resulted in removing him from the superintendence of that department. It would be ludicrous in me to pay such a compliment to the leader of my own party, were it not notoriously true. And I must not forget that the noble lord, his successor, deserves our thanks for his Act of last year, of which I do not pretend to approve of the details, but which has the great merit of having fixed the disposal of colonial lands on the basis of an Act of Parliament.

By these aids, Sir, these views have met with such general acceptance, that I think I may take their elementary principles as now being the admitted basis of colonization. Hardly any man that ever I met with now talks of colonization without assuming that the lands in the colonies are to be sold instead of given away; that the proceeds are to be applied to emigration; and that the emigrants are to be carried out at the public expense, and are to be selected

from the fittest among the applicants. But what is even
more satisfactory is that, owing to the measures taken by
our government, these principles have received so much of a
trial as at any rate shows that they are capable of producing
some of the greatest results at which they professed to aim.
No one can doubt that the sale of lands, instead of deterring
persons from taking them, has very greatly increased the
amount, I will not say nominally appropriated, but actually
taken into use. No one can doubt that emigration to our
colonies has received a very great impulse since the regulations of 1832 came into operation. Compare the emigration
that took place to the Australian colonies, to which alone the
system has been applied, in the eight years preceding the
application of the new system, with that which has taken
place since. In the first eight years, the total number of
persons who emigrated to these colonies was 11,711, giving
an average of 1464 emigrants a-year. In the ten subsequent
years the total emigration to the Australian colonies, including New Zealand, which had in the meantime been colonized on the same principles, amounted to 104,487, or
10,448 a-year, being an increase of more than sevenfold.
Nor must you regard this as at all subtracted from the
general amount of unassisted emigration, inasmuch as during
the first period the total emigration to all other parts was
352,580, giving an average of 44,072 a-year; and in the
second 661,039, giving an average of no less than 66,104
a-year; and this, though during a considerable portion of
the latter period emigration to the Canadas was almost
stopped by the disturbances in those colonies. And it is
also put beyond a doubt, that the fund thus derivable from
the sale of lands is a very large one. The sum raised by
sales of land in Australia, during a period of nine years,
beginning with 1833, and ending with the end of 1841,
including the New-Zealand Company's sales, which are on
the same principle, and may be reckoned as effected by the
government, through the agency of a company, amounts to
a few hundreds short of two millions; a sum saved out of
the fire—a sum which has been received without making
any body poorer, but actually by adding immensely to the
value of everybody's property in those colonies — a sum
which, if applied entirely to emigration, would have carried
out comfortably more than 110,000 emigrants. The results
in one single colony—that of New South Wales—have been
most remarkable and most satisfactory. In these nine years,
the land fund has produced 1,100,000l.; and though only

partially applied to emigration, has been the means of carrying out as many as 52,000 selected emigrants, making two-fifths, and two valuable fifths, of the present population of the colony, added to it in the space of little more than three years.

The possibility, however, of raising a very large fund by the sale of land required no proof from actual experience in our colonies; because that fact, at least, had been ascertained by a long and large experiment in the United States. In 1795, the federal government put an end to gratuitous grants; and commenced the plan of selling the waste lands of their vast territory at a system of auction, which has, however, in fact, ended in their selling the whole at the upset price, which for some years was two dollars, and latterly a dollar and a quarter per acre. The proceeds of these sales has, during the whole period, amounted to the vast sum of 23,366,434*l.* of our money; being an average of more than half a million a-year for the whole of that time. In the last twenty years of this period, the total sum produced was nearly 19,000,000*l.*, giving an average of more than 900,000*l.* a-year. In the last ten years of the period, the total amount was 16,000,000*l.*, and the annual average 1,600,000*l.*; and in the last seven years of which I can get an account—the years from 1834 to 1840, both included—the total amount realized was more than 14,000,000*l.* of our money, or upwards of 2,000,000*l.* a·year.* This is what

---

* Lord Stanley, in answer to this, stated that the large proceeds of these land sales had been produced by the excessive speculations of the years 1835 and 1836, since which "the bubble had burst," and there had been a great falling off. The proceeds of the different years were—

					£.	s.	d.
In 1835	.	.	.	.	3,333,292	10	0
In 1836	.	.	.	.	5,243,296	9	2
In 1837	.	.	.	.	1,459,900	12	6
In 1838	.	.	.	.	896,992	10	1
In 1839	.	.	.	.	1,346,772	10	0
In 1840	.	.	.	.	581,264	7	6

The facts stated by Lord Stanley are perfectly correct; but they do not controvert the conclusions drawn by Mr. Buller. The sales of 1835 and 1836 were no doubt swelled by the speculative spirit of the period; but it is just as obvious that the great falling off in the latter years has been the result of the extraordinary commercial distress that has pressed on the United States all the time. The only subject for wonder is that during such a period of distress as that from 1837 to 1840 there should have been so much as £4,284,930 to spare for the purchase of land.—*Foot note in Mr. Murray's Publication.*

actually has been done in the United States; and done, let me remark, without the object of promoting emigration, almost without that of getting revenue: for it is very clear that the primary object with which the system of sale was established was not that of getting money, but of preventing that jobbing and favouritism which cannot be avoided where the government has the power of making gratuitous grants of land. The experiment cannot be regarded as a test of the largest amount which could be got for the land, consistently with a due regard to other public objects, because, in the first place, there have been large exceptional grants, which have brought a great amount of unbought land into the market. There has been a large amount of additional land, not under the control of the general government, and which had been sold by the old states, particularly Maine. And, above all, the price has, as I said, never been fixed with a view to getting the greatest amount of revenue. There is not the slightest reason to doubt that the same amount of land might have been sold at a higher price. Indeed, we know that the amount of land sold did not increase in consequence of the great diminution of price from two dollars to a dollar and a quarter in 1819; but actually fell off very considerably, and did not recover itself for the next ten years. I have very little doubt that the same amount of land would have been sold at our price of a pound; and that the sum of eighty millions might thus have been realized in forty-five years as easily as that of twenty-three millions actually was.

I tell you what has actually been done, and what we may safely infer might have been done by a country, which, with all its vast territory, possesses actually a less amount of available land than is included within our empire; which has now a much less, and had when all this began, a very much less population than ours; and with a far less proportion even of that available for emigration; and which, with all its activity and prosperity, possesses an amount of available capital actually insignificant when compared with ours. Imagine what would have been the result, had we at the period in which the American government commenced its sales, applied the same principle with more perfect details to the waste lands of our colonies, and used the funds derived from such sales in rendering our Far West as accessible to our people as the valleys of the Ohio and Missouri to the settlers in the United States. Hundreds of thousands of our countrymen, who now with their families people the territory of the United States, would have been subjects of the British Crown; as many—ay, even more—who have passed their wretched existence in our workouses or crowded cities, or perished in Irish famines, or pined away in the more lingering torture of such destitution as Great Britain has too often seen, would have been happy and thriving on fertile soils and under genial climates, and making really our country that vast empire which encircles the globe. In every part of the world would have risen fresh towns, inhabited by our people; fresh ports would have been crowded by our ships; and harvests would have waved where the silence of the forest still reigns. What now would have been our commerce! What the population and revenue of our empire! This, Sir, is one of those subjects on which we may not embody in precise form the results which calculation justifies us in contemplating, lest sober arithmetic should assume the features of sanguine fancy. But this much I think I may say, that the experience of America justifies us in believing that if we, like the people of that country, had begun half a century ago, to turn our waste lands to account, we should have had a larger population, and a greater accumulation of wealth than we now have; and yet that over-population and over-production, and low wages, and low profits, and destitution, and distress, and discontent, would have been words of as little familiarity and meaning in our ears, as they are in those of the people of the United States.

We need, then, feel little doubt but that the new system of colonization has shown itself capable of producing all the economical results which it professes to attain. But I cannot quit the subject of its practical working, without calling your attention to effects quite as important, which it has shown itself capable of realizing in the way of changing the character and spirit in which our colonization has hitherto been conducted. If you wish colonies to be rendered generally useful to all classes in the mother-country—if you wish them to be prosperous, to reflect back the civilization, and habits, and feelings of their parent stock, and to be and long to remain integral parts of your empire—care should be taken that society should be carried out in something of the form in which it is seen at home—that it should contain some, at least, of all the elements that go to make it up here, and that it should continue under those influences that are found effectual for keeping us together in harmony. On such principles alone have the foundations of successful

colonies been laid.   Neither Phœnician, nor Greek, nor
Roman, nor Spaniard—no, nor our own great forefathers—
when they laid the foundations of an European society on
the continent, and in the islands of the Western World, ever
dreamed of colonizing with one class of society by itself,
and that the most helpless for shifting by itself.   The fore-
most men of the ancient republics led forth their colonies;
each expedition was in itself an epitome of the society which
it left; the solemn rites of religion blessed its departure
from its home; and it bore with it the images of its country's
gods, to link it for ever by a common worship to its ancient
home.   The government of Spain sent its dignified clergy
out with some of its first colonists.   The noblest families in
Spain sent their younger sons to settle in Hispaniola, and
Mexico, and Peru.   Raleigh quitted a brilliant court, and
the highest spheres of political ambition, in order to lay the
foundation of the colony of Virginia; Lord Baltimore and
the best Catholic families founded Maryland; Penn was a
courtier before he became a colonist; a set of noble proprietors established Carolina, and intrusted the framing of its
constitution to John Locke; the highest hereditary rank in
this country below the peerage was established in connexion
with the settlement of Nova Scotia; and such gentlemen as
Sir Harry Vane, Hampden, and Cromwell did not disdain
the prospect of a colonial career.   In all these cases the
emigration was of every class.   The mass, as does the mass
everywhere, contributed its labour alone; but they were
encouraged by the presence, guided by the counsels, and
supported by the means of the wealthy and educated, whom
they had been used to follow and honour in their own
country.   In the United States the constant and large
migration from the old to the new states is a migration of
every class; the middle classes go in quite as large proportion as the labouring; the most promising of the educated
youth are the first to seek the new career.   And hence it is
that society sets itself down complete in all its parts in the
back settlements in the United States; that every political,
and social, and religious institution of the old society is
found in the new at the outset: that every liberal profession
is abundantly supplied; and that, as Captain Marryat
remarks, you find in a town of three or four years' standing,
in the back part of New York or Ohio, almost every luxury
of the old cities.

And thus was colonization always conducted, until all our
ideas on the subject were perverted by the foundation of

convict colonies; and emigration being associated in men's minds with transportation, was looked upon as the hardest punishment of guilt, or necessity of poverty.   It got to be resorted to as the means of relieving parishes of their paupers; and so sprung up that irregular, ill-regulated emigration of a mere labouring class which has been one of the anomalies of our time.   The state exercised not the slightest control over the hordes whom it simply allowed to leave want in one part of the empire for hardship in another; and it permitted the conveyance of human beings to be carried on just as the avidity and rashness of shipowners might choose.   I am drawing no picture of a mere fanciful nature, but am repeating the solemn assertions of the legislature of Lower Canada, confirmed by Lord Durham's report, when I say that the result of this careless, shameful neglect of the emigrants was, that hundreds and thousands of pauper families walked in their rags from the quays of Liverpool and Cork into ill-found, unsound ships, in which human beings were crammed together in the empty space which timber was to be stowed in on the homeward voyage. Ignorant themselves, and misinformed by the government of the requisites of such a voyage, they suffered throughout it from privations of necessary food and clothing; such privations, filth, and bad air were sure to engender disease; and the ships that reached their destination in safety, generally deposited some contagious fever, together with a mass of beggary, on the quays of Quebec and Montreal.   No medical attendance was required by law, and the provision of it in some ships was a creditable exception to the general practice.   Of course, where so little thought was taken of men's physical wants, their moral wants were even less cared for; and as the emigrants went without any minister of religion or schoolmaster in their company, so they settled over the vacant deserts of Canada without church or school among them.   Respectable tradesmen and men possessed of capital shrunk from such associations; and if their necessities compelled them to quit their own country for a new one, they went as a matter of course to the United States.   The idea of a gentleman emigrating was almost unheard of, unless he emigrated for a while as a placeman; and I recollect when Colonel Talbot was regarded as a kind of innocent monomaniac, who, from some strange caprice, had committed the folly of residing on his noble Canadian estate.

Within the last ten or twelve years a great change has

come over this state of things; within the last three or four years our colonization has entirely altered its character. The emigration to Port Philip, South Australia, and New Zealand, has been an emigration of every class, with capital in due proportion to labourers; with tradesman and artisans of every kind, and with the framework of such social institutions as the settlers have been used to in their native land. Clergymen and schoolmasters, and competent men of every liberal profession, are among the earliest emigrants; artists and men of science resort to a new field for their labours; in the foundation of the settlement you find funds set apart for public works, for religious endowments, and even for colleges. Associations of a religious and charitable and literary nature are formed at the outset; and these are intended to benefit not only the poor emigrants, but the helpless native, who is brought into contact with a superior race. To such settlements men of birth and refinement are tempted to emigrate; they do so in great numbers. I will be bound to say, that more men of good family have settled in New Zealand in the three years since the beginning of 1840, than in British North America in the first thirty years of the present century. It is notorious that the greatest change has taken place in the public feeling on this point, and that a colonial career is now looked upon as one of the careers open to a gentleman. This change in the character of colonization—this great change in the estimation in which it is held, is of greater moment than the mere provision of means for conducting emigration without cost to the public. It makes colonization, indeed, an extension of civilized society, instead of that mere emigration which aimed at little more than shovelling out your paupers to where they might die, without shocking their betters with the sight or sound of their last agony.

I come, then, before you to-night as the advocate of no new fancy of my own, of no untried scheme for the realization of unattainable results. The remedy which I propose is one which the experience of the world has approved; and the mode in which I would apply it is one which sufficient experience justifies me in describing as of recognised efficacy in the opinion of all practical authorities. The great principles of the plan of colonization which I urge have been formally but unequivocally adopted by the government of this country; they have been adopted with the general sanction of public opinion here; and the colonies, as we well know, are clamorous for the extension of a system which they feel to have already given an amazing stimulus to their prosperity, and to which they look as the only means of enabling their progress to be steady. I ask, then, for no experiment. The thing has been tried, and I call upon you to make more use of the remedy, which has proved to be sound. If you think that on the system which is now recognised as the sound one, the benefits of colonization may be practically secured, then I say that the only question that remains for us is, whether and how that system can be so far extended as to realize its utmost results. For it is clear that, if it contains the means of greater relief, the condition of the country requires its extended application. It is equally clear that, though it has done great good already, it has been put in operation with no system or steadiness, not always quite heartily, certainly with no readiness to profit by experience for the purpose of either amending or extending it. It has, nevertheless, called into existence a large fund, which was not in being before. Those lands, which from all time had been barren and nominal domains—the mere materials for jobbing, this discovery has converted into a valuable property ; and it has also shown you how to apply them, so as to make them most productive to the general good of the colonies, by effecting the importation of labour. But I think I am justified in saying that, under such circumstances, the system has never been turned to full account; that if the people of the United States can purchase two millions of pounds' worth of land a-year, there is spare capital in this country to purchase something more than one-eighth of that amount; and if they can dispose of some seven or eight millions a-year, we could dispose of more than one-thirtieth of that quantity; that if they can take annually from us 50,000 emigrants, besides at least as large a number from their own country, our Australian colonies could take more than one-seventh of that total amount. If we could only realize the same results as actually are realized in the United States, we should get two millions, on the average, instead of 250,000l. a-year, from the sale of our lands ; and the means of sending out, free of cost, some 110,000 instead of 10,000 or 12,000 poor persons every year, in addition to the large unassisted emigration that goes on. If, with our vastly superior wealth and immeasurably larger emigrant population, we fall so lamentably short of the results actually realized in the United States—nay, if with such superior powers we do not realize much greater results—I say it is sufficient proof that there is some defect in the mode of applying a sound principle.

It is no defect of inclination on the part of the people to better their fortunes in another part of the empire; the amount of voluntary emigration shows that. It is no defect of inclination on the part of capitalists to invest their money in the purchase of colonial lands; there is never any difficulty in getting money in any sound system of colonization. The defect must be in the mode of facilitating the access of labour to the colonies; it must be from our not making the most of the good principles on which we go. 1 say it is our bounden duty to have the matter investigated thoroughly; and to discover and remove the faults of detail that prevent our satisfying our present most extreme need, by devising, from a sound principle, the utmost benefits that colonization can produce. It is clear that the public—not the ignorant and thoughtless—but men of the greatest speculative research—men of the greatest practical knowledge and interest in commerce, such as those who have signed the recent memorials to the right honourable baronet, from this great city, and the other principal parts of the kingdom; it is clear, I say, that the public look to colonization as affording a means of relief for our national difficulties. It is our business to prove whether that hope is sound or unsound; and either without delay to expose its want of truth, and clear it out from the public mind as a delusion that can only do harm; or, seeing it to be sound, to take care that it shall be realized, and that the means of good which God has placed at our disposal shall be turned to their full account. To do one of these things is our imperative duty. Above all, it is a duty most binding on her Majesty's government, who alone can be the instrument of thoroughly sifting such matter—who alone can give practical effect to the results of such inquiry. It is a duty of which, if they should, contrary to my hopes, neglect it, it becomes this House to remind them. And it is with this view that I have ventured to bring forward the motion of to-night.

It is not my purpose to propose any specific measure to the House. And in the first place let me guard myself against the supposition that I mean to propose anything of a kind to which I have the very strongest objection—namely, compulsory emigration. Most assuredly I have no thought of proposing that any one should be compelled to emigrate. So far from proposing compulsory emigration, I should object to holding out to any man any inducement to quit his country. On this ground I deprecate anything like making emigration an alternative for the Union Workhouse. I am very dubious of the propriety of even applying parish rates in aid of emigration. My object would be that the poor of this country should be accustomed to regard the means of bettering their condition in another part of the empire as a great boon offered them—not a necessity imposed on them by government. I do not wonder that in the old days of convict colonies and pauper emigration they shrank from colonization, and responded to Mr. Cobbett's denunciation of the attempt of their rulers to transport them. But a better feeling has now sprung up, together with a better knowledge of the subject. The difficulty is now not to inveigle emigrants, but to select among the crowds of eager applicants; and the best portion of the labouring classes are now as little inclined to look on the offer of a passage to the colonies as a punishment, or a degradation, as a gentleman would be to entertain the same view of an offer of cadetship or writership for one of his younger sons. The prejudice is gone ; and I did imagine that the attempt to appeal to it by the agency of stale nick-names was not likely to be made in our day, had I not been undeceived by some most furious invectives against the gentlemen who signed the City memorials, which were recently delivered at Drury Lane theatre, on one of those nights on which the legitimate drama is not performed. I cannot imagine that my esteemed friend the member for Stockport (Mr. Cobden), who is reported on that occasion to have been very successful in representing the character of a bereaved grandmother, can help, on sober reflection, feeling some compunction for having condescended to practice on the ignorance of his audience by the use of clap-traps so stale, and representations so unfounded; and for bringing just the same kind of unjust charges against honest men engaged in an honest cause, as he brushes so indignantly out of his own path when he finds them opposed to him in his own pursuit of a great public cause. I must attribute this deviation from his usual candour to the influence of the unseen genius of the place in which he spoke, and suppose that he believed it would be out of keeping in a theatre to appeal to men's passions otherwise than by fiction.

It is not my purpose to suggest interference on the part of government to induce emigration, except by merely facilitating access to the colonies by the application of th e land-fund to that object. To do this more effectually than it now does is what I ask of it, and for this purpose I only ask it to perfect the details of the system now in force. Carry out, I say of her Majesty's government, the system which was begun by the Regulations of 1832, and by the appointment of Land and Emigration Commission, to which you made a valuable addition when you sanctioned the principle of the Act of last session, which secured the system of disposing of the lands of the colonies against the caprice of Colonial Governors, and even of Secretaries of State. Carry it out with the same sound purpose at bottom, but with more deliberate consideration of details than it was possible for the noble lord to apply to a matter of so difficult a nature, which he brought in a few months after entering on the duties of his department. I suppose that the noble lord cannot set such store by the details of a measure so rapidly prepared, that he will deny that they may be possibly amended on reconsideration ; that in fact many of the details of a sound and large system of colonization are not touched by his Act ; and that, until they are matured by assiduous inquiry, the principle can never be fairly tried, or rendered productive of the full amount of good of which it was capable.

There are some most important questions which require to be fully investigated before the system of colonization can with prudence be placed on any permanent footing ; and I think it right to mention the most important of them, in order to impress upon the house how much of the success of any scheme must depend on their being rightly adjusted. There is, in the first place, a very important question as to the possibility of applying to the rest of our colonies the system which is now in force only in the Australian. It has never yet been satisfactorily explained what causes prevent the application of the principle to the land that lies open for settlement at the Cape of Good Hope, speaking not merely of the present limits of the colony, but of the boundless unappropriated extent which adjoins it—superior, apparently, in natural fertility, and free from all proprietary claims on the part of individuals. With respect to the North American colonies, I am aware that some difficulties are presented by the partial cession of the crown lands contained within them to the control of their respective legislatures. With the control of these legislatures I should not be disposed to interfere, even if the Imperial Government retain the strict legal right ; but I am so convinced that the interests of the mother-country and the colonies with respect to emigration are identical, that I have no doubt that the colonial legisla-tures would rejoice to co-operate with the imperial govern-ment in the adoption of the general principles of such a plan as might be deemed most conducive to the good of the empire. At any rate, viewing the magnitude and importance of these colonies, and their proximity to Great Britain, they ought not to be excluded from the general plan without the fullest inquiry.

But there are very important questions with respect to the mode of applying the principles, which are still matters of doubt and controversy. Thus it is yet a question what is the " *sufficient price* " which the government should endeavour to secure from the lands in each colony. It is obvious that no more should be asked than may be applied so as to attract labourers to the colony ; whatever more is imposed is a partial tax on immigrants and agriculture for the general purposes of the community, and would actually deter instead of attract settlers. On the other hand, it is contended that the price is in many instances still so low as to lead to too great an accumulation of land in private hands at the first formation of settlements ; and to the subsequent drying up of government sales and land-fund when the first purchasers are compelled to bring their lands back into the market. It will be seen that it is of the utmost importance to the right working of the system that the right price should be ascertained, not only in a rough and general way, but in the case of each colony.

Another question of considerable importance is, how this sufficient price should be got—whether by fixing it on all lands as both minimum and maximum, or by trying to get the highest price which may be offered at an auction. By the latter plan it is said that the full worth of the land is most sure to be got. While it is objected to it that, besides operating with peculiar unfairness on all persons of known enterprise and skill, the tendency of the auction system is to encourage great competition for favoured town lots, lavish expenditure at the outset, an exhaustion of the capital necessary to give value to the purchase, and a consequent stagnation of the settlement after the first feverish burst of speculative ardour ; that the system of uniform price, by giving to the purchaser all the advantages derivable from the possession of peculiarly advantageous sites, presents the greatest attraction to purchasers, and gives the surest stimulus to energy in developing the resources of the colony ; and that though the auction system may bring in the greatest amount of money to government at first, it will be found that, in the course of a few years, the steady produce of a fixed price will make the largest return. A subsidiary question to this is, whether the same principle of price should be uniformly applied to all kinds of land, or any distinction made between different qualities.

But a far more important matter, still in dispute, is, whether the whole of the land fund shall be devoted to the introduction of labourers, or whether a portion shall be applied to the general expenses of the colony. It is said, on the one hand, that if the object be to apply the land-fund so as to render the colony attractive to settlers, the formation of roads and public works is as requisite to that end as the supply of labour. To this it is answered, that the applying of the largest possible amount of money to the importation of labour is the surest way of increasing the population, the increase of population the surest way of raising the ordinary revenue from taxes, out of which all necessary works may be provided; and that applying any portion of the land-fund to the general expenses of the colony is merely placing at the disposal of irresponsible authority an additional and easily-acquired fund, which will be sure to be expended with that shameless extravagance, which, whether in New South Wales, or South Australia, or New Zealand, is the curse of our colonies, and the scandal of our colonial system.

There is a question of even greater magnitude and difficulty than any of these; and that is, the question whether, viewing the great necessity of supplying labour in the early period of the colony's existence, it may not be advisable to anticipate the proceeds of the land sales by a loan raised on the security of future sales; and in this instance only has aid been demanded from the mother country in the form of a guarantee, which would enable the colony to raise money at a moderate interest. If the principle on which this suggestion is made be sound, it is of paramount importance, because it would really be bridging over the ocean, and enabling the future purchasers to repair at once to the spot which they are to render productive. No doubt great caution would be requisite in thus forestalling the resources of a colony; and I should deprecate such extravagant suggestions of large loans as have been sometimes proposed. But, on the other hand, a debt contracted for such a purpose is not unproductive waste of capital, such as our national debt, nor is it to be likened to the debts of individuals contracted for the enjoyment of the moment. It is rather to be compared to those debts which wise landlords often deliberately contract, for the purpose of giving an additional value to their estates, or to the loans by which half the enterprises of trade are undertaken, and which are to be regarded as resources of future wealth, not embarrassment.

The proposal of a loan in anticipation of the land-fund has been recently urged on the government from a quarter deserving of great weight—I mean the legislative council of New South Wales—in a report, which, I trust, has been successful in correcting an erroneous notion most fatal to colonial interests, to which the noble lord (Lord Stanley) gave rather an incautious expression last year,—I mean the notion that the Australian colonies were at that time rather over-supplied with labour. It appears that the term over-supply is correct only as respects the means of paying the cost of emigration out of the land sales of the year; that the colony exhausted its means of bringing over labourers, but that it is still, in fact, craving for it as much as ever; that the supply of nearly 24,000 labourers in one year, far from overstocking the labour-market, had produced no material reduction of wages; that the labourers and artisans imported that year were getting ample wages, and that the colony still continued capable of absorbing an annual free importation of 10,000 or 12,000 of the labouring classes.

I have briefly adverted to these important points without suggesting the decision which, I think, ought to be made with respect to any of them. The details of a plan of colonization are obviously matters in which it would be idle for any one not a member of the executive government to make any specific suggestions. To discuss the general bearings of such a question, and to impress its general importance on the general government, is all that appears to me to lie practically within the competence of this House. It is with the government that the investigation of such details as I have adverted to, and the preparation of specific measures must rest. They have the best means of collecting the most correct information and the soundest opinions on the subject. I have no wish to take the discharge of their duties on myself. I think this a stage of the question in which it would tend to no good purpose to call in the cumbrous and indecisive action of a committee of this House: but that I have done my duty when,—after thus explaining the grave necessities of our condition, and sifting the practicability of the remedy which seems most efficient,—I leave the question, with its niceties of detail and responsibilities of execution, in the hands of the advisers of the Crown. But I leave it not as a question to be discussed by one particular department as a matter of detail, or as a mere

colonial question, but as one of general import to the condition of England.   The remedy, which I thus call on her
Majesty's ministers to investigate, is one on which inquiry
can excite no illusory hopes; for, though I believe that its
adoption would give an immediate impulse to enterprise, it
is one of which the greater results cannot be expected for
some few years.   It is one, too, which, if it fails of giving
relief to the extent that I have contemplated, cannot fail of
bettering the condition of many, and of extending the
resources and widening the basis of our empire.

The honourable and learned Member proposed the following motion :—" That an humble address be presented to
Her Majesty, praying that she will take into her most
gracious consideration the means by which extensive and
systematic colonization may be most effectually rendered
available for augmenting the resources of Her Majesty's
empire, giving additional employment to capital and labour,
both in the United Kingdom and in the colonies, and
thereby bettering the condition of her people."

APPENDIX No. II.

A LETTER FROM CERTAIN NEW-ZEALAND COLONISTS

TO MR. HAWES,

UNDER-SECRETARY OF STATE FOR THE COLONIES.

70, *Jermyn Street, 5th Oct.*, 1846.

SIR,—In accordance with the suggestions so courteously expressed by you to some of our number that we should write down some of our ideas, on the subject of the Orders in Council to be framed in pursuance of the recent New Zealand Government Act, we beg to submit to you the following observations.

We have, however, to request that you will excuse the rough form in which they appear, owing to the necessity which there has been for their prompt consideration and arrangement; and also that, if in the course of them you should remark any freedom in urging opinions somewhat at variance with those pre-conceived by her Majesty's Government, you will ascribe the fact to our wish to meet in a cordial spirit the invitation which you have made to us to state, without reservation, views which we believe will be approved by the leading members of the communities with which we are connected.

Our attention has been first called to the powers which are to be granted to the proposed Municipal Corporations. Putting aside, for the present, their function of electing representatives to a Provincial Assembly, we fear that the local powers which may be granted under the act to the Municipal Corporation of each settlement are not sufficiently large.

The settlements now existing in New Zealand are scattered at a considerable distance one from the other; and the next settlement which is likely to be founded, that of the

Free Church of Scotland, is intended to be placed at Otago, four hundred miles from the nearest of the others. From the varying nature of the country, and the different classes of colonists who are likely to proceed in large bodies from this side of the world, each body to found a distinct plantation, the settlements may, in a short time, vary as much in character and circumstances as they are actually distant from one another. We may here again instance the proposed Scotch colony, which will consist entirely of emigrants from Scotland, who are as little acquainted with the details and forms of English law as the English settlers of Wellington and Nelson are with those to which the Scotchmen have been accustomed. We may remark that, while discussing the details of the proposed institutions, we have discovered that these colonists are not acquainted with the duties of a Coroner or of a Recorder, at any rate under these names. In some other points the difference will be equally striking. We can conceive, for instance, that a much lower rate of franchise would secure as desirable a class of voters among the Scotchmen as could only be attained by a high rate among the mixed British population of the Cook's Strait settlements, which already number many immigrants from the neighbouring penal colonies, and which may probably be for the next few years subject to such immigration. A colony such as has been proposed in particular connexion with the Church of England, to be founded in the plain of Wairarapa, near Wellington, might require certain local institutions different from those of its neighbour. A still more striking instance would occur, if the success of the few French colonists who have taken root at Akaroa, in Banks's Peninsula, should encourage others to follow them in large numbers, willing to submit to a general British allegiance, provided that they may enjoy, in their own particular locality, the peculiar usages and privileges to which they have been accustomed in their native country. Again, one community may, from its position, be almost exclusively pastoral, another agricultural, and a third manufacturing or commercial; while present appearances promise that some districts may derive their prosperity in great measure from mining operations.

We are inclined to believe that the toleration of these distinctive features in the different plantations of a new country will be productive of no mischief; but that, on the contrary, each separate community will flourish the more, and even contribute the more to the general prosperity, the more it is allowed to manage its own affairs in its own way.

We conceive Burke to have been of this opinion, when he wrote the words quoted by Sir Robert Peel in the debate on New Zealand, during the session of 1845, praising the municipal institutions which laid the foundations of representative government in our old colonies of North America, and which still exist in the United States under the name of " townships."

We have reason to believe that Governor Grey is so far of our opinion that he has recommended the division of the present general government of New Zealand into as many subordinate governments of the same form, each with a lieutenant-governor, and legislative council, as there are separate settlements. He has already, indeed, introduced the great improvement of publishing the revenue and expenditure of each settlement, separately from the general accounts of the colony; and he promised the inhabitants of Nelson that he would " eventually recommend a local council, with powers to enact laws, subject to the approval of the Governor, in accordance with the wants and wishes of the settlers;" thus almost advocating the establishment of a provincial assembly, rather than a mere municipal corporation, in each settlement.

We therefore earnestly desire that each distinct settlement or "township" should have power to make all laws and regulations for its own local government, not being repugnant to the laws of Great Britain, or to those of the General Assembly on the nine points reserved for its jurisdiction, by section 7th of the Act, or to those made by the provincial assembly for the peace, order, and good government of the province in which it is situated, as provided for by the 5th section.

We fear that under the present Act such powers could not be at once given to " municipal corporations" constituted here by letters patent, as they would exceed those " which in pursuance of the statutes in that behalf made and provided, it is competent to her Majesty to grant to the inhabitants of any town or borough in England and Wales in virtue of such statutes."—(sect. 2.)

But if we are not mistaken in conceiving that it would be expedient to grant such extensive powers, for local purposes, to the " municipal corporation" of each separate settlement, we can suggest a means by which this may be 'done without exceeding the limits of the Act.—The " municipal corporations" may be constituted at first only for the purpose of electing members to a Provincial House of Representatives, and the provincial assembly may then legislate for the powers to be enjoyed by each separate c rporation, or may pass a law to the effect that these bodies shall have the power of legislating on all local purposes, such legislation not being repugnant, &c., as before recommended.

We are the more impressed with the expediency of some such arrangement, because we are convinced that it is essential to secure in each settlement the services of the leading colonists as officers of its corporation, since those officers are to chose the members for the Representative Chamber of their Provincial Assembly.   The colonists who are most fit for this important trust might be unwilling to exercise it, if with its exercise were coupled the necessity of acting as Common Councilman or Alderman of a Borough, confined in its powers like those of England and Wales.

We should even desire to see a provision for the erection of any one or more "Municipal Corporations" into a separate Province, as soon as it or they should apply for it, and could fairly show an ability to provide the necessary civil list.   We imagine that the power of enacting such a change might be vested in the General Assembly, subject of course to the approval of the Government in England, like all its other measures.   This provision would at any rate act as a remedy, should it be found that too many communities were included in one Province, and that the Provincial Assembly was legislating for matters beyond the powers of the particular Municipal Corporations, which could be better managed by persons more immediately and locally interested.   To give an instance, it would be desirable that Otakou should, upon its application for the change, and production of evidence that it could provide its own civil list, have a right to be separated from an Assembly consisting of members from many communities of different character from its own, and legislating at a distance of four hundred miles for matters comparatively local:—or again, Nelson might complain of being taxed by a Provincial Assembly which should include it along with Wellington and New Plymouth, for the expense of making a road between the two latter settlements.

We are anxious that, if possible, the settlements in the north part of the islands should enjoy the same civil rights as those which are to be granted to the southern settlements. We should regret to see any use made of the 9th Section, which provides for the continuance of the present form of government in the northern part of the islands until 1854, should such a course appear advisable. We are aware of the difficulties arising from the fact that extensive tracts of land in their neighbourhood are held by individuals under title from the Crown, so as to obstruct a system of colonization similar to that pursued in the Company's settlements. And we are aware that what is termed the "native question," in that part of the country where the natives, credulous in the intrinsic value of the waste lands which they have learned to claim, and indisposed to submit to British authority, are very numerous, may prevent the immediate establishment of Municipal Corporations legislating for the local wants of extensive districts like those in the south. But we would suggest that "Municipal Corporations" be established in the northern districts, within boundaries, at first, as small as the Governor (with whom the settlement of the "native question" rests) may think fit to determine, but that within these necessarily circumscribed boundaries the inhabitants should receive privileges of local self-government similar to those of the south. The boundaries might be afterwards extended as the natives might either abandon their immediate vicinity, or request to be admitted within the pale of British law.

We cannot refrain from expressing our doubts as to the expediency of the proposed election of Members to the Provincial House of Representatives by the officers of the Corporations. We freely own that we should have preferred two distinct elections, one for the officers of the Corporations, and another for the Representatives to the Assembly. But in proportion as larger local powers are granted to the Municipal Corporations, and these bodies thus become in fact, if not in name, inferior Provincial Assemblies, our mistrust of this rather novel provision diminishes. If the officers of the Corporation are to perform duties such as those of an alderman or common councilman of an English town or borough, we object strongly to their having a main voice in choosing members for the Provincial House of Representatives, because, as we before stated, the best colonists will not have consented to perform the ungenial duties in order to secure the vote. But if the "Municipal Corporation" possess the "Township" powers which we have above recommended, its offices would confer sufficient dignity and importance to induce the best colonists to accept them; and they, being the *élite*, as it were, of the general body of electors, might, without disadvantage, be empowered to select the Representatives.

We approach the question of franchise with some diffi-
dence, because we are unaware how far our views as to the
large local powers necessary for the "Municipal Corporations" will be agreed to by her Majesty's Government. We
should, however, be unwilling to give an opinion as to what
qualification would secure success to the scheme, if the
Municipal Corporations were to have only the powers of
bodies which bear that name in England and Wales; because we should conceive that the functions of such bodies
were totally distinct from those of choosing a representative.
The suggestions, therefore, that we offer on this point, are
based on the assumption that each Municipal Corporation is
to enjoy those powers of local legislation for which we have
been pleading.

The object of any qualification is to secure that the men
most fitted for the duties should be chosen as officers of the
corporations.   They must be the men most fitted, not only
to carry on the local legislation of the "township," but also
to select members for the representative house of an Assembly, which makes all laws for the whole province, except on
the nine points reserved for the General Assembly.

We are of opinion that, at any rate in the existing settlements and for the present, it would be very dangerous to extend the franchise too much by making the qualification for
a voter too low, trusting to a higher qualification for the person to be elected.   This arrangement allows mischievous
and intriguing individuals, who have no difficulty in providing themselves with the higher qualification, to obtain the
suffrages of a low and comparatively ignorant class of voters
through bribery or other corrupting means.   A remarkable
instance of this occurred at the election which took place at
Wellington in October 1842, for the officers of a corporation
which possessed very limited powers.   Every male adult
who chose to pay 1l. sterling to have his name registered,
was privileged to vote; and any voter was qualified for election : 350 persons obtained the franchise ; and of course
the small sum of money was paid for many of them by
parties who wished to secure their votes.   In one case, a
committee for the election of certain persons had given 25l.
to a colonist who had great influence over a number of High-
land labourers, in order that he should register twenty-five
of their votes, and make them vote for the committee's list.
The leader of the opposing candidates, however, knew the
laird's failing—set to drinking with him at breakfast-time till
he had won his heart, and then marched reeling arm-in-arm

with him to the poll, followed by the twenty-five High-
landers, who were in the same state; and who all voted for
the man who had so disgraced himself and them. He was
an auctioneer, who had joined the community of Wellington
from Van Diemen's Land, and who had always distinguished
himself by courting the admiration of the most ignorant portion of the inhabitants. He was comparatively uneducated;
and very unfit, at any rate, to exercise such influence as he
would do, among voters qualified by a small stake in the
country. A high qualification for candidates would not have
excluded him; he would easily have procured that qualification, and then have resorted to the same means of procuring
votes, so long as the voters included a class comparatively
ignorant, careless of their reputation, and easily swayed by
mere mob oratory and dishonourable artifice.

We should be content, then, to allow of a qualification
for candidate no higher than that for voter, provided that
the franchise is only extended so as to include those labourers
who shall have earned sufficient money to buy some land,
or to hold a considerable quantity as tenants ; thus proving,
to a certain degree, not only their steadiness and intelligence,
but their determination to retain an interest in the country.
Supposing the franchise to be so arranged, we can conceive
no reason why such persons should not be perfectly eligible
to the office of a councilman. On the contrary, we should
be glad to see, if possible, a certain proportion of such men
in the governing body of each municipality, because we
distinctly consider them to be included among the best
colonists.

We are thus averse to a qualification for a candidate
higher than that for a voter, but strongly in favour of a
qualification for both which shall depend on holding a
sufficient stake in the colony to prevent the selection of unfit
persons. With our knowledge and experience of the present
population of the existing settlements, we are in favour of a
scale of qualification which may at first sight appear very
high ; but we will begin by stating it, and afterwards adduce
some reasons to justify it. The right to vote should, in our
opinion, be confined to persons :—

1st. Owning a freehold estate in land of the value of *fifty
pounds sterling*, clear of all charges and encumbrances.

2nd. Deriving a *beneficial* interest from land, to the amount
of *five pounds sterling* annually.

3rd. Occupiers or tenants of land, houses, or other tenements to the value of *fifty pounds sterling* annually.

Provided always that for the purposes of this arrangement, land shall never be estimated at less than the price originally paid for it to the New Zealand Company in their settlements, or to the Crown, or to the natives with the sanction of the Crown, elsewhere. And provided also, that any land to be estimated for these purposes must be held by title derived from the Crown; that not even, for instance, the occupation of native reserves by natives should give them the franchise, still less that natives admitted on their own application with their own lands (formerly constituting an exceptional territory) should be able to qualify, until the land has been distributed in freehold among individuals of their number by title from the Crown. This will give the Crown the power of determining how soon natives may be competent to enjoy the electoral franchise.

It is necessary that we should here explain that the customary rate of interest on money in New-Zealand and the neighbouring Colonies, is ten per cent., while it is only three per cent. in England, and that the wages of labour are also ordinarily much higher. A freehold qualification in these new settlements of the value of 6*l.* 13*s.* per annum, is, therefore, equal to a 40*s.* per annum freehold qualification in England; and the freehold ownership of land of the value of fifty pounds which we advocate is worth five pounds a year there, but is actually equal to a smaller freehold qualification in England. We do not, however, found our estimate of the scale desirable at present only on this calculation, but on a practical view of that scale which will include the most suitable class of voters, and we only adduce the undeniable difference in the value as at least worthy of consideration.

We have not failed to seek for precedents as to franchise in some new communities. We find that the qualification for voters in New South Wales is a freehold estate in lands and tenements of the clear value of *two hundred pounds sterling*, though this high qualification is rendered almost null by the granting of the franchise also to householders occupying dwelling houses of the yearly value of 20*l.* in a Colony where scarcely any dwelling house is worth less than this sum.

Even in some of the States of the American Union, the qualification is as high as that which we recommend, and in others not far below it.

In Massachusets, it is necessary to have an income of 3*l.* sterling, or a capital of 60*l.*

In Rhode Island, a man must possess landed property to the amount of 133 dollars.

In Connecticut, he must have property which gives an income of 17 dollars.

In New Jersey, an elector must have a property of 50*l. a year.*

In South Carolina and Maryland, the elector must possess *fifty acres of land.*

It is also of importance to observe, that there is great difficulty in restricting a franchise once established and exercised, while there is comparatively none in extending it; so that a fault on the side of fixing too high a qualification will be easily remedied, but one in the opposite direction will be almost irretrievable.

We are of opinion that, under the before-mentioned conditions, "Municipal Corporations" under the Act might be advantageously established at once in the existing settlements of Wellington, Nelson, New Plymouth, and Petre, to form a southern province, and in those of Auckland and Russell, to form a northern province. We have included Petre among those, although it contains no more than 200 European inhabitants. But it has a town and country district of its own under the Company's arrangements; it is upwards of a hundred miles from the nearest of the other settlements; it numbers among its inhabitants four gentlemen who were thought fit for the office of Justice of the Peace under the existing form of government; and, the "Native question" having been recently arranged there by Governor Grey, we have little doubt that its population will rapidly increase; and even in its present state, it will be good economy to let the inhabitants manage their little local matters without having to refer to Wellington or New Plymouth. The boundary in this case may be left to be fixed by the Governor, as in the cases of Auckland and Russell; and the Provincial Assembly may be trusted to determine what local powers the little " township" shall exercise.

In the case of Wellington, we should recommend that the "Municipal Corporation" extend its jurisdiction over all to the south of a line as follows:—The latitude of 40° 30′ S., from the east coast to the highest ridge of the Tararua mountains; then southwards along that ridge to the point nearest to any waters of the Waikanae river; then along that river to its mouth in Cook's Strait; together with the islands of *Kapiti* and *Mana.* But the Governor might be allowed to use his discretion in excepting for the present any districts within this boundary, as provided for by the 10th section of the Act, so as to meet the difficulties which may arise from the continuance of Rangihaiata in a troublesome attitude.

In the case of Nelson, we should recommend the " Municipal Corporation" to extend over all that part of the Middle Island which lies between Cook's Strait and the latitude of 42° south.

In the case of New Plymouth, we approve of the boundary recommended in Mr. E. G. Wakefield's letter to Mr. Gladstone, dated in February, 1846. Although, as we believe Governor Grey has found some difficulty in overcoming the obstacles which his predecessor threw in the way of adjusting the " Native Question" at that settlement, the boundary might, in this case also, be left to be fixed by the Governor for the present.

We should also desire that a " Municipal Corporation" be constituted at once for Otakou, to include within its boundaries at least the whole block purchased in that neighbourhood by the Company.

We also think it very advisable that some of these extensive " Boroughs" should be divided into " Hundreds" or " Wards," with a view to the election of councillors from each such subdivision in proportion to its population. Some of these subdivisions might return no councillor for the present, but any person holding qualification therein should vote in that " Hundred" nearest to his qualification.

It would be necessary, with a view to the numerous changes in the state of population which are sure to take place in a country under the process of a rapid colonization, that the powers now possessed by her Majesty to constitute " Municipal Corporations," to extend the boundaries of those first established, or to erect any one sub-division or more of a " borough," into a separate " Municipal Corporation," or to alter and amend the boundaries in any way, be delegated to the Governor, if, as we apprehend, such delegation be possible under the Act. If the proposed Church of England Colony, for instance, should intend to settle in a part of the Wellington borough, at present only inhabited by squatters, and only placed under its jurisdiction in order to include them within the pale of law, the person sent out to order the land to be surveyed for such a settlement might also carry out an application to the Governor to constitute such sub-division of an already existing " borough" into a separate one. Or if, upon the settlement of the " native question," the population in the valley of the Hutt, or at Porirua, should so rapidly increase as that the local matters could be better managed by a separate municipality, the Governor might be empowered to grant the application for that boon of a certain amount of population, say *one* or *two* thousand souls.

We may here observe that the average population of a " township" in the state of Massachusets is about 2000 souls.

With regard to the provinces, we are content to propose that at first there should be two.

1. All north of the latitude of the mouth of the Mokau River, including the municipal corporations of Auckland and Russell.

2. All south of the same parallel, including the municipalities of Wellington, Nelson, New Plymouth, Petre, and Otakou.

We are of opinion that the same qualification which we have recommended as calculated to secure the best class of voters in each municipality, is sufficient for a representative to the provincial assembly, no less than for a councilman; and this is on the principle before advocated, that you are more secure of a correct choice when the whole body of electors is of a station secured by property, than when you provide that the few persons chosen shall be possessed of a certain property, and leave the choice to a larger body of electors, having less stake in the country, and a lower position to maintain by upright conduct.

The representatives from each " municipal corporation" should be in proportion to its population.

We are inclined to desire that no *ex-officio* members should sit in the Provincial House of Representatives; but that officers of the government should offer themselves to the suffrages of the electors, in the same way as in England. Such an arrangement would go far to secure that the officers of the provincial governments should be chosen from among the most estimable of the colonists, and not from among strangers and new comers careless of their welfare, as has almost always been the case under the old form of government.

We should desire, above all, that the legislative councils be composed of persons having a very important stake in the country. At the beginning, indeed, it may be expedient to allow the Governor perfect *carte blanche* in the selection of legislative councillors; because the late troubles of the colony have left many persons fitted for so high a station with comparatively little property. We should not, therefore, be sorry to leave this discretion entirely with the Governor for at least three years. But during the succeeding three years, no one should be eligible to the legislative council, who had not resided at least two years in the colony, and who did not possess property to the clear value of three thousand pounds sterling, of which at least one thousand should be in real property, in the province to whose legislative council he might be nominated. After these six years no one should be eligible who had not resided at least five years in the colony, and who did not possess property to the clear value of six thousand pounds sterling, of which two thousand must be in real property in the province.

All nominations, excepting those made during the first six years, should, in our opinion, be for life, or at any rate for the duration of the Provincial Assembly as then constituted. But it should be at the option of the Governor to nominate or not for life, at the end of the six years, any of the persons who had served during any part of that time, but who at the end of it might not possess the highest qualification required. It may be necessary that some Government officers not possessed of the above qualification, should hold seats in the Legislative Council by virtue of their office, as the Judge of the highest Court in the Province, &c.; and perhaps that the Governor should always preside; though we should prefer to see him so completely a representative of her Majesty as only to appear even in the Upper House on occasions of dissolution, prorogation, and re-assemblage, and as to introduce Government measures into either House through the medium of responsible Executive Officers. We are convinced that the office of Colonial Governor loses much of its dignity and usefulness, when its holder appears as a violent partisan in a legislative chamber, and the discussion of public objects is converted into an occasion of personal dispute between the representative of royalty and one of the Queen's subjects.

We would apply precisely the same principles to the representatives and legislative councillors of the General Assembly as to those of the Provincial Assemblies. The House of Representatives of each Province should be empowered to choose those of their number to be sent to that of the General Assembly.

But it appears to us most essential that the number of members thus deputed by each province should be in proportion to the *bonâ fide* tax-paying population of such province; and this would be still more requisite, should it be determined against our wish to continue the present form of government in the northern part of the north island; for in that case, by the 9th section, the Government would be enabled to send to the General House of Representatives a number of mere Government nominees from the northern Province, equal to that of the members really representing the more populous southern Province, and there would be only a mockery of Representative Government on the nine points of legislation reserved for the General Assembly of the islands. *Bonâ fide* Representatives, indeed, from any of the settlements, would probably not be found to, give their countenance to its deliberations; as they have on many occasions heretofore refused a seat among the non-official minority in the Legislative Council as at present constituted.

Although there are some other matters relating to the affairs of New Zealand on which, at some future time, we should be glad of the opportunity of submitting our views to her Majesty's government, we have thought it of importance to confine ourselves at present to that subject which is more immediately under the consideration of Earl Grey, the Orders in Council to be framed under the New Zealand Government Act; and we beg to repeat that the above suggestions have been expressed in some haste, although they contain, as the principles on which they are founded, our deliberate and carefully considered opinions. We would, therefore, respectfully request that we may be allowed to explain or reconsider any points which may not seem sufficiently clear in this rough statement; and we may add that we have also turned our attention to some of the more minute details of the proposed arrangements, with which we have not thought fit to encumber this letter.—We have the honour to be, Sir, your most obedient servants,

(Signed)   W. CARGILL, leader of the proposed Colony at Otago.

E. S. HALSWELL, ex-member of the Legislative Council, N. Z.

H. MOREING, four years Resident and Magistrate, N. Z.

E. JERNINGHAM WAKEFIELD, four years and a half resident in New Zealand.

Benjamin Hawes, Esq., M.P.

200497897